Applied Deep Learning

A Case-Based Approach to Understanding Deep Neural Networks

Umberto Michelucci

Apress®

Applied Deep Learning: A Case-Based Approach to Understanding Deep Neural Networks

Umberto Michelucci
toelt.ai, Dübendorf, Switzerland

ISBN-13 (pbk): 978-1-4842-3789-2 ISBN-13 (electronic): 978-1-4842-3790-8
https://doi.org/10.1007/978-1-4842-3790-8

Library of Congress Control Number: 2018955206

Managing Director, Apress Media LLC: Welmoed Spahr
Acquisitions Editor: Celestin Suresh John
Development Editor: Matthew Moodie
Coordinating Editor: Aditee Mirashi

Cover designed by eStudioCalamar

Cover image designed by Freepik (www.freepik.com)

Distributed to the book trade worldwide by Springer Science+Business Media New York, 233 Spring Street, 6th Floor, New York, NY 10013. Phone 1-800-SPRINGER, fax (201) 348-4505, e-mail orders ny@springer-sbm.com, or visit www.springeronline.com. Apress Media, LLC is a California LLC and the sole member (owner) is Springer Science+Business Media Finance Inc (SSBM Finance Inc). SSBM Finance Inc is a **Delaware** corporation.

For information on translations, please e-mail rights@apress.com, or visit www.apress.com/rights-permissions.

Apress titles may be purchased in bulk for academic, corporate, or promotional use. eBook versions and licenses are also available for most titles. For more information, reference our Print and eBook Bulk Sales web page at www.apress.com/bulk-sales.

Any source code or other supplementary material referenced by the author in this book is available to readers on GitHub via the book's product page, located at www.apress.com/9781484237892. For more detailed information, please visit www.apress.com/source-code.

I dedicate this book to my daughter, Caterina,
and my wife, Francesca. Thank you for the inspiration,
the motivation, and the happiness you bring to my life every day.
Without you, this would not have been possible.

Table of Contents

About the Author

Umberto Michelucci currently works in innovation and artificial intelligence (AI) at the leading health insurance company in Switzerland. He leads several strategic initiatives related to AI, new technologies, machine learning, and research collaborations with universities. Formerly, he worked as a data scientist and lead modeler for several large projects in health care and has had extensive hands-on experience in programming and algorithm design. He managed projects in business intelligence and data warehousing, enabling data-driven solutions to be implemented in complicated production environments. More recently, Umberto has worked extensively with neural networks and has applied deep learning to several problems linked to insurance, client behavior (such as customer churning), and sensor science. He studied theoretical physics in Italy, the United States, and in Germany, where he also worked as a researcher. He also undertook higher education in the UK. He presents scientific results at conferences regularly and publishes research papers in peer-reviewed journals.

About the Technical Reviewer

Jojo Moolayil is an Artificial Intelligence, Deep Learning, Machine Learning & Decision Science professional with over 5 years of industrial experience and published author of the book - **Smarter Decisions – The Intersection of IoT and Decision Science**. He has worked with several industry leaders on high impact and critical data science and machine learning projects across multiple verticals. He is currently associated with **General Electric**, the pioneer and leader in data science for Industrial IoT and lives in Bengaluru—the silicon-valley of India.

He was born and raised in Pune, India and graduated from the University of Pune with a major in Information Technology Engineering. He started his career with Mu Sigma Inc., the world's largest pure-play analytics provider and worked with the leaders of many Fortune 50 clients. One of the early enthusiasts to venture into IoT analytics, he converged his learnings from decision science to bring the problem-solving frameworks and his learnings from data and decision science to IoT Analytics.

To cement his foundations in data science for industrial IoT and scale the impact of the problem-solving experiments, he joined a fast-growing IoT Analytics startup called Flutura based in Bangalore and headquartered in the valley. After a short stint with Flutura, Jojo moved on to work with the leaders of Industrial IoT - General Electric, in Bangalore, where he focused on solving decision science problems for Industrial IoT use cases. As a part of his role in GE, Jojo also focuses on developing data science and decision science products and platforms for Industrial IoT.

Apart from authoring books on Decision Science and IoT, Jojo has also been Technical Reviewer for various books on Machine Learning, Deep Learning and Business Analytics with Apress and Packt publications. He is an active Data Science tutor and maintains a blog at `http://www.jojomoolayil.com/web/blog/`.

Profile

- `http://www.jojomoolayil.com/`
- `https://www.linkedin.com/in/jojo62000`

I would like to thank my family, friends and mentors.

—Jojo Moolayil

Acknowledgments

It would be unfair if I did not thank all the people who helped me with this book. While writing, I discovered that I did not know anything about book publishing, and I also discovered that even when you think you know something well, putting it on paper is a completely different story. It is unbelievable how one's supposedly clear mind becomes garbled when putting thoughts on paper. It was one of the most difficult things I have done, but it was also one of the most rewarding experiences of my life.

First, I must thank my beloved wife, Francesca Venturini, who spent countless hours at night and on weekends reading the text. Without her, the book would not be as clear as it is. I must also thank Celestin Suresh John, who believed in my idea and gave me the opportunity to write this book. Aditee Mirashi is the most patient editor I have ever met. She was always there to answer all my questions, and I had quite a few, and not all of them good. I particularly would like to thank Matthew Moodie, who had the patience of reading every single chapter. I have never met anyone able to offer so many good suggestions. Thanks, Matt; I own you one. Jojo Moolayil had the patience to test every single line of code and check the correctness of every explanation. And when I mean every, I really mean every. No, really, I mean it. Thank you, Jojo, for your feedback and your encouragement. It really meant a lot to me.

Finally, I am infinitely grateful to my beloved daughter, Caterina, for her patience when I was writing and for reminding me every day how important it is to follow your dreams. And of course I have to thank my parents, that have always supported my decisions, whatever they were.

Introduction

Why another book on applied deep learning? That is the question I asked myself before starting to write this volume. After all, do a Google search on the subject, and you will be overwhelmed by the huge number of results. The problem I encountered, however, is that I found material only to implement very basic models on very simple datasets. Over and over again, the same problems, the same hints, and the same tips are offered. If you want to learn how to classify the Modified National Institute of Standards and Technology (MNIST) dataset of ten handwritten digits, you are in luck. (Almost everyone with a blog has done that, mostly copying the code available on the TensorFlow web site). Searching for something else to learn how logistic regression works? Not so easy. How to prepare a dataset to perform an interesting binary classification? Even more difficult. I felt there was a need to fill this gap. I spent hours trying to debug models for reasons as silly as having the labels wrong. For example, instead of 0 and 1, I had 1 and 2, but no blog warned me about that. It is important to conduct a proper metric analysis when developing models, but no one teaches you how (at least not in material that is easily accessible). This gap needed to be filled. I find that covering more complex examples, from data preparation to error analysis, is a very efficient and fun way to learn the right techniques. In this book, I have always tried to cover complete and complex examples to explain concepts that are not so easy to understand in any other way. It is not possible to understand why it is important to choose the right learning rate if you don't see what can happen when you select the wrong value. Therefore, I always explain concepts with real examples and with fully fledged and tested Python code that you can reuse. Note that the goal of this book is not to make you a Python or TensorFlow expert, or someone who can develop new complex algorithms. Python and TensorFlow are simply tools that are very well suited to develop models and get results quickly. Therefore, I use them. I could have used other tools, but those are the ones most often used by practitioners, so it makes sense to choose them. If you must learn, better that it be something you can use in your own projects and for your own career.

The goal of this book is to let you see more advanced material with new eyes. I cover the mathematical background as much as I can, because I feel that it is necessary for a complete understanding of the difficulties and reasoning behind many concepts. You cannot comprehend why a large learning rate will make your model (strictly speaking, the cost function) diverge, if you don't know how the gradient descent algorithm works mathematically. In all real-life projects, you will not have to calculate partial derivatives or complex sums, but you will have to understand them to be able to evaluate what can work and what cannot (and especially why). Appreciating why a library such as TensorFlow makes your life easier is only possible if you try to develop a trivial model with one neuron from scratch. It is a very instructive thing to do, and I will show you how in Chapter 10. Once you have done it once, you will remember it forever, and you will really appreciate libraries such as TensorFlow.

I suggest that you really try to understand the mathematical underpinnings (although this is not strictly necessary to profit from the book), because they will allow you to fully understand many concepts that otherwise cannot be understood completely. Machine learning is a very complicated subject, and it is utopic to think that it is possible to understand it thoroughly without a good grasp of mathematics or Python. In each chapter, I highlight important tips to develop things efficiently in Python. There is no statement in this book that is not backed up by concrete examples and reproducible code. I will not discuss anything without offering related real-life examples. In this way, everything will make sense immediately, and you will remember it.

Take the time to study the code that you find in this book and try it for yourself. As every good teacher knows, learning works best when students try to resolve problems themselves. Try, make mistakes, and learn. Read a chapter, type in the code, and try to modify it. For example, in Chapter 2, I will show you how to perform binary classification recognition between two handwritten digits: 1 and 2. Take the code and try two different digits. Play with the code and have fun.

By design, the code that you will find in this book is written as simply as possible. It is not optimized, and I know that it is possible to write much better-performing code, but by doing so, I would have sacrificed clarity and readability. The goal of this book is not to teach you to write highly optimized Python code; it is to let you understand the fundamental concepts of the algorithms and their limitations and give you a solid basis with which to continue your learning in this field. Regardless, I will, of course, point out important Python implementation details, such as, for example, how you should avoid standard Python loops as much as possible.

All the code in this book is written to support the learning goals I have set for each chapter. Libraries such as NumPy and TensorFlow have been recommended because they allow mathematical formulations to be translated directly into Python. I am aware of other software libraries, such as TensorFlow Lite, Keras, and many more that may make your life easier, but those are merely tools. The significant difference lies in your ability to understand the concepts behind the methods. If you get them right, you can choose whatever tool you want, and you will be able to achieve a good implementation. If you don't understand how the algorithms work, no matter the tool, you will not be able to undertake a proper implementation or a proper error analysis. I am a fierce opponent of the concept of data science for everyone. Data science and machine learning are difficult and complex subjects that require a deep understanding of the mathematics and subtelties behind them.

I hope that you will have fun reading this book (I surely had a lot in writing it) and that you will find the examples and the code useful. I hope, too, that you will have many Eureka! moments, wherein you will finally understand why something works the way you expect it to (or why it does not). I hope you will find the complete examples both interesting and useful. If I help you to understand only one concept that was unclear to you before, I will be happy.

There are a few chapters of this book that are more mathematically advanced. In Chapter 2, for example, I calculate partial derivatives. But don't worry, if you don't understand them, you can simply skip the equations. I have made sure that the main concepts are understandable without most of the mathematical details. However, you should really know what a matrix is, how to multiply matrices, what a transpose of a matrix is, and so on. Basically, you need a good grasp of linear algebra. If you don't have one, I suggest you review a basic linear algebra book before reading this one. If you have a solid linear algebra and calculus background, I strongly advise you not to skip the mathematical parts. They can really help in understanding why we do things in specific ways. For example, it will help you immensely in understanding the quirks of the learning rate, or how the gradient descent algorithm works. You should also not be scared by a more complex mathematical notation and feel confident with an equation as complex as the following (this is the mean square error we will use for the linear regression algorithm and will be explained in detail later, so don't worry if you don't know what the symbols mean at this point):

$$J(w_0, w_1) = \frac{1}{m}\sum_{i=1}\left(y_i - f\left(w_0, w_1, x^{(i)}\right)\right)^2$$

You should understand and feel confident with such concepts as a sum or a mathematical series. If you feel unsure about these, review them before starting the book; otherwise, you will miss some important concepts that you must have a firm grasp on to proceed in your deep-learning career. The goal of this book is not to give you a mathematical foundation. I assume you have one. Deep learning and neural networks (in general, machine learning) are complex, and whoever tries to convince you otherwise is lying or doesn't understand them.

I will not spend time in justifying or deriving algorithms or equations. You will have to trust me there. Additionally, I will not discuss the applicability of specific equations. For those of you with a good understanding of calculus, for example, I will not discuss the problem of the differentiability of functions for which we calculate derivatives. Simply assume that you can apply the formulas I give you. Many years of practical implementations have shown the deep-learning community that those methods and equations work as expected and can be used in practice. The kind of advanced topics mentioned would require a separate book.

In Chapter 1, you will learn how to set up your Python environment and what computational graphs are. I will discuss some basic examples of mathematical calculations performed using TensorFlow. In Chapter 2, we will look at what you can do with a single neuron. I will cover what an activation function is and what the most used types, such as sigmoid, ReLU, or tanh, are. I will show you how gradient descent works and how to implement logistic and linear regression with a single neuron and TensorFlow. In Chapter 3, we will look at fully connected networks. I will discuss matrix dimensions, what overfitting is, and introduce you to the Zalando dataset. We will then build our first real network with TensorFlow and start looking at more complex variations of gradient descent algorithms, such as mini-batch gradient descent. We will also look at different ways of weight initialization and how to compare different network architectures. In Chapter 4, we will look at dynamic learning rate decay algorithms, such as staircase, step, or exponential decay, then I will discuss advanced optimizers, such as Momentum, RMSProp, and Adam. I will also give you some hints on how to develop custom optimizers with TensorFlow. In Chapter 5, I will discuss regularization, including such well-known methods as l_1,l_2, dropout, and early stopping. We will look at the mathematics behind these methods and how to implement them in TensorFlow. In Chapter 6, we will look at such concepts as human-level performance and Bayes error. Next, I will introduce a metric analysis workflow that will allow you to identify problems having to do with your dataset. Additionally, we will look at k-fold cross-validation as a tool to validate your results. In Chapter 7, we will look at the black box class of problems and what hyperparameter tuning is. We will look at such algorithms as grid and random search and at which is more efficient and why. Then we will look at some tricks, such as coarse-to-fine optimization. I have dedicated most of the chapter to Bayesian optimization—how to use it and what an acquisition function is. I will offer a few tips, such as how to tune hyperparameters on a logarithmic scale, and then we will perform hyperparameter tuning on the Zalando dataset, to show you how it may work. In Chapter 8, we will look at convolutional and recurrent neural networks. I will show you what it means to perform convolution and pooling, and I will show you a basic TensorFlow implementation of both architectures. In Chapter 9, I will give you an insight into a real-life research project that I am working on with the Zurich University of Applied Sciences, Winterthur, and how deep learning can be used in a less standard way. Finally, in Chapter 10, I will show you how to perform logistic regression with a single neuron in Python—without using TensorFlow—entirely from scratch.

I hope you enjoy this book and have fun with it.

CHAPTER 1

Computational Graphs and TensorFlow

Before we delve into the extended examples later in this book, you will require a Python environment and a working knowledge of TensorFlow. Therefore, this chapter will show you how to install a Python environment ready to run the code in this book. Once that's in place, I'll cover the basics of the TensorFlow machine-learning library.

How to Set Up Your Python Environment

All the code in this book was developed with the Python distribution Anaconda and Jupyter notebooks. To set up Anaconda, first download and install it for your operating system. (I used Windows 10, but the code is not dependent on this system. Feel free to use a version for Mac, if you prefer.) You may retrieve Anaconda by accessing `https://anaconda.org/`.

On the right side of the web page, you will find a Download Anaconda link, as shown in Figure 1-1 (top right).

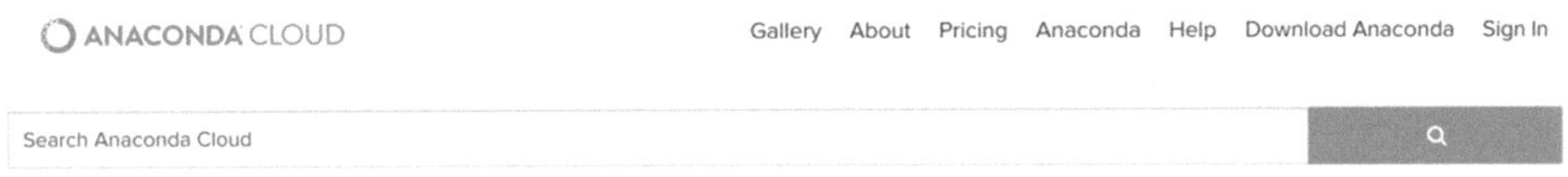

Figure 1-1. *On the Anaconda web site, at the top right of the page, you will find a link to download the required software*

Simply follow the instructions to install it. When you start it after the installation, you will be presented with the screen shown in Figure 1-2. In case you don't see this screen, simply click the Home link on the navigation pane at left.

U. Michelucci, *Applied Deep Learning*, https://doi.org/10.1007/978-1-4842-3790-8_1

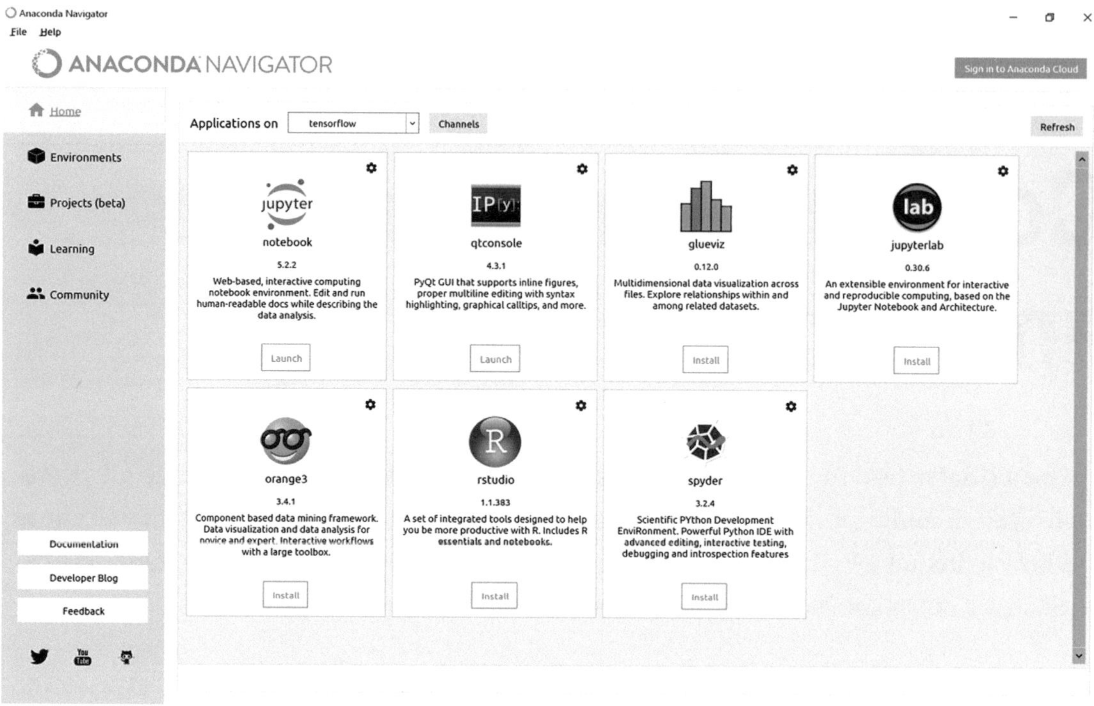

Figure 1-2. *The screen you see when you start Anaconda*

Python packages (like NumPy) are updated regularly and very often. It can happen that a new version of a package makes your code stop working. Functions are deprecated and removed, and new ones are added. To solve this problem, in Anaconda, you can create what is called an environment. This is basically a container that holds a specific Python version and specific versions of the packages you decide to install. With this, you can have a container for Python 2.7 and NumPy 1.10 and another with Python 3.6 and NumPy 1.13, for example. You may have to work with existing code that has been developed with Python 2.7, and, therefore, you must have a container with the right Python version. But, at the same time, it may be that you require Python 3.6 for your projects. With containers, you can ensure all this at the same time. Sometimes different packages conflict with each other, so you must be careful and avoid installing all packages you find interesting in your environment, especially if you are developing packages under a deadline. Nothing is worse than discovering that your code is no longer working, and you don't know why.

Note When you define an environment, try to install only the packages you really need, and pay attention when you update them, to make sure that any upgrade does not break your code. (Remember: Functions are deprecated, removed, added, or frequently changed.) Check the documentation of updates before upgrading, and do so only if you really need the updated features.

You can create an environment from the command line, using the `conda` command, but to get an environment up and running for our code, everything can be done from the graphical interface. This is the method I will explain here, because it is the easiest. I suggest that you read the following page on the Anaconda documentation, to understand in detail how to work within its environment: `https://conda.io/docs/user-guide/tasks/manage-environments.html`.

Creating an Environment

Let's get started. First, click the Environments link (the one that has a small icon representing a box) from the left navigation panel (Figure 1-3).

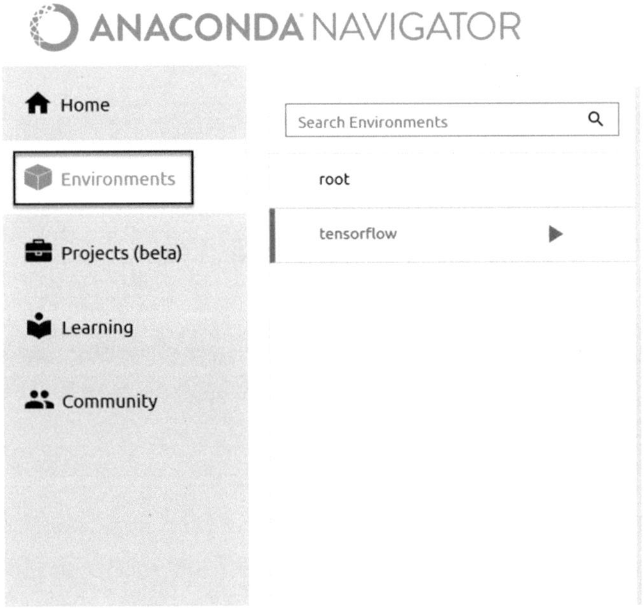

***Figure 1-3.** To create a new environment, you first must go into the Environments section of the application, by clicking the related link from the left navigation pane (indicated in the figure by a black rectangle)*

Then click the Create button in the middle navigation pane (as indicated in Figure 1-4).

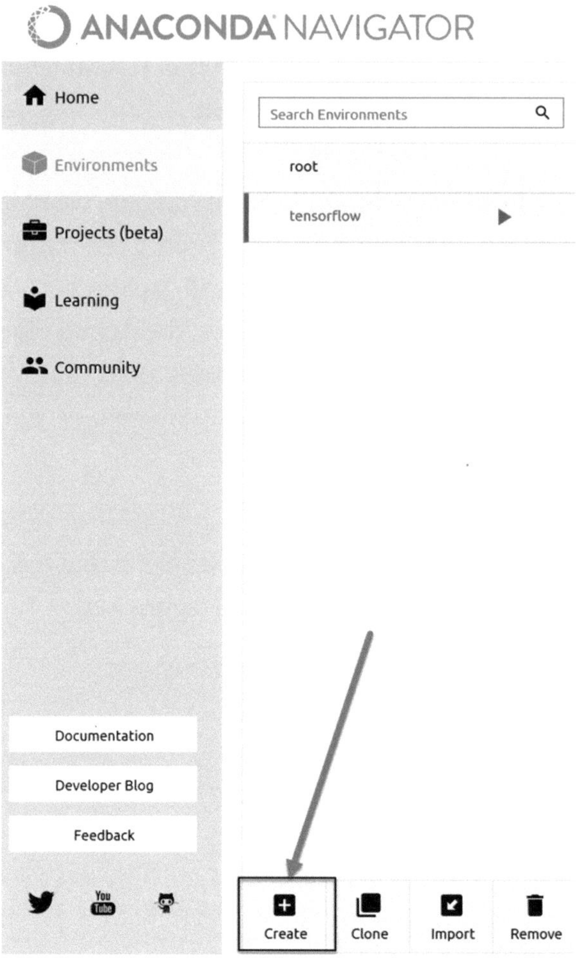

Figure 1-4. *To create a new environment, you must click the Create button (indicated with a plus sign) from the middle navigation pane. In the figure, a red arrow indicates the location of the button.*

When you click the Create button, a small window will pop up (see in Figure 1-5).

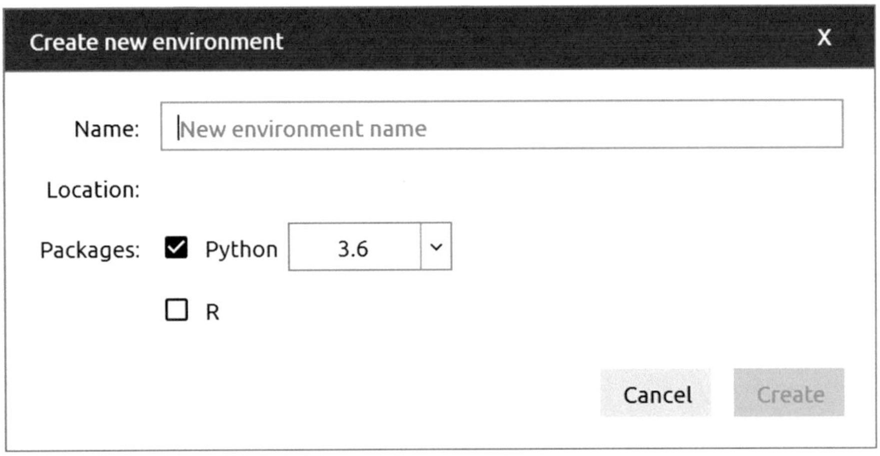

Figure 1-5. *The window you will see when you click the Create button indicated in Figure 1-4*

You can choose any name. In this book, I used the name *tensorflow*. As soon as you type a name, the Create button becomes active (and green). Click it and wait a few minutes until all the necessary packages are installed. Sometimes, you may get a pop-up window telling you that a new version of Anaconda is available and asking if you want to upgrade. Feel free to click yes. Follow the on-screen instructions until Anaconda navigator starts again, in the event you received this message and clicked yes.

We are not done yet. Click again the Environments link on the left navigation pane (as shown in Figure 1-3), then click the name of the newly created environment. If you've followed the instructions until now, you should see an environment named "tensorflow." After a few seconds, you will see on the right panel a list of all installed Python packages that you will have at your disposal in the environment. Now we must install some additional packages: NumPy, matplotlib, TensorFlow, and Jupyter. To do this, first select Not installed from the drop-down menu, as illustrated in Figure 1-6.

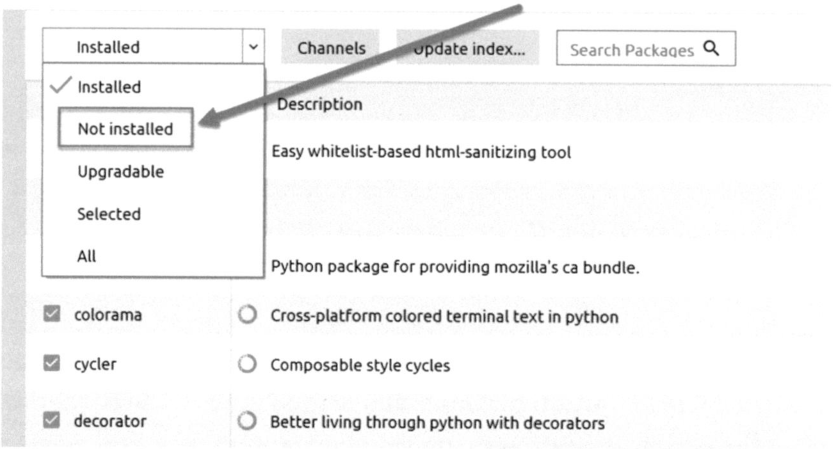

Figure 1-6. *Selecting the Not installed value from the drop-down menu*

Next, in the Search Packages field, type the package name you want to install (Figure 1-7 shows that `numpy` has been selected).

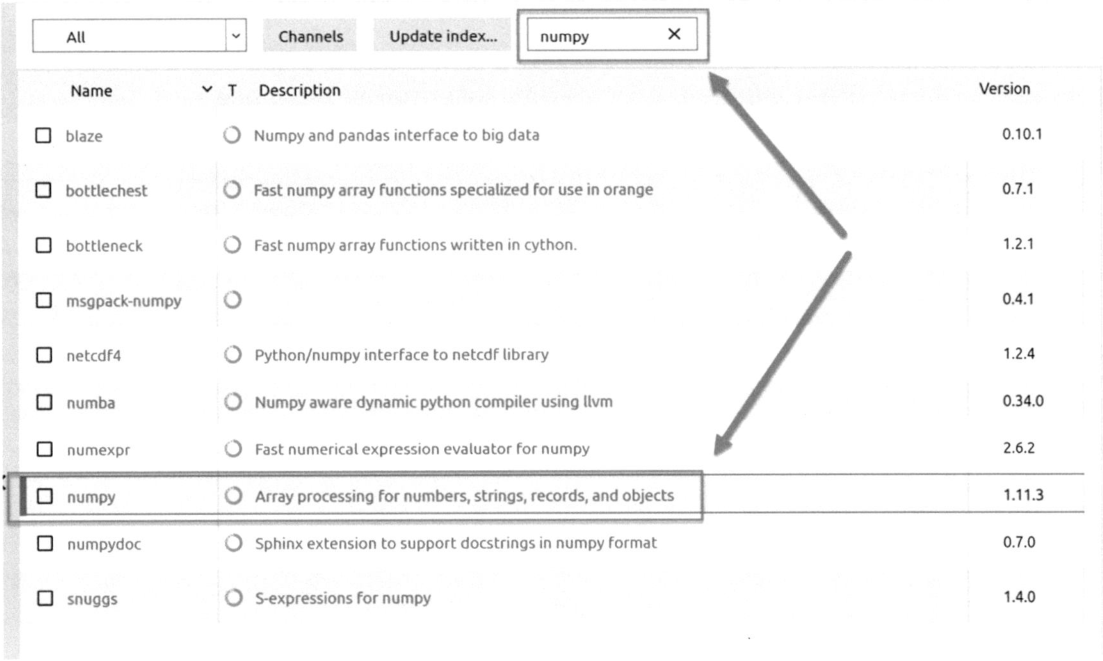

Figure 1-7. *Type "numpy" in the search field, to include it in the package repository*

Anaconda navigator will automatically show you all packages that have the word *numpy* in the title or in the description. Click the small square to the left of the name of the package that has the name *numpy*. It will become a small downward-pointing arrow (indicating that it is marked for installation). Then you can click the green Apply button at the lower right corner of the interface (see Figure 1-8).

Figure 1-8. *After you have selected the* `numpy` *package for installation, click the green Apply button. The button is at the lower right of the interface.*

Anaconda navigator is smart enough to determine if other packages are needed by `numpy`. You may get an additional window asking if it is OK to install the additional packages. Just click Apply. Figure 1-9 shows what this window looks like.

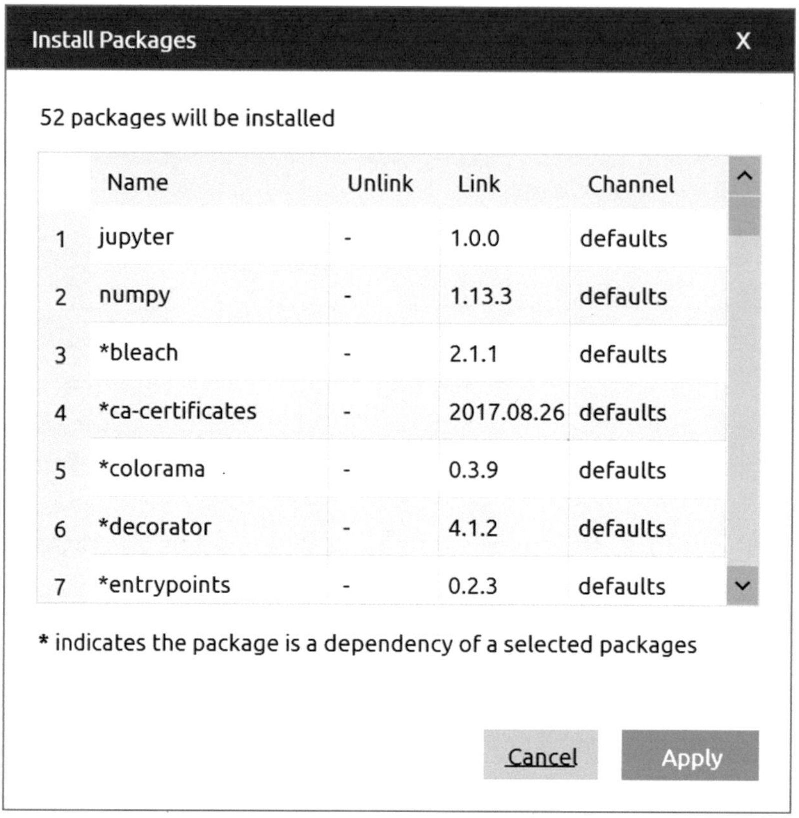

Figure 1-9. *When installing a package, the Anaconda navigator will check if what you want to install depends on other packages that are not installed. In such a case, it will suggest that you install the missing (but necessary) packages from an additional window. In our case, 52 additional packages were required by the NumPy library on a newly installed system. Simply click Apply to install all of them.*

You must install the following packages to be able to run the code in this book. (I added within parentheses the versions I used for testing the code in this book; subsequent versions are fine.)

- `numpy` (1.13.3): For doing numerical calculations
- `matplotlib` (2.1.1): To produce nice plots, as the ones you will see in this book
- `scikit-learn` (0.19.1): This package contains all the libraries related to machine learning and that we use, for example, to load datasets.
- `jupyter` (1.0.0): To be able to use the Jupyter notebooks

Installing TensorFlow

Installing TensorFlow is slightly more complex. The best way to do this is to follow the instructions given by the TensorFlow team, available at the following address: `www.tensorflow.org/install/`.

On this page, click your operating system, and you will receive all the information you need. I will provide here instructions for Windows, but the same can be done using a macOS or Ubuntu (Linux) system. The installation with Anaconda is not officially supported but works perfectly (it is community supported) and is the easiest way to get up and running and check the code in this book. For more advanced applications, you may want to consider other installation options. (For that, you will have to check the TensorFlow web site.) To begin, go to the Start menu in Windows and type "anaconda." Under Apps, you should see the Anaconda Prompt item, as in Figure 1-10.

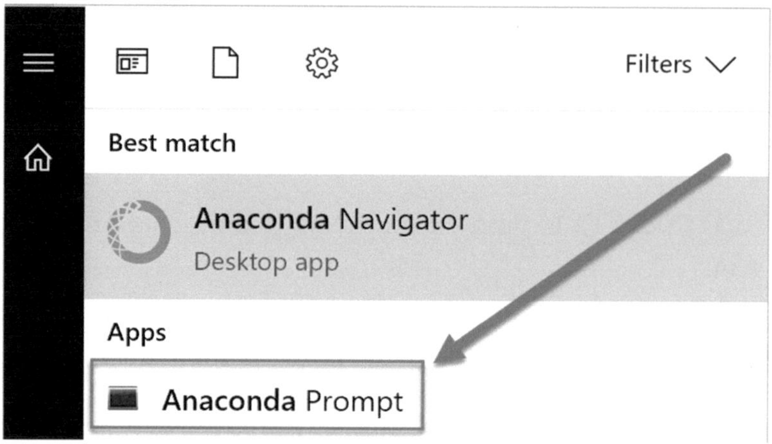

Figure 1-10. *If you type "anaconda" in the Start menu search field in Windows 10, you should see at least two entries: Anaconda Navigator, where you created the TensorFlow environment, and Anaconda Prompt*

Start the Anaconda Prompt. A command line interface should appear (see Figure 1-11). The difference between this and the simple `cmd.exe` command prompt is that here, all the Anaconda commands are recognized, without setting up any Windows environment variable.

Figure 1-11. *This is what you should see when you select Anaconda Prompt. Note that the user name will be different. You will see not* `umber` *(my username) but your username.*

At the command prompt, you first must activate your new "tensorflow" environment. This is necessary to let the Python installation know in which environment you want to install TensorFlow. To do this, simply type the following command: `activate tensorflow`. Your prompt should change to this: `(tensorflow) C:\Users\umber>`.

Remember: Your username will be different (you will see not umber in your prompt but your username). I will assume here that you will install the standard TensorFlow version that uses only the CPU (and not the GPU) version. Just type the following command: `pip install --ignore-installed --upgrade tensorflow`.

Now let the system install all the necessary packages. This may take a few minutes (depending on several factors, such as your computer speed or your Internet connection). You should not receive any error message. Congratulations! Now you have an environment in which you can run code using TensorFlow.

Jupyter Notebooks

The last step to be able to type code and let it run is to start a Jupyter notebook. The Jupyter notebook can be described (according to the official web site) as follows:

> *The Jupyter Notebook is an open-source web application that allows you to create and share documents that contain live code, equations, visualizations and narrative text. Uses include: data cleaning and transformation, numerical simulation, statistical modeling, data visualization, machine learning, and much more.*

It is widely used in the machine learning community, and it is a good idea to learn how to use it. Check the Jupyter project web site at `http://jupyter.org/`.

This site is very instructive and includes many examples of what is possible. All the code you find in this book has been developed and tested using Jupyter notebooks. I assume that you already have some experience with this web-based development environment. In case you need a refresher, I suggest you check the documentation you can find on the Jupyter project web site at the following address: `http://jupyter.org/documentation.html`.

To start a notebook in your new environment, you must go back to Anaconda navigator in the Environments section (see Figure 1-3). Click the triangle to the right of your "tensorflow" environment (in case you have used a different name, you will have to click the triangle to the right of your new environment), as shown in Figure 1-12. Then click Open with Jupyter Notebook.

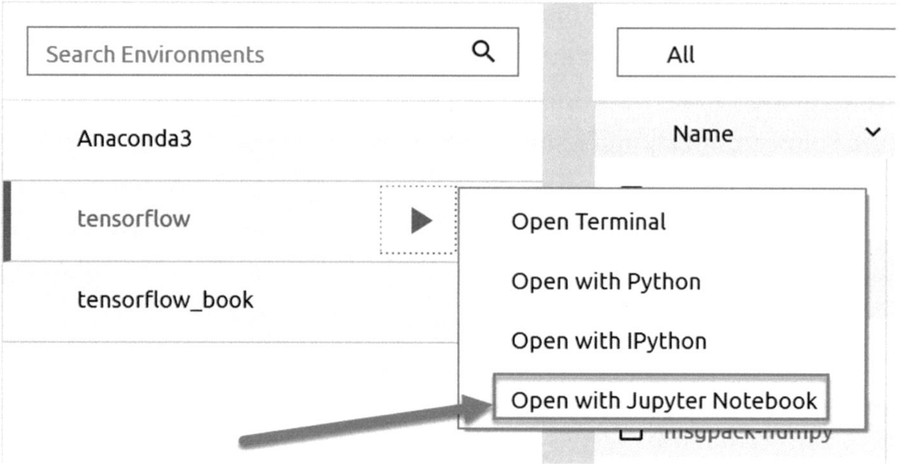

***Figure 1-12.** To start a Jupyter notebook in your new environment, click the triangle to the right of the "tensorflow" environment name and click Open with Jupyter Notebook*

Your browser will start with a list of all the folders you have in your user folder. (If you are using Windows, this is usually located under `c:\Users\<YOUR USER NAME>`, within which you must substitute `<YOUR USER NAME>` with your username.) From there, you should navigate to a folder where you want to save your notebook files and from which you can create a new notebook by clicking the New button, as illustrated in Figure 1-13.

***Figure 1-13.** To create a new notebook, click the New button located at the top-right corner of the page and select Python 3*

A new page will open that should look like the one in Figure 1-14.

***Figure 1-14.** When you create an empty notebook, an empty page will open that should look like this one*

For example, you can type the following code in the first "cell" (the rectangular box in which you can type).

```
a=1
b=2
print(a+b)
```

To evaluate the code, simply press Shift+Enter, and you should see the result (3) immediately (Figure 1-15).

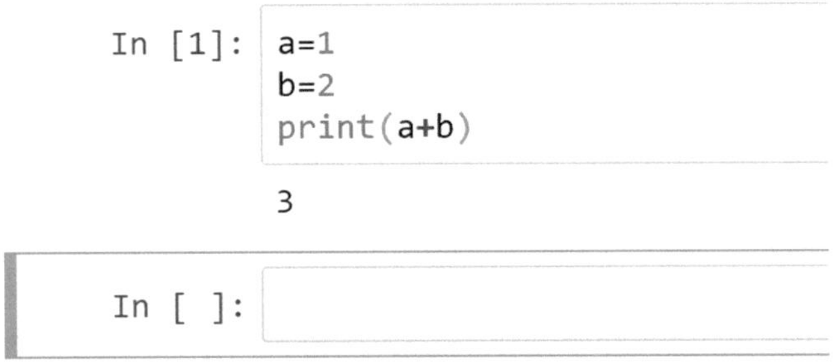

***Figure 1-15.** After typing some code in the cell, pressing Shift+Enter will evaluate the code in the cell*

The preceding code gives the result of `a+b`, that is, `3`. A new empty cell for you to type in is automatically created after the result is given. For more information on how to add comments, equations, inline plots, and much more, I suggest that you visit the Jupyter web site and check the documentation provided.

Note In case you forget the folder your notebook is in, you can check the URL of the page. For example, in my case, I have `http://localhost:8888/notebooks/Documents/Data%20Science/Projects/Applied%20advanced%20deep%20learning%20(book)/chapter%201/AADL%20-%20Chapter%201%20-%20Introduction.ipynb`. You will notice that the URL is simply a concatenation of the folders in which the notebook is located, separated by a forward slash. A `%20` character simply means a space. In this case, my notebook is in the folder: `Documents/Data Science/Projects/`... and so forth. I often work with several notebooks at the same time, and it is useful to know where each notebook is located in case you forget (I sometimes do).

Basic Introduction to TensorFlow

Before starting to use TensorFlow, you must understand the philosophy behind it. The library is heavily based on the concept of computational graphs, and unless you understand how those work, you cannot understand how to use the library. I will give you a quick introduction to computational graphs and show you how to implement simple calculations with TensorFlow. At the end of the next section, you should understand how the library works and how we will use it in this book.

Computational Graphs

To understand how TensorFlow works, you must understand what a computational graph is. A computational graph is a graph in which each node corresponds to an operation or a variable. Variables can feed their values into operations, and operations can feed their results into other operations. Usually, nodes are plotted as a circle (or ellipsis), with variable names or operations inside, and when one node's value is the input to another node, an arrow goes from one to another. The simplest graph that can exist is simply one with a single node that is simply a variable. (Remember: A node can be a variable or an operation.) The graph in Figure 1-16 simply computes the value of the variable *x*.

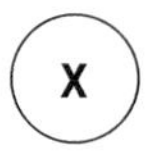

***Figure 1-16.** The simplest graph that we can build, showing a simple variable*

Not very interesting! Now let's consider something slightly more complex, such as the sum of two variables x and y: $z = x + y$. It can be done as in the following graph (Figure 1-17):

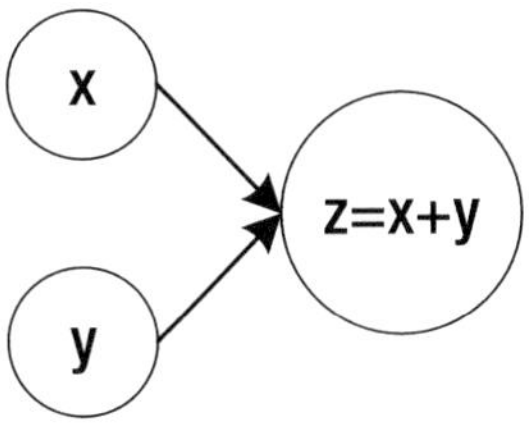

***Figure 1-17.** A basic computational graph for the sum of two variables*

The nodes at the left of Figure 1-17 (the ones with x and y inside) are variables, while the bigger node indicates the sum of the two variables. The arrows show that the two variables, x and y, are inputs to the third node. The graph should be read (and computed) in topological order, which means that you should follow the arrows that will indicate in which order you have to compute the different nodes. The arrow will also tell you the dependencies between the nodes. To evaluate z, you first must evaluate x and y. We can also say that the node that performs the sum is dependent on the input nodes.

An important aspect to understand is that such a graph only defines the operations (in this case, the sum) to perform on two input values (in this case, x and y) to obtain a result (in this case, z). It basically defines the "how." You must assign values to the input x and y and then perform the sum to obtain z. The graph will give you a result only when you evaluate all the nodes.

Note In this book, I will refer to the "construction" phase of a graph, when defining what each node is doing, and the "evaluation" phase, when we will actually evaluate the related operations.

This is a very important aspect to understand. Note that the input variables do not need to be real numbers. They can be matrices, vectors, and so on. (We will mostly use matrices in this book.) A slightly more complex example can be found in Figure 1-18 and uses a graph to calculate the quantity $A(x + y)$, given three input quantities: x, y, and A.

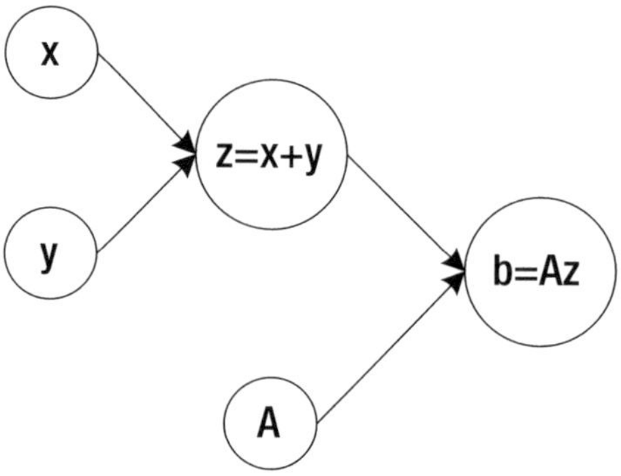

Figure 1-18. *A computational graph to calculate the quantity A(x + y), given three input quantities: x, y, and A*

We can evaluate this graph by assigning values to the input nodes (in this case, x, y, and A) and evaluate the nodes through the graph. For example, if you consider the graph in Figure 1-18 and assign the values $x = 1$, $y = 3$, and $A = 5$, we will get the result $b = 20$ (as plotted in Figure 1-19).

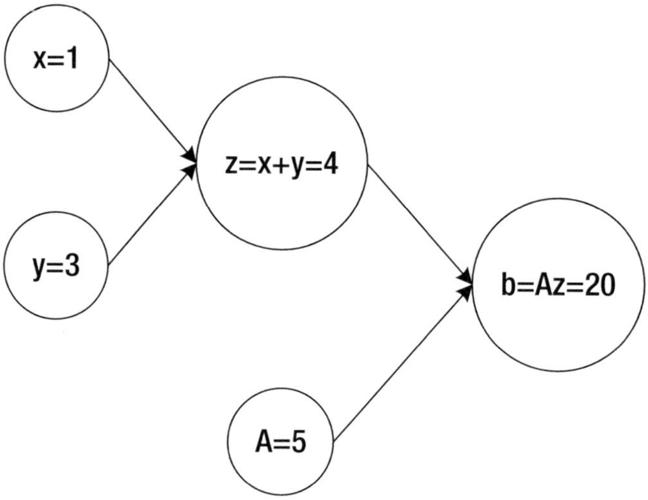

Figure 1-19. *To evaluate the graph in Figure 1-18, we must assign values to the input nodes x, y, and A and then evaluate the nodes through the graph*

A neural network is basically a very complicated computational graph, in which each neuron is composed by several nodes in the graph that feed its output to a certain number of other neurons, until a certain output is reached. In the next section, we will build the simplest neural network of all: one with a single neuron. Even with such a simple network, we will be able to do some pretty fun stuff.

`TensorFlow` allows you to build very complicated computational graphs very easily. And by construction, it separates their evaluation from the construction. (Remember that to compute a result, you must assign values and evaluate all the nodes.) In the next sections, I will show you how this works: how to build computational graphs and how to evaluate them.

Note Remember that `tensorflow` first builds a computational graph (in the so-called construction phase) but does not automatically evaluate it. The library keeps the two steps separate, so that you can compute your graph several times with different inputs, for example.

Tensors

The basic unit of data handled by `tensorflow` is—try to guess from its name—a tensor. A tensor is simply a collection of primitive types (such as, for example, floating numbers) shaped as an n-dimensional array. Here are some examples (with relative Python definitions) of tensors:

- 1 → a scalar
- [1,2,3] → a vector
- [[1,2,3], [4,5,6]] → a matrix or a two-dimensional array

A tensor has a static type and dynamic dimensions. You cannot change its type while evaluating it, but the dimensions can be changed dynamically before evaluating it. (Basically, you declare the tensors without specifying some of the dimensions, and `tensorflow` will infer the dimensions from the input values.) Usually, one talks about the rank of a tensor, which is simply the number of dimensions of the tensor (whereas a scalar is intended to have a rank of 0). Table 1-1 may help in understanding what the different ranks of tensors are.

***Table 1-1.** Examples of Tensors with Ranks 0, 1, 2, and 3*

Rank	Mathematical Entity	Python Example
0	Scalar (for example, length or weight)	L=30
1	A vector (for example, the speed of an object in a two-dimensional plane)	S=[10.2,12.6]
2	A matrix	M=[[23.2, 44.2], [12.2, 55.6]]
3	A 3D matrix (with three dimensions)	C = [[[1],[2]],[[3],[4]], [[5], [6]]]

Supposing you import `tensorflow` with the statement `import tensorflow as tf`, the basic object, a tensor, is the class `tf.tensor`. A `tf.tensor` has two properties:

- data type (for example, float32)
- shape (for example, [2,3], meaning a tensor with two rows and three columns)

An important aspect is that each element of a tensor always has the same data type, while the shape need not be defined at declaration time. (This will be clearer in the practical examples in the next chapters.) The main types of tensors (there are more) that we will see in this book are

- `tf.Variable`
- `tf.constant`
- `tf.placeholder`

The `tf.constant` and the `tf.placeholder` values are, during a single-session run (more on that later), immutable. Once they have a value, they will not change. For example, a `tf.placeholder` could contain the dataset you want to use for training your neural network. Once assigned, it will not change during the evaluation phase. A `tf.Variable` could contain the weights of your neural networks. They will change during training, to find their optimal values for your specific problem. Finally, a `tf.constant` will never change. I will show you in the next section how to use the three different types of tensors and what aspect you should consider when developing your models.

Creating and Running a Computational Graph

Let's start using `tensorflow` to create a computational graph.

Note Remember: We always keep the construction phase (when we define what a graph should do) and its evaluation (when we perform the calculations) separate. `tensorflow` follows the same philosophy: first you construct a graph, and then you evaluate it.

Let's consider something very easy: the sum of two tensors

$$x_1 + x_2$$

that can be calculated with the computational graph depicted in Figure 1-20.

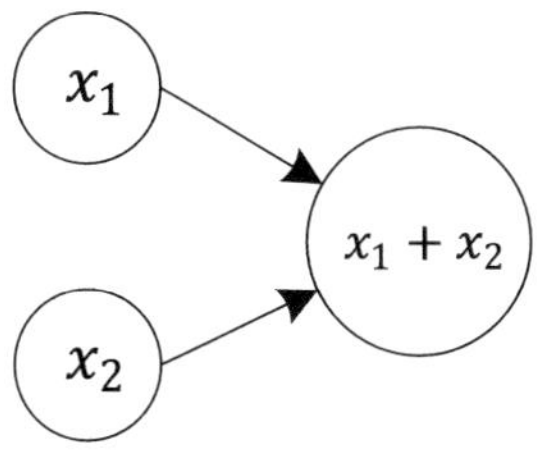

Figure 1-20. *The computational graph for the sum of two tensors*

Computational Graph with tf.constant

As discussed, first we must create this computational graph with `tensorflow`. (Remember: We begin with the construction phase.) Let's start using the `tf.constant` tensor type. We need three nodes: two for the input variables and one for the sum. This can be achieved with the following code:

```
x1 = tf.constant(1)
x2 = tf.constant(2)
z = tf.add(x1, x2)
```

The preceding code creates the computational graph in Figure 1-20 and, at the same time, tells `tensorflow` that `x1` should have the value `1` (the value in the parentheses in the declaration), and `x2` should have the value `2`. Now, to evaluate the code, we must create what `tensorflow` calls a session (wherein an actual evaluation can take place), and then we can ask the session class to run our graph with the following code:

```
sess = tf.Session()
print(sess.run(z))
```

This will simply give you the evaluated result of `z` that is, as expected, `3`. This version of the code is rather simple and does not require much, but it is not very flexible. `x1` and `x2` are fixed and cannot be changed during the evaluation, for example.

Note In `TensorFlow`, you first must create a computational graph, then create a session, and finally run your graph. These three steps must always be followed to evaluate your graph.

Remember: You can also ask `tensorflow` to evaluate only an intermediate step. For example, you might want to evaluate `x1` (not very interesting, but there are many cases in which it will be useful, for example, when you want to evaluate your graph and, at the same time, the accuracy and the cost function of a model), as follows: `sess.run(x1)`.

You will get the result 1, as expected (you expected that, right?). At the end, remember to close the session with `sess.close()` to free up used resources.

Computational Graph with tf.Variable

The same computational graph (the one in Figure 1-20) can be created with variables, but that requires a bit more work. Let's re-create our computational graph.

```
x1 = tf.Variable(1)
x2 = tf.Variable(2)
z = tf.add(x1,x2)
```

We want to initialize the variables with the values `1` and `2`, as before.[1] The problem is that when you run the graph, as we did before, with the code

```
sess = tf.Session()
print(sess.run(z))
```

[1]To learn more about variables, check the official documentation at `www.tensorflow.org/versions/master/api_docs/python/tf/Variable`.

you will receive an error message. It is a very long error message, but near the end, you will find the following message:

```
FailedPreconditionError (see above for traceback): Attempting to use
uninitialized value Variable
```

This occurs because `tensorflow` does not automatically initialize the variables. To do this, you could use this approach:

```
sess = tf.Session()
sess.run(x1.initializer)
sess.run(x2.initializer)
print(sess.run(z))
```

This works now without errors. Line `sess.run(x1.initializer)` will initialize the variable `x1` with the value `1`, and the line `sess.run(x2.initializer)` will initialize the variable `x2` with the value `2`. But this is rather cumbersome. (You don't want to write a line for each variable you need to initialize.) A much better approach is to add a node to your computational graph that has the goal of initializing all the variables you define in your graph with the code

```
init = tf.global_variables_initializer()
```

and then again create and run your session, running this node (`init`) before evaluating `z`.

```
sess = tf.Session()
sess.run(init)
print(sess.run(z))
sess.close()
```

This will work and give you the result `3`, as you would expect.

Note When working with variables, remember always to add a global initializer (`tf.global_variables_initializer()`) and run the node in your session at the beginning, before any other evaluation. We will see in many examples during the book how this works.

Computational Graph with tf.placeholder

Let's declare `x1` and `x2` as placeholders.

```
x1 = tf.placeholder(tf.float32, 1)
x2 = tf.placeholder(tf.float32, 1)
```

Note that I have not provided any value in the declaration.[2] We will have to assign a value to `x1` and `x2` at evaluation time. That is the main difference between placeholders and the other two tensor types. The sum, then, is given again by

```
z = tf.add(x1,x2)
```

Note that if you try to see what is in `z` using, for example, `print(z)`, you will get

```
Tensor("Add:0", shape=(1,), dtype=float32)
```

Why this strange result? First, we have not given `tensorflow` the values for `x1` and `x2` and, second, `TensorFlow` has not yet run any calculation. Remember: Graph construction and evaluation are separate steps. Now let's create a session in `TensorFlow`, as before.

```
sess = tf.Session()
```

Now we can run the actual calculation, but to do that, we must first have a way of assigning values to the two inputs `x1` and `x2`. This can be achieved by using a Python dictionary that contains all the placeholders' names as keys and assign to them values. In this example, we assign to `x1` the value `1` and to `x2` the value `2`.

```
feed_dict={ x1: [1], x2: [2]}
```

Feeding this code to the `TensorFlow` session can be done with the following command:

```
print(sess.run(z, feed_dict))
```

[2]It is always a good idea to check the official documentation for the datatypes: `www.tensorflow.org/versions/master/api_docs/python/tf/placeholder`.

You finally get the result you expected: `3`. Note that `tensorflow` is rather smart and can handle more complicated inputs. Let's redefine our placeholder to be able to use arrays with two elements. (Here, we report the entire code, to make it easier to follow the example.)

```
x1 = tf.placeholder(tf.float32, [2])
x2 = tf.placeholder(tf.float32, [2])

z = tf.add(x1,x2)
feed_dict={ x1: [1,5], x2: [1,1]}

sess = tf.Session()
sess.run(z, feed_dict)
```

This time, you will get an array with two elements as output.

```
array([ 2., 6.], dtype=float32)
```

Remember that `x1=[1,5]` and `x2=[1,1]` meaning that `z=x1+x2=[1,5]+[1,1]=[2,6]`, because the sum is done element by element.

To summarize, here are some guidelines on when to use which tensor type:

- Use `tf.placeholder` for entities that will not change at each evaluation phase. Usually, those are input values or parameters that you want to keep fixed during the evaluation but may change with each run. (You will see several examples later in the book.) Examples include input dataset, learning rate, etc.
- Use `tf.Variable` for entities that will change during the calculation, for example, the weights of our neural networks, as you will see later in the book.
- Use `tf.constant` for entities that will never change, for example, fix values in your model that you don't want to change anymore.

Figure 1-21 depicts a slightly more complex example: the computational graph for the calculation $x_1w_1 + x_2w_2$.

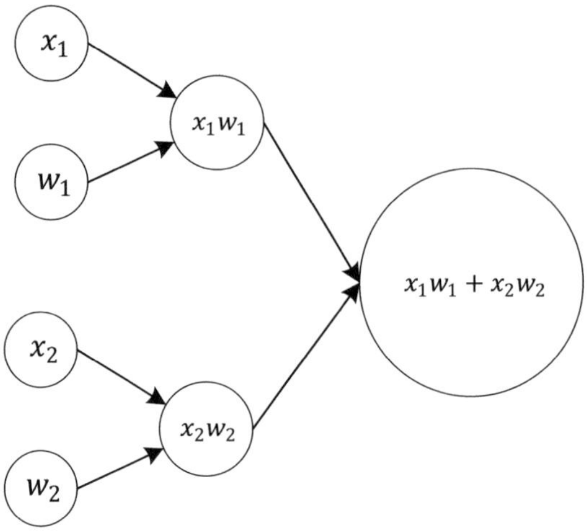

Figure 1-21. *The computational graph for the calculation* $x_1w_1 + x_2w_2$

In this case, I defined x_1, x_2, w_1, and w_2 as placeholders (they will be our inputs) containing scalars (remember: when defining placeholders, you must always pass the dimensions as second input parameters, in this case, the `1`).

```
x1 = tf.placeholder(tf.float32, 1)
w1 = tf.placeholder(tf.float32, 1)
x2 = tf.placeholder(tf.float32, 1)
w2 = tf.placeholder(tf.float32, 1)

z1 = tf.multiply(x1,w1)
z2 = tf.multiply(x2,w2)
z3 = tf.add(z1,z2)
```

Running the calculations means simply (as before) defining the dictionary containing the input values, creating a session, and then running it.

```
feed_dict={ x1: [1], w1:[2], x2:[3], w2:[4]}
sess = tf.Session()
sess.run(z3, feed_dict)
```

As expected, you will get the following result:

```
array([ 14.], dtype=float32)
```

This is simply $1 \times 2 + 3 \times 4 = 2 + 12 = 14$ (remember that we have fed the values 1, 2, 3, and 4 in `feed_dict`, in the previous step). In the Chapter 2, we will draw the computational graph for a single neuron and apply what we have learned in this chapter to a very practical case. Using that graph, we will be able to do linear and logistic regression on a real dataset. As always, remember to close the session with `sess.close()` when you are done.

Note In `TensorFlow`, it can happen that the same piece of code runs several times, and you can end up with a computational graph with multiple copies of the same node. A very common way of avoiding such a problem is to run the code `tf.reset_default_graph()` before the code that constructs the graph. Note that if you separate your construction code from your evaluation code appropriately, you should be able to avoid such problems. We will see later in the book in many examples how this is working.

Differences Between run and eval

If you look at blogs and books, you may find two ways of evaluating a computational graph with `tensorflow`. The one we have used up to now is `sess.run()`, in which the function wants as argument the name of the node you want to evaluate. We have chosen this method because it has a nice advantage. To understand it, consider the following code (the same you have seen previously)

```
x1 = tf.constant(1)
x2 = tf.constant(2)
z = tf.add(x1, x2)
init = tf.global_variables_initializer()
sess = tf.Session()
sess.run(init)
sess.run(z)
```

This will only give you the evaluated node z, but you can also evaluate several nodes at the same time, using the following code:

```
sess.run([x1,x2,z])
```

This will give you

```
[1, 2, 3]
```

And that is very useful, as will become clear in the next section about the life cycle of a node. Additionally, evaluating many nodes at the same time will make your code shorter and more readable.

The second method of evaluating a node in a graph is to use the `eval()` call. This code

```
z.eval(session=sess)
```

will evaluate `z`. But this time, you must explicitly tell `TensorFlow` which session you want to use (you may have several defined). This is not very practical, and I prefer to use the `run()` method to get several results at the same time (for example, the cost function, accuracy, and F1 score). There is also a performance reason to prefer the first method, as explained in the next section.

Dependencies Between Nodes

As I mentioned before, `TensorFlow` evaluates a graph in topological order, which means that when you ask it to evaluate a node, it automatically determines all the nodes that are required to evaluate what you are asking and evaluate them first. The problem is that `TensorFlow` might evaluate some nodes multiple times. Consider the following code, for example:

```
c = tf.constant(5)
x = c + 1
y = x + 1
z = x + 2
sess = tf.Session()
print(sess.run(y))
print(sess.run(z))
sess.close()
```

This code will build and evaluate the computational graph in Figure 1-22.

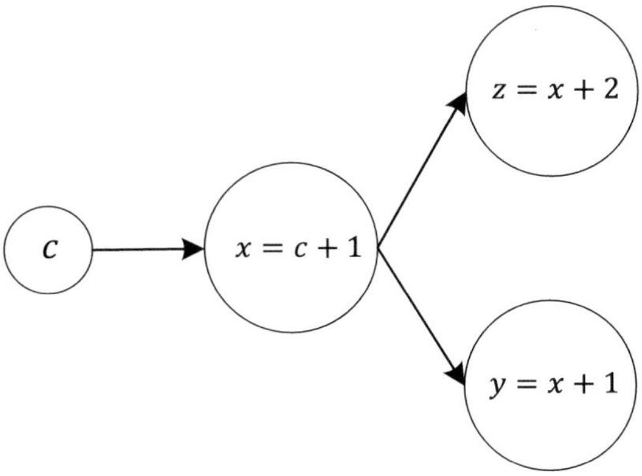

Figure 1-22. *The computational graph that the code cited at the beginning of the section builds*

As you can see, *z* and *y* both depend from *x*. The problem with the code as we have written, is that `TensorFlow` will not reuse the result of the previous evaluation of *c* and *x*. This means that it will evaluate the node for *x* one time when evaluating *z* and again when evaluating *y*. In this case, for example, using the code `yy, zz = sess.run([y,z])` will evaluate *y* and *z* in one run, and *x* only once.

Tips on How to Create and Close a Session

I showed you how to create a session with the template

```
sess = tf.Session()
# Code that does something
```

At the end, you should always close a session, to free up used resources. The syntax is quite easy:

```
sess.close()
```

Keep in mind that the moment you close the session, you cannot evaluate anything else. You must create a new session and perform your evaluation again. In a Jupyter environment, this method has the advantage of allowing you to split your evaluation code in several cells and then close the session at the very end. But it is useful to know that there is a slightly more compact way of opening and using a session, using the following template:

```
With tf.Session() as sess:
# code that does something
```

For example, the code

```
sess = tf.Session()
print(sess.run(y))
print(sess.run(z))
sess.close()
```

from the previous section could have been written as

```
with tf.Session() as sess:
    print(sess.run(y))
    print(sess.run(z))
```

In this case, the session would automatically be closed at the end of the `with` clause. Using this method makes using `eval()` easier. For example, the code

```
sess = tf.Session()
print(z.eval(session=sess))
sess.close()
```

will look like this with the `with` clause

```
with tf.Session() as sess:
    print(z.eval())
```

There are some cases in which the explicit declaration of the session is preferred. For example, it is rather common to write a function that performs the actual graph evaluation and that returns the session, so that additional evaluation (for example, of the accuracy or similar metrics) can be done after the main training has finished. In this case, you cannot use the second version, because it would close the session immediately after finishing the evaluation, therefore making additional evaluations with the session results impossible.

Note If you are working in an interactive environment such as Jupyter notebooks and you want to split your evaluation code on multiple notebook cells, it is easier to declare the session as `sess = tf.Session()`, perform the calculations needed, and then, at the end, close it. In this way, you can intercalate evaluations, graphs, and text. In case you are writing code that will not be interactive, it is sometimes preferable (and less error-prone) to use the second version, to make sure that the session is closed at the end. Additionally, with the second method, you don't have to specify the session when using the `eval()` method.

The material covered in this chapter should give you all you need to build your neural networks with `tensorflow`. What I explained here is by no means complete or exhaustive. You should really take some time and go on the official TensorFlow web site and study the tutorials and other materials there.

Note In this book I use a *lazy programming approach*. That means that I explain only what I want you to understand, nothing more. The reason is that I want you to focus on the learning goals for each chapter, and I don't want you to be distracted by the complexity that lies behind the methods or the programming functions. Once you understand what I am trying to explain, you should invest some time and dive deeper into the methods and libraries, using the official documentation.

CHAPTER 2

Single Neuron

In this chapter, I will discuss what a neuron is and what its components are. I will clarify the mathematical notation we will require and cover the many activation functions that are used today in neural networks. Gradient descent optimization will be discussed in detail, and the concept of learning rate and its quirks will be introduced. To make things a bit more fun, we will then use a single neuron to perform linear and logistic regression on real datasets. I will then discuss and explain how to implement the two algorithms with `tensorflow`.

To keep the chapter focused and the learning efficient, I have left out a few things on purpose. For example, we will not split the dataset into training and test parts. We simply use all the data. Using the two would force us to do some proper analysis, and that would distract from the main goal of this chapter and make it way too long. Later in the book, I will conduct a proper analysis of the consequences of using several datasets and see how to do this properly, especially in the context of deep learning. This is a subject that requires its own chapter.

You can do wonderful, amazing, and fun things with deep learning. Let's start to have fun!

The Structure of a Neuron

Deep learning is based on large and complex networks made up of a large number of simple computational units. Companies on the forefront of research are dealing with networks with 160 billion parameters [1]. To put things in perspective, this number is half that of the stars in our galaxy, or 1.5 times the number of people who ever lived. On a basic level, neural networks are a large set of differently interconnected units, each performing a specific (and usually relatively easy) computation. They recall LEGO toys, with which you can build very complex things using very simple and basic units. Neural networks are similar. Using relatively simple computational units, you can build

U. Michelucci, *Applied Deep Learning*, https://doi.org/10.1007/978-1-4842-3790-8_2

very complex systems. We can vary the basic units, changing how they compute the result, how they are connected to each other, how they use the input values, and so on. Roughly formulated, all those aspects define what is known as the network architecture. Changing it will change how the network learns, how accurate the predictions are, and so on.

Those basic units are known, due to a biological parallel with the brain [2], as neurons. Basically, each neuron does a very simple thing: takes a certain number of inputs (real numbers) and calculates an output (also a real number). In this book, our inputs will be indicated by $x_i \in R$ (real numbers), with $i = 1, 2, \ldots, n_x$, where $i \in N$ is an integer and n_x is the number of input attributes (often called features). As an example of input features, you can imagine the age and weight of a person (so, we would have $n_x = 2$). x_1 could be the age, and x_2 could be the weight. In real life, the number of features easily can be very big. In the dataset that we will use for our logistic regression example later in the chapter, we will have $n_x = 784$.

There are several kinds of neurons that have been extensively studied. In this book, we will concentrate on the most commonly used one. The neuron we are interested in simply applies a function to a linear combination of all the inputs. In a more mathematical form, given n_x, real parameters $w_i \in R$ (with $i = 1, 2, \ldots, n_x$), and a constant $b \in R$ (usually called bias), the neuron will calculate first what is usually indicated in literature and in books by z.

$$z = w_1 x_1 + w_2 x_2 + \cdots + w_{n_x} x_{n_x} + b$$

It will then apply a function f to z, giving the output $\hat{y}$.

$$\hat{y} = f(z) = f\left(w_1 x_1 + w_2 x_2 + \cdots + w_{n_x} x_{n_x} + b\right)$$

Note Practitioners mostly use the following nomenclature: w_i refers to weights, b bias, x_i input features, and f the activation function.

Owing to a biological parallel, the function f is called the neuron activation function (and sometimes transfer function), which will be discussed at length in the next sections.

Let's summarize the neuron computational steps again.

1. Combine linearly all inputs x_i, calculating $z = w_1x_1 + w_2x_2 + \cdots + w_{n_x}x_{n_x} + b$;
2. Apply f to z, giving the output $\hat{y} = f(z) = f\left(w_1x_1 + w_2x_2 + \cdots + w_{n_x}x_{n_x} + b\right)$.

You may remember that in Chapter 1, I discussed computational graphs. In Figure 2-1, you will find the graph for the neuron described previously.

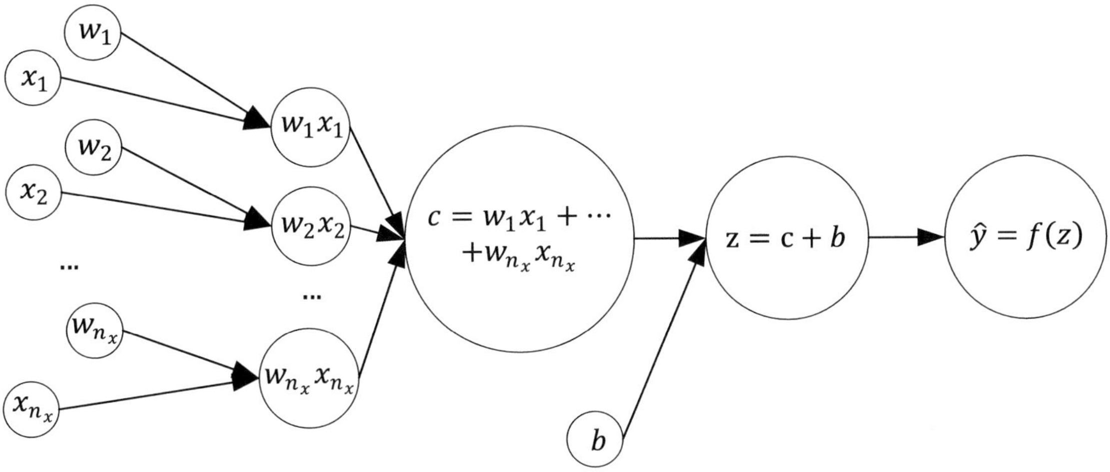

***Figure 2-1.** The computational graph for the neuron described in the text*

This is not what you usually find in blogs, books, and tutorials. It is rather complicated and not very practical to use, especially when you want to draw networks with many neurons. In the literature, you can find numerous representations for neurons. In this book, we will use the one shown in Figure 2-2, because it is widely used and is easy to understand.

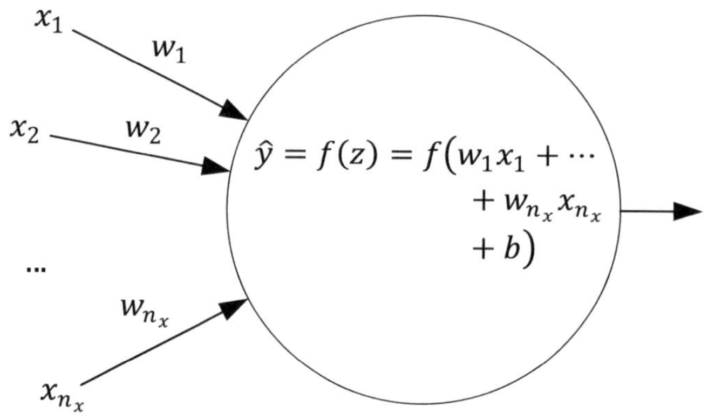

Figure 2-2. *The neuron representation mostly used by practitioners*

Figure 2-2 must be interpreted in the following way:

- The inputs are not put in a bubble. This is simply to distinguish them from nodes that perform an actual calculation.
- The weights' names are written along the arrow. This means that before passing the inputs to the central bubble (or node), the input first will be multiplied by the relative weight, as labeled on the arrow. The first input, x_1, will be multiplied by w_1, x_2, by w_2, and so on.
- The central bubble (or node) will perform several calculations at the same time. First, it will sum the inputs (the x_iw_i for $i = 1, 2, \ldots, n_x$), then sum to the result the bias b, and, finally, apply to the resulting value the activation function.

All neurons we will deal with in this book will have exactly this structure. Very often, an even simpler representation is used, as in Figure 2-3. In such a case, unless otherwise stated, it is understood that the output is

$$\hat{y} = f(z) = f\left(w_1x_1 + w_2x_2 + \cdots + w_{n_x}x_{n_x} + b\right)$$

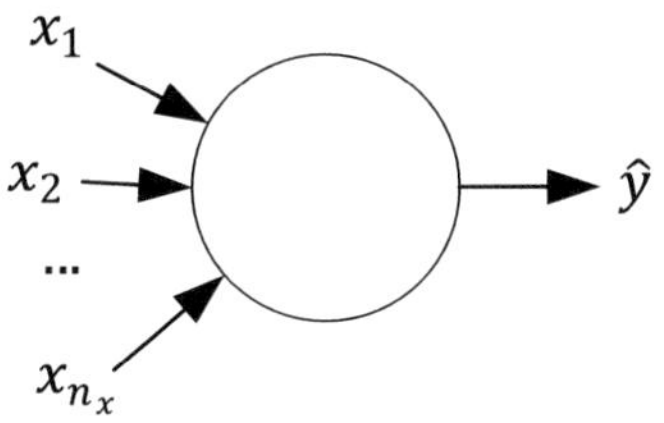

Figure 2-3. *The following representation is a simplified version of Figure 2-2. Unless otherwise stated, it is usually understood that the output is* $\hat{y} = f(z) = f\left(w_1x_1 + w_2x_2 + \ldots + w_{n_x}x_{n_x} + b\right)$. *The weights are often not explicitly reported in the neuron representation.*

Matrix Notation

When dealing with big datasets, the number of features is large (n_x will be big), and so it is better to use a vector notation for the features and the weights, as follows:

$$\boldsymbol{x} = \begin{pmatrix} x_1 \\ \vdots \\ x_{n_x} \end{pmatrix}$$

where we have indicated the vector with a boldfaced $\boldsymbol{x}$. For the weights, we use the same notation:

$$\boldsymbol{w} = \begin{pmatrix} w_1 \\ \vdots \\ w_{n_x} \end{pmatrix}$$

For consistency with formulas that we will use later, to multiply $\boldsymbol{x}$ and $\boldsymbol{w}$, we will use matrix multiplication notation, and, therefore, we will write

$$\boldsymbol{w}^T\boldsymbol{x} = \left(w_1 \ldots w_{n_x}\right)\begin{pmatrix} x_1 \\ \vdots \\ x_{n_x} \end{pmatrix} = w_1x_1 + w_2x_2 + \cdots + w_{n_x}x_{n_x}$$

where $\boldsymbol{w}^T$ indicates the transpose of $\boldsymbol{w}$. z can then be written with this vector notation as

$$z = \boldsymbol{w}^T \boldsymbol{x} + b$$

and the neuron output $\hat{y}$ as

$$\hat{y} = f(z) = f\left(\boldsymbol{w}^T \boldsymbol{x} + b\right) \# (3)$$

Let's now summarize the different components that define our neuron and the notation we will use in this book.

- $\hat{y}$ → neuron output
- $f(z)$ → activation function (or transfer function) applied to z
- $\boldsymbol{w}$ → weights (vector with n_x components)
- b → bias

Python Implementation Tip: Loops and NumPy

The calculation that we have outlined in the equation (3) can be done in Python by standard lists and with loops, but those tend to be very slow, as the number of variables and observations grows. A good rule of thumb is to avoid loops, when possible, and to use `NumPy` (or `TensorFlow`, as we will see later) methods as often as possible.

It is easy to get an idea of how fast `NumPy` can be (and how slow loops are). Let's start by creating two standard lists of random numbers in Python with 10^7 elements in each.

```
import random
lst1 = random.sample(range(1, 10**8), 10**7)
lst2 = random.sample(range(1, 10**8), 10**7)
```

The actual values are not relevant for our purposes. We are simply interested in how fast Python can multiply two lists, element by element. The times reported were measured on a 2017 Microsoft surface laptop and will vary greatly, depending on the hardware the code runs on. We are not interested in the absolute values, but only on how much faster `NumPy` is in comparison with standard Python loops. To time Python code in a Jupyter notebook, we can use a "magic command." Usually, in a Jupyter notebook, these commands start with %% or %. A good idea is to check the official documentation, accessible from `http://ipython.readthedocs.io/en/stable/interactive/magics.html`, to better understand how they work.

Going back to our test, let's measure how much time a standard laptop takes to multiply, element by element, the two lists with standard loops. Using the code

```
%%timeit
ab = [lst1[i]*lst2[i] for i in range(len(lst1))]
```

gives us the following result (note that on your computer, you will probably get a different result):

```
2.06 s ± 326 ms per loop (mean ± std. dev. of 7 runs, 1 loop each)
```

Over seven runs, the code needed roughly two seconds on average. Now let's try to do the same multiplication, but, this time, using `NumPy` where we have first converted the two lists to `NumPy` arrays, with the following code:

```
import numpy as np
list1_np = np.array(lst1)
list2_np = np.array(lst2)

%%timeit
Out2 = np.multiply(list1_np, list2_np)
```

This time, we get the following result:

```
20.8 ms ± 2.5 ms per loop (mean ± std. dev. of 7 runs, 10 loops each)
```

The `numpy` code needed only 21 ms, or, in other words, was roughly 100 times faster than the code with standard loops. `NumPy` is faster for two reasons: the underlying routines are written in C, and it uses vectorized code as much as possible to speed up calculations on big amounts of data.

Note Vectorized code refers to operations that are performed on multiple components of a vector (or a matrix) at the same time (in one statement). Passing matrices to `NumPy` functions is a good example of vectorized code. `NumPy` will perform operations on big chunks of data at the same time, obtaining a much better performance with respect to standard Python loops, which must operate on one element at a time. Note that part of the good performance `NumPy` is showing is also owing to the underlying routines being written in C.

While training deep learning models, you will find yourself doing this kind of operation over and over, and, therefore, such a speed gain will make the difference between having a model that can be trained and one that will never give you a result.

Activation Functions

There are many activation functions at our disposal to change the output of our neuron. Remember: An activation function is simply a mathematical function that transforms z in the output $\hat{y}$. Let's have a look at the most used.

Identity Function

This is the most basic function that you can use. Usually, it is indicated by $I(z)$. It returns simply the input value unchanged. Mathematically we have

$$f(z) = I(z) = z$$

This simple function will come in handy when I discuss linear regression with one neuron later in the chapter. Figure 2-4 shows what it looks like.

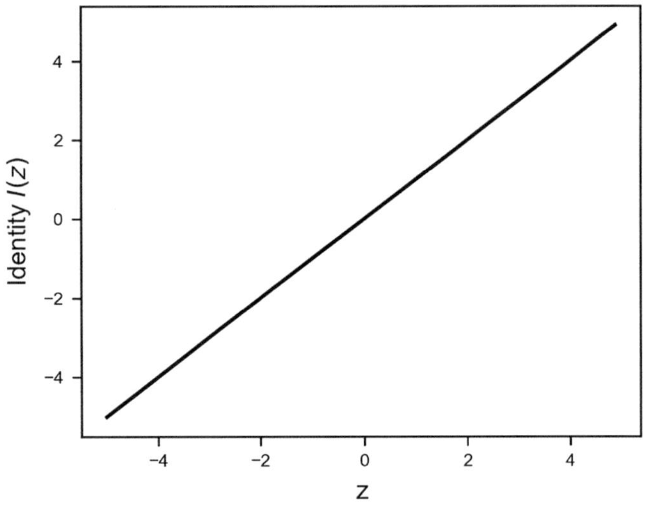

Figure 2-4. *The identity function*

Implementing an identity function in Python with `numpy` is particularly simple.

```
def identity(z):
    return z
```

Sigmoid Function

This is a very commonly used function that gives only values between 0 and 1. It is usually indicated by $\sigma(z)$.

$$f(z)=\sigma(z)=\frac{1}{1+e^{-z}}$$

It is especially used for models in which we must predict the probability as an output (remember that a probability may only assume values between 0 and 1). You can see its shape in Figure 2-5. Note that in Python, if z is big enough, it can happen that the function returns exactly 0 or 1 (depending on the sign of z) for rounding errors. In classification problems, we will calculate $\log\sigma(z)$ or $\log(1 - \sigma(z))$ very often, and, therefore, this can be a source of errors in Python, because it will try to calculate log 0, which is not defined. For example, you can start seeing `nan` appearing while calculating the cost function (more on that later). We will see a practical example of this phenomenon later in the chapter.

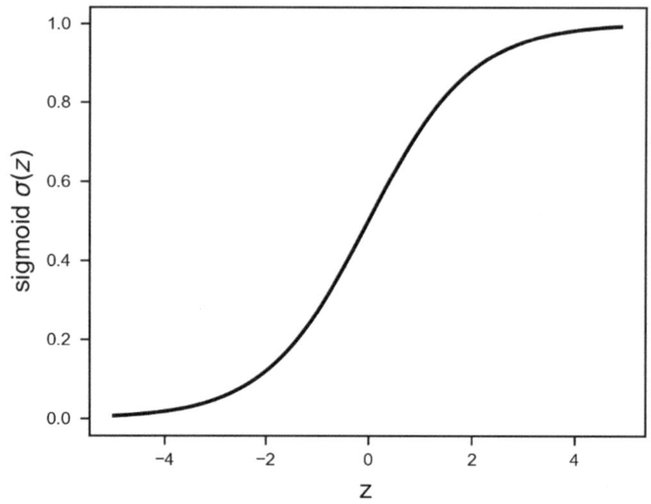

***Figure 2-5.** The sigmoid activation function is an s-shaped function that goes from 0 to 1*

Note Although $\sigma(z)$ should never be exactly 0 or 1, while programming in Python, the reality can be quite different. due to a very big z (positive or negative), Python may round the results to exactly 0 or 1. This could give you errors while calculating the cost function (I will give you a detailed explanation and practical example later in the chapter) for classification, because we will need to calculate $\log \sigma(z)$ and $\log(1 - \sigma(z))$ and, therefore, Python will try to calculate $\log 0$, which is not defined. This may occur, for example, if we don't normalize our input data correctly, or if we don't initialize our weights correctly. For the moment, it is important to remember that although mathematically everything seems under control, the reality while programming can be more difficult. It is something that is good to keep in mind while debugging models that, for example, give `nan` as a result for the cost function.

The behavior with z can be seen in Figure 2-5. The calculation can be written in this form using numpy functions:

```
s = np.divide(1.0, np.add(1.0, np.exp(-z)))
```

Note It is very useful to know that if we have two numpy arrays, A and B, the following are equivalent: `A/B` is equivalent to `np.divide(A,B)`, A+B is equivalent to `np.add(A,B)`, `A-B` is equivalent to `np.subtract(A,B)`, and A*B is equivalent to `np.multiply(A,B)`. In case you are familiar with object-oriented programming, we say that in numpy, basic operations, such as /, *, +, and -, are overloaded. Note also that all of these four basic operations in numpy act element by element.

We can write the sigmoid function in a more readable (at least for humans) form as follows:

```
def sigmoid(z):
    s = 1.0 / (1.0 + np.exp(-z))
    return s
```

As stated previously, `1.0 + np.exp(-z)` is equivalent to `np.add(1.0, np.exp(-z))`, and `1.0 / (np.add(1.0, np.exp(-z)))` to `np.divide(1.0, np.add(1.0, np.exp(-z)))`. I want to draw your attention to another point in the formula. `np.exp(-z)` will have the dimensions of `z` (usually a vector that will have a length equal to the number of observations), while 1.0 is a scalar (a one-dimensional entity). How can Python sum the two? What happens is what is called *broadcasting*.[1] Python, subject to certain constraints, will "broadcast" the smaller array (in this case, the 1.0) across the larger one, so that at the end, the two have the same dimensions. In this case, the 1.0 becomes an array of the same dimension as `z`, all filled with 1.0. This is an important concept to understand, as it is very useful. You don't have to transform numbers in arrays, for example. Python will take care of it for you. The rules on how broadcasting works in other cases are rather complex and beyond the scope of this book. However, it is important to know that Python is doing something in the background.

Tanh (Hyperbolic Tangent Activation) Function

The hyperbolic tangent is also an s-shaped curve that goes from -1 to 1.

$$f(z) = \tanh(z)$$

[1] You can find a more extensive explanation of how numpy uses broadcasting in the official documentation, available at `https://docs.scipy.org/doc/numpy-1.13.0/user/basics.broadcasting.html`.

In Figure 2-6, you can see its shape. In Python, this can be easily implemented, as follows:

```
def tanh(z):
    return np.tanh(z)
```

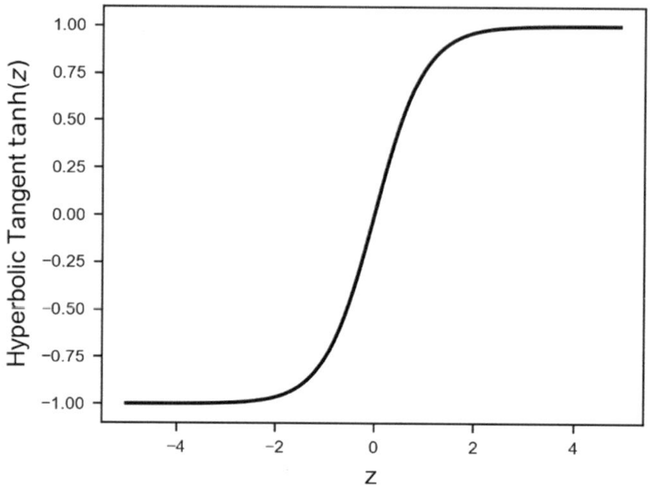

Figure 2-6. *The tanh (or hyperbolic function) is an s-shaped curve that goes from -1 to 1*

ReLU (Rectified Linear Unit) Activation Function

The ReLU function (Figure 2-7) has the following formula:

$$f(z) = \max(0, z)$$

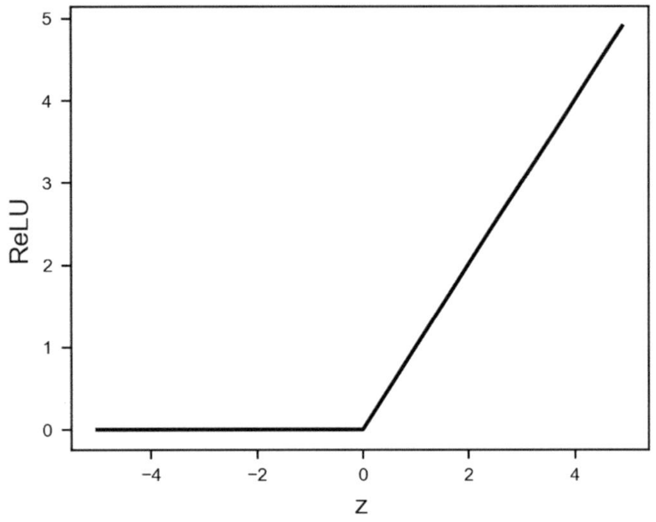

Figure 2-7. *The ReLU function*

It is useful to spend a few moments exploring how to implement the ReLU function in a smart way in Python. Note that when we will start using `TensorFlow`, we will have it already implemented for us, but it is very instructive to observe how different Python implementations can make a difference when implementing complex deep-learning models.

In Python, you can implement the ReLU function in several ways. Listed below are four different methods. (Try to understand why they work before proceeding.)

1. `np.maximum(x, 0, x)`
2. `np.maximum(x, 0)`
3. `x * (x > 0)`
4. `(abs(x) + x) / 2`

The four methods have very different execution speeds. Let's generate a `numpy` array with 10^8 elements, as follows:

```
x = np.random.random(10**8)
```

Now let's measure the time needed by the four different versions of the ReLU function when applied to it. Let the following code run:

```
x = np.random.random(10**8)
print("Method 1:")
%timeit -n10 np.maximum(x, 0, x)

print("Method 2:")
%timeit -n10 np.maximum(x, 0)

print("Method 3:")
%timeit -n10 x * (x > 0)

print("Method 4:")
%timeit -n10 (abs(x) + x) / 2
```

The results follow:

```
Method 1:
2.66 ms ± 500 µs per loop (mean ± std. dev. of 7 runs, 10 loops each)
Method 2:
6.35 ms ± 836 µs per loop (mean ± std. dev. of 7 runs, 10 loops each)
Method 3:
4.37 ms ± 780 µs per loop (mean ± std. dev. of 7 runs, 10 loops each)
Method 4:
8.33 ms ± 784 µs per loop (mean ± std. dev. of 7 runs, 10 loops each)
```

The difference is stunning. The Method 1 is four times faster than the Method 4. The `numpy` library is highly optimized, with many routines written in C. But knowing how to code efficiently still makes a difference and can have a great impact. Why is `np.maximum(x, 0, x)` faster than `np.maximum(x, 0)`? The first version updates x in place, without creating a new array. This can save a lot of time, especially when arrays are big. If you don't want to (or can't) update the input vector in place, you can still use the `np.maximum(x, 0)` version.

An implementation could look like this:

```
def relu(z):
    return np.maximum(z, 0)
```

Note Remember: When optimizing your code, even small changes may make a huge difference. In deep-learning programs, the same chunk of code will be repeated millions and billions of times, so even a small improvement will have a huge impact in the long run. Spending time to optimize your code is a necessary step that will pay off.

Leaky ReLU

The Leaky ReLU (also known as a parametric rectified linear unit) is given by the formula

$$f(z) = \begin{cases} \alpha z & for \quad z < 0 \\ z & for \quad z \geq 0 \end{cases}$$

with α a parameter typically of the order of 0.01. In Figure 2-8, you can see an example for $\alpha = 0.05$. This value has been chosen to make the difference between $x > 0$ and $x < 0$ more marked. Usually, smaller values for α are used, but testing with your model is required to find the best value.

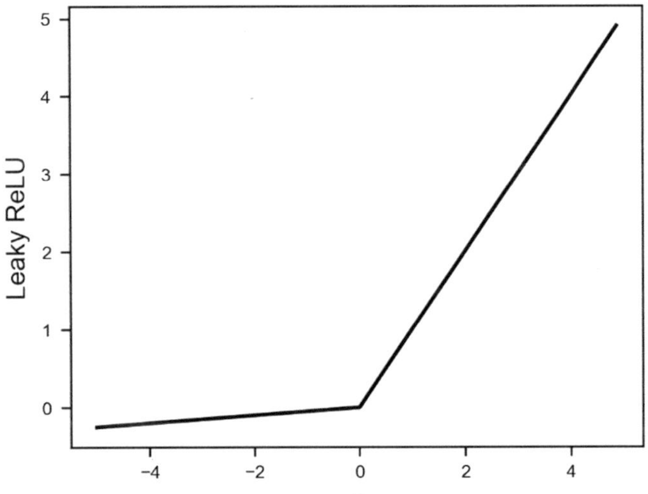

***Figure 2-8.** The Leaky ReLU activation function with α = 0.05*

In Python, for example, this can be implemented if the `relu(z)` function has already been defined as

```
def lrelu(z, alpha):
  return relu(z) - alpha * relu(-z)
```

Swish Activation Function

Recently, Ramachandran, Zopf, and Le at Google Brain [4] studied a new activation function, called Swish, that shows great promise in the deep-learning world. It is defined as

$$f(z) = z\sigma(\beta z)$$

where β is a learnable parameter. In Figure 2-9, you can see how this activation function looks for three values of the parameter β: 0.1, 0.5, and 10.0. The team's studies have shown that simply replacing ReLU activation functions with Swish improves classification accuracy on ImageNet by 0.9%. In today's deep-learning world, that is a lot. You can find more information on ImageNet at `www.image-net.org/`.

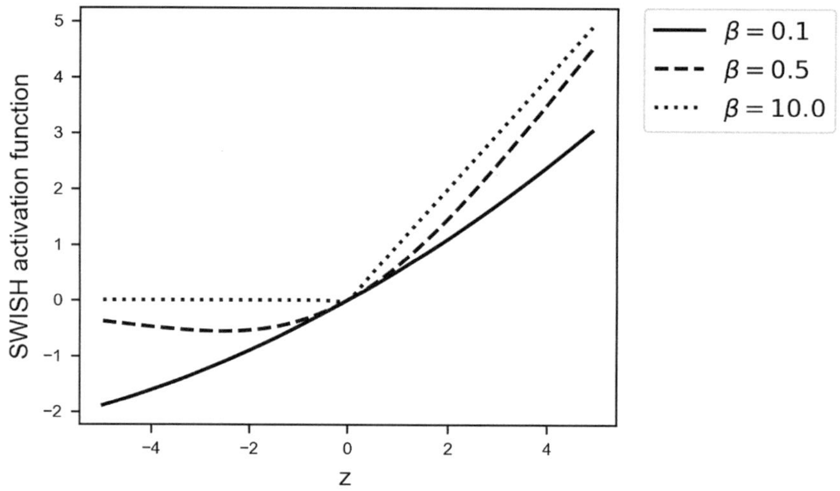

Figure 2-9. *The Swish activation function for three different values of the parameter β*

ImageNet is a large database of images that is often used to benchmark new network architectures or algorithms, such as, in this case, networks with a different activation function.

Other Activation Functions

There are many other activation functions, but these are rarely used. As a reference, following are some additional ones. The list is by no means comprehensive but should serve the purposes of giving you an idea of the variety of activation functions that can be used when developing neural networks.

- ArcTan

$$f(z) = \tan^{-1} z$$

- Exponential Linear unit (ELU)

$$f(z) = \begin{cases} \alpha\left(e^z - 1\right) & for \quad z < 0 \\ z & for \quad z \geq 0 \end{cases}$$

- Softplus

$$f(z) = \ln\left(1 + e^z\right)$$

Note Practitioners almost always use only two activation functions: the sigmoid and the ReLU (the ReLU probably most often). With both, you can achieve good results, and, given a complex enough network architecture, both can approximate any nonlinear function [5,6]. Remember that when using `tensorflow`, you will not have to implement the functions by yourself. `tensorflow` will offer an efficient implementation for you to use. But it is important to know how each activation function behaves, to understand when to use which one.

Cost Function and Gradient Descent: The Quirks of the Learning Rate

Now that you understand clearly what a neuron is, I will discuss what it means for it (and, in general, for a neural network) to learn. This will allow us to introduce concepts such as hyperparameters and learning rate. In almost all neural network problems, learning simply means finding the weights (remember that a neural network is composed of many neurons, and each neuron will have its own set of weights) and biases of the network that minimize a chosen function, which is usually called the cost function and typically indicated by J.

In calculus, there are several methods for finding the minimum of a given function analytically. Unfortunately, in all neural network applications, the number of weights is so big that it is not possible to use these methods. Numerical methods must be relied on, the most famous being gradient descent. It is the easiest method to understand, and it will give you the perfect basis from which to understand the more complex algorithms that you will see later in the book. Let me give a brief overview on how it works, because it is one of the best algorithms in machine learning to introduce the reader to the concept of learning rate and its quirks.

Given a generic function $J(\boldsymbol{w})$, where $\boldsymbol{w}$ is a vector of weights, the minimum location in weight space (meaning the value for $\boldsymbol{w}$ for which $J(\boldsymbol{w})$ has a minimum) can be found with an algorithm based on the following steps:

1. Iteration 0: Choose a random initial guess $\boldsymbol{w_0}$
2. Iteration $n + 1$ (with n starting from 0): The weights at iteration $n + 1$, $\boldsymbol{w}_{n+1}$ will be updated from the previous values at iteration n, $\boldsymbol{w}_n$, using the formula

$$\boldsymbol{w}_{n+1} = \boldsymbol{w}_n - \gamma \nabla J(\boldsymbol{w}_n)$$

With $\nabla J(\boldsymbol{w})$, we have indicated the gradient of the cost function, which is a vector whose components are the partial derivatives of the cost function with respect to all the components of the weight vector $\boldsymbol{w}$, as follows:

$$\nabla J(\boldsymbol{w}) = \begin{pmatrix} \partial J(\boldsymbol{w}) / \partial w_1 \\ \vdots \\ \partial J(\boldsymbol{w}) / \partial w_{n_x} \end{pmatrix}$$

To decide when to stop, we could check when the cost function $J(\boldsymbol{w})$ stops changing too much, or, in other words, you could define a threshold ϵ and stop at any iteration $q > k$ (with k an integer that you have to find) that satisfies $|J(w_{q+1}) - J(w_q)| < \epsilon$ for all $q > k$. The problem with this approach is that it is complicated, and this check is very expensive in terms of performance when implemented in Python (remember: you will have to do this step a very large number of times), so, usually, people simply let the algorithm run for a fixed big number of iterations and check the final results. If the result is not what is expected, they increase the fixed big number. How big? Well, that depends on your problem. What you do is choose a certain number of iterations (for example, 10,000 or 1,000,000) and let the algorithm run. At the same time, you plot the cost function vs. the number of iterations, and you check that the number of iterations you have chosen is sensible. Later in this chapter, you will see a practical example in which I will show you how to check if the number you chose was big enough. For the moment, you should know that you simply stop the algorithm after a fixed number of iterations.

Note Why this algorithm converges toward the minimum (and how to show it) is beyond the scope of this book, would make this chapter too long, and distract the reader from the main learning goal, which is to make you understand what the effect of choosing a specific learning rate is and what the consequences are of choosing too big or too small a rate.

We will assume here that the cost function is differentiable. This is not usually the case, but a discussion of this issue goes well beyond the scope of this book. People tend to use a practical approach in this case. The implementations work very well, and so these kinds of theoretical problems are usually ignored by a large number of practitioners. Remember that in deep-learning models, the cost function becomes an incredibly complex function, and studying it is almost impossible.

The series $\boldsymbol{w}_n$ will hopefully converge toward the minimum location, after a reasonable amount of iterations. The parameter γ is called the learning rate and is one of the most important parameters required in the neural network learning process.

Note To distinguish it from weights, the learning rate is called a hyperparameter. We will encounter more of those. A hyperparameter is a parameter whose value is not determined by training and usually set before the learning process begins. In contrast, the values of parameters $\boldsymbol{w}$ and b are derived via training.

The word *hopefully*, has been chosen for good reason. It is possible that the algorithm will not converge toward the minimum. It is even possible that the series $\boldsymbol{w}_n$ will oscillate between values without converging at all—or diverge outright. Choose γ too big or too small, and your model will not converge (or converge too slowly). To understand why this is the case, let's consider a practical case and see how the method works while choosing different learning rates.

Learning Rate in a Practical Example

Let's consider the dataset formed by $m = 30$ observations y generated by the code.

```
m = 30
w0 = 2
w1 = 0.5
x = np.linspace(-1,1,m)
y = w0 + w1 * x
```

As a cost function, we choose the classical mean squared error (MSE)

$$J(w_0,w_1)=\frac{1}{m}\sum_{i=1}^{m}\left(y_i - f\left(w_0,w_1,x^{(i)}\right)\right)^2$$

where we have indicated with the superscript (i) the ith observation. Remember that with the subscript i (x_i), we have indicated the ith feature. To recap our notation, we have indicated with $x_j^{(i)}$ the jth feature and the ith observation. In the example here, we have just one feature, so we don't need the subscript j. The cost function can be implemented in Python easily as

```
np.average((y-hypothesis(x, w0, w1))**2, axis=2)/2
```

where we have defined

```
def hypothesis(x, w0, w1):
    return w0 + w1*x
```

Our goal is to find the values for w_0 and w_1 that minimize $J(w_0, w_1)$.

To apply the gradient descent method, we must calculate the series for $w_{0,n}$ and $w_{1,n}$. We have the following equations:

$$
\begin{cases}
w_{0,n+1} = w_{0,n} - \gamma \dfrac{\partial J(w_{0,n}, w_{1,n})}{\partial w_0} = w_{0,n} + \gamma \dfrac{1}{m} \displaystyle\sum_{i=1}^{m} 2\left(y_i - f(w_{0,n}, w_{1,n}, x_i)\right) \dfrac{\partial f(w_0, w_1, x_i)}{\partial w_0} \\
w_{1,n+1} = w_{1,n} - \gamma \dfrac{\partial J(w_{0,n}, w_{1,n})}{\partial w_1} = w_{1,n} + \gamma \dfrac{1}{m} \displaystyle\sum_{i=1}^{m} 2\left(y_i - f(w_{0,n}, w_{1,n}, x_i)\right) \dfrac{\partial f(w_0, w_1, x_i)}{\partial w_1}
\end{cases}
$$

Simplifying equations by calculating the partial derivatives gives

$$
\begin{cases}
w_{0,n+1} = w_{0,n} + \dfrac{\gamma}{m} \displaystyle\sum_{i=1}^{m} \left(y_i - f(w_{0,n}, w_{1,n}, x_i)\right) = w_{0,n}(1-\gamma) + \dfrac{\gamma}{m} \displaystyle\sum_{i=1}^{m} \left(y_i - w_{1,n} x_i\right) \\
w_{1,n+1} = w_{1,n} + \dfrac{\gamma}{m} \displaystyle\sum_{i=1}^{m} \left(y_i - f(w_{0,n}, w_{1,n}, x_i)\right) x_i = w_{1,n} - \gamma w_{0,n} + \dfrac{\gamma}{m} \displaystyle\sum_{i=1}^{m} \left(y_i - w_{1,n} x_i\right) x_i
\end{cases}
$$

Because $\partial f(w_0, w_1, x_i)/\partial w_0 = 1$ and $\partial f(w_0, w_1, x_i)/\partial w_1 = x_i$, the previous equations are the ones that must be implemented in Python, if we want to code the gradient descent algorithm by ourselves.

Note The derivation of the equations in (2.11) has the goal of showing how the equations for gradient descent become very complicated very quickly, even for a very easy case. In the next section, we will build our first model with `tensorflow`. One of the best aspects of the library is that all those formulas are calculated automatically, and you don't have to bother calculating anything. Implementing equations such as the ones in shown here and debugging them can take quite some time and prove to be impossible the moment you are dealing with large neural networks of interconnected neurons.

I have omitted in this book the complete Python implementation of the example, because it would require too much space.

It is instructive to check how the model works, by varying the learning rate. In Figures 2-10, 2-11, and 2-12, the contour lines[2] of the cost functions have been drawn, and on top of these, the series $(w_{0,n}, w_{1,n})$ has been plotted, as points to visualize how the series converges (or doesn't). In the figures, the minimum is indicated by a circle placed approximately at the center. We will consider the values $\gamma = 0.8$ (in Figure 2-10), $\gamma = 2$ (in Figure 2-11), and $\gamma = 0.05$ (in Figure 2-12). The different estimates, $\boldsymbol{w}_n$, are indicated with points. The minimum is indicated by the circle approximately in the middle of the image.

In the first case (in Figure 2-10), the converging is well behaved, and in just eight steps, the method converges toward the minimum. When $\gamma = 2$ (Figure 2-11), the method makes steps that are too big (remember: the steps are given by $-\gamma\nabla J(\boldsymbol{w})$ and therefore the bigger γ the bigger the steps) and unable to get close to the minimum. It keeps oscillating around it, without reaching it. In this case, the model will never converge. In the last case, when $\gamma = 0.05$ (Figure 2-12), the learning is so slow that it will take many more steps to get close to the minimum. In some cases, the cost function may be so flat around the minimum that the method takes such a big number of iterations to converge that, practically, you will not get close enough to the real minimum in a reasonable amount of time. In Figure 2-12, 300 iterations are plotted, but the method is not even very close to the minimum.

Note Choosing the right learning rate is of paramount importance when coding the learning part of a neural network. Choose too big a rate, and the method may just bounce around the minimum, without ever reaching it. Choose too small a rate, and the algorithm may become so slow that you will not be able to find the minimum in a reasonable amount of time (or number of iterations). A typical sign of a learning rate that is too big is that the cost function may become `nan` ("not a number," in Python slang). Printing the cost function at regular intervals during the training process is a good way of checking such kind of problems. This will give you a chance to stop the process and avoid wasting time (in case you see `nan` appearing). A concrete example appears later in the chapter.

---

[2]A contour line of a function is a curve along which the function has a constant value.

In deep-learning problems, each iteration will cost time, and you will have to perform this process several times. Choosing the right learning rate is a key part of designing a good model, because it will make training much faster (or make it impossible).

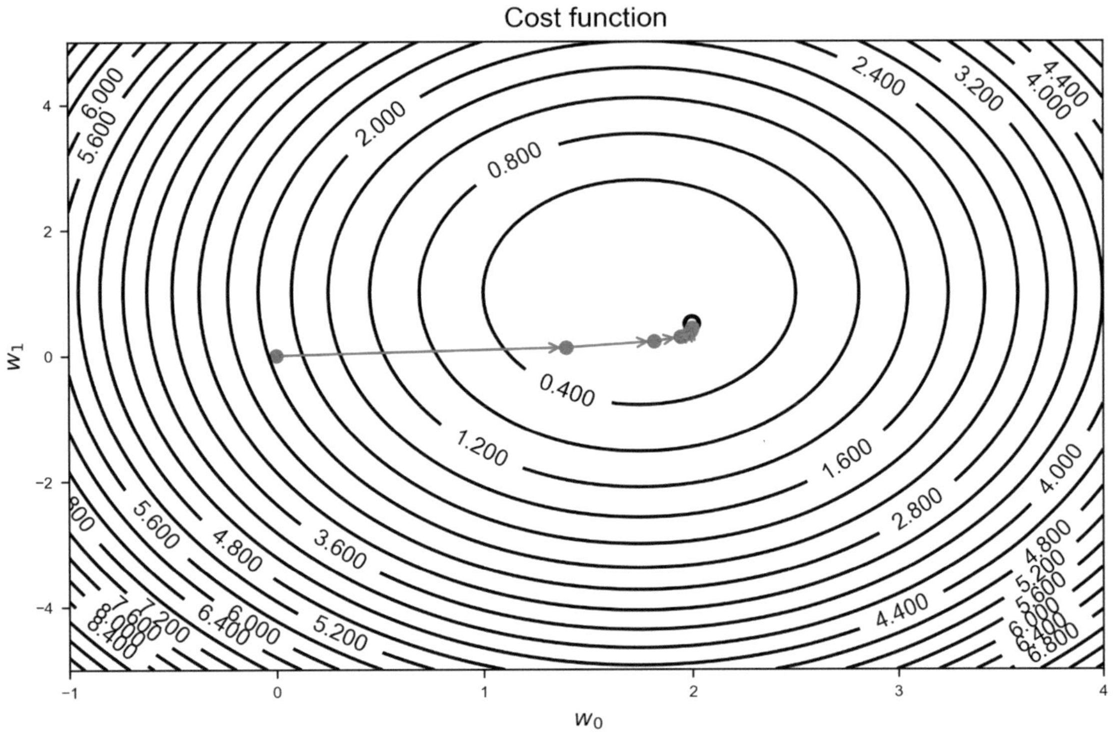

Figure 2-10. *Illustration of a gradient descent algorithmwith well-behaved convergence*

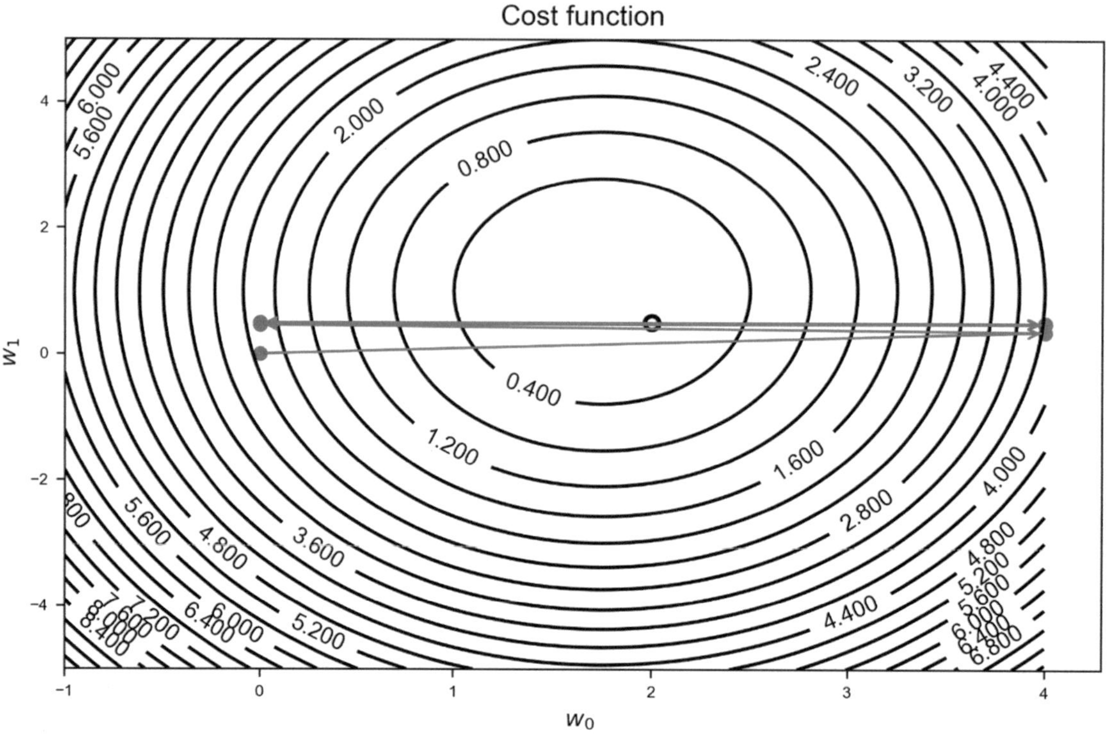

Figure 2-11. *Illustration of a gradient descent algorithm when the learning rate is too big. The method is not able to converge toward the minimum.*

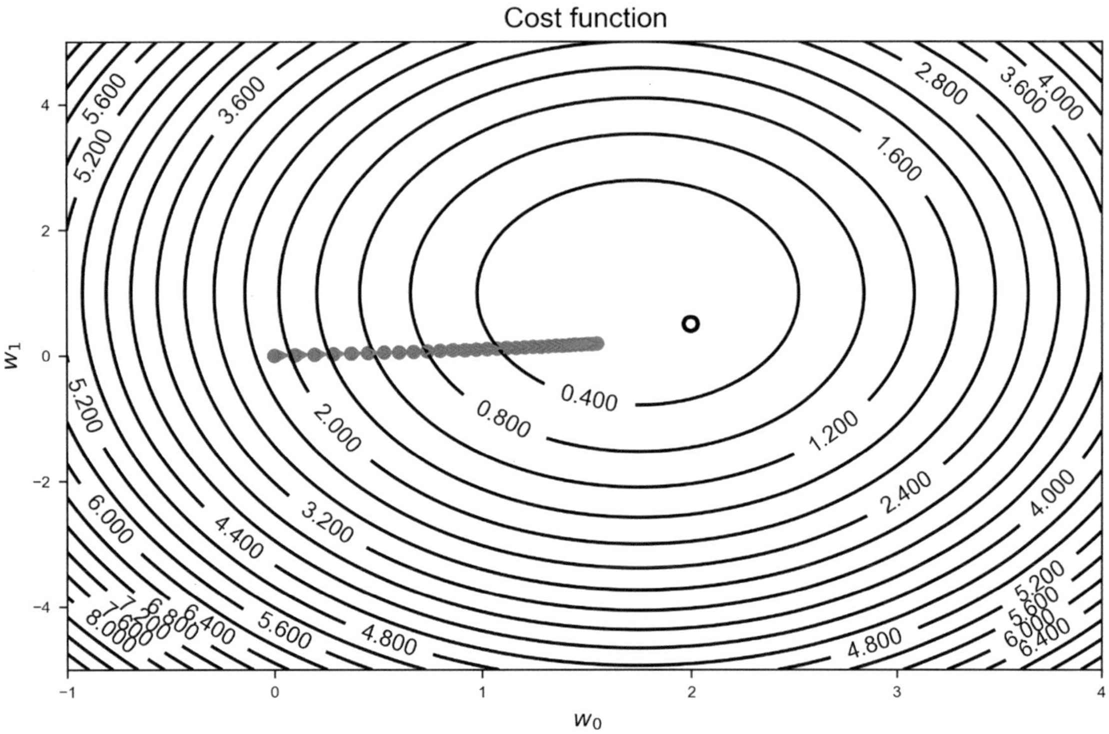

***Figure 2-12.** Illustration of a gradient descent algorithm when the learning rate is too small. The method is so slow that it will take a huge number of iterations to converge toward the minimum.*

Sometimes it is efficient to change the learning rate during the process. You start with a bigger value to get close to the minimum faster, and then you reduce it progressively, to make sure that you get as close as possible to the real minimum. I will discuss this approach later in the book.

Note There are no fixed rules on how to choose the right learning rate. It depends on the model, on the cost function, on the starting point, and so on. A good rule of thumb is to start with $\gamma = 0.05$ and then see how the cost function behaves. It is rather common to plot $J(\boldsymbol{w})$ vs. the number of iterations, to check that it decreases and the speed at which it is decreasing.

A good way of checking the convergence is to plot the cost function vs. the number of iterations. In this way, you can check its behavior. How the cost function looks in our three learning rates for the preceding example is shown in Figure 2-13. You can clearly see how the case with $\gamma = 0.8$ goes to zero rather quickly, indicating that we have reached a minimum. The case with $\gamma = 2$ does not even start to go down. It continues to remain at almost the same initial value. And, finally, the case with $\gamma = 0.05$ starts to go down, but it is a lot slower than the first case.

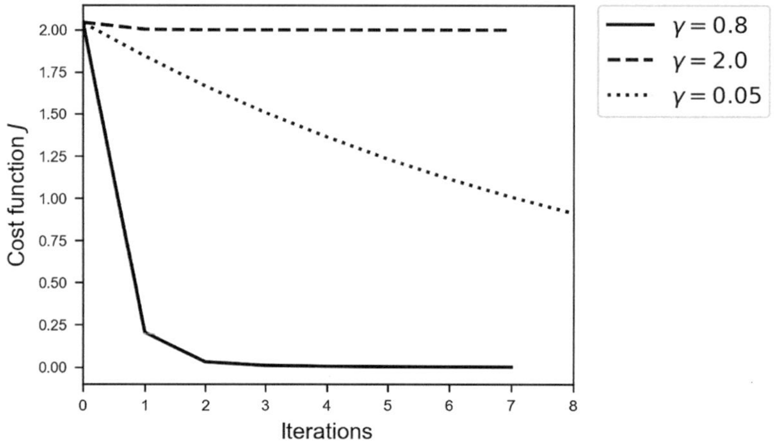

Figure 2-13. *The cost function vs. the number of iterations (only the first eight are considered)*

So, here are the conclusions we should draw from Figure 2-13 for the three cases:

- $\gamma = 0.05 \rightarrow J$ is decreasing, which is good, but after eight iterations, we have not reached a plateau, so we must use many more iterations, until we see that J is not changing much anymore.
- $\gamma = 2 \rightarrow J$ is not decreasing. We should check our learning rate to see if it helps. Trying smaller values would be a good starting point.
- $\gamma = 0.8 \rightarrow$ The cost function decreases rather quickly and then remains constant. That is a good sign and indicates that we have reached a minimum.

Remember also that the absolute value of the learning rate is not relevant. What is important is the behavior. We can multiply our cost function by a constant, and that would not influence our learning at all. Don't look at the absolute values; check how fast and how the cost function is behaving. Additionally, the cost function will almost never reach zero, so don't expect it. The value of J at its minimum is almost never zero (it depends on the functions itself). In the section about linear regression, you will see an example in which the cost function will not reach zero.

Note When training your models, remember to always check the cost function vs. the number of iterations (or number of swipes over the entire training set, called epochs). This will give you an efficient way of estimating if the training is efficient, if it is working at all, and give you hints on how to optimize it.

Now that we have defined the basis, we will use a neuron to solve two simple problems with machine learning: linear and logistic regression.

Example of Linear Regression in tensorflow

The first type of regression will offer an opportunity to understand how to build a model in `tensorflow`. To explain how to perform linear regression efficiently with one neuron, I must first explain some additional notation. In the previous sections, I discussed inputs $\boldsymbol{x} = \left(x_1, x_2, \ldots, x_{n_x}\right)$. These are the so-called features that describe an observation. Normally, we have many observations. As briefly explained before, we will use an upper index to indicate the different observations between parentheses. Our i^{th} observation will be indicated with $\boldsymbol{x}^{(i)}$, and the jth feature of the ith observations will be indicated as $\boldsymbol{x}_j^{(i)}$. We will indicate the number of observations with m.

Note In this book, m is the number of observations, and n_x is the number of features. Our j^{th} feature of the ith observation will be indicated with $x_j^{(i)}$. In deep-learning projects, the bigger the m the better. So be prepared to deal with a huge number of observations.

You will remember that I have said many times that `numpy` is highly optimized to perform several parallel operations at the same time. To get the best performance possible, it is important to write our equations in matrix form and feed the matrices to `numpy`. In this way, our code will be as efficient as possible. Remember: Avoid loops at all costs whenever possible. Let's spend some time now in writing all our equations in matrix form. In this way, our Python implementation will be much easier later.

The entire set of inputs (features and observations) can be written in matrix form. We will use the following notation:

$$X = \begin{pmatrix} x_1^{(1)} & \dots & x_1^{(m)} \\ \vdots & \ddots & \vdots \\ x_{n_x}^{(1)} & \dots & x_{n_x}^{(m)} \end{pmatrix}$$

where each column is an observation and each row represents a feature in the matrix X, which has dimensions $n_x \times m$. We can also write the output values $\hat{y}^{(i)}$ in matrix form. If you recall our neuron discussion, we have defined a $z^{(i)} = \boldsymbol{w}^T\boldsymbol{x}^{(i)} + b$ for one observation i. Putting each observation in a column, we can use the following notation:

$$\boldsymbol{z} = \left(z^{(1)}\ z^{(2)} \dots z^{(m)}\right) = \boldsymbol{w}^T X + \boldsymbol{b}$$

where we have $\boldsymbol{b} = (b\ b \dots b)$. We will define $\hat{\boldsymbol{y}}$ as

$$\hat{\boldsymbol{y}} = \left(\hat{y}^{(1)}\ \hat{y}^{(2)} \dots \hat{y}^{(m)}\right) = \left(f\left(z^{(1)}\right)\ f\left(z^{(2)}\right)\ \dots\ f\left(z^{(m)}\right)\right) = f(\boldsymbol{z})$$

where with $f(\boldsymbol{z})$, we intend the function f be applied element by element to the matrix $\boldsymbol{z}$.

Note Although $\boldsymbol{z}$ has dimensions $1 \times m$, we will use the term *matrix* for it and not *vector*, to use consistent names in the book. This will also help you to remember that we should always use matrix operations. For our purposes, $\boldsymbol{z}$ is simply a matrix with just one row.

You know from Chapter 1 that in `tensorflow`, you must declare explicitly the dimensions of our matrices (or tensors), so it is a good idea to have them well under control. Here is an overview of the dimensions of all the vectors and matrices we will use:

- X has dimensions $n_x \times m$
- $\boldsymbol{z}$ has dimensions $1 \times m$
- $\hat{\boldsymbol{y}}$ has dimensions $1 \times m$
- $\boldsymbol{w}$ has dimensions $n_x \times 1$
- $\boldsymbol{b}$ has dimensions $1 \times m$

Now that the formalism is clear, we will prepare the dataset.

Dataset for Our Linear Regression Model

To make things a bit more interesting, let's use a real dataset. We will use the so-called Boston dataset.[3] This contains information collected by the US Census Bureau concerning housing around Boston. Each record in the database describes a Boston suburb or town. The data was drawn from the Boston Standard Metropolitan Statistical Area (SMSA) in 1970. The attributes are defined as follows [3]:

- *CRIM*: Per capita crime rate by town
- *ZN*: Proportion of residential land zoned for lots over 25,000 square feet
- *INDUS*: Proportion of non-retail business acres per town
- *CHAS*: Charles River dummy variable (= 1 if tract bounds river; 0 otherwise)
- *NOX*: Nitric oxides concentration (parts per 10 million)
- *RM*: Average number of rooms per dwelling
- *AGE*: Proportion of owner-occupied units built prior to 1940
- *DIS*: Weighted distances to five Boston employment centers
- *RAD*: Index of accessibility to radial highways
- *TAX*: Full-value property-tax rate per $10,000
- *PTRATIO*: Pupil-teacher ratio by town
- B - 1000(Bk - 0.63)^2 - Bk: Proportion of blacks by town
- *LSTAT*: % lower status of the population
- *MEDV*: Median value of owner-occupied homes in $1000s

Our target variable MEDV, the one we want to predict, is the median price of the house in $1000s for each suburb. For our example, we don't have to understand or study the features. My goal here is to show you how to build a linear regression model with what you have learned. Normally, in a machine-learning project, you would first

[3]Delve (Data for Evaluating Learning in Valid Experiments), "The Boston Housing Dataset," `www.cs.toronto.edu/~delve/data/boston/bostonDetail.html`, 1996.

study your input data, check their distribution, quality, missing values, and so on; however, I will skip this part to concentrate on how to implement what you learned with `tensorflow`.

Note In machine learning, the variable we want to predict is usually called the *target variable*.

Let's import the usual libraries, including `sklearn.datasets`. Importing the data and getting features and target is very easy with the help of the `sklearn.datasets` package. You don't have to download CSV files and import them. Simply run the following code:

```
import matplotlib.pyplot as plt
%matplotlib inline
import tensorflow as tf
import numpy as np
from sklearn.datasets import load_boston

boston = load_boston()
features = np.array(boston.data)
labels = np.array(boston.target)
```

Every dataset in the `sklearn.datasets` package comes with a description. You can check it with the following command:

```
print(boston["DESCR"])
```

Now let's check how many observations and features we have.

```
n_training_samples = features.shape[0]
n_dim = features.shape[1]
print('The dataset has',n_training_samples,'training samples.')
print('The dataset has',n_dim,'features.')
```

Linking the mathematical notation with the Python code `n_training_samples` is m and `n_dim` is n_x. The code will give the following results:

```
The dataset has 506 training samples.
The dataset has 13 features.
```

It is a good idea to normalize each numerical feature defining normalized features $x^{(i)}_{norm,j}$ according to the formula

$$x^{(i)}_{norm,j} = \frac{x^{(i)}_j - \left\langle x^{(i)}_j \right\rangle}{\sigma^{(i)}_j}$$

where $\left\langle x^{(i)}_j \right\rangle$ is the average of the jth feature, and $\sigma^{(i)}_j$ is its standard deviation. This can be easily calculated in numpy with the following function:

```
def normalize(dataset):
    mu = np.mean(dataset, axis = 0)
    sigma = np.std(dataset, axis = 0)
    return (dataset-mu)/sigma
```

To normalize our features numpy array, we must simply call the function `features_norm = normalize(features)`. Now each feature contained in the `numpy array` `features_norm` will have an average of zero and a standard deviation of one.

Note It is generally a good idea to normalize the features, so that their average is zero, and the standard deviation is one. Sometimes, some features are much bigger than others and can have a stronger influence on the model, thus bringing wrong predictions. Particular care is needed when the dataset is split into training and test datasets, to have consistent normalizations.

For this chapter, we will simply use all the data for the training, to concentrate on implementation details.

```
train_x = np.transpose(features_norm)
train_y = np.transpose(labels)

print(train_x.shape)
print(train_y.shape)
```

The last two prints will give us the dimensions of our new matrices.

```
(13, 506)
(506,)
```

The `train_x` array has dimensions of (13, 506), and that is exactly what we expect. Remember for our discussion that X has dimensions $n_x \times m$.

The training target `train_y` has dimensions of `(506,)`, which is how numpy describes one-dimensional arrays. `tensorflow` wants to have dimensions of `(1, 506)` (remember our previous discussion?), so we must reshape the array in this way:

```
train_y = train_y.reshape(1,len(train_y))
```

```
print(train_y.shape)
```

and our print statements give us what we need:

```
(1, 506)
```

Neuron and Cost Function for Linear Regression

A neuron that can perform linear regression uses the identity activation function. The cost function that needs to be minimized is the MSE (mean square error) that can be written as

$$J(\boldsymbol{w},b)=\frac{1}{m}\sum_{i=1}^{m}\left(y^{(i)}-\boldsymbol{w}^T\boldsymbol{x}^{(i)}-b\right)^2$$

where the sum is over all m observations.

The `tensorflow` code to build this neuron and define the cost function is actually very simple.

```
tf.reset_default_graph()

X = tf.placeholder(tf.float32, [n_dim, None])
Y = tf.placeholder(tf.float32, [1, None])
learning_rate = tf.placeholder(tf.float32, shape=())
W = tf.Variable(tf.ones([n_dim,1]))
b = tf.Variable(tf.zeros(1))

init = tf.global_variables_initializer()
y_ = tf.matmul(tf.transpose(W),X)+b
cost = tf.reduce_mean(tf.square(y_-Y))
training_step = tf.train.GradientDescentOptimizer(learning_rate).minimize(cost)
```

Note that in `tensorflow`, you don't have to explicitly declare the number of observations. You can use `None` in the code. In this way, you will be able to run the model on any dataset independently of the number of observations, without modifying your code.

In the code, we have indicated the neuron output $\hat{y}$ as `y_`, because we don't have a hat in Python. Let me clarify a bit which line of code does what.

- `X = tf.placeholder(tf.float32, [n_dim, None])` → contains the matrix X, which must have dimensions $n_x \times m$. Remember that in our code, `n_dim` is n_x and that m is not declared explicitly in `tensorflow`. In its place, we use `None`.
- `Y = tf.placeholder(tf.float32, [1, None])` → contains the output values $\hat{y}$, which must have dimensions $1 \times m$. Here, this means that instead of m, we use `None`, because we want to use the same model for different datasets (that will have a different number of observations).
- `learning_rate = tf.placeholder(tf.float32, shape=())` → contains the learning rate as a parameter instead of a constant, so that we can run the same model varying it, without creating a new neuron each time.
- `W = tf.Variable(tf.zeros([n_dim, 1]))` → defines and initializes the weights, $\boldsymbol{w}$, with zeros. Remember that the weights, $\boldsymbol{w}$, must have dimensions $n_x \times 1$.
- `b = tf.Variable(tf.zeros(1))` → defines and initializes the bias, b, with zero.

Remember that in `tensorflow`, a placeholder is a tensor that will not change during the learning phase, whereas a variable is one that will change. Weights, $\boldsymbol{w}$, and bias, b, will be updated during the learning. Now we must define what to do with all those quantities. Remember: We must calculate $\boldsymbol{z}$. The chosen activation function is the identity function, so $\boldsymbol{z}$ will also be the output of our neuron.

- `init = tf.global_variables_initializer()` → creates a piece of the graph that initializes the variable and adds it to the graph.
- `y_ = tf.matmul(tf.transpose(W),X)+b` → calculates the output of the neuron. The output of a neuron is $\hat{\boldsymbol{y}} = f(\boldsymbol{z}) = f(\boldsymbol{w}^T X + b)$. Because the activation function for linear regression is the identity, the output is $\hat{\boldsymbol{y}} = \boldsymbol{w}^T X + b$. Remember that b being a scalar is not a problem. Python broadcasting will take care of it, expanding it to the right dimensions, to make the sum between a vector $\boldsymbol{w}^T X$ and a scalar b possible.
- `cost = tf.reduce_mean(tf.square(y_-Y))` → defines the cost function. `tensorflow` provides an easy and efficient way of calculating the average—`tf.reduce_mean()`—that simply performs the sum of all the elements of the tensor and divides it by the number of elements.
- `training_step = tf.train.GradientDescentOptimizer (learning_rate).minimize(cost)` → tells `tensorflow` which algorithm to use to minimize the cost function. In `tensorflow` language, the algorithms used to minimize the cost function are called optimizers. We now use gradient descent with the given learning rate. Later in the book, other optimizers will be extensively studied.

You will remember from the introduction in Chapter 1 that the previous code will not run any model. It simply defines the computational graph. Let's define a function that will perform the actual learning and will run our model. It is easier to define it in a function, so that we can rerun it, changing, for example, the learning rate or the number of iterations we want to use.

```
def run_linear_model(learning_r, training_epochs, train_obs, train_labels,
debug = False):
    sess = tf.Session()
    sess.run(init)

    cost_history = np.empty(shape=[0], dtype = float)
```

```
for epoch in range(training_epochs+1):
    sess.run(training_step, feed_dict = {X: train_obs, Y: train_labels,
    learning_rate: learning_r})
    cost_ = sess.run(cost, feed_dict={ X:train_obs, Y: train_labels,
    learning_rate: learning_r})
    cost_history = np.append(cost_history, cost_)

    if (epoch % 1000 == 0) & debug:
        print("Reached epoch",epoch,"cost J =", str.format('{0:.6f}',
        cost_))

return sess, cost_history
```

Let's go through the code again, line by line.

- `sess = tf.Session()` → creates a `tensorflow` session.
- `sess.run(init)` → runs the initialization of the different element of the graphs.
- `cost_history = np.empty(shape=[0], dtype = float)` → creates an empty vector (for the moment with zero elements) in which the value of our cost function at each iteration is stored.
- `for loop...` → In this loop, `tensorflow` performs the gradient descent steps that we have discussed earlier and updates the weights and the bias. In addition, it will save in the array `cost_history` the value of the cost function each time: `cost_history = np.append(cost_history, cost_)`.
- `if (epoch % 1000 == 0)...` → Every 1000 epochs we will print the value of the cost function. This is an easy way of checking if the cost function is really decreasing or if `nan`s are appearing. If you perform some initial tests in an interactive environment (such as a Jupyter notebook), you can stop the process if you see that the cost function is not behaving as you expect.
- `return sess, cost_history` → returns the session (in case you want to calculate something else) and the array containing the cost function values (we will use this array to plot it).

Running the model is as easy as using the call.

```
sess, cost_history = run_linear_model(learning_r = 0.01,
                                      training_epochs = 10000,
                                      train_obs = train_x,
                                      train_labels = train_y,
                                      debug = True)
```

The output of the command will be the cost function every 1000 epochs (check in the function definition the `if`, starting with `if (epoch % 1000 == 0)`).

```
Reached epoch 0 cost J = 613.947144
Reached epoch 1000 cost J = 22.131165
Reached epoch 2000 cost J = 22.081099
Reached epoch 3000 cost J = 22.076544
Reached epoch 4000 cost J = 22.076109
Reached epoch 5000 cost J = 22.07606
Reached epoch 6000 cost J = 22.076057
Reached epoch 7000 cost J = 22.076059
Reached epoch 8000 cost J = 22.076059
Reached epoch 9000 cost J = 22.076054
Reached epoch 10000 cost J = 22.076054
```

The cost function clearly decreases and then reaches a value and stays almost constant. You can see a plot of it in Figure 2-14. That is a good sign, indicating that the cost function has reached a minimum. That does not mean that our model is good or that it will give good predictions. This tells us only that the learning has worked efficiently.

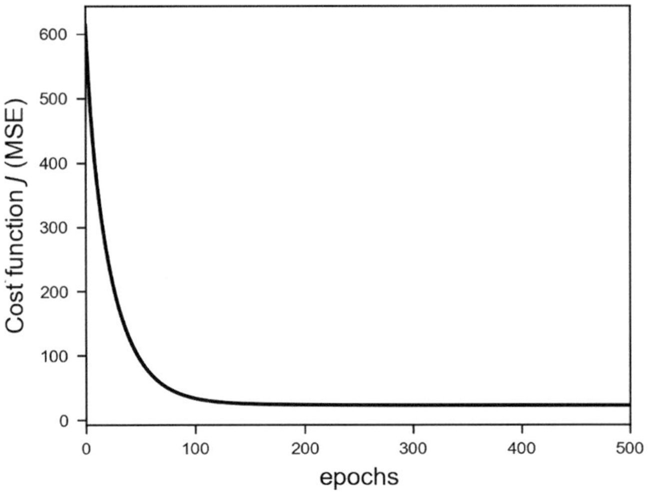

Figure 2-14. *The cost function resulting in our model applied to the Boston dataset with a learning rate of γ=0.01. We plot only the first 500 epochs, since the cost function has almost already reached its final value.*

It would be nice to be able to visualize graphically how good our fit is. Because we have 13 features, it is not possible to plot the price vs. the other features. However, it is helpful to get a feel of how good the model predicts the observed values. This can be done by plotting our predicted target variable vs. the observed one, as I have done in Figure 2-15. If we can perfectly predict our target variable, all the points should be on a diagonal line in the plot. The more spread the points are around the line, the worse our model is at predicting. Let's check how our model is doing.

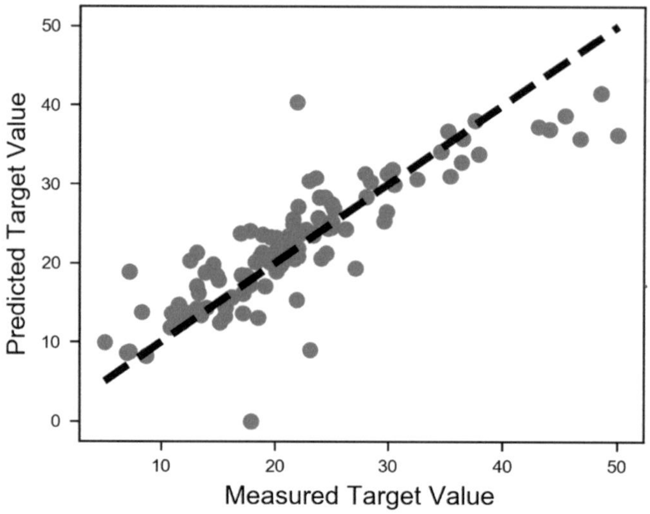

Figure 2-15. *The predicted target value vs. the measured target value for our model, applied to our trianing data*

The points lay reasonably well around the line, so it seems we can predict our price to a certain degree. A more qualitative method for estimating the accuracy of our regression is the MSE itself (which, in our case, is simply our cost function). Whether the value we are obtaining (22.08 in 1000 USD) is good enough depends on the problem you are trying to solve, or the constraint and requirements you have been given.

Satisficing and Optimizing a Metric

We have seen that it is not easy to decide whether a model is good. Figure 2-15 will not allow us to describe quantitively how good (or not good) our model is. For this, we must define a metric.

The easiest way is to set up what is called a *single number evaluation metric*. That means that you calculate one single number and base your model evaluation on that number. It is easy and very practical. For example, you could use the accuracy or the F1 score, in the case of classification, or the MSE, in the case of regression. Normally, in real life, you will receive goals and constraints for your model. For example, your company may want to predict house prices with an MSE < 20 (in 1000 USD), and your model should be able to run on an iPad, or in less than 1 second. It is useful, therefore, to distinguish between two types of metrics:

- **Satisficing metric** → Searching through available alternatives until an acceptability threshold is met, for example, code running (RT) time, which minimizes the cost function subject to RT < 1 sec, or choosing among modes the one that has an RT < 1 sec
- **Optimizing metric** → Searching through available alternatives to maximize a specific metric, for example, choosing the model (or the hyperparameters) that maximize accuracy

---

Note If you have several metrics, you should always choose one optimizing and the rest satisficing.

We have written our code to be able to run our model with different parameters. It is very instructive now to do that. Here is how the cost function behaves for three different learning rates: 0.1, 0.01, and 0.001. You can check the different behaviors in Figure 2-16.

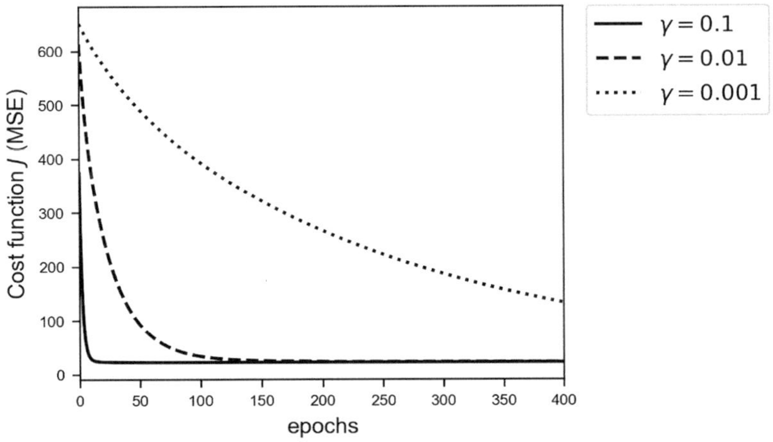

Figure 2-16. *The cost function for linear regression applied to the Boston dataset for three learning rates: 0.1 (solid line), 0.01 (dashed line), and 0.001 (dotted line). The smaller the learning rate, the slower the learning process.*

As expected for very small learning rates (0.001), the gradient descent algorithm is very slow in finding the minimum, whereas with a bigger value (0.1), the method works quickly. This kind of plot is very useful for giving you an idea of how fast and how good the learning process is going. You will see cases later in the book where the cost function is much less well behaved. For example, when applying dropout regularization, the cost function will not be smooth anymore.

Example of Logistic Regression

Logistic regression is a classic classification algorithm. To keep it simple, we will consider here a binary classification. This means that we will deal with the problem of recognizing two classes, which we will label as 0 or 1, only. We will need an activation function different from the one we used for linear regression, a different cost function to minimize, and a slight modification of the output of our neuron. Our goal is to be able to build a model that can predict if a certain new observation is of one of two classes. The neuron should give as output the probability $P(y = 1|x)$ of the input x to be of class 1. We will then classify our observation as of class 1, if $P(y = 1|x) > 0.5$, or of class 0, if $P(y = 1|x) < 0.5$.

Cost Function

As a cost function, we will use the cross entropy.[4] The function for one observation is

$$L\left(\hat{y}^{(i)},y^{(i)}\right)=-\left(y^{(i)}\log\hat{y}^{(i)}+\left(1-y^{(i)}\right)\log\left(1-\hat{y}^{(i)}\right)\right)$$

In the presence of more than one observation, the cost function is the sum over all observations

$$J(\boldsymbol{w},b)=\frac{1}{m}\sum_{i=1}^{m}L\left(\hat{y}^{(i)},y^{(i)}\right)$$

[4]A discussion of the meaning of cross-entropy is beyond the scope of this book. A nice introduction can be found at `https://rdipietro.github.io/friendly-intro-to-cross-entropy-loss/` and in many introductory books on machine learning.

In Chapter 10, I will provide a complete derivation of logistic regression from scratch, but for the moment, `tensorflow` will take care of all the details—derivatives, gradient descent implementation, and so on. We only have to build the right neuron, and we will be on our way.

Activation Function

Remember: We want our neuron to output the probability of our observation to be of class 0 or 1. Therefore, we need an activation function that can assume only values between 0 and 1. Otherwise, we cannot regard it as a probability. For our logistic regression, we will use the sigmoid function as the activation function.

$$\sigma(z) = \frac{1}{1+e^{-z}}$$

The Dataset

To build an interesting model, we will use a modified version of the MNIST dataset. You will find all relevant information from the following link: `http://yann.lecun.com/exdb/mnist/`.

The MNIST database is a large database of handwritten digits that we can use to train our model. The MNIST database contains 70,000 images. "The original black and white (bilevel) images from NIST were size normalized to fit in a 20×20 pixel box while preserving their aspect ratio. The resulting images contain grey levels as a result of the anti-aliasing technique used by the normalization algorithm. The images were centered in a 28×28 image by computing the center of mass of the pixels, and translating the image so as to position this point at the center of the 28×28 field" (source: `http://yann.lecun.com/exdb/mnist/`).

Our features will be the gray value for each pixel, so we will have $28 \times 28 = 784$ features whose values will go from 0 to 255 (gray values). The dataset contains all ten digits, from 0 to 9. With the following code, you can prepare the data to use in the sections below. As usual, let's first import the necessary library.

```
from sklearn.datasets import fetch_mldata
```

Then let's load the data.

```
mnist = fetch_mldata('MNIST original')
X,y = mnist["data"], mnist["target"]
```

Now X contains the input images and y the target labels (remember that the value we want to predict is called target in machine-learning jargon). Just typing `X.shape` will give you the shape of X: (70000, 784). Note that X has 70,000 rows (each row is an image) and 784 columns (each column is a feature, or a pixel gray value, in our case). Let's check how many digits we have in our dataset.

```
for i in range(10):
    print ("digit", i, "appears", np.count_nonzero(y == i), "times")
```

That gives us the following:

```
digit 0 appears 6903 times
digit 1 appears 7877 times
digit 2 appears 6990 times
digit 3 appears 7141 times
digit 4 appears 6824 times
digit 5 appears 6313 times
digit 6 appears 6876 times
digit 7 appears 7293 times
digit 8 appears 6825 times
digit 9 appears 6958 times
```

It is useful to define a function to visualize the digits, to get an idea of how they look.

```
def plot_digit(some_digit):

    some_digit_image = some_digit.reshape(28,28)

    plt.imshow(some_digit_image, cmap = matplotlib.cm.binary, interpolation
    = "nearest")
    plt.axis("off")
    plt.show()
```

For example, we can plot one randomly (see Figure 2-17).

```
plot_digit(X[36003])
```

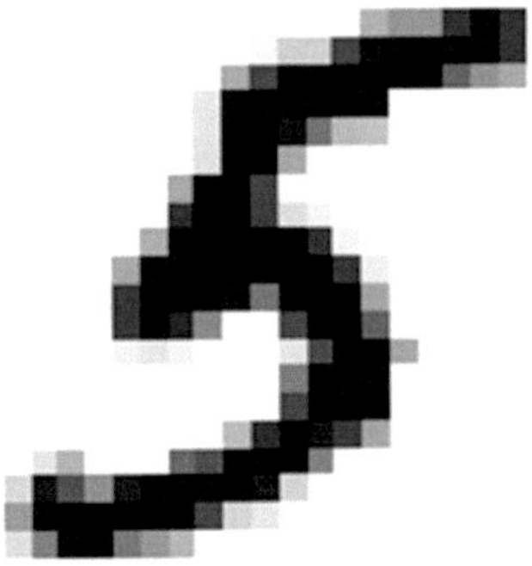

Figure 2-17. *The 36,003rd digit in the dataset. It is easly recognizable as a 5*

The model we want to implement here is a simple logistic regression for binary classification, so the dataset must be reduced to two classes, or in this case, to two digits. We choose ones and twos. Let's extract from our dataset only the images that represent a 1 or a 2. Our neuron will try to recognize if a given image is of class 0 (a digit 1) or of class 1 (a digit 2).

```
X_train = X[np.any([y == 1,y == 2], axis = 0)]
y_train = y[np.any([y == 1,y == 2], axis = 0)]
```

Next, the input observations must be normalized. (Remember: You don't want your input data to be too big when using the sigmoid activation function, because you have 784 of them.)

```
X_train_normalised = X_train/255.0
```

We chose 255, because each feature is the gray value of a pixel in the image, and gray levels in the source images go from 0 to 255. Later in the book I will discuss at length why we need to normalize the input features. For now, trust me that this is a necessary step. In each column, we want to have an input observation, and each row should represent a feature (a pixel gray value), so we must reshape the tensors

```
X_train_tr = X_train_normalised.transpose()
y_train_tr = y_train.reshape(1,y_train.shape[0])
```

and we can define a variable `n_dim` to contain the number of features

```
n_dim = X_train_tr.shape[0]
```

Now comes a very important point. The labels in our dataset as imported will be 1 or 2 (they simply tell you which digit the image represents). However, we will build our cost function with the assumptions that our class's labels are 0 and 1, so we must rescale our `y_train_tr` array.

Note When doing binary classification, remember to check the values of the labels you are using for training. Sometimes, using the wrong labels (not 0 and 1) may cost you quite some time in understanding why the model is not working.

```
y_train_shifted = y_train_tr - 1
```

Now all images representing a 1 will have a label of 0, and all images representing a 2 will have a label of 1. Finally, let's use some proper names for our Python variables.

```
Xtrain = X_train_tr
ytrain = y_train_shifted
```

Figure 2-18 shows some of the digits we are dealing with.

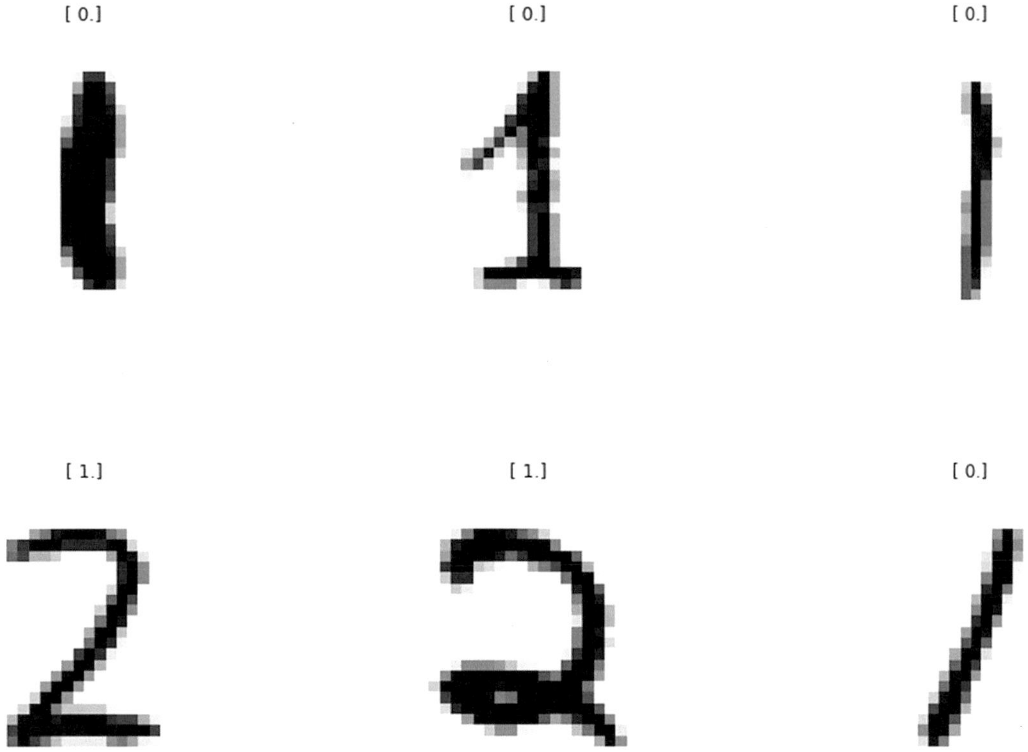

Figure 2-18. *Six random digits chosen from the dataset. The relative rescaled labels (remember: labels in our dataset are now 0 or 1) are given in brackets.*

tensorflow Implementation

The `tensorflow` implementation is not difficult and is almost the same as for the linear regression. First, let's define placeholders and variables.

```
tf.reset_default_graph()

X = tf.placeholder(tf.float32, [n_dim, None])
Y = tf.placeholder(tf.float32, [1, None])
learning_rate = tf.placeholder(tf.float32, shape=())

W = tf.Variable(tf.zeros([1, n_dim]))
b = tf.Variable(tf.zeros(1))

init = tf.global_variables_initializer()
```

Note that the code is the same we used for the linear regression model. However, we must define a different cost function (as discussed earlier) and a different neuron output (the sigmoid function).

```
y_ = tf.sigmoid(tf.matmul(W,X)+b)
cost = - tf.reduce_mean(Y * tf.log(y_)+(1-Y) * tf.log(1-y_))
training_step = tf.train.GradientDescentOptimizer(learning_rate).minimize(cost)
```

We have used the sigmoid function for the output of our neuron, with `tf.sigmoid()`. The code that will run the model is the same as that we have used for the linear regression. We have only changed the name of the function.

```
def run_logistic_model(learning_r, training_epochs, train_obs,
train_labels, debug = False):
    sess = tf.Session()
    sess.run(init)

    cost_history = np.empty(shape=[0], dtype = float)

    for epoch in range(training_epochs+1):
        sess.run(training_step, feed_dict = {X: train_obs, Y: train_labels,
        learning_rate: learning_r})
        cost_ = sess.run(cost, feed_dict={ X:train_obs, Y: train_labels,
        learning_rate: learning_r})
        cost_history = np.append(cost_history, cost_)

        if (epoch % 500 == 0) & debug:
            print("Reached epoch",epoch,"cost J =", str.format('{0:.6f}',
            cost_))

    return sess, cost_history
```

Let's run the model and see the results. We will choose to start with a learning rate of 0.01.

```
sess, cost_history = run_logistic_model(learning_r = 0.01,
                                training_epochs = 5000,
                                train_obs = Xtrain,
                                train_labels = ytrain,
                                debug = True)
```

The output of our code (stopped after 3000 epochs) follows:

```
Reached epoch 0 cost J = 0.678598
Reached epoch 500 cost J = 0.108655
Reached epoch 1000 cost J = 0.078912
Reached epoch 1500 cost J = 0.066786
Reached epoch 2000 cost J = 0.059914
Reached epoch 2500 cost J = 0.055372
Reached epoch 3000 cost J = nan
```

What happened? Suddenly, at some point, our cost function assumes the value nan (not a number). It seems that the model does not do well after a certain point. If the learning rate is too big, or you initialize your weights wrongly, your values for $\hat{y}^{(i)} = P\left(y^{(i)} = 1|\boldsymbol{x}^{(i)}\right)$ may get very close to zero or one (the sigmoid function assumes values very close to 0 or 1 for very big negative or positive values of z). Remember that in the cost function, you have the two terms `tf.log(y_)` and `tf.log(1-y_)`, and because the log function is not defined for a value of zero, if y_ is 0 or 1, you will get a nan, because the code will try to evaluate `tf.log(0)`. As an example, we can run the model with a learning rate of 2.0. After only one epoch, you already will get a nan value for the cost function. And it is easy to understand why, if you print out the value for b before and after the first training step. Simply modify your model code and use the following version:

```
def run_logistic_model(learning_r, training_epochs, train_obs, train_
labels, debug = False):
    sess = tf.Session()
    sess.run(init)

    cost_history = np.empty(shape=[0], dtype = float)

    for epoch in range(training_epochs+1):

        print ('epoch: ', epoch)
        print(sess.run(b, feed_dict={X:train_obs, Y: train_labels,
        learning_rate: learning_r}))

        sess.run(training_step, feed_dict = {X: train_obs, Y: train_labels,
        learning_rate: learning_r})
```

```
        print(sess.run(b, feed_dict={X:train_obs, Y: train_labels,
        learning_rate: learning_r}))

        cost_ = sess.run(cost, feed_dict={ X:train_obs, Y: train_labels,
        learning_rate: learning_r})
        cost_history = np.append(cost_history, cost_)

        if (epoch % 500 == 0) & debug:
            print("Reached epoch",epoch,"cost J =", str.format('{0:.6f}',
            cost_))
    return sess, cost_history
```

You will get the following result (after stopping the training after just one epoch):

```
epoch:  0
[ 0.]
[-0.05966223]
Reached epoch 0 cost J = nan
epoch:  1
[-0.05966223]
[ nan]
```

You see how b goes from 0 to -0.05966223 and then to nan? Therefore, $\boldsymbol{z} = \boldsymbol{w}^T\boldsymbol{X} + \boldsymbol{b}$ turns into nan, then $\boldsymbol{y} = \sigma(\boldsymbol{z})$ also turns into nan, and, finally, the cost function, being a function of $\boldsymbol{y}$, will also result in nan. This is simply because the learning rate is way too big.

What is the solution? You should try a different (read: much smaller) learning rate.

Let's try and see if we can get a result that is more stable after 2500 epochs. We run the model with the call, as follows:

```
sess, cost_history = run_logistic_model(learning_r = 0.005,
                                        training_epochs = 5000,
                                        train_obs = Xtrain,
                                        train_labels = ytrain,
                                        debug = True)
```

The output of the command is

```
Reached epoch 0 cost J = 0.685799
Reached epoch 500 cost J = 0.154386
Reached epoch 1000 cost J = 0.108590
Reached epoch 1500 cost J = 0.089566
Reached epoch 2000 cost J = 0.078767
Reached epoch 2500 cost J = 0.071669
Reached epoch 3000 cost J = 0.066580
Reached epoch 3500 cost J = 0.062715
Reached epoch 4000 cost J = 0.059656
Reached epoch 4500 cost J = 0.057158
Reached epoch 5000 cost J = 0.055069
```

No more `nan` in our output. You can see a plot of the cost function in Figure 2-19. To evaluate our model, we must choose an optimizing metric (as discussed before). For a binary classification problem, a classical metric is the accuracy (which we can indicate with a) that can be understood as a measure of the difference between a result and its "true" value. Mathematically, it can be calculated as

$$a = \frac{number\ of\ cases\ correctly\ identified}{total\ number\ of\ cases}$$

To get the accuracy, we can run the following code. (Remember: We will classify an observation i of class 0 if $P(y^{(i)} = 1 | \boldsymbol{x}^{(i)}) < 0.5$, or in class 1 if $P(y^{(i)} = 1 | \boldsymbol{x}^{(i)}) > 0.5$.)

```
correct_prediction1 = tf.equal(tf.greater(y_, 0.5), tf.equal(Y,1))
accuracy = tf.reduce_mean(tf.cast(correct_prediction1, tf.float32))
print(sess.run(accuracy, feed_dict={X:Xtrain, Y: ytrain, learning_rate:
0.05}))
```

With this model, we reach an accuracy of 98.6%. Not bad for a network with only one neuron.

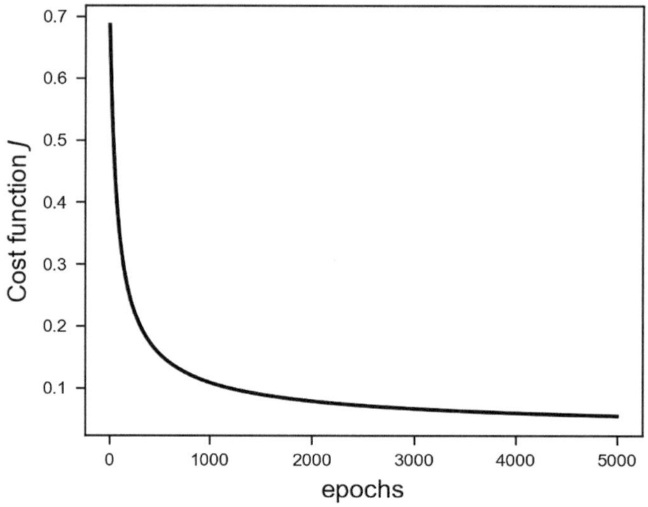

Figure 2-19. *The cost function vs. epochs for a learning rate of 0.005*

You could also try to run the previous model (with a learning rate of 0.005) for more epochs. You will discover that at about 7000 epochs, the `nan` will reappear. The solution here would be to reduce the learning rate with an increasing number of epochs. A simple approach, such as halving the learning rate every 500 epochs, will get rid of the `nan`s. I will discuss a similar approach in more detail later in the book.

References

[1] Jeremy Hsu, "Biggest Neural Network Ever Pushes AI Deep Learning," `https://spectrum.ieee.org/tech-talk/computing/software/biggest-neural-network-ever-pushes-ai-deep-learning`, 2015.

[2] Raúl Rojas, *Neural Networks: A Systematic Introduction*, Berlin: Springer-Verlag, 1996.

[3] Delve (Data for Evaluating Learning in Valid Experiments), "The Boston Housing Dataset," `www.cs.toronto.edu/~delve/data/boston/bostonDetail.html`, 1996.

[4] Prajit Ramachandran, Barret Zoph, Quoc V. Le, "Searching for Activation Functions," arXiv:1710.05941 [cs.NE], 2017.

[5] Guido F. Montufar, Razvan Pascanu, Kyunghyun Cho, and Yoshua Bengio, "On the Number of Linear Regions of Deep Neural Networks," https://papers.nips.cc/paper/5422-on-the-number-of-linear-regions-of-deep-neural-networks.pdf, 2014.

[6] Brendan Fortuner, "Can Neural Networks Solve Any Problem?", https://towardsdatascience.com/can-neural-networks-really-learn-any-function-65e106617fc6, 2017.

CHAPTER 3

Feedforward Neural Networks

In Chapter 2, we did some amazing things with one neuron, but that is hardly flexible enough to tackle more complex cases. The real power of neural networks comes to light when several (thousand, even million) neurons interact with each other to solve a specific problem. The network architecture (how neurons are connected to each other, how they behave, and so on) plays a crucial role in how efficient the learning of a network is, how good its predictions are, and what kind of problems it can solve.

There are many kinds of architectures that have been extensively studied and are very complex, but from a learning perspective, it is important to start from the most simple kind of neural network with multiple neurons. It makes sense to begin with so-called feedforward neural networks, in which data enters at the input layer and passes through the network, layer by layer, until it arrives at the output layer. (This gives the networks their name: feedforward neural networks.) In this chapter, we will consider networks in which each neuron in a layer gets its input from all neurons from the preceding layer and feeds their output into each neuron of the next layer.

As is easy to imagine, with more complexity come more challenges. It is more difficult to achieve fast learning and good accuracy; the number of hyperparameters that are available grows, due to the increased network complexity; and a *simple* gradient descent algorithm will no longer cut it when dealing with big datasets. When developing models with many neurons, we will need to have at our disposal an expanded set of tools that will allow us to deal with all the challenges that these networks present. In this chapter, we will start to look at some more advanced methods and algorithms that will allow us to work efficiently with big datasets and big networks. These complex networks become good enough to do some interesting multiclass classification, one of the most

U. Michelucci, *Applied Deep Learning*, https://doi.org/10.1007/978-1-4842-3790-8_3

frequent tasks that big networks are required to perform (for example, handwriting recognition, face recognition, image recognition, and so on), so I have chosen a dataset that will allow us to do some interesting multiclass classification and study its difficulties.

I will start the chapter by discussing the network architecture and the needed matrix formalism. A short overview of the new hyperparameters that come with this new type of network is then given. How to implement multiclass classification using the `softmax` function, and what kind of output layer is needed, is then explained. Then, before starting with Python code, a brief digression is taken to explain in detail what exactly overfitting is, with a simple example, and how to conduct a basic error analysis with complex networks. Then we will start to use TensorFlow to construct bigger networks, applying them to a MNIST-similar dataset, based on images of clothing items (which will be lots of fun). We will look at how to make the gradient descent algorithm covered in Chapter 2 faster, introducing two new variations: stochastic and mini-batch gradient descent. Then we will look at how to add many layers in an efficient way and how to initialize the weights and the biases in the best way possible, to make training fast and stable. In particular, we will look at Xavier and He initialization for sigmoid and the ReLU activation function, respectively. Finally, a rule of thumb on how to compare complexity of networks going beyond only the number of neurons is offered, and the chapter concludes with some tips on how to choose the right networks.

Network Architecture

Neural network architecture is quite easy to understand. It consists of an input layer (the inputs $x_j^{(i)}$), several layers (called hidden, because they are sandwiched between the input and the output layers, so they are "invisible" from the outside, so to speak), and an output layer. In each layer, you may have one to several neurons. The main property of such a network is that each neuron receives input from each neuron in the preceding layer and feeds its output to every neuron in the next layer. In Figure 3-1, you can see a graphical representation of such a network.

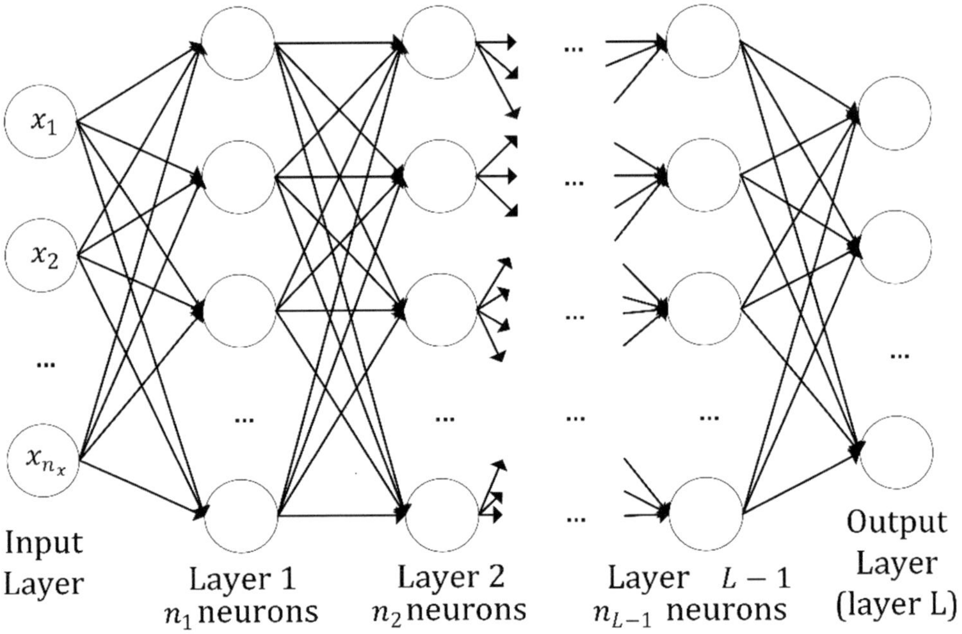

Figure 3-1. *Diagram of a multilayered deep feedforward neural network, in which each neuron receives input from each neuron in the preceding layer and feeds its output to every neuron in the subsequent layer*

To jump from one neuron, as in Chapter 2, to this is quite a big step. To build the model, we will have to work with matrix formalism, and, therefore, we must get all the matrix dimensions right. First, I'll discuss some new notation.

- L: Number of hidden layers, excluding the input layer but including the output layer
- n_l: Number of neurons in layer l

In a network such as the one in Figure 3-1, we will indicate the total number of neurons with $N_{neurons}$, which can be written as

$$N_{neurons} = n_x + \sum_{i=1}^{L} n_i = \sum_{i=0}^{L} n_i$$

where, by convention, we defined $n_0 = n_x$. Each connection between two neurons will have its own weight. Let's indicate the weight between neuron i in layer l and neuron j in layer $l-1$ with $w_{ij}^{[l]}$. In Figure 3-2, I have drawn only the first two layers (input and layer 1) of our generic network of Figure 3-1, with the weights between the first neuron in the input layer and all the others in layer 1. All other neurons are grayed out for clarity.

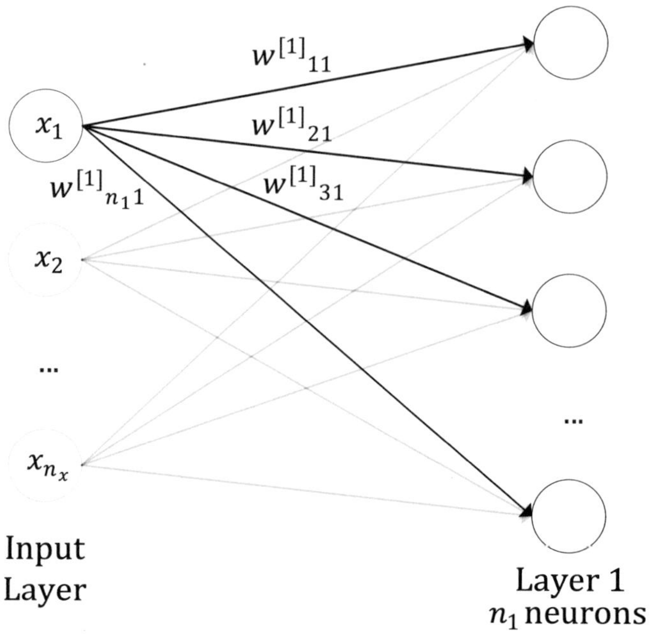

***Figure 3-2.** The first two layers of a generic neural network, with the weights of the connections between the first neuron in the input layers and the others in the second layer. All other neurons and connections are drawn in light gray, to make the diagram clearer.*

The weights between the input layer and layer 1 can be written as a matrix, as follows:

$$W^{[1]} = \begin{pmatrix} w_{11}^{[1]} & \cdots & w_{1n_x}^{[1]} \\ \vdots & \ddots & \vdots \\ w_{n_1 1}^{[1]} & \cdots & w^{[1]}{}_{n_1 n_x} \end{pmatrix}$$

This means that our matrix $W^{[1]}$ has dimensions $n_1 \times n_x$. Of course, this can be generalized between any two layers l and $l - 1$, meaning that the weight matrix between two adjacent layers l and $l - 1$, indicated by $W^{[l]}$, will have dimensions $n_l \times n_{l-1}$. By convention, $n_0 = n_x$ is the number of input features (not the number of observations that we indicate with m).

Note The weight matrix between two adjacent layers l and $l-1$, which we indicate with $W^{[l]}$, will have dimensions $n_l \times n_{l-1}$, where, by convention, $n_0 = n_x$ is the number of input features.

The bias (indicated by b in Chapter 2) will be a matrix this time. Remember that each neuron that receives inputs will have its own bias, so when considering our two layers, l and $l-1$, we will require n_l different values of b. We will indicate this matrix with $b^{[l]}$, and it will have dimensions $n_l \times 1$.

Note The bias matrix for two adjacent layers l and $l-1$, which we indicate with $b^{[l]}$, will have dimensions $n_l \times 1$.

Output of Neurons

Now let's start considering the output of our neurons. To begin, we will consider the ith neuron of the first layer (remember that our input layer is by definition layer 0). Let's indicate its output with $\hat{y}_i^{[1]}$ and assume that all neurons in layer l use the same activation function, which we will indicate by $g^{[l]}$. Then we will have

$$\hat{y}_i^{[1]} = g^{[1]}\left(z_i^{[1]}\right) = g^{[i]}\left(\sum_{j=1}^{n_x}\left(w_{ij}^{[1]}\, x_j + b_i^{[1]}\right)\right)$$

where we have indicated, as you will remember from Chapter 2, z_i as

$$z_i^{[1]} = \sum_{j=1}^{n_x}\left(w_{ij}^{[1]}\, x_j + b_i^{[1]}\right)$$

As you can imagine, we want to have a matrix for all the output of layer 1, so we will use the notation

$$Z^{[1]} = W^{[1]}X + b^{[1]}$$

where $Z^{[1]}$ will have dimensions $n_1 \times 1$, and where with X, we have indicated our matrix with all our observations (rows for the features, and columns for observations), as I have already discussed in Chapter 2. We assume here that all neurons in layer l will use the same activation function that we will indicate with $g^{[l]}$.

We can easily generalize the previous equation for a layer l

$$Z^{[l]} = W^{[l]} Z^{[l-1]} + b^{[l]}$$

because layer l will get its input from layer $l - 1$. We just need to substitute X with $Z^{[l-1]}$. $Z^{[l]}$ will have dimensions $n_l \times 1$. Our output in matrix form will then be

$$Y^{[l]} = g^{[l]}\left(Z^{[l]}\right)$$

where the activation function acts, as usual, element by element.

Summary of Matrix Dimensions

Following is a summary of the dimensions of all the matrices we have described so far.

- $W^{[l]}$ has dimensions $n_l \times n_{l-1}$ (where we have $n_0 = n_x$ by definition)
- $b^{[l]}$ has dimensions $n_l \times 1$
- $Z^{[l-1]}$ has dimensions $n_{l-1} \times 1$
- $Z^{[l]}$ has dimensions $n_l \times 1$
- $Y^{[l]}$ has dimensions $n_l \times 1$

In each case, l goes from 1 to L.

Example: Equations for a Network with Three Layers

To make this discussion a bit more concrete, let's consider an example of a network with three layers (so $L = 3$), with $n_1 = 3$, $n_2 = 2$, and $n_3 = 1$, as depicted in Figure 3-3.

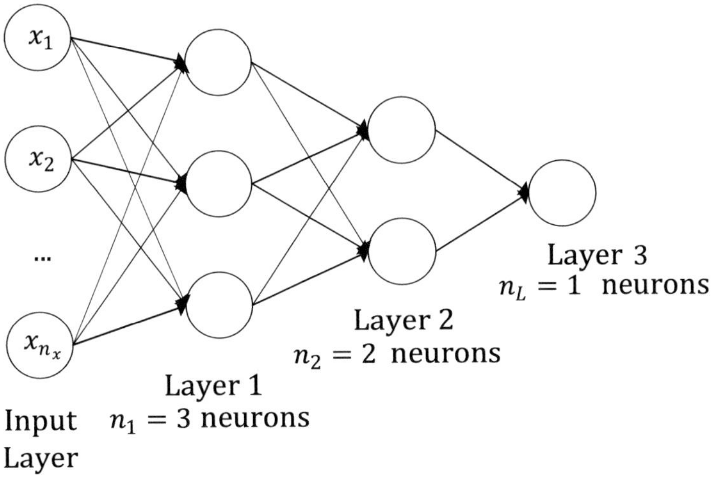

***Figure 3-3.** A practical example of a feedforward neural network*

In this case, we will have to calculate the following quantities:

- $\hat{Y}^{[1]} = g^{[1]}\left(W^{[1]}X + b^{[1]}\right)$, where $W^{[1]}$ has dimensions $3 \times n_x$, b has dimensions 3×1, and X has dimensions $n_x \times m$
- $\hat{Y}^{[2]} = g^{[2]}\left(W^{[2]}Z^{[1]} + b^{[2]}\right)$, where $W^{[2]}$ has dimensions 2×3, b has dimensions 2×1, and $Z^{[1]}$ has dimensions $3 \times m$
- $\hat{Y}^{[3]} = g^{[3]}\left(W^{[3]}Z^{[2]} + b^{[3]}\right)$, where $W^{[3]}$ has dimensions 1×2, b has dimensions 1×1, and $Z^{[2]}$ has dimensions $2 \times m$

and your network output, $\hat{Y}^{[3]}$, will have, as expected, dimensions $1 \times m$.

All this may seem rather abstract (and, in fact, it is). You will see later in the chapter how easy it is to implement in TensorFlow, simply by building the right computational graph, based on the steps just discussed.

Hyperparameters in Fully Connected Networks

In networks such as the ones just discussed, there are quite a few parameters that you can tune to find the best model for your problem. You will remember from Chapter 2 that parameters that you fix at the beginning and then don't change during the training phase are called hyperparameters. You will have to tune the additional following hyperparameters for feed forward networks:

- Number of layers: L
- Number of neurons in each layer: n_i for i from 1 to L
- Choice of activation function for each layer: $g^{[l]}$

Then, of course, you still have the following hyperparameters that you encountered in Chapter 2:

- Number of iterations (or epochs)
- Learning rate

softmax Function for Multiclass Classification

You will still have to suffer a bit more theory before getting to some TensorFlow code. The kinds of networks described in this chapter start to be complex enough to be able to perform some multiclass classification with reasonable results. To do this, we must first introduce the `softmax` function.

Mathematically speaking, the `softmax` function S is one that transforms a k dimensional vector into another k dimensional vector of real values, each between 0 and 1, and that sum up to 1. Given k real values z_i for $i = 1, \ldots, k$, we define the vector $\boldsymbol{z} = (z_1, \ldots, z_k)$, and we define the `softmax` vector function $\boldsymbol{S}(\boldsymbol{z}) = (S(\boldsymbol{z})_1 \;\; S(\boldsymbol{z})_2 \ldots \;\; S(\boldsymbol{z})_k)$ as

$$S(\boldsymbol{z})_i = \frac{e^{z_i}}{\sum_{j=1}^{k} e^{z_j}}$$

Because the denominator is always bigger than the nominator, $S(\boldsymbol{z})_i < 1$. Additionally, we have

$$\sum_{i=1}^{k} S(\boldsymbol{z})_i = \sum_{i=1}^{k} \frac{e^{z_i}}{\sum_{j=1}^{k} e^{z_j}} = \frac{\sum_{i=1}^{k} e^{z_i}}{\sum_{j=1}^{k} e^{z_j}} = 1$$

So, $S(\mathbf{z})_i$ behaves like a probability, because its sum over i is 1, and its elements are all less than 1. We will consider $S(\mathbf{z})_i$ as a probability distribution over k possible outcomes. For us, $S(\mathbf{z})_i$ will simply be the probability of our input observation of being of class i. Let's suppose we are trying to classify an observation into three classes. We may get the following output: $S(\mathbf{z})_1 = 0.1$, $S(\mathbf{z})_2 = 0.6$, and $S(\mathbf{z})_3 = 0.3$. That means that our observation has a 10% probability of being of class 1, a 60% probability of being of class 2, and 30% probability of being of class 3. Normally, one chooses to classify the input observation into the class with the higher probability, in this example, class 2, with 60% probability.

Note We will look at $S(\mathbf{z})_i$ as a probability distribution over k with $i = 1, \ldots, k$ possible outcomes. For us, $S(\mathbf{z})_i$ will simply be the probability of our input observation being of class i.

To be able to use the `softmax` function for classification, we will have to use a specific output layer. We will have to use ten neurons, each of which will give z_i as its output, and then one neuron that will output $\mathbf{S}(\mathbf{z})$. This neuron will have the `softmax` function as activation function and will have as inputs the 10 outputs, z_i, of the last layer with 10 neurons. In TensorFlow, you use the `tf.nn.softmax` function applied to the last layer with 10 neurons. Remember that this `tensorflow` function will act element by element. Later in the chapter, you will find a concrete example showing how to implement this from start to finish.

A Brief Digression: Overfitting

One of the most common problems that you will encounter when training deep neural networks will be overfitting. What can happen is that your network may, owing to its flexibility, learn patterns that are due to noise, errors, or simply wrong data. It is very important to understand what overfitting is, so I will give you a practical example of what can happen, to give you an intuitive understanding of it. To make it easier to visualize, I will work with a simple two-dimensional dataset, which I will create for the purpose. I hope that at the end of the next section, you will have a clear idea of what overfitting is.

A Practical Example of Overfitting

Networks described in the previous sections are rather complex and can easily lead to overfitting of the dataset. Let me explain briefly the concept of overfitting. To understand it, consider the following problem: find the best polynomial that approximates a given dataset. Given a set of two-dimensional points $(x^{(i)}, y^{(i)})$, we want to find the best polynomial of degree K in the form

$$f\left(x^{(i)}\right)=\sum_{j=0}^{K} a_j x^{(i)j}$$

that minimizes the mean square error

$$\frac{1}{m}\sum_{i=1}^{m}\left(y^{(i)}-f\left(x^{(i)}\right)\right)^2$$

where, as usual, m indicates the number of data points we have. I don't want only to determine all the parameters a_j, but also the value of K that best approximates our data. K, in this case, measures our model complexity. For example, for $K = 0$, we simply have $f(x^{(i)}) = a_0$ (a constant), the simplest polynomial we can think of. For higher K, we have higher order polynomials, meaning that our function is more complex, having more parameters available for training.

Here is an example of our function for $K = 3$:

$$f\left(x^{(i)}\right)=\sum_{j=0}^{3} a_j x^{(i)j}=a_0+a_1 x^{(i)}+a_2\left(x^{(i)}\right)^2+a_3\left(x^{(i)}\right)^3$$

where we have four parameters that can be tuned during our training models. Let's generate some data, starting from a second order polynomial ($K = 2$)

$$1+2x^{(i)}+3x^{(i)^2}$$

and adding some random error (this will make overfitting visible). Let's first import our standard libraries with the addition of the `curve_fit` function, which will minimize automatically the standard error and find the best parameters. Don't worry too much about this function. The goal here is to show you what can happen when you use a model that is too complex.

```
import numpy as np
import matplotlib.pyplot as plt
from scipy.optimize import curve_fit
```

Let's define a function for a second-degree polynomial

```
def func_2(p, a, b, c):
    return a+b*p + c*p**2
```

then let's generate our dataset

```
x = np.arange(-5.0, 5.0, 0.05, dtype = np.float64)
y = func_2(x, 1,2,3)+18.0*np.random.normal(0, 1, size=len(x))
```

To add some random noise to the function, we have used the function `np.random.normal(0, 1, size=len(x))`, which generates a `numpy` array of random values from a normal distribution of length `len(x)`, with average `0` and standard deviation `1`.

In Figure 3-4, you can see what the data looks like for $a = 1$, $b = 2$, and $c = 3$.

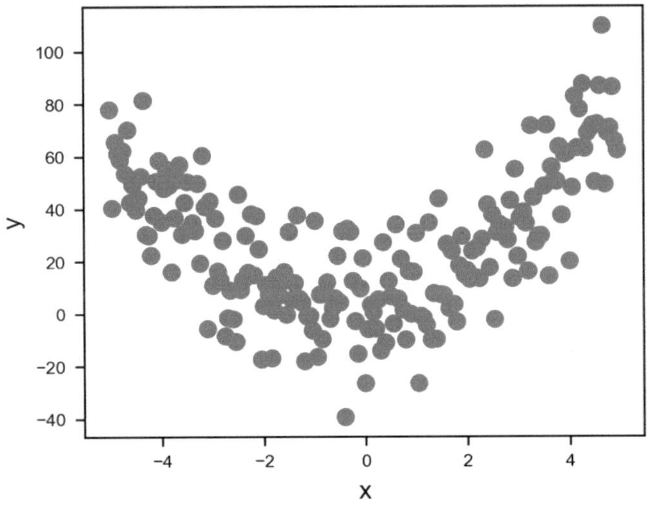

***Figure 3-4.** The data we have generated with a = 1, b = 2, and c = 3, as described in the text*

Now let's consider a model that is too simple to capture the feature of the data, meaning that we will see what a model with high bias[1] can do. Let's consider a linear model ($K = 1$). The code will be

```
def func_1(p, a, b):
    return a+b*p
popt, pcov = curve_fit(func_1, x, y)
```

That will give the best values for a and b that minimize the standard error. In Figure 3-5, it is clear how this model completely misses the main feature of the data, being too simple.

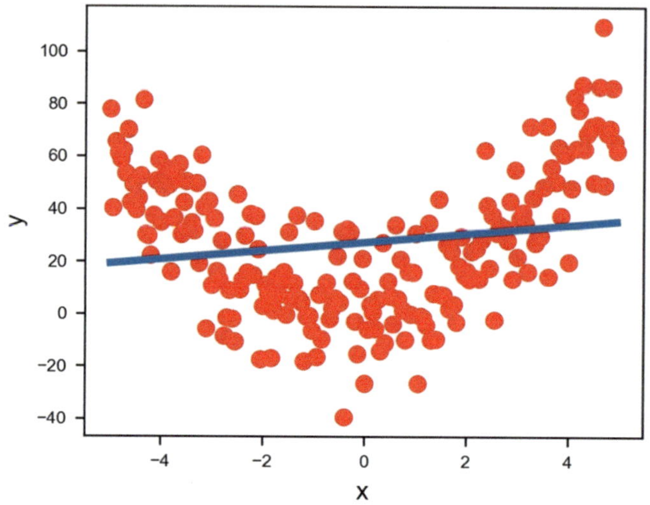

Figure 3-5. *The linear model misses the main feature of the data, being too simple. In this case, the model has high bias.*

Let's try to fit a two-degree polynomial ($K = 2$). The results appear in Figure 3-6.

[1]Bias is a measure of the error originating from models that are too simple to capture the real features of the data.

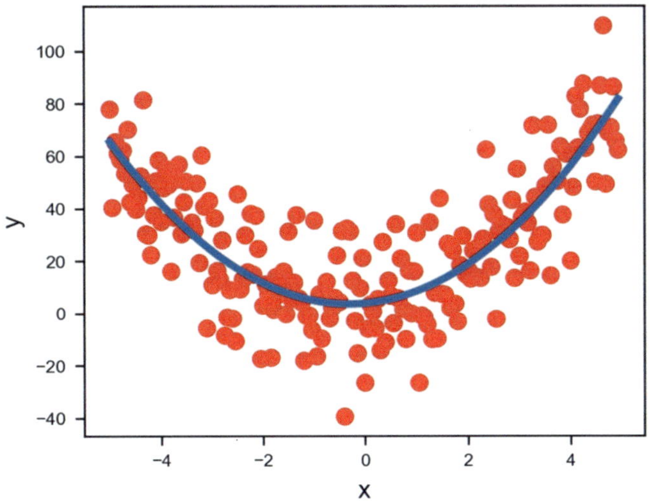

Figure 3-6. *The results for a 2-degree polynomial*

That is better. This model seems to capture the main features of the model, ignoring the random noise. Now let's try a very complex model—a 21-degree polynomial ($K = 21$). The results are shown in Figure 3-7.

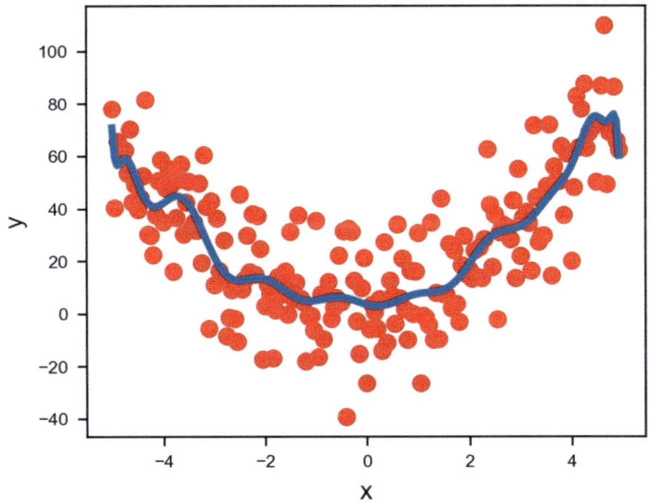

Figure 3-7. *The results for a 21-degree polynomial model*

Now, this model shows features that we know are wrong, because we created our data. These features are not present, but the model is so flexible that it captures the random variability that we have introduced with noise. Here, I am referring to the oscillations that have appeared using this high-ordered polynomial.

In this case, we talk about overfitting, meaning we start capturing with our model features owing, for example, to random error. It is easy to understand that this generalizes quite badly. If we applied this 21-degree polynomial model to new data, it would not work well, because the random noise would be different in new data, and so the oscillations we see in Figure 3-7 would make no sense on new data. In Figure 3-8, I have plotted the best 21-degree polynomial models obtained by fitting data generated with 10 different random noise values added. You can clearly see how much it varies. It is not stable and is strongly dependent on the random noise present. The oscillations are always different! In this case, we are talking about *high variance*.

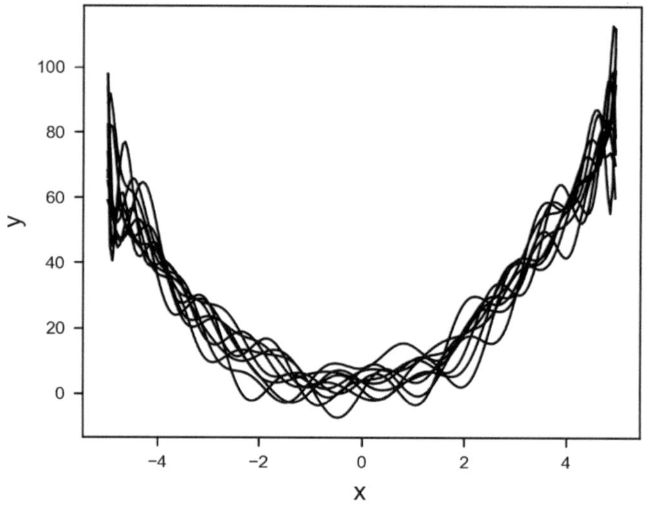

Figure 3-8. *Result of our model, with a 21-degree polynomial fitted to 10 different datasets generated with different random noise values added*

Now let's create the same plot with our linear model, while varying our random noise, as we did in Figure 3-8. You can check the results in Figure 3-9.

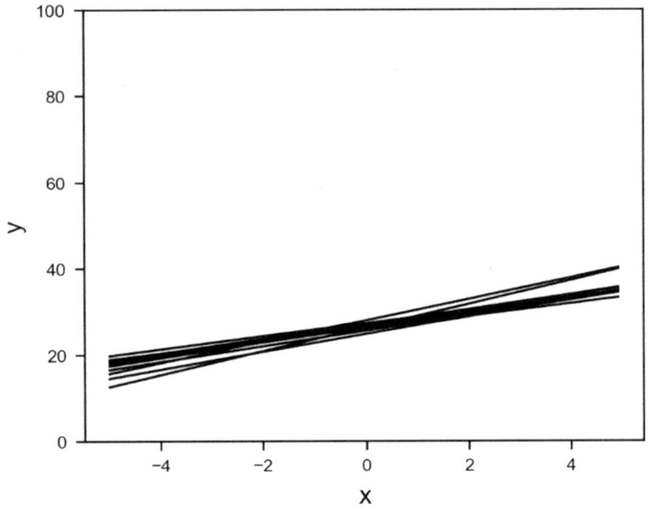

Figure 3-9. *Results of our linear model applied to data in which we have randomly changed the random noise. For easier comparison with Figure 3-8, I have used the same scale.*

You can see that our model is much more stable. Our linear model does not capture any feature that is dependent on our noise, but it misses the main features of our data (the concave nature). We are talking here of *high bias.*

Figure 3-10 should help you to gain an intuitive understanding of bias and variance. Bias is a measure of how close our measurements are to the true values (the center of the figure), and variance is a measure of how spread the measurements are around the average (not necessarily the true value, as you can see on the right).

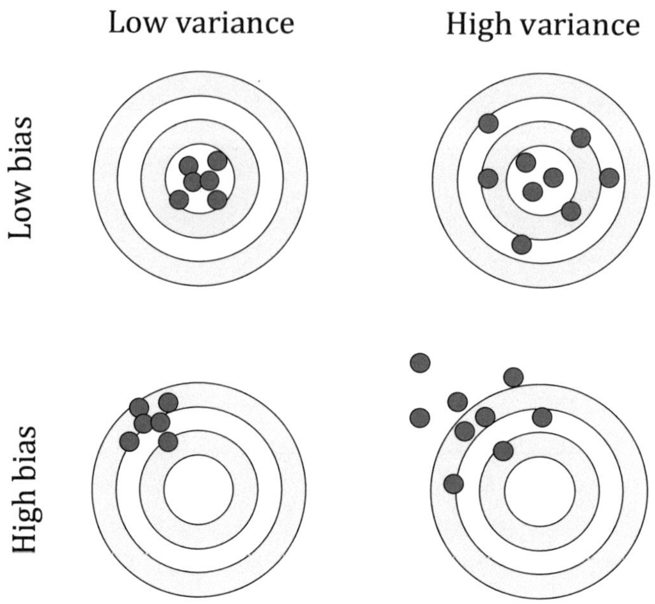

Figure 3-10. *Bias and variance*

In the case of neural networks, we have many hyperparameters (number of layers, number of neurons in each layer, activation function, and so on), and it is very difficult to know in which regime we are. How can we tell if our model has a high variance or a high bias, for example? I will dedicate an entire chapter to this subject, but the first step in performing this error analysis is to split our dataset into two different ones. Let's see what this means and why we do it.

Note The essence of overfitting is to have unknowingly extracted some of the residual variation (i.e., the noise) as if that variation represented the underlying model structure (see Burnham, K. P.; Anderson, D. R., *Model Selection and Multimodel Inference*, 2nd ed., New York; Springer-Verlag, 2002). The opposite is called underfitting—when the model cannot capture the structure of the data.

The problem with overfitting and deep neural networks is that there is no way of visualizing easily the results, and, therefore, we require a different approach to determine if our model is overfitting, underfitting, or is just right. This can be achieved by splitting our dataset into different parts and evaluating and comparing the metrics on all of them. Let's explore the basic idea in the next section.

Basic Error Analysis

To check how our model is doing, and to do a proper error analysis, we must split our dataset into the following two parts:[2]

- *Training dataset*: The model is trained on this dataset, using the inputs and the relative labels, by an optimizer algorithm such as gradient descent, as we did in Chapter 2. Often, this set is called the "train set."
- *Development (or validation) set*: The trained model will then be used on this dataset, to check how it is doing. On this dataset, we will test different hyperparameters. For example, we can train two different models with a different number of layers on the training dataset and test them on this dataset, to check how they are doing. Often, this set is termed the "dev set."

I will devote an entire chapter to error analysis, but it is a good idea to offer you an overview of why it is important to split the dataset. Let's suppose we are dealing with classification, and let's suppose that the metric we use to judge the quality of our model is 1 minus the accuracy, or, in other words, the percentage of the cases that are wrongly classified. Let's consider the following three cases (Table 3-1):

Table 3-1. *Four different cases to show how to recognize overfitting from the training and the dev set error*

Error	Case A	Case B	Case C	Case D
Training set error	1%	15%	14%	0.3%
Dev set error	11%	16%	32%	1.1%

- *Case A*: Here, we are overfitting (high variance), because we are doing very well on the training set, but our model generalizes very badly to our dev set (refer again to Figure 3-8).
- *Case B*: Here, we see a problem with high bias, meaning that our model is not doing very well generally, on both datasets (refer again to Figure 3-9).

[2]To conduct a proper error analysis, we will require at least three parts, perhaps four. But to get a basic understanding of the process, two parts suffice.

- *Case C*: Here, we have a high bias (the model cannot predict very well the training set) and high variance (the model does not generalize well on the dev set).
- *Case D*: Here, everything seems OK. The error is good on the train set and good on the dev set. That is a good candidate for our best model.

I will explain all these concepts more thoroughly later in the book, where I will provide recipes for how to solve problems of high bias, high variances, both, or even more complex cases.

To recap: To perform a very basic error analysis, you will have to split your dataset into at least two sets: train and dev. You should then calculate your metric on both sets and compare them. You want to have a model that has low error on the train set and on the dev set (as in Case D, in the preceding example), and the two values should be comparable.

Note Your main takeaways from this section should be (1) a set of recipes and guidelines is required for understanding how your model is doing (is it overfitting, underfitting, or is it just right?); (2) to answer the preceding questions, you must split your dataset in two, to perform the relevant analysis. Later in the book, you will see what you can do with a dataset split into three, or even four, parts.

The Zalando Dataset

Zalando SE is a German e-commerce company based in Berlin. The company maintains a cross-platform store that sells shoes, clothing, and other fashion items.[3] For a kaggle competition (if you don't know what this is, check the website `www.kaggle.com`, from which you can participate in many competitions that have the goal of solving problems with data science), Zalando prepared a MNIST-similar dataset of images of its clothing, for which they provided 60,000 training images and 10,000 test images. As in MNIST, each image was 28 × 28 pixels in grayscale. Zalando grouped all images in ten different classes and provided the labels for each image. The dataset has 785 columns. The first column is the class label (an integer going from 0 to 9), and the

[3]Wikipedia, "Zalando," `https://en.wikipedia.org/wiki/Zalando`, 2018.

remaining 784 contain the pixel gray value of the image (you can calculate that as $28 \times 28 = 784$), exactly as we have seen in Chapter 2, in the discussion related to the MNIST dataset of handwritten digits.

Each training and test sample is assigned one of the following labels (per the documentation):

- 0: T-shirt/top
- 1: Trouser
- 2: Pullover
- 3: Dress
- 4: Coat
- 5: Sandal
- 6: Shirt
- 7: Sneaker
- 8: Bag
- 9: Ankle boot

In Figure 3-11, you can see an example of each class, chosen randomly from the dataset.

Figure 3-11. *One example from each of the ten classes in the Zalando dataset*

The dataset has been provided under the MIT License.[4] The data file can be downloaded from kaggle (`www.kaggle.com/zalando-research/fashionmnist/data`) or directly from GitHub (`https://github.com/zalandoresearch/fashion-mnist`). If you choose the second option. you will have to prepare the data a bit. (You can convert it to CSV with the script located at `https://pjreddie.com/projects/mnist-in-csv/`.) If you download it from kaggle, the data will already be in the correct format. You will find two CSV files zipped on the kaggle web site. When unzipped, you will have `fashion-mnist_train.csv`, with 60,000 images (roughly 130MB), and `fashion-mnist_test.csv`, with 10,000 (roughly 21MB). Let's fire up a Jupyter notebook and start coding!

We will need the following imports in our code:

```
import pandas as pd
import numpy as np
import tensorflow as tf
%matplotlib inline
import matplotlib
import matplotlib.pyplot as plt
from random import *
```

Put the CSV files in the same directory as your notebook. Then, you can simply load the files with the `pandas` function.

```
data_train = pd.read_csv('fashion-mnist_train.csv', header = 0)
```

You can also read the file with standard NumPy functions (such as `loadtxt()`), but using `read_csv()` from pandas gives you a lot of flexibility in slicing and analyzing your data. Additionally, it is a lot faster. Reading the file (that is, roughly 130MB) with pandas takes about 10 seconds, while with NumPy, it takes 1 minute, 20 seconds on my laptop. So, if you are dealing with big datasets, keep this in mind. It is common practice to use pandas to read and prepare the data. If you aren't familiar with pandas, don't worry. All you need to understand will be explained in detail.

[4] Wikipedia, "MIT License," `https://en.wikipedia.org/wiki/MIT_License`, 2018.

Note Remember: You should not focus on the Python implementation. Focus on the model, on the concepts behind the implementation. You can achieve the same results using pandas, NumPy, or even C. Try to concentrate on how to prepare the data, how to normalize it, how to check the training, and so on.

With the command

```
data_train.head()
```

you can see the first five lines of your dataset, as shown in Figure 3-12.

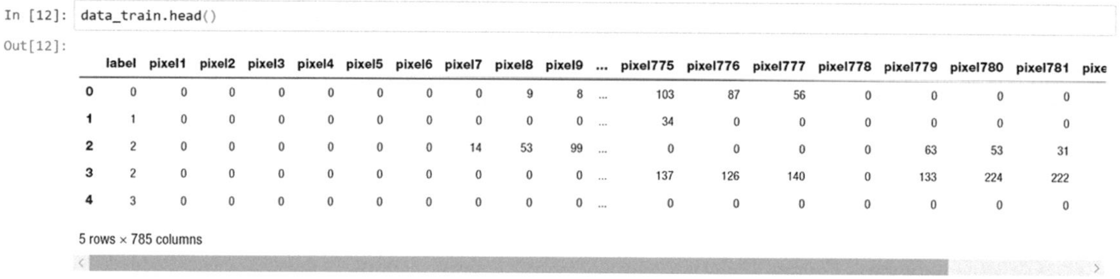
In [12]: data_train.head()

Out[12]:

	label	pixel1	pixel2	pixel3	pixel4	pixel5	pixel6	pixel7	pixel8	pixel9	...	pixel775	pixel776	pixel777	pixel778	pixel779	pixel780	pixel781	pixe
0	0	0	0	0	0	0	0	0	9	8	...	103	87	56	0	0	0	0	
1	1	0	0	0	0	0	0	0	0	0	...	34	0	0	0	0	0	0	
2	2	0	0	0	0	0	0	14	53	99	...	0	0	0	0	63	53	31	
3	2	0	0	0	0	0	0	0	0	0	...	137	126	140	0	133	224	222	
4	3	0	0	0	0	0	0	0	0	0	...	0	0	0	0	0	0	0	

5 rows × 785 columns

Figure 3-12. *With `data_train.head()` the command, you can check the first five rows of your dataset*

You will see that each column has a name. pandas retrieves it from the first line in the file. Checking the column name, you know immediately what is in which column. For example, in the first, we have the class label. Now we must create an array with the labels and one with the 784 features (remember that we have all the pixel gray values as features). For this, we can simply write the following:

```
labels = data_train['label'].values.reshape(1, 60000)
train = data_train.drop('label', axis=1).transpose()
```

Let's discuss briefly what the code does, starting with the labels. In pandas, each column has a name (as you can see in Figure 3-12), which in our case, is automatically inferred from the first line of the CSV file. The first column ("label") contains the class label, an integer from 0 to 9. In pandas, to select this column only, we can simply use the following syntax:

```
data_train['label']
```

giving the column name in square brackets.

If you check the shape of this array with

```
data_train['label'].shape
```

you get the value (60000), as expected. As we have already seen in Chapter 2, we want a tensor for our labels with the dimensions $1 \times m$, where m is the number of observations (in this case 60000). So, we must reshape it with the command

```
labels = data_train['label'].values.reshape(1, 60000)
```

Now the tensor labels have the dimension (1, 60000), as we want.

The tensor that should contain the features should contain all columns, except the labels. So, we simply remove the label column with `drop('label', axis=1)`, take all the others, and then transpose the tensor. In fact, `data_train.drop('label', axis=1)` has the dimensions (60000, 784), and we want a tensor with the dimensions $n_x \times m$, where here $n_x = 784$ is the number of the features. Following is a summary of our tensors so far.

- *Labels*: This has the dimensions $1 \times m$ (1×60000) and contains the class labels (integers from 0 to 9).
- *Train*: This has the dimensions $n_x \times m$ (784×60000) and contains the features, in which each row contains the grayscale value of a single pixel in the image (remember $28 \times 28 = 784$).

Refer again to Figure 3-11 for an idea of how the images look. Finally, let's normalize the input, so that instead of having values from 0 to 255 (the grayscale values), it has only values between 0 and 1. This is very easy to do with the following code:

```
train = np.array(train / 255.0)
```

Building a Model with tensorflow

Now it is time to expand what we did with TensorFlow in Chapter 2 with one neuron to networks with many layers and neurons. Let's first discuss the network architecture and what kind of output layer we need, and then let's build our model with TensorFlow.

Network Architecture

We will start with a network with just one hidden layer. We will have an input layer with 784 features, then a hidden layer (in which we will vary the number of neurons), then an output layer of ten neurons that will feed their output into a neuron that will have as an activation function the `softmax` function. See first Figure 3-13, for a graphical representation of the network, and then I will spend some time explaining the various parts, especially the output layers.

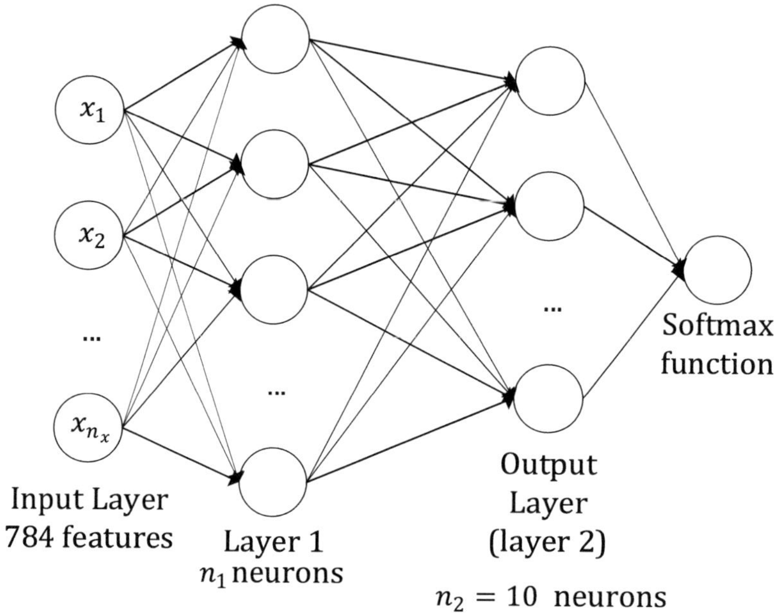

Figure 3-13. *The network architecture with a single hidden layer. During our analysis, we will vary the number of neurons, n_1, in the hidden layer.*

Let me explain why there is this strange output layer with ten neurons and why there is a need for an additional neuron for the `softmax` function. Remember that for each image, we want to be able to determine to which class it belongs. To do this, as explained when discussing the `softmax` function, we will have to get ten outputs for each observation: each being the probability of the image of being of each of the classes. So, given an input $\boldsymbol{x}^{(i)}$, we will need the ten values: $P(y^{(i)} = 1|\boldsymbol{x}^{(i)})$, $P(y^{(i)} = 2|\boldsymbol{x}^{(i)})$, …., $P(y^{(i)} = 10|\boldsymbol{x}^{(i)})$ (probability of the observation class $y^{(i)}$ being one of the ten possibilities given the input $\boldsymbol{x}^{(i)}$), or, in other words, our output should be a tensor of dimensions 1×10 in the form

$$\hat{\boldsymbol{y}} = \left(P\left(y^{(i)} = 1|\boldsymbol{x}^{(i)}\right) \quad P\left(y^{(i)} = 2|\boldsymbol{x}^{(i)}\right) \quad \dots \quad P\left(y^{(i)} = 10|\boldsymbol{x}^{(i)}\right) \right)$$

And because the observation must be of one single class the condition

$$\sum_{j=1}^{10} P\left(y^{(i)} = j | \boldsymbol{x}^{(i)}\right) = 1$$

must be satisfied. This can be understood as follows: the observation has a 100% probability of being of one of the ten classes, or, in other words, all the probabilities must add to 1. We solve this problem in two steps:

- We create an output layer with ten neurons. In this way, we will have our ten values as output.
- Then we feed the ten values to a new neuron (let's call it "softmax" neuron) that will take the ten inputs and give as output ten values that are all less than 1 and that add up to 1.

Figure 3-14 shows our "softmax" neuron in detail.

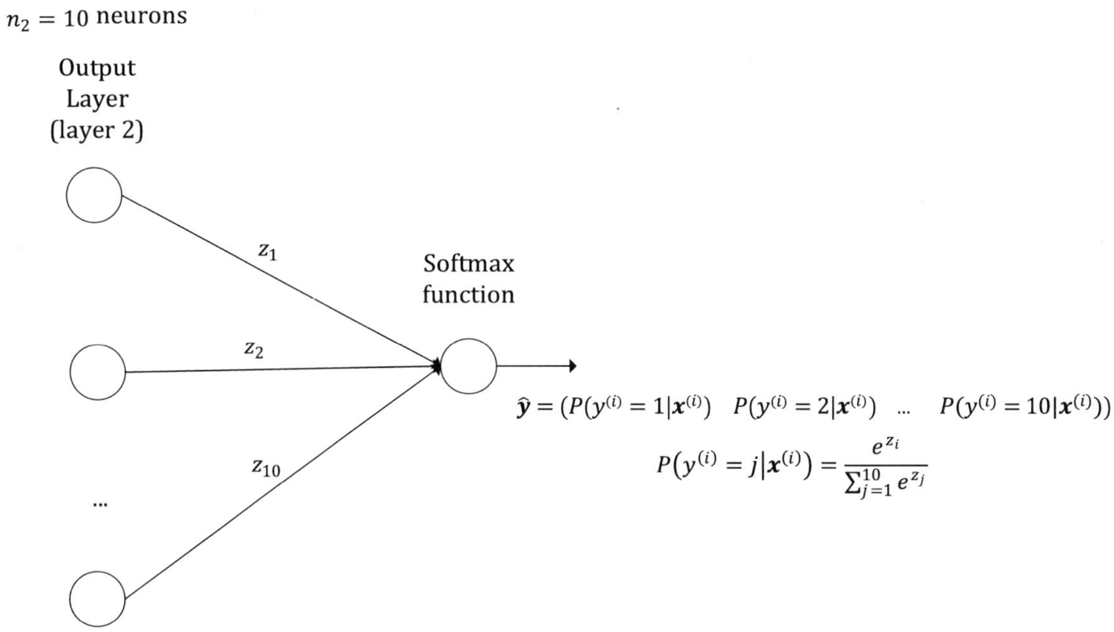

Figure 3-14. *The final neuron in our network that transforms the ten inputs in probabilities*

Calling z_i the output of the ith neuron in the last layer (with i going from 1 to 10), we will have

$$P\left(y^{(i)} = j \mid \boldsymbol{x}^{(i)}\right) = \frac{e^{z_i}}{\sum_{j=1}^{10} e^{z_j}}$$

That is exactly what the `tensorflow` function `tf.nn.softmax()` does. It takes a tensor as input and returns a tensor with the same dimensions as the input but "normalized," as discussed previously. In other words, if we feed $\boldsymbol{z} = (z_1 \quad z_2 \quad \dots \quad z_{10})$ to the function, it will return a tensor with the same dimensions as $\boldsymbol{z}$, meaning 1×10, where each element is the last equation.

Modifying Labels for the softmax Function—One-Hot Encoding

Before developing our network, first we must solve another problem. You will remember from Chapter 2 that in classification, we will use the following cost function:

```
cost = - tf.reduce_mean(Y * tf.log(y_)+(1-Y) * tf.log(1-y_))
```

where `Y` contains our labels and `y_` is the result of our network. So, the two tensors must have the same dimensions. In our case, I explained to you that our network will give as output a vector with ten elements, while a label in our dataset is simply a scalar. Therefore, we have `y_` that has dimensions (10,1) and `Y` that has dimensions (1,1). This will not work if we don't do something smart. We must transform our labels in a tensor that has dimensions (10,1). A vector with a value for each class is also required, but what value should we use?

We must perform what is known as *one-hot encoding*.[5] This means that we will transform our labels (integers from 0 to 9) to tensors with dimensions (1,10) with the following algorithm: our one-hot encoded vector will have all zeros, except at the index of the label. For example, for a label 2, our 1×10 tensor will have all zeros, except at the position of index 2, or, in other words, it will be (0,0,1,0,0,0,0,0,0,0). Try some other examples (see Table 3-2), and the concept will become clear immediately.

[5]As a side note, this technique is often used to feed categorical variables to machine-learning algorithms.

Table 3-2. *Examples of How One-Hot Encoding Works (Remember that labels go from 0 to 9 as indexes.)*

Label	One-Hot Encoded Label
0	(1,0,0,0,0,0,0,0,0,0)
2	(0,0,1,0,0,0,0,0,0,0)
5	(0,0,0,0,0,1,0,0,0,0)
7	(0,0,0,0,0,0,0,1,0,0)

In Figure 3-15, you can see a graphical representation of the process of one-hot encoding a label. In the figure, two labels (2 and 5) are one-hot encoded in two tensors. The grayed element of the tensor (in this case, a one-dimensional vector) is the one that becomes one, while the white ones remain zero.

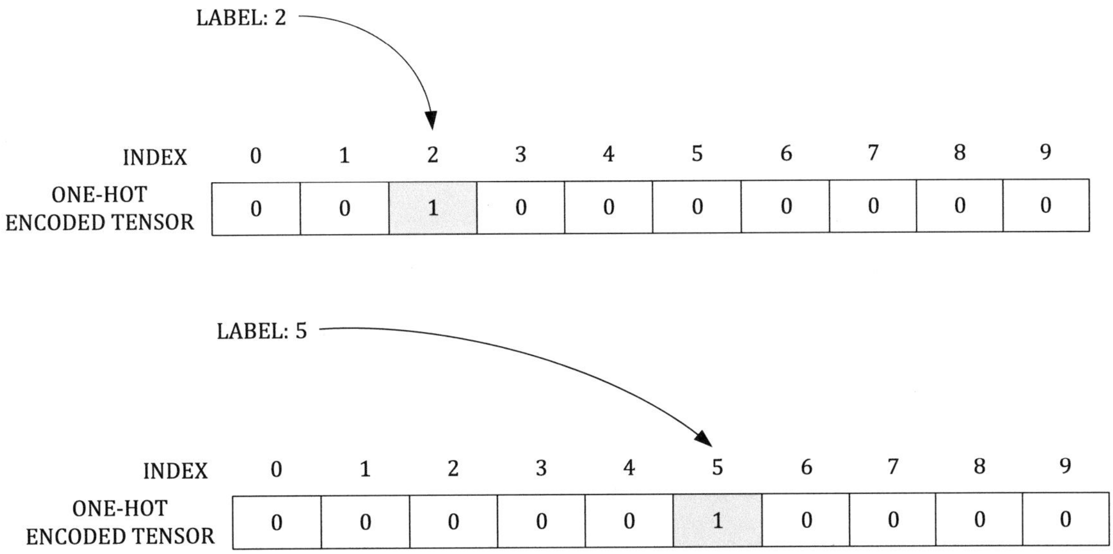

Figure 3-15. *Graphical representation of the process of one-hot encoding a label*

Sklearn has several ways of doing this automatically (check, for example, the function `OneHotEncoder()`), but I think it is instructive to undertake the process manually, to really see how it is done. Once you understand why you need it, and in which format you need it, you can use the function you like most. The Python code to do this is very simple (the last line just converts the pandas data frame into a NumPy array):

```
labels_ = np.zeros((60000, 10))
labels_[np.arange(60000), labels] = 1
labels_ = labels_.transpose()
labels_ = np.array(labels_)
```

First, you create a new array with the right dimensions: (60000,10), then you fill it with zeros with the NumPy function `np.zeros((60000,10))`. Next, you set to 1 only the columns related to the label itself, using pandas functionalities to slice data frames with the line `labels_[np.arange(60000), labels] = 1`. Then you transpose it, to have the dimensions we want at the end: (10, 60000), where each column indicates a different observation.

Now in our code, we can finally compare `Y` and `y_`, because both now have the dimensions (10,1) for one observation, or when considering the entire training dataset of (10, 60000). Each row in y_ will now represent the probability of our observation as being of a specific class. At the very end, when calculating the accuracy of our model, we will assign the class with the highest probability to each observation.

Note Our network will give us the ten probabilities for the observation as being of each of the ten classes. At the end, we will assign to the observation the class that has the highest probability.

The tensorflow Model

Now is time to build our model with `tensorflow`. The following code will do the job:

```
n_dim = 784
tf.reset_default_graph()

# Number of neurons in the layers
n1 = 5 # Number of neurons in layer 1
n2 = 10 # Number of neurons in output layer
```

```
cost_history = np.empty(shape=[1], dtype = float)
learning_rate = tf.placeholder(tf.float32, shape=())

X = tf.placeholder(tf.float32, [n_dim, None])
Y = tf.placeholder(tf.float32, [10, None])
W1 = tf.Variable(tf. truncated_normal ([n1, n_dim], stddev=.1))
b1 = tf.Variable(tf.zeros([n1,1]))
W2 = tf.Variable(tf. truncated_normal ([n2, n1], stddev=.1))
b2 = tf.Variable(tf.zeros([n2,1]))

# Let's build our network...
Z1 = tf.nn.relu(tf.matmul(W1, X) + b1)
Z2 = tf.nn.relu(tf.matmul(W2, Z1) + b2)
y_ = tf.nn.softmax(Z2,0)

cost = - tf.reduce_mean(Y * tf.log(y_)+(1-Y) * tf.log(1-y_))
optimizer = tf.train.AdamOptimizer(learning_rate).minimize(cost)

init = tf.global_variables_initializer()
```

I will not go through each line of code, because you should understand by now what a placeholder or a variable is. But there are a few details of the code that I would like you to notice.

- When we initialize the weights, use the code `tf.Variable(tf. truncated_normal ([n1, n_dim], stddev=.1))`. The `truncated_normal()` function will return values from a normal distribution, with the peculiarity that values that are more than 2 standard deviation from the average will be dropped and repicked. The reason for choosing a small `stddev` of 0.1 is to avoid that the output of the ReLU activation function becomes too big and, therefore, `nan`s start to appear, owing to Python not being able to calculate properly numbers that are too big. I will discuss a better way of choosing the right `stddev` later in the chapter.
- Our last neuron will use the `softmax` function: `y_ = tf.nn.softmax(Z2,0)`. Remember that `y_` will not be a scalar but a tensor of the same dimensions as `Z2`. The second parameter, `0`, tells `tensorflow` that we want to apply the `softmax` function along the vertical axis (the rows).

- The two parameters n1 and n2 define the number of neurons in the different layers. Remember that the second (output) layer must have ten neurons to be able to use the softmax function. But we will play with the value for n1. Increasing n1 will increase the complexity of the network.

Now let's try to perform the training, as we did in Chapter 2. We can reuse the code we already wrote. Try to run the following code on your laptop:

```
sess = tf.Session()
sess.run(tf.global_variables_initializer())

training_epochs = 5000

cost_history = []
for epoch in range(training_epochs+1):

    sess.run(optimizer, feed_dict = {X: train, Y: labels_, learning_rate:
    0.001})
    cost_ = sess.run(cost, feed_dict={ X:train, Y: labels_, learning_rate:
    0.001})
    cost_history = np.append(cost_history, cost_)

    if (epoch % 20 == 0):
        print("Reached epoch",epoch,"cost J =", cost_)
```

You should immediately notice one thing: it is *very* slow. Unless you have a very powerful CPU or have installed TensorFlow with GPU support and you have a powerful graphic card, this code will take, on a 2017 laptop, a few hours (from a couple to several, depending on the hardware you have). The problem is that the model, as we coded it, will create a huge matrix for all observations (that is 60,000) and then will modify the weights and bias only after a complete sweep over all observations. This requires quite some resources, memory, and CPU. If that were the only choice we had, we would be doomed. Keep in mind that in the deep-learning world, 60,000 examples of 784 features is not a big dataset at all. So, we must find a way of letting our model learn faster.

The last piece of code you need is the one you can use to calculate the accuracy of your model. You can do it easily with the following code:

```
correct_predictions = tf.equal(tf.argmax(y_,0), tf.argmax(Y,0))
accuracy = tf.reduce_mean(tf.cast(correct_predictions, "float"))
print ("Accuracy:", accuracy.eval({X: train, Y: labels_, learning_rate:
0.001}, session = sess))
```

The `tf.argmax()` function returns the index with the largest value across axes of a tensor. You will remember that when I discussed the `softmax` function, I said that we will assign an observation to the class that has the highest probability (y_ is a tensor with ten values, each containing the probability for the observation of being of each class). So, `tf.argmax(y_,0)` will give us the most probable class for each observation. `tf.argmax(Y,0)` will do the same for our labels. Remember that we one-hot encoded our labels, so that, for example, class 2 will now be (0,0,2,0,0,0,0,0,0). Therefore, `tf.argmax([0,0,2,0,0,0,0,0,0],0)` will return 2 (the index with the highest value, in this case, the only one different than zero).

I have shown you how to load and prepare the train dataset. To do some basic error analysis, you will also need the dev dataset. Following is the code that you can use. I will not discuss it, since it is exactly the same as that we used for the train dataset.

```
data_dev = pd.read_csv('fashion-mnist_test.csv', header = 0)
labels_dev = data_test['label'].values.reshape(1, 10000)

labels_dev_ = np.zeros((10000, 10))
labels_dev_[np.arange(10000), labels_dev] = 1
labels_dev_ = labels_dev_.transpose()

dev = data_dev.drop('label', axis=1).transpose()
```

Don't get confused by the fact that the file name contains the word *test*. Sometimes, the dev dataset is called test dataset. Later in the book, when I discuss error analysis, we will use three datasets: train, dev, and test. To remain consistent throughout the book, I prefer to stick with the name dev, so as not to confuse you with different names in different chapters.

Finally, to calculate accuracy on the dev dataset, you simply reuse the same code I provided previously.

```
correct_predictions = tf.equal(tf.argmax(y_,0), tf.argmax(Y,0))
accuracy = tf.reduce_mean(tf.cast(correct_predictions, "float"))
print ("Accuracy:", accuracy.eval({X: dev, Y: labels_dev_, learning_rate:
0.001}, session = sess))
```

A good exercise would be to include this calculation in your model, so that your `model()` function automatically returns the two values.

Gradient Descent Variations

In Chapter 2, I described the very basic gradient descent algorithm (also called batch gradient descent). This is not the smartest way of finding the cost function minimum. Let's have a look at the variations that you need to know, and let's compare how efficient they are, using the Zalando dataset.

Batch Gradient Descent

The gradient descent algorithm described in Chapter 2 calculates the weights and bias variations for each observation but performs the learning (weights and bias update) only after all observations have been evaluated, or, in other words, after a so-called epoch. (Remember that a cycle through the entire dataset is called an epoch.)

Following is an advantage:

- Fewer weights and bias updates mean a more stable gradient, which usually results in a more stable convergence.

Here are the downsides:

- Usually, this algorithm is implemented in such a way that all the datasets must be in memory, which computationally is quite intensive.
- This algorithm is typically very slow for very big datasets.

A possible implementation could look like this:

```
sess = tf.Session()
sess.run(tf.global_variables_initializer())

training_epochs = 100

cost_history = []
for epoch in range(training_epochs+1):

    sess.run(optimizer, feed_dict = {X: train, Y: labels_, learning_rate: 
    0.01})
    cost_ = sess.run(cost, feed_dict={ X:train, Y: labels_, learning_rate: 
    0.01})
    cost_history = np.append(cost_history, cost_)

    if (epoch % 50 == 0):
        print("Reached epoch",epoch,"cost J =", cost_)
```

Running the code for 100 epochs would give a result similar to the following:

```
Reached epoch 0 cost J = 0.331401
Reached epoch 50 cost J = 0.329093
Reached epoch 100 cost J = 0.327383
```

This code ran in roughly 2.5 minutes, but the cost function barely changed. To see the cost function start decreasing, you must run your training for a few thousand epochs, and that will require quite some time. With the following code we can calculate the accuracy:

```
correct_predictions = tf.equal(tf.argmax(y_,0), tf.argmax(Y,0))
accuracy = tf.reduce_mean(tf.cast(correct_predictions, "float"))
print ("Accuracy:", accuracy.eval({X: train, Y: labels_, learning_rate: 
0.001}, session = sess))
```

After 100 epochs, we only reached an accuracy of 16% on our training set!

Stochastic Gradient Descent

The Stochastic[6] gradient descent (abbreviated SGD) calculates the gradient of the cost function and then updates weights and biases for each observation in the dataset.

The advantages are that

- The frequent updates allow an easy check on how the model learning is going. (You don't have to wait until all the datasets have been considered.)
- In a few problems, this algorithm may be faster than batch gradient descent.
- The model is intrinsically noisy, and that may allow it to avoid local minima when trying to find the absolute minimum of the cost function.

Among the downsides are that

- On large datasets, this method is quite slow, because it is very computationally intensive, owing to the continuous updates.
- The fact that the algorithm is noisy can make it hard for it to settle on a minimum for the cost function, and the convergence may not be as stable as expected.

A possible implementation could look like this:

```
sess = tf.Session()
sess.run(tf.global_variables_initializer())

cost_history = []
for epoch in range(100+1):
    for i in range(0, features.shape[1], 1):
        X_train_mini = features[:,i:i + 1]
        y_train_mini = classes[:,i:i + 1]

        sess.run(optimizer, feed_dict = {X: X_train_mini,
                                         Y: y_train_mini,
                                         learning_rate: 0.0001})
```

[6] *Stochastic* means that the updates have a random probability distribution and cannot be predicted exactly.

```
        cost_ = sess.run(cost, feed_dict={ X:features,
                                           Y: classes,
                                           learning_rate: 0.0001})
    cost_history = np.append(cost_history, cost_)

    if (epoch % 50 == 0):
        print("Reached epoch",epoch,"cost J =", cost_)
```

If you let the code run, you will get a result that should look like the following (the exact numbers will be different each time, because we initialize the weights and biases randomly, but the speed of decrease should be the same):

```
Reached epoch 0 cost J = 0.31713
Reached epoch 50 cost J = 0.108148
Reached epoch 100 cost J = 0.0945182
```

As mentioned, this method can be quite unstable. For example, using a learning rate of `1e-3` will make nan appear before having reached epoch 100. Try to play with the learning rate and see what happens. You require a rather small value for the method to converge nicely. In comparison, with bigger learning rates (as big as 0.05, for example), a method such as batch gradient descent converges without problems. As I mentioned before, the method is quite computationally intensive and for 100 epochs, requires roughly 35 minutes on my laptop. With this variation, after only 100 epochs, we already would have reached an accuracy of 80%. With this variation, learning is, in terms of epochs, very efficient but also very slow.

Mini-Batch Gradient Descent

With this variation of the gradient descent, datasets are split into a certain number of small (from here the term *mini* is used) groups of observations (called batches), and weights and biases are updated only after each batch has been fed to the model. This is by far the method most commonly used in the field of deep learning.

The advantages are that

- The model update frequency is higher than with batch gradient descent but lower than SGD. Therefore, allow for a more robust convergence.
- This method is computationally much more efficient than batch gradient descent, or SGD, because fewer calculations and resources are needed.
- This variation is by far (as we will see later) the fastest of the three.

Among the downsides are that

- The use of this variation introduces a new hyperparameter that must be tuned: the batch size (number of observations in the mini-batch).

A possible implementation could look like this for a batch size of 50:

```
sess = tf.Session()
sess.run(tf.global_variables_initializer())

cost_history = []
for epoch in range(100+1):
    for i in range(0, features.shape[1], 50):
        X_train_mini = features[:,i:i + 50]
        y_train_mini = classes[:,i:i + 50]

        sess.run(optimizer, feed_dict = {X: X_train_mini,
                                         Y: y_train_mini,
                                         learning_rate: 0.001})
        cost_ = sess.run(cost, feed_dict={ X:features,
                                           Y: classes,
                                           learning_rate: 0.001})
    cost_history = np.append(cost_history, cost_)

    if (epoch % 50 == 0):
        print("Reached epoch",epoch,"cost J =", cost_)
```

Note that the code is the same as that for the stochastic gradient descent. The only difference is the size of the batches. In this example, we use 50 observations each time before updating weights and biases. Running it will give you a result that should look like this (remember that your numbers will be different, due to the random initialization of weights and biases):

```
Reached epoch 0 cost J = 0.322747
Reached epoch 50 cost J = 0.193713
Reached epoch 100 cost J = 0.141135
```

In this case, we have used a learning rate of `1e-3`—much bigger than the one in SGD—and reached a cost function value of 0.14—a bigger value than the 0.094 reached with SGD but much smaller than the 0.32 value reached with batch gradient descent—and it requires only 2.5 minutes. So, with a factor of 14, it is faster than SGD. After 100 epochs, we achieved an accuracy of 66%.

Comparison of the Variations

Following is a summary of the findings for our three variations of gradient descent for 100 epochs (Table 3-3).

Table 3-3. *Summary of the Findings for Three Variations of Gradient Descent for 100 Epochs*

Gradient Descent Variation	Running Time	Final Value of Cost Function	Accuracy
Batch gradient descent	2.5 min	0.323	16%
Mini-batch gradient descent	2.5 min	0.14	66%
Stochastic gradient descent (SGD)	35 min	0.094	80%

Now you can see that SGD is the algorithm that achieves the lowest value of cost function with the same number of epochs, although it is by far the slowest. For the mini-batch gradient descent to reach a value of 0.094 for the cost function, it takes 450 epochs and roughly 11 minutes. Still, this is a huge improvement over SGD—31% of the time for the same results.

In Figure 3-16, you can see the difference in how the cost function decreases with different mini-batch sizes. It is clear how, with respect to the number of epochs, the smaller the mini-batch size, the faster the decrease (though not in time). The learning rate used for this figure was $\gamma=0.001$. Note that the time required in each case is not the same, and the smaller the mini-batch size, the more time is required for the algorithm.

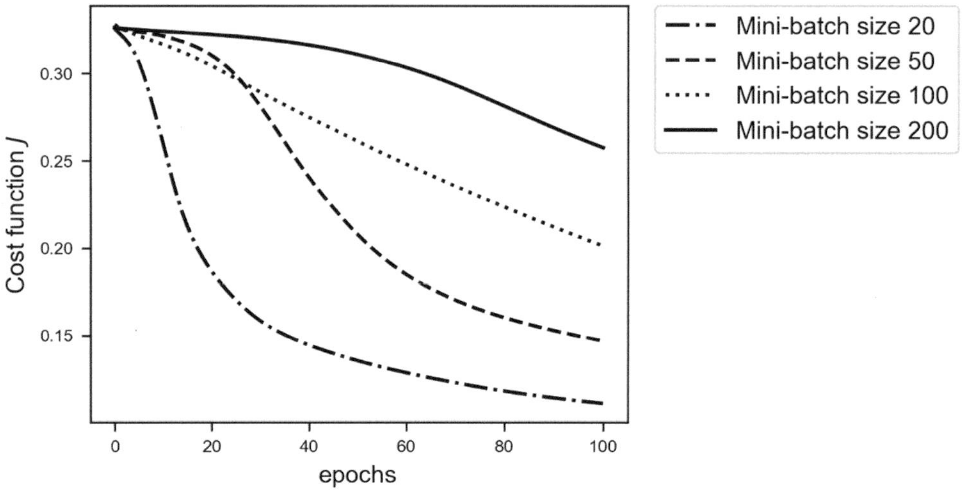

Figure 3-16. *Comparison of the speed of convergence of a mini-batch gradient descent algorithm with different mini-batch sizes*

Note The best compromise between running time and convergence speed (with respect to number of epochs) is achieved by mini-batch gradient descent. The optimal size of the mini-batches is dependent on your problem, but, usually, small numbers, such as 30 or 50, are a good option. You will find a compromise between running time and convergence speed.

To give you an idea of how the running time depends on the value the cost function can reach after 100 epochs, see Figure 3-17. Each point is labeled with the size of the mini-batch used in that run. Note that the points are single runs, and the plot is only indicative of the dependency. Running time and cost function value have a small variance when evaluated over several runs. This variance is not shown in the plot. You can see that decreasing the mini-batch size from 300 quickly decreases the value of J after 100 epochs, without increasing the running time significantly, until you arrive at a value for the mini-batch size that is about 50. At that point, the time starts to increase quickly, and the value for *J* after 100 epochs no longer decreases as quickly and flattens out. Intuitively, the best compromise is to choose a value for the mini-batch size when the curve is closer to zero (small running time and small cost function value), and that is at a mini-batch size value between 50 and 30. This is why those are the values chosen most frequently. After that point, the increase in running time becomes very quick and is no longer worth decreasing the mini-batch size. Note that for other datasets, the optimal value may be very different. So, it is worth trying different values, to see which one works best. In very big datasets, you may want to try bigger values, such as 200, 300, or 500. In our case, we have 60,000 observations and a mini-batch size of 50, which gives 1200 batches. If you have much more data, for example `1e-6` observations, a mini-batch size of 50 would give 20,000 batches. Keep that in mind and try different values, to see which works best.

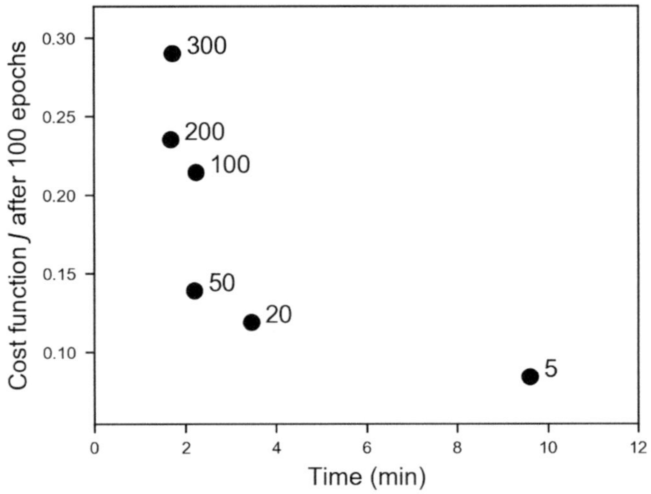

Figure 3-17. *Plot for the Zalando dataset, showing the value of the cost function after 100 epochs vs. the running time required to run through 100 epochs*

It is good programming practice to write a function that runs your evaluations. In this way, you can tune your hyperparameters (such as the mini-batch size) without copying and pasting the same chunk of code over and over. The following function is one you can use to train our model:

```
def model(minibatch_size, training_epochs, features, classes, logging_step
= 100, learning_r = 0.001):
    sess = tf.Session()
    sess.run(tf.global_variables_initializer())
```

```
    cost_history = []
    for epoch in range(training_epochs+1):
        for i in range(0, features.shape[1], minibatch_size):
            X_train_mini = features[:,i:i + minibatch_size]
            y_train_mini = classes[:,i:i + minibatch_size]

            sess.run(optimizer, feed_dict = {X: X_train_mini,
                                            Y: y_train_mini,
                                            learning_rate: learning_r})
        cost_ = sess.run(cost, feed_dict={ X:features, Y: classes,
        learning_rate: learning_r})
        cost_history = np.append(cost_history, cost_)

        if (epoch % logging_step == 0):
                print("Reached epoch",epoch,"cost J =", cost_)

    return sess, cost_history
```

The `model()` function will accept the following parameters:

- `minibatch_size`: The number of observations we want in each batch. Note that if we choose for this hyperparameter a number q that is not a divisor of m (number of observations), or, in other words, m/q is not an integer, we will have the last mini-batch with a different number of observations than all the others. But this will not be an issue for the training. For example, suppose we have a hypothetical dataset with m=100, and you decide to use mini-batch sizes of 32 observations. Then, with m=100, you will have 3complete mini-batches with 32 observations and 1 with just 4, since 100 = 3*32+4. Now you may wonder what will happen with a line such as

  ```
  X_train_mini = features[:,i:i + 32]
  ```

  when i=96 and `features` has only 100 elements. Are we not going over the limits of the array? Fortunately, Python is nice to programmers and takes care of this. Consider the following code:

  ```
  l = np.arange(0,100)
  for i in range (0, 100, 32):
      print (l[i:i+32])
  ```

The result is

```
[ 0 1 2 3 4 5 6 7 8 9 10 11 12 13 14 15 16 17 18 19 20
21 22 23 24 25 26 27 28 29 30 31]

[32 33 34 35 36 37 38 39 40 41 42 43 44 45 46 47 48 49
50 51 52 53 54 55 56 57 58 59 60 61 62 63]

[64 65 66 67 68 69 70 71 72 73 74 75 76 77 78 79 80 81
82 83 84 85 86 87 88 89 90 91 92 93 94 95]

[96 97 98 99]
```

And as you see, the last batch has only four elements, and we don't get any error. So, you should not worry about this, and you can choose any mini-batch size that works better for your problem.

- `training_epochs`: The number of epochs we want
- `features`: The tensor that contains our features
- `classes`: The tensor that contains our labels
- `logging_step`: This tells the function to print the value of the cost function every `logging_step` epoch
- `learning_r`: The learning rate we want to use

Note Writing a function with the hyperparameters as inputs is common practice. This allows you to test different models with different values for the hyperparameters and check which one is better.

Examples of Wrong Predictions

Running the model with batch gradient descent, one hidden layer with 5 neurons for 1000 epochs, and learning rate of 0.001 will give us an accuracy on the training set of 82.3%. You can increase the accuracy by using more neurons in your hidden layer. For example, using 50 neurons, using 1000 epochs and a learning rate of 0.001, will allow you to reach 86.4% on the training set and 86.1% on the test set. It is interesting to check a few examples of wrongly classified images, to see if we can understand something from the errors. Figure 3-18 shows an example of wrongly classified images for each class. Over each image, the `True` class (labeled as "True:") and the predicted (labeled as "Pred:") class are reported. The model used here has one hidden layer with five neurons and has been run for 1000 epochs with a learning rate of 0.001.

***Figure 3-18.** Example of wrongly classified images for each class*

Some errors are understandable, such as, for example, that at the lower left of the figure. A shirt has been wrongly classified as a coat. It is also difficult to determine which item is which, and I could easily have made the same mistake. The wrongly classified bag is, on the other hand, easy for a human to sort out.

Weight Initialization

If you have tried to run the code, you will have realized that the convergence of the algorithm is strongly dependent on the way you initialize your weights. You will remember that we use the following line to initialize weights:

```
W1 = tf.Variable(tf.truncated_normal([n1, n_dim], stddev=.1))
```

But why choose a standard deviation of 0.1?

You will surely have wondered why. In the previous sections, I wanted you to focus on understanding how such a network works, without the distraction of additional information, but it is now time to look at this problem a bit more closely, because it plays a fundamental role with many layers. Basically, we initialize the weights with a small standard deviation to prevent the gradient descent algorithm from exploding and starting to return nans. For example, in our first layer for the ith neuron, we will have to calculate the ReLU activation function of the quantity (refer to the beginning of the chapter for an explanation, if you've forgotten why), as follows:

$$z_i = \sum_{j=1}^{n_x} \left(w_{ij}^{[1]} x_j + b_i^{[1]} \right)$$

Normally in a deep network, the number of weights is quite big, so you can easily imagine that if the $w_{ij}^{[1]}$ are big, the quantity z_i, too, can be quite big, and the ReLU activation function can return a nan value, because the argument is too big for Python to calculate it properly. So, you want the z_i to be small enough to avoid an explosion of the output of the neurons and big enough to prevent the outputs from dying out and, therefore, making the convergence a very slow process.

The problem has been researched extensively,[7] and there are different initialization strategies, depending on the activation function you are using. A few are outlined in the Table 3-4, in which it is assumed that the weights will be initialized with a normal distribution with mean 0 and standard deviation. (Note that the standard deviation will depend on the activation function you want to use.)

[7]See, for example, Xavier Glorot and Yoshua Bengio, "Understanding the Difficulty of Training Deep Feedforward Neural Networks," available at `https://goo.gl/bHB5BM`.

Table 3-4. *Different Initialization Strategies, Depending on Activation Functions*

Activation Function	Standard Deviation σ for a Given Layer
Sigmoid	$\sigma = \sqrt{\frac{2}{n_{inputs} + n_{outputs}}}$ Usually called Xavier Initialization
ReLU	$\sigma = \sqrt{\frac{4}{n_{inputs} + n_{outputs}}}$ Usually called He Initialization

In a layer l, the number of inputs will be the number of neurons of the preceding layer $l - 1$, and the number of outputs will be the number of neurons in the layer coming next: $l + 1$. So, we will have

$$n_{inputs} = n_{l-1}$$

and

$$n_{outputs} = n_{l+1}$$

Very often, deep networks such as the one discussed before will have several layers, all with the same number of neurons. Therefore, you will have, for most of the layers, $n_{l-1} = n_{l+1}$, and, therefore, you will have the following for Xavier initialization:

$$\sigma_{Xavier} = \sqrt{1/n_{l+1}} \quad or \quad \sqrt{1/n_{l-1}}$$

For the ReLU activation functions, the He initialization will be

$$\sigma_{He} = \sqrt{2/n_{l+1}} \quad or \quad \sqrt{2/n_{l-1}}$$

Let's consider the ReLU activation function (the one we have used in this chapter). Every layer, as has been discussed, will have n_l neurons. A way of initializing the weights for layer 3, for example, would be

```
stddev = 2 / np.sqrt(n4+n2)
W3=tf.Variable(tf.truncated_normal([n3,n2], stddev = stddev)
```

Or, if all layers have the same number of neurons, and, therefore, n2=n3=n4, you could simply use the following:

```
stddev = 2 / np.sqrt(2.0*n2)
W3=tf.Variable(tf.truncated_normal([n3,n2], stddev = stddev)
```

Typically, to make evaluation and construction of networks easier, the most typical initialization form used is for ReLU activation function

$$\sigma_{He} = \sqrt{2 / n_{l-1}}$$

and

$$\sigma_{Xavier} = \sqrt{1 / n_{l-1}}$$

For a sigmoid activation function, for example, the code for the weight initialization for the network we have used previously with one layer would look like this:

```
W1 = tf.Variable(tf.random_normal([n1, n_dim], stddev= 2.0 / np.sqrt
(2.0*n_dim)))
b1 = tf.Variable(tf.ones([n1,1]))
W2 = tf.Variable(tf.random_normal([n2, n1], stddev= 2.0 / np.sqrt(2.0*n1)))
b2 = tf.Variable(tf.ones([n2,1]))
```

Using this initialization can speed up training considerably and is the standard way in which many libraries initialize weights (for example, the Caffe library).

Adding Many Layers Efficiently

Repeatedly typing all this code each time is a bit tedious and error-prone. Usually, what one does is define a function that creates a layer. This can be done easily with this code:

```
def create_layer (X, n, activation):
    ndim = int(X.shape[0])
    stddev = 2 / np.sqrt(ndim)
    initialization = tf.truncated_normal((n, ndim), stddev = stddev)
    W = tf.Variable(init)
    b = tf.Variable(tf.zeros([n,1]))
    Z = tf.matmul(W,X)+b
    return activation(Z)
```

Let's go through the code:

- First, we get the dimension of the inputs, to be able to define the right weight matrix.
- Then, we initialize the weights with the He initialization discussed in the previous section.
- Next, we create the weights `W` and bias `b`.
- Then, we evaluate the quantity `Z` and return the activation function evaluated on `Z`. (Note that in Python, you can pass functions as parameters to other functions. In this case, `activation` may be `tf.nn.relu`.)

So, to create our networks, we can simply write our construction code (in this example, with two layers), as follows:

```
n_dim = 784
n1 = 300
n2 = 300
n_outputs = 10

X = tf.placeholder(tf.float32, [n_dim, None])
Y = tf.placeholder(tf.float32, [10, None])

learning_rate = tf.placeholder(tf.float32, shape=())

hidden1 = create_layer (X, n1, activation = tf.nn.relu)
hidden2 = create_layer (hidden1, n2, activation = tf.nn.relu)
outputs = create_layer (hidden2, n3, activation = tf.identity)
y_ = tf.nn.softmax(outputs)

cost = - tf.reduce_mean(Y * tf.log(y_)+(1-Y) * tf.log(1-y_))
optimizer = tf.train.GradientDescentOptimizer(learning_rate).minimize(cost)
```

To run our model, we again define a `model()` function, as discussed previously.

```
def model(minibatch_size, training_epochs, features, classes, logging_step
= 100, learning_r = 0.001):
    sess = tf.Session()
    sess.run(tf.global_variables_initializer())

    cost_history = []
    for epoch in range(training_epochs+1):
        for i in range(0, features.shape[1], minibatch_size):
            X_train_mini = features[:,i:i + minibatch_size]
            y_train_mini = classes[:,i:i + minibatch_size]

            sess.run(optimizer, feed_dict = {X: X_train_mini, Y: y_train_
            mini, learning_rate: learning_r})
        cost_ = sess.run(cost, feed_dict={ X:features, Y: classes,
        learning_rate: learning_r})
        cost_history = np.append(cost_history, cost_)

        if (epoch % logging_step == 0):
                print("Reached epoch",epoch,"cost J =", cost_)

    return sess, cost_history
```

Now the code is much easier to understand, and you can use it to create networks as big as you wish.

With the preceding functions, it is very easy to run several models and compare them, as I have done in Figure 3-19, which illustrates five different tested models.

- One layer and ten neurons each layer
- Two layers and ten neurons each layer
- Three layers and ten neurons each layer
- Four layers and ten neurons each layer
- 4 layers and 100 neurons each layer

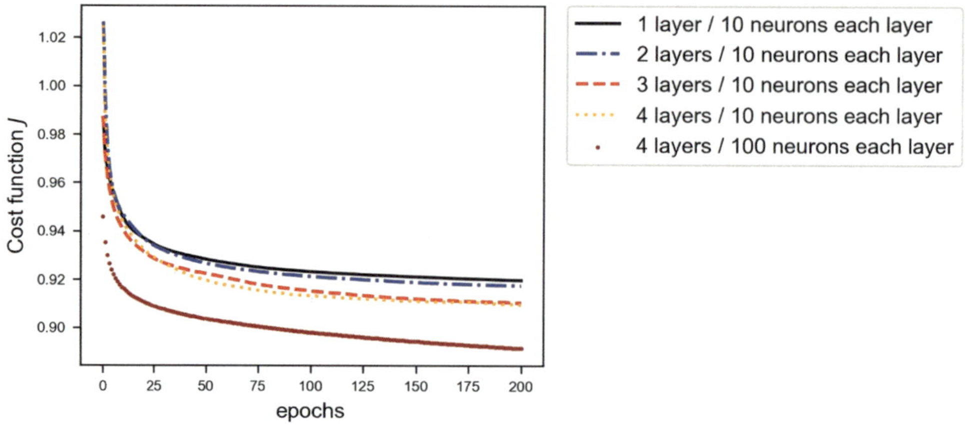

Figure 3-19. *The cost function vs. epochs for five models, as described in the legend*

In case you are wondering, the model with four layers, each with 100 neurons, which seems much better than the others, is starting to go in the overfitting regime, with a train set accuracy of 94% and of 88% on the dev set (after only 200 epochs).

Advantages of Additional Hidden Layers

I suggest you play with the models. Try varying the number of layers, number of neurons, how to initialize the weights, and so on. If you invest some time, you can achieve an accuracy of more than 90% in a few minutes of running time, but that requires some work. If you try several models, you may realize that in this case, using several layers does not seem to accrue benefits vs. a network with just one. This is often the case.

Theoretically speaking, a one-layer network can approximate every function you can imagine, but the number of neurons needed may be very large, and, therefore, the model becomes much less useful. The catch is that the ability to approximate a function does not mean that the network is able to learn to do it, owing, for example, to the sheer number of neurons involved or the time required.

Empirically, it has been shown that networks with more layers require much smaller numbers of neurons to reach the same results and usually generalize better to unknown data.

Note Theoretically speaking, you don't need to have multiple layers in your networks, but often, in practice, you should. It is almost always a good idea to try a network of several layers with a few neurons in each, instead of a network with one layer populated by a huge number of neurons. There is no fixed rule on how to decide how many neurons or layers are best. You should try starting with low numbers of layers and neurons and then increase these until your results stop improving.

In addition, having more layers may allow your network to learn different aspects of your inputs. For example, one layer may learn to recognize vertical edges of an image, and another, horizontal ones. Remember that in this chapter, I have discussed networks in which each layer is identical (up to the number of neurons) to all the others. You will see later, in Chapter 4, how you can build networks in which each layer performs very different tasks and is also structured very differently from another, making this kind of network much more powerful for certain tasks that have been discussed previously in this chapter.

You may remember that in Chapter 2, we tried to predict the selling prices of houses in the Boston area. In that case, a network with several layers might reveal more information about how the features relate to the price. For example, the first layer might reveal basic relationships, such as bigger houses equal higher prices. But the second layer might reveal more complex relationships, such as big houses with a smaller numbers of bathrooms equal low selling prices.

Comparing Different Networks

Now you should know how to build neural networks with a huge number of layers or neurons. But it is relatively easy to lose yourself in a forest of possible models without knowing which are worth trying. Suppose you start with a network (as I have done in the previous sections) with one hidden layer with five neurons, one layer with ten neurons (for our "softmax" function) and our "softmax" neuron. Suppose you have reached some accuracy and would like to try different models. At first, you should try increasing the number of neurons in your hidden layers, to see what you can achieve. In Figure 3-20, I have plotted the cost function as it decreases for different numbers of neurons. The calculations have been performed with a mini-batch gradient descent with a batch size of 50, one hidden layer with respectively 1, 5, 15, and 30 neurons, and a learning rate of 0.05. You can see how moving from one neuron to five immediately makes the convergence faster. But further increasing the number of neurons doesn't result in much improvement. For example, increasing the neurons from 15 to 30 adds almost no improvement.

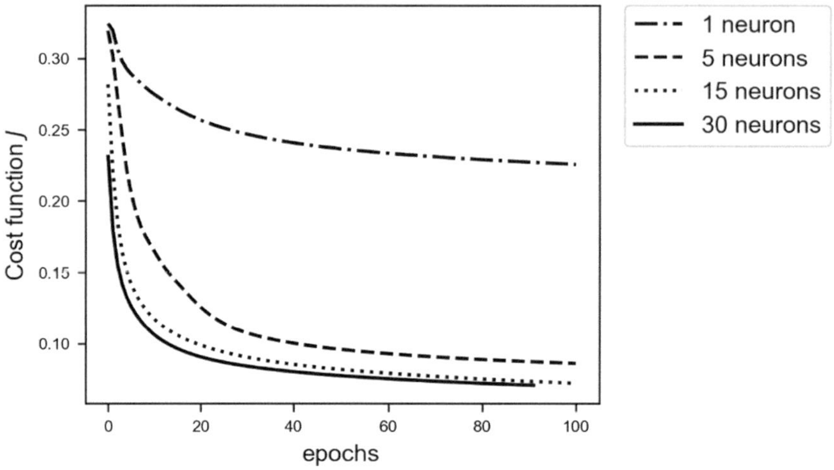

Figure 3-20. *Cost function decrease vs. epochs for a neural network of one hidden layer with, respectively, 1, 5, 15, and 30 neurons, as indicated in the legend. The calculations have been performed with mini-batch gradient descent, with a batch size of 50 and a learning rate of 0.05.*

Let's first try to find a way of comparing these networks. Comparing only the number of neurons can be very misleading, as I will show you shortly. Remember that your algorithm is trying to find the best combinations of weights and biases to minimize your cost function. But how many learnable parameters do we have in our model? We have the weights and the biases. You will remember from our theoretical discussion that we can associate a certain number of weights to each layer, and the number of learnable parameters in our layer l that we will indicate with $Q^{[l]}$ is given by the total number of elements in the matrix $W^{[l]}$, that is, $n_l n_{l-1}$ (where we have $n_0 = n_x$ by definition), plus the number of biases we have (in each layer we will have n_l biases). The number $Q^{[l]}$ can then be written as

$$Q^{[l]} = n_l n_{l-1} + n_l = n_l \left(n_{l-1} + 1 \right)$$

so that the total number of learnable parameters in our network (indicated here with Q) can be written as

$$Q = \sum_{j=1}^{L} n_l \left(n_{l-1} + 1 \right)$$

where by definition $n_0 = n_x$. Please note that the parameter Q of our network is strongly architecture-dependent. Let's calculate it in some examples, so that you understand what I mean (Table 3-5).

Table 3-5. *A comparison of the values of Q for different network architectures*

Network Architecture	Parameter Q (Number of learnable parameters)	Number of Neurons
Network A: 784 features, 2 layers: $n_1 = 15$, $n_2 = 10$	$QA = 15(784 + 1) + 10 * (15 + 1) = 11935$	25
Network B: 784 features, 16 layers: $n_1 = n_2 = \ldots = n_{15} = 1$, $n_{16} = 10$	$QB = 1 * (784 + 1) + 1 * (1 + 1) + \ldots + 10 * (1 + 1) = 923$	25
Network C: 784 features, 3 layers: $n_1 = 10$, $n_2 = 10$, $n_3 = 10$	$QC = 10 * (784 + 1) + 10 * (10 + 1) + 10 * (10 + 1) = 8070$	30

I would like to draw your attention to networks A and B. Both have 25 neurons, but the parameter Q_A is much bigger (more than a factor of ten) than Q_B. You can easily imagine how network A will be much more flexible in learning than network B, even if the number of neurons is the same.

Note I would be misleading you if I told you that this number *Q* is a measure of how complex or how good a network is. This is not the case, and it may well happen that of all the neurons, only a few will play a role. Therefore, calculating only as I told you will not tell the entire story. There is a vast amount of research on the so-called effective degrees of freedom of deep neural networks, but that goes way beyond the scope of this book. Nonetheless, this parameter will provide a good rule of thumb in deciding if the set of models you want to test are in a reasonable complexity progression.

Checking Q for the model you want to test may give you some hints on which you should neglect and which you should try. For example, let's consider the cases we have tested in Figure 3-20 and calculate the parameter Q for each network (Table 3-6).

Table 3-6. *A comparison of the values of Q for different network architectures*

Network Architecture	Parameter Q	Number of Neurons
784 features, 1 layer with 1 neuron, 1 layer with 10 neurons	$Q = 1 * (784 + 1) + 10 * (1 + 1) = 895$	11
784 features, 1 layer with 5 neuron, 1 layer with 10 neurons	$Q = 5 * (784 + 1) + 10 * (5 + 1) = 3985$	15
784 features, 1 layer with 15 neuron, 1 layer with 10 neurons	$Q = 15 * (784 + 1) + 10 * (15 + 1) = 11935$	25
784 features, 1 layer with 30 neuron, 1 layer with 10 neurons	$Q = 30 * (784 + 1) + 10 * (30 + 1) = 23860$	40

From Figure 3-20, let's suppose we choose the model with 15 neurons as our candidate as our best model. Now let's suppose we want to try a model with 3 layers, all with the same number of neurons, that should compete (and possibly be better) than our (for the moment) candidate model with 1 layer and 15 neurons. What should we choose as a starting point for the number of neurons in the three layers? Let's indicate as model A the one with 1 layer with 15 neurons and as B a model with 3 layers with an (as of yet) unknown number of neurons in each layer, indicated with n_B. We can easily calculate the parameter Q for both networks

$$Q_A = 15 * (784 + 1) + 10 * (15 + 1) = 11935$$

and

$$Q_B = n_B * (784 + 1) + n_B * (n_B + 1) + n_B * (n_B + 1) + 10 * (n_B + 1) = 2n_B^2 + 797n_B + 10$$

What value for n_B will give $Q_B \approx Q_A$? We can easily solve the equation.

$$2n_B^2 + 797n_B + 10 = 11935$$

You should be able to solve a quadratic equation, so I will only give the solution here (hint: try to solve it). This equation is solved for a value of $n_B = 14.4$, but because we cannot have 14.4 neurons, we will have to use the closest integer, which would be $n_B = 14$. For $n_B = 14$, we will have $Q_B = 11560$, a value very close to 11935.

Note Please let me say it again. The fact that the two networks have the same number of learnable parameters does not mean that they can reach the same accuracy. It does not even mean that if one learns very fast the second will learn at all!

Our model with 3 layers with each 14 neurons could, however, be a good starting point for further testing.

Let's discuss another point that is important when dealing with a complex dataset. Consider our first layer. Suppose we consider the Zalando dataset and we create a network with two layers: the first with one neuron and the second with many. All the complex features that your dataset has may well be lost in your single first neuron, because it will combine all features in one single value and pass the same exact value to all other neurons of the second layer.

Tips for Choosing the Right Network

I hear you crying, "You've discussed a lot of cases, given us a lot of formulas, but how can we decide how to design our network?"

Unfortunately, there is no fixed set of rules. But you may consider the following tips:

- When considering a set of models (or network architectures) that you want to test, a good rule of thumb is to start with the less complex one and move to more complex ones. Another is to estimate the relative complexity (to make sure that you are moving in the right direction) of the use of the parameter Q.
- In case you cannot achieve good accuracy, check if any of your layers has a particularly low number of neurons. This layer may kill the effective capacity of learning from a complex dataset of your network. Consider, for example, the case with one neuron in Figure 3-20. The model cannot reach low values for the cost function because the network is too simple to learn from a dataset as complex as the Zalando one.

- Remember that a low or high number of neurons is always relative to the number of features you have. If you have only two features in your dataset, one neuron may well be sufficient, but if you have few hundred (like in the Zalando dataset where $n_x = 784$), you should not expect one neuron to be enough.
- Which architecture you need is also dependent on what you want to do. It is always worth checking online literature to see what others have already discovered about specific problems. For example, it is well known that for image recognition, convolutional networks are very good, so they would be an excellent choice.

Note When moving from a model with L layers to one with $L + 1$ layers, it is always a good idea to start with the new model, using a slightly lower number of neurons in each layer, and then increasing them step by step. Remember that more layers have a chance of learning complex features more effectively, so if you are lucky, fewer neurons may be enough. It is something worth trying. Always keep track of your optimizing metric (remember this from Chapter 2?) for all your models. When you are no longer getting much improvement, it may be worth trying completely different architectures (maybe convolutional neuronal networks, etc.).

CHAPTER 4

Training Neural Networks

Building complex networks with TensorFlow is quite easy, as you have probably realized by now. A few lines of code are enough to construct networks with thousands (and even more) parameters. It should be clear by now that problems arise while training such networks. It is difficult, unstable, and slow to test hyperparameters, because a run over a few hundred epochs may take hours. This is not only a performance problem; otherwise, it would suffice to use faster and faster hardware. The problem is that very often, the convergence process (the learning) does not work at all. It stops, it diverges, or it never gets close to the minimum of the cost function. We need ways of making the training process efficient, fast, and reliable. You will look at two of the main strategies that will help with the training of complex networks: dynamic learning rate decay and optimizers that are smarter than plain gradient descent ([GD] such as RMSProp, Momentum, and Adam).

Dynamic Learning Rate Decay

I mentioned several times that the learning rate γ is a very important parameter and that choosing it badly will make your model not perform. Refer again to Figure 2-12, which shows you how choosing a learning rate that is too big will make your gradient descent algorithm bounce around the minimum and not converge. Without discussing them, let's rewrite the equations that describe the weight and bias update described in Chapter 2 when discussing the gradient descent algorithm. (Remember: I described the algorithm for a problem with two weights w_0 and w_1.)

$$w_{0,[n+1]} = w_{0,[n]} - \gamma \frac{\partial J\left(w_{0,[n]}, w_{1,[n]}\right)}{\partial w_0}$$

$$w_{1,[n+1]} = w_{1,[n]} - \gamma \frac{\partial J\left(w_{0,[n]}, w_{1,[n]}\right)}{\partial w_1}$$

U. Michelucci, *Applied Deep Learning*, https://doi.org/10.1007/978-1-4842-3790-8_4

As a reminder, following is an overview of the notation. (Please refer again to Chapter 2, if you don't remember how the gradient descent is working.)

- $w_{0,[n]}$: Weight 0 at iteration n
- $w_{1,[n]}$: Weight 1 at iteration n
- $J(w_{0,[n]}, w_{1,[n]})$: Cost function at iteration n
- γ: Learning rate

To show the effect of what I will discuss, we will consider the same problem described in the section "Learning Rate in a Practical Example," in Chapter 2. Plotting the weights $w_{0,n}$, $w_{1,n}$ on the contour lines of the cost function for $\gamma = 2$ (see Figure 4-1) shows (as you will remember from Chapter 2) how the values of weights oscillate around the minimum of $(w_{0,n}, w_{1,n})$. Here, the problem of a learning rate that is too big is clearly visible. The algorithm cannot converge, because the steps that it takes are too big to be able to get close to the minimum. The different estimates $\boldsymbol{w_n}$ are indicated with points in Figure 4-1. The minimum is indicated by the circle approximately in the middle of the image.

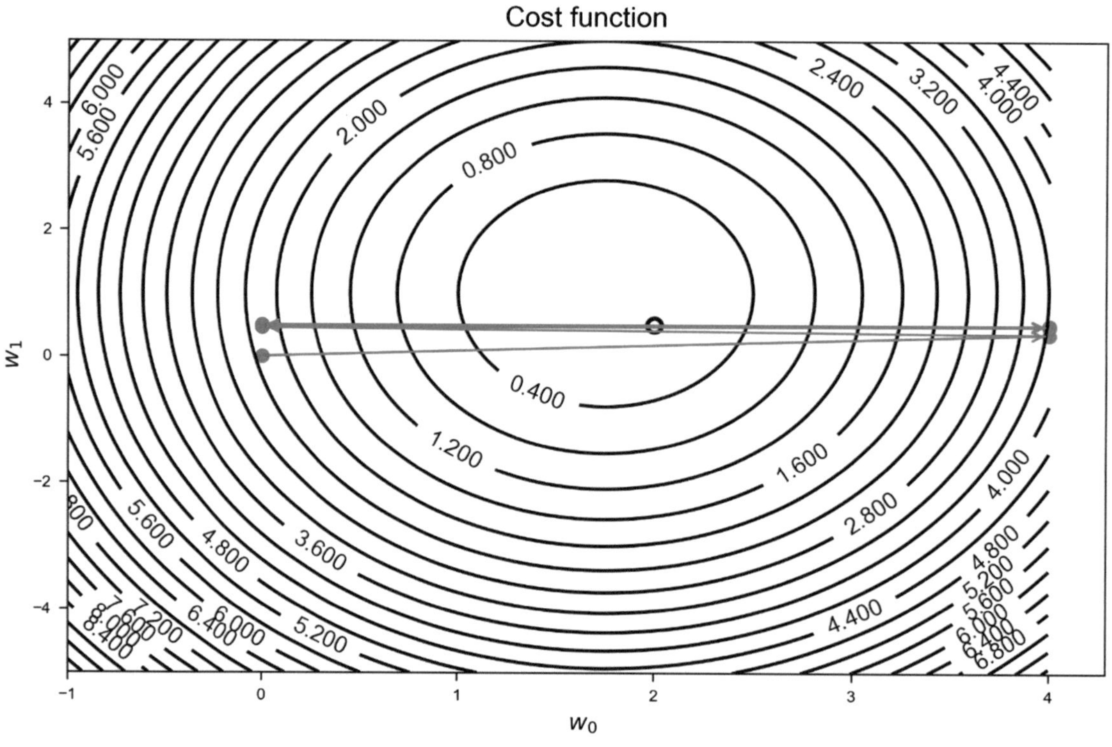

***Figure 4-1.** Illustration of the gradient descent algorithm. Here, the learning rate of $\gamma = 2$ has been chosen*

But you may have noticed that in our algorithm, we made a pretty important decision (without stating it explicitly): *we keep the learning rate constant for each iteration*. But there is no reason for doing so. On the contrary, it is quite a bad idea. Intuitively, a big learning rate will make the convergence move fast at the beginning, but as soon as you are around the minimum, you will want to use a much smaller learning rate, to allow the algorithm to converge in the most efficient way toward the minimum. We want to have a learning rate that starts (relatively) big and then decreases with the iterations. But how should it decrease? There are several methods that are used today, and in the next section, we will look at those used most frequently and how to implement them in Python and TensorFlow. We will use the same problem with which Figure 4-1 and 2-12 were generated and compare the behavior of the different algorithms. Please take some time to review the section in Chapter 2 on gradient descent, to have the material clear in your head before reading the next sections.

Iterations or Epochs?

Before looking at the various methods, I would like to shed some light on the question: what are the iterations we are talking about? Are they epochs? Technically, this is not the case. An iteration is when you update your weights. Consider, for example, mini-batch gradient descent. In that case, an iteration occurs after each mini-batch (when you update the weights). Consider the Zalando dataset in Chapter 3: 60,000 training cases and a mini-batch size of 50. In that case, you would have 1200 iterations in an epoch. What is important for the decrease of the learning rate is the number of updates you perform on the weights, not the number of epochs. If you used stochastic gradient descent (SGD) on the Zalando dataset (update the weights after each observation), you would have 60,000 iterations, and you might need to decrease the learning more than with mini-batch gradient descent, because it is updated more often. In the case of batch gradient descent, where you update your weight after one complete sweep over the training data, you would update the learning rate exactly once each epoch.

Note Iterations in dynamic learning rate decay refer to the step in the algorithm in which the weights are updated. For example, if you use SGD on the Zalando dataset in Chapter 3, with a mini-batch size of 50, in one epoch (a sweep over the 60,000 training observations), you have 1200 iterations.

This is very important to understand correctly. If you do, you can choose the parameters of the different algorithms for learning rate decay properly. If you choose them thinking that the learning rate is updated only after each epoch, you may make big mistakes.

Note For each algorithm that decreases dynamically, the learning rate will introduce new hyperparameters that you must optimize, adding some complexity to your model-selection process.

Staircase Decay

The staircase decay method is the most basic one to use. It consists of reducing the learning rate manually in the code and hard-coding the changes, based on what seems to work. For example, how can we make the GD algorithm converge in Figure 4-1, starting with a $\gamma = 2$? Let's consider the following decay (in which we have indicated with j the iteration number):

$$\gamma = \begin{cases} 2 & j < 4 \\ 0.4 & j \geq 4 \end{cases}$$

Simply including this with the Python code

```
gamma0 = 2.0
if (j < 4):
        gamma = gamma0
    elif j>=4:
        gamma = gamma0 /5.0
```

will give a converging algorithm (see Figure 4-2). Here, the initial learning rate of $\gamma_0 = 2$ has been chosen, and from the iteration 4, $\gamma = 0.4$ has been used. The different estimates $\boldsymbol{w}_n$ are indicated with points. The minimum is indicated by the circle approximately in the middle of the image. The algorithm is now able to converge. Each point has been labeled with the iteration number, to make following the weights update easier.

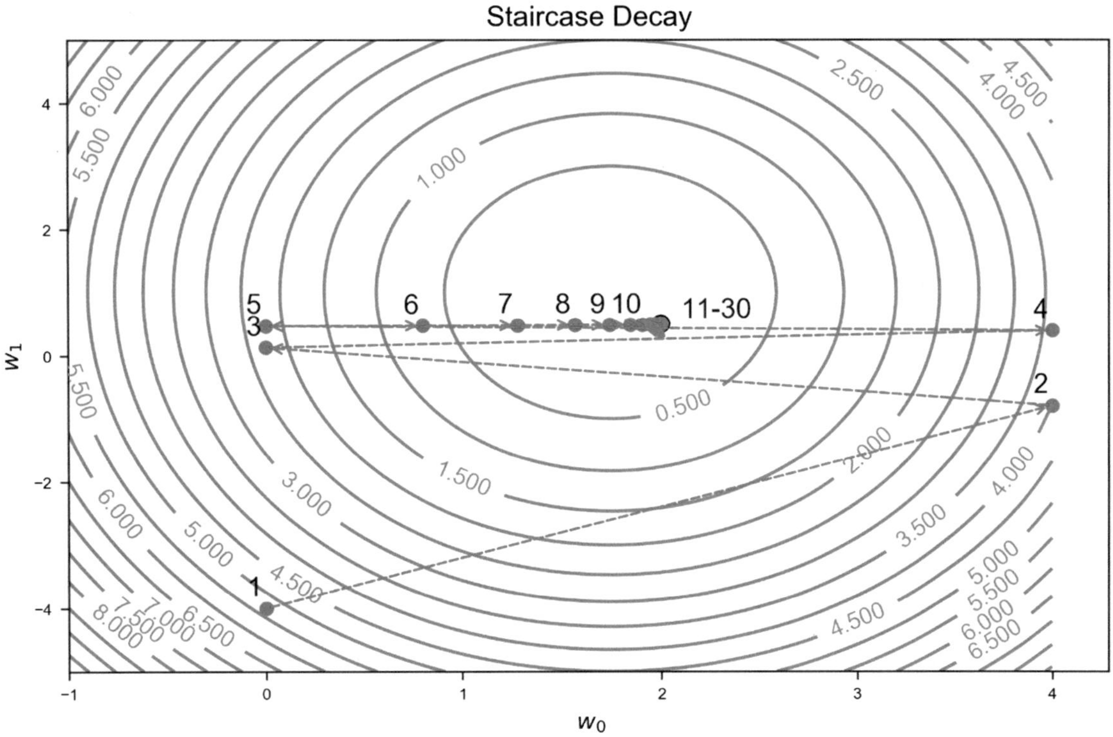

Figure 4-2. *Illustration of gradient descent algorithm with a staircase decay method*

The first steps are big, and then, as we decrease the learning rate to 0.4 at iteration 4, they become smaller, and the GD is able to converge toward the minimum. With this simple modification, we have achieved a nice result. The problem is that when dealing with complicated datasets and models (such as we did in Chapter 3), this process requires (if it works) a lot of tests. You will have to reduce the learning rate several times, and finding the right iteration and values for the learning rate decrease is a really challenging task, so much so that it is actually not usable, unless you are dealing with very easy datasets and networks. The method is also not very stable, and, depending on the data you have, may require continuous tuning. TL;DR[1]: don't use it.

[1]In case you don't know, TL;DR is short for "too long; didn't read." This is Internet slang to describe text that has been ignored because it is too long. (Source: `https://en.wikipedia.org/wiki/TL;DR`)

Table 4-1. *Additional Hyperparameters Introduced*

Hyperparameter	Example
The iteration at which the algorithm will update the learning rate	In this example, we choose iteration number 4
The values of the learning rate after each change (multiple values)	In this example, we had, from iteration 1 to 3, $\gamma = 2$, and, from iteration 4, $\gamma = 0.4$.

Step Decay

Something slightly more automatic is the so-called step decay. This method reduces the learning rate by a constant factor every certain number of iterations. Mathematically, it can be written as

$$\gamma = \frac{\gamma_0}{\lfloor j/D+1 \rfloor}$$

where $\lfloor a \rfloor$ indicates the integer part of a, and D (indicated in the code later with `epoch_drop`) is an integer constant that we can tune. For example, using the following code:

```
epochs_drop = 2
gamma = gamma0 / (np.floor(j/epochs_drop)+1)
```

will again give a convergent algorithm. In Figure 4-3, the initial learning rate of $\gamma_0 = 2$ has been chosen, and every 2 iterations, the learning rate decreases according to $\gamma_0 / \lfloor j/2+1 \rfloor$. The different estimates $\boldsymbol{w}_n$ are indicated with points. The minimum is indicated by the circle approximately in the middle of the image. The algorithm is now able to converge. Each point has been labeled with the iteration number, to make following the weights update easier.

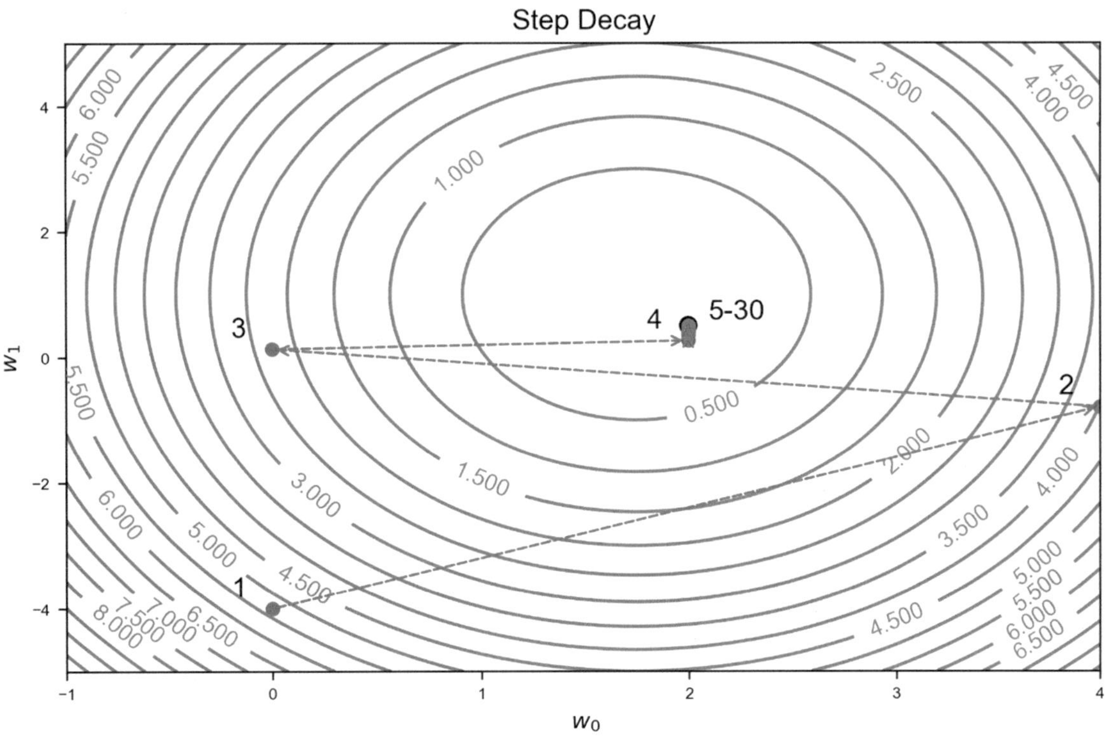

Figure 4-3. *Illustration of gradient descent algorithm with step decay*

It is important to have an idea of how fast the learning rate is decreasing. You don't want to have a learning rate close to zero after only a few iterations; otherwise, your convergence will never succeed. In Figure 4-4, you can see a comparison of how fast (or slow) the learning rate is decreasing for three values for *D*.

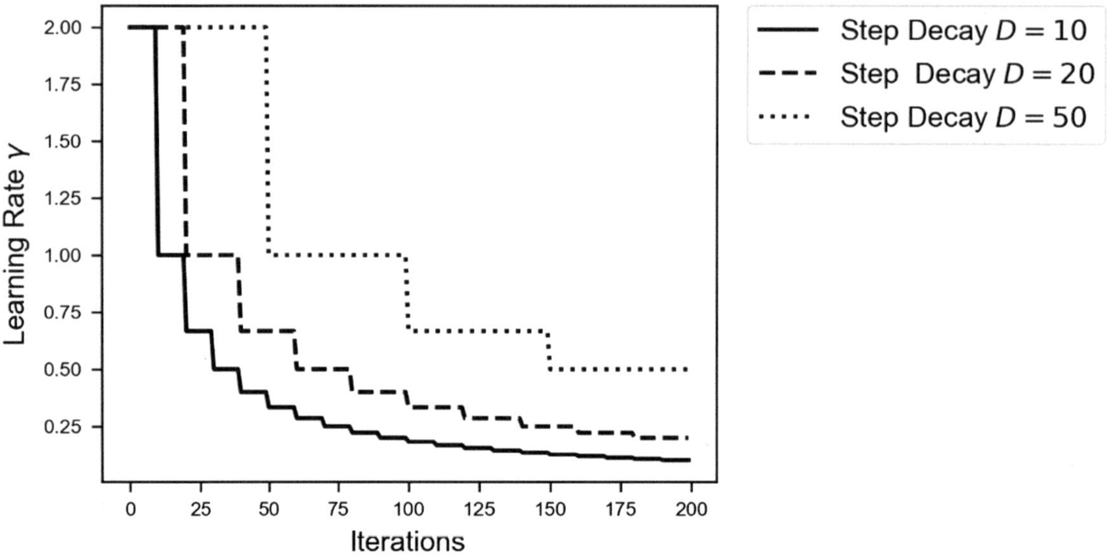

***Figure 4-4.** Decrease in the learning rate for three values of D: 10, 20, and 50, using the step decay algorithm*

Note, for example, how with $D = 10$, the learning rate is roughly 10 times smaller after only 100 iterations! If you make your learning rate decrease too fast, you may see your convergence grind to a halt after only a few iterations. Always try to get an idea of how fast your γ is decreasing.

Note A good way of getting a feel for how fast your learning rate is decreasing is to try to determine after how many iterations γ is ten times smaller than the initial value. Keep in mind that if you get a $\gamma = \gamma_0/10$ after $10D$ iterations, you will get $\gamma = \gamma_0/100$ after only $100D$ iterations, and $\gamma = \gamma_0/10^3$ after only 10^3D iterations, and so on. If this occurs, what is needed can be answered only by testing the rate properly with several values of D.

Let's consider a concrete example. Suppose you are training your model with `1e-5` observations for 5000 epochs, with a mini-batch sizes of 50 and a starting learning rate of $\gamma_0 = 0.2$. If you choose $D = 10$ without thinking, you will have

$$\gamma = \frac{\gamma_0}{20000} = \frac{0.2}{20000} = 10^{-5}$$

after only 100 epochs, so you will not gain much by using 5000 epochs if you reduce the learning rate so quickly.

Table 4-2. *Additional Hyperparameters Introduced*

Hyperparameter	Example
Parameter D	$D = 10$

Inverse Time Decay

Another way of updating the learning rate is with the formula called inverse time decay

$$\gamma = \frac{\gamma_0}{1+\nu j}$$

where ν is a parameter called the decay rate. In Figure 4-5, you can see a comparison of the learning rate decrease for three parameters of ν: 0.01, 0.1, and 0.8. In Figure 4-5, you also can see how the learning rate decreases for the three different values of ν. Note that the y axis has been plotted in logarithmic scale, to make the entity of the changes easier to compare. Note that the *y* axis is logarithmic.

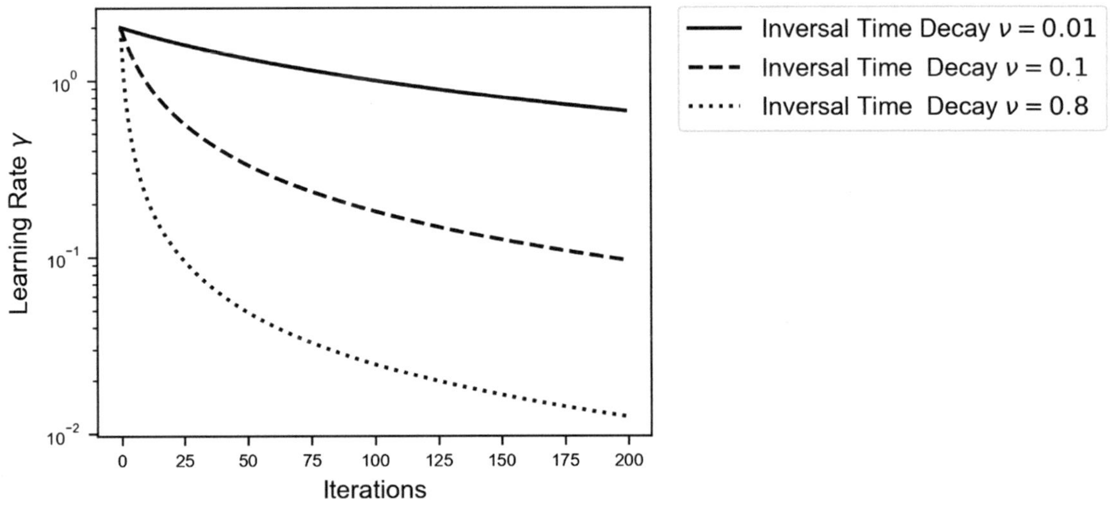

Figure 4-5. *Decreased learning rate for three values of ν: 0.01, 0.1, and 0.8, using the inverse time decay algorithm*

This method also makes the GD algorithm discussed in Chapter 2 converge. In Figure 4-6, you can see how the weights converge toward the minimum location after only a few iterations when choosing $\nu = 0.2$. In Figure 4-6, the initial learning rate of $\gamma_0 = 2$ has been chosen, and an inverse time decay algorithm with $\nu = 0.2$ has been used. The different estimates $\boldsymbol{w}_n$ are indicated with points. The minimum is indicated by the circle approximately in the middle of the image. The algorithm is now able to converge. Each point has been labeled with the iteration number, to make following the weights update easier.

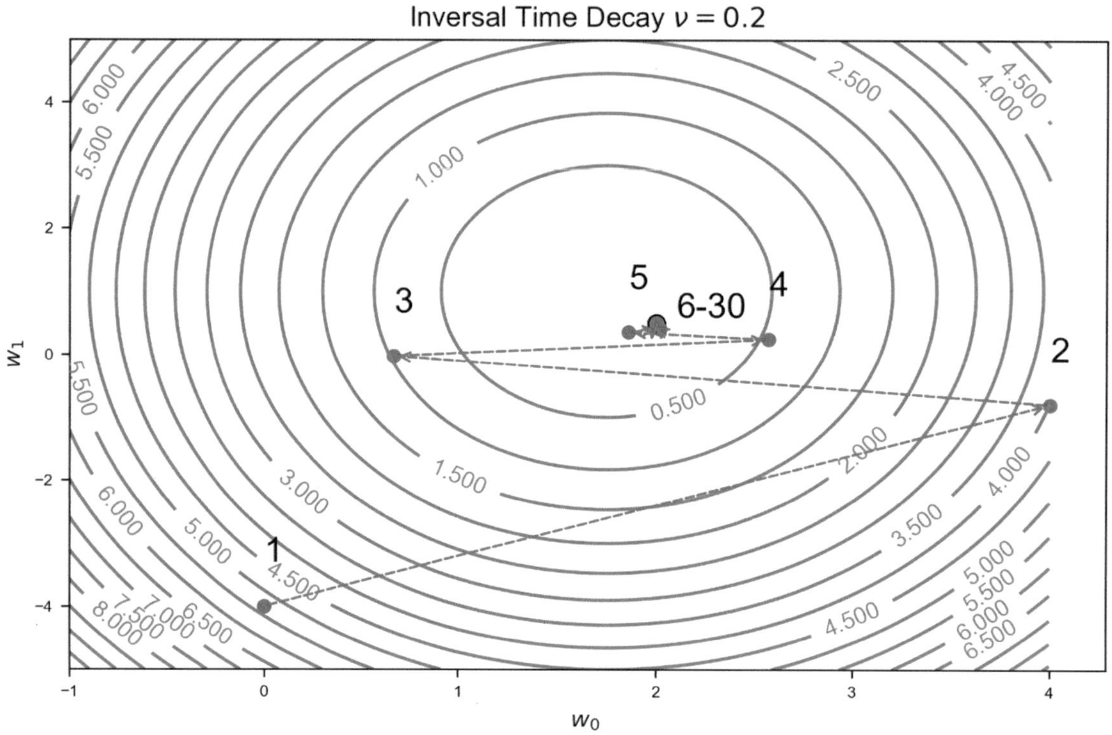

***Figure 4-6.** Illustration of gradient descent algorithm with inverse time decay for $\nu = 0.2$*

It is very interesting to see what happens if we choose a bigger value for ν. In Figure 4-7, the initial learning rate of $\gamma_0 = 2$ has been chosen, and an inverse time decay algorithm with $\nu = 1.5$ has been used. The different estimates $\boldsymbol{w}_n$ are indicated with points. The minimum is indicated by the circle approximately in the middle of the image. The algorithm is now able to converge. Each point has been labeled with the iteration number, to make following the weights update easier.

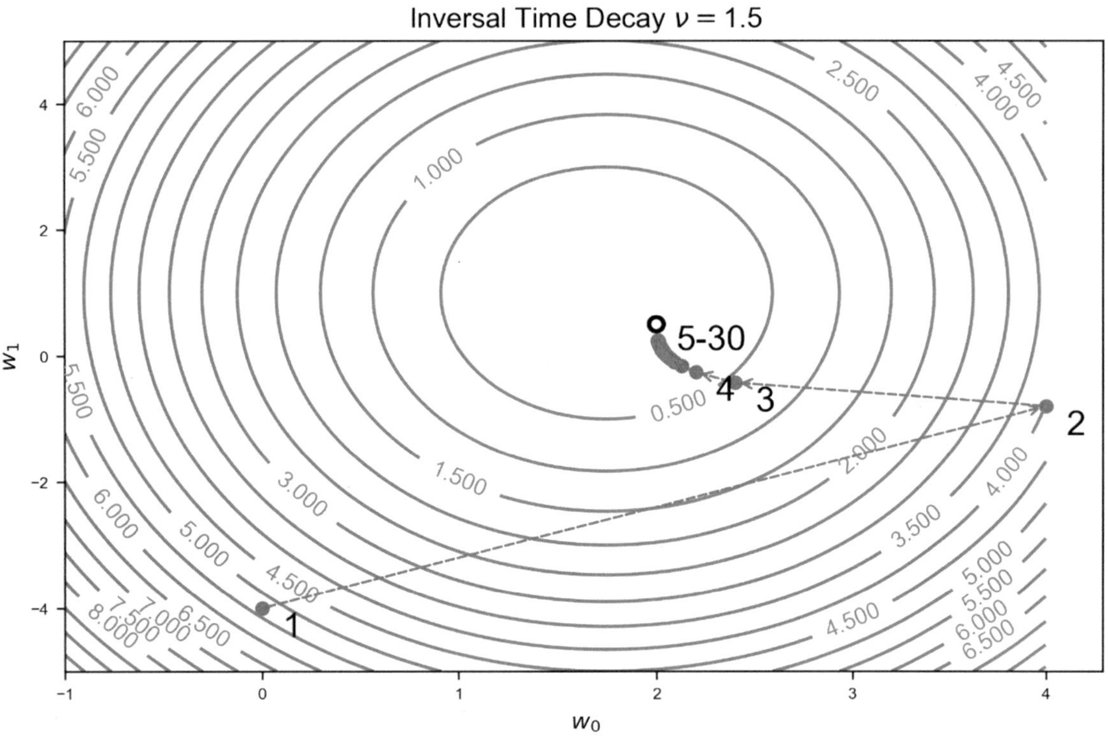

Figure 4-7. *Illustration of the gradient descent algorithm for $\nu = 1.5$*

What we observe in Figure 4-7 makes perfect sense. Increasing ν makes the learning rate decrease faster, and, therefore, more steps are required to reach the minimum, because the learning rate is increasingly smaller, in comparison to what happens in Figure 4-6. We can compare the behavior of the cost functions for the two values of ν. In Figure 4-8, you can see in plot (A) the cost function vs. the number of epochs. At first sight, the two seem to converge equally as fast. But let's zoom around $J = 0$ in plot (B). You can clearly see how with $\nu = 0.2$ the convergence is much faster, because the learning rate is bigger than for $\nu = 1.5$.

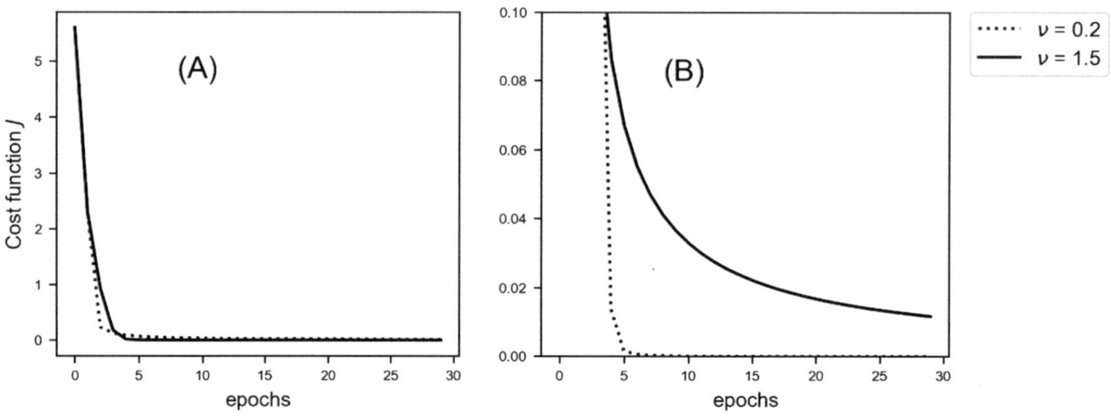

***Figure 4-8.** Cost function vs. the number of epochs. In plot (A), the entire range of values that the cost functions assume are plotted. In plot (B), the area around $J = 0$ has been zoomed in to show how the cost functions decrease much faster for smaller values of ν.*

***Table 4-3.** Additional Hyperparameters Introduced*

Hyperparameter	Example
Decay rate ν	$\nu = 0.2$

Exponential Decay

Another way of reducing the learning rate is according to the formula called exponential decay

$$\gamma = \gamma_0 \nu^{j/T}$$

See Figure 4-9 to get an idea of the speed of the learning rate. Note that the y axis has been plotted in logarithmic scale, to make the entity of the changes easier to compare. Note how for $\nu = 0.01$, after 200 iterations (not epochs), the learning rate is already a factor 1000 smaller than that at the start!

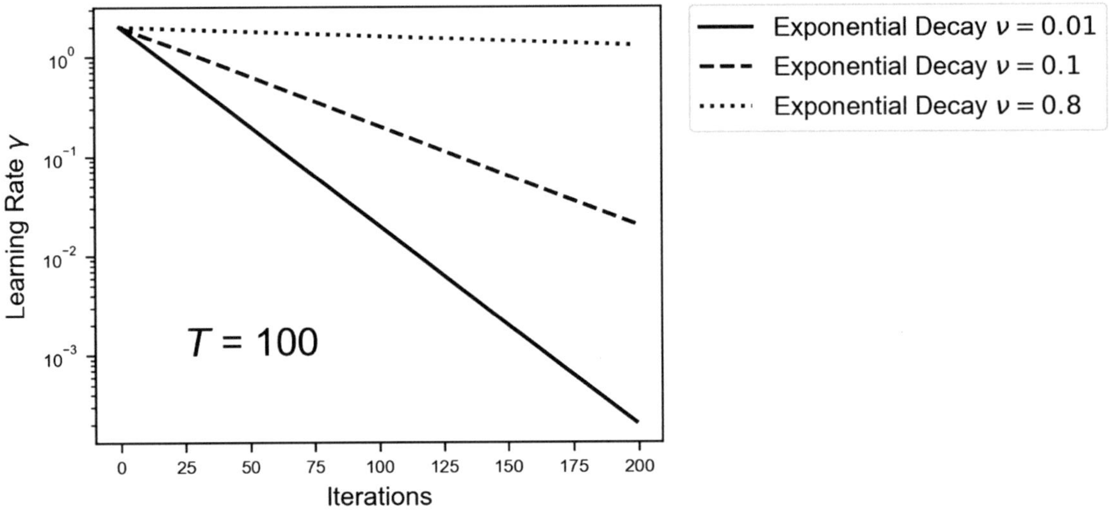

***Figure 4-9.** Decrease in the learning rate for three values of ν: 0.01, 0.1, and 0.8, and $T = 100$, using the exponential decay algorithm*

We can apply this method to our problem with $\nu = 0.2$ and $T = 3$ and, again, the algorithm converges. In Figure 4-10, the initial learning rate of $\gamma_0 = 2$ has been chosen, and an exponential decay algorithm with $\nu = 0, 2$ and $T = 3$ has been used. The different estimates $\boldsymbol{w}_n$ are indicated with points. The minimum is indicated by the circle approximately in the middle of the image. The algorithm is now able to converge. Each point has been labeled with the iteration number, to make following the weights update easier.

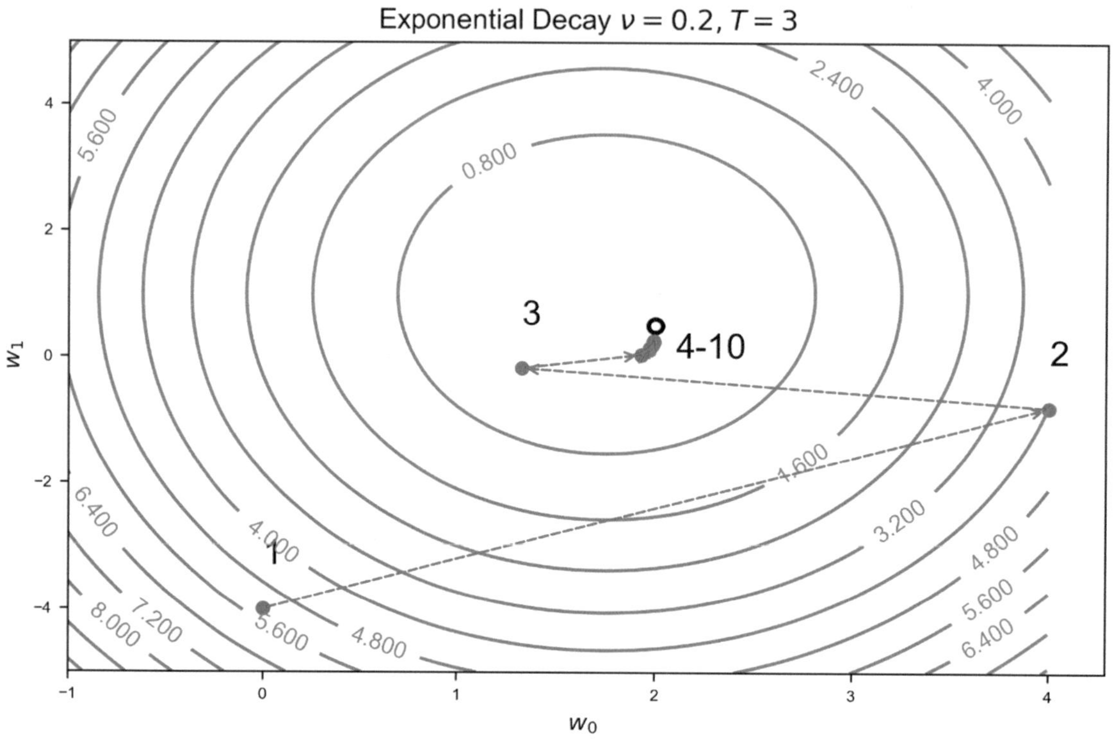

Figure 4-10. Illustration of the gradient descent algorithm for exponential decay

Table 4-4. Additional Hyperparameters Introduced

Hyperparameter	Example
Decay rate ν	$\nu = 0.2$
Decay steps T	$T = 3$

Natural Exponential Decay

Another way of reducing the learning rate is according to the formula called natural exponential decay

$$\gamma = \gamma_0 e^{-\nu j}$$

This case is particularly interesting because it allows you to learn a few important things. Consider first Figure 4-11, to compare how different values of ν relate to different decreases in speed for the learning rate.

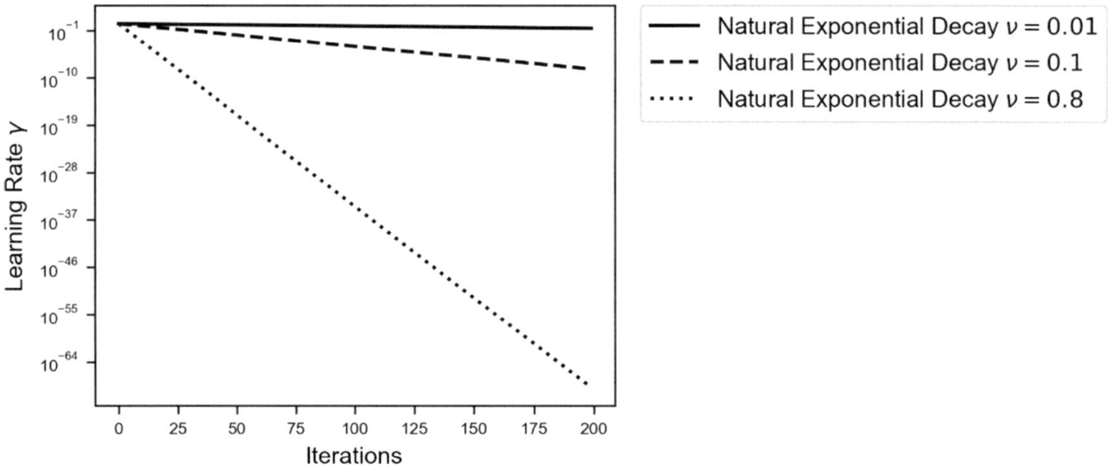

***Figure 4-11.** Decreased learning rate for three values of ν: 0.01, 0.1, and 0.8 and T = 100, using the natural exponential decay algorithm. Note that the y axis has been plotted in logarithmic scale, to make the entity of the changes easier to compare. Note how for ν = 0.8 after 200 iterations (not epochs), the learning rate is already a factor 10^{64} smaller than that at the start.*

I would like to draw your attention to the values on the y axis (note that it is using a logarithmic scale). For $\nu = 0.8$ after 200 iterations, the learning rate is a factor of 10^{-64} of the initial value! Practically zero. That means that already after a few iterations, no more updates can occur, because the learning rate is too small. To give you an idea of the scale of 10^{-64}, a hydrogen atom is "only" roughly 10^{-11} *m*! So, unless you are very careful with the choice of ν, you will not get very far.

Consider Figure 4-12, for which I have plotted our weights, as they are updated with the GD algorithm, for two values of the learning rate: 0.2 (dotted) and 0.5 (continuous).

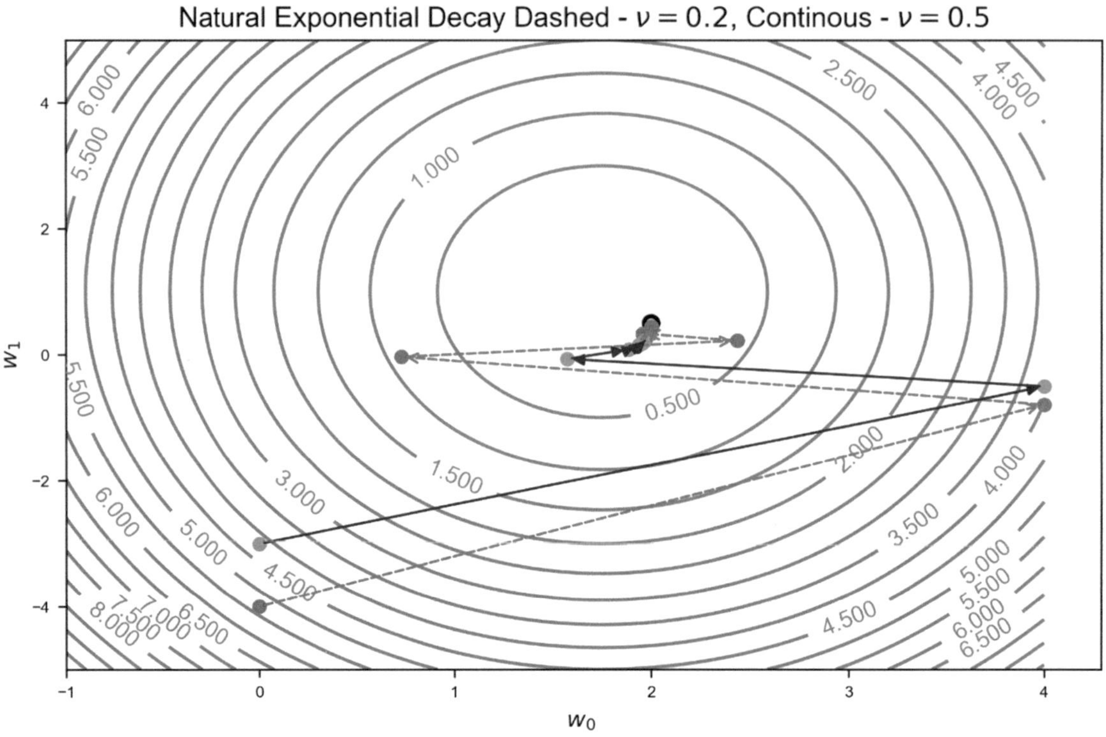

Figure 4-12. *Illustration of the gradient descent algorithm with natural exponential decay*

To check the convergence, we need to zoom in around the minimum. You'll see that in Figure 4-13. In case you are wondering why the minimum seems to be in a different position relative to the contour lines as in Figure 4-12, this is because the contour lines are not the same, because in Figure 4-13, we are much closer to the minimum.

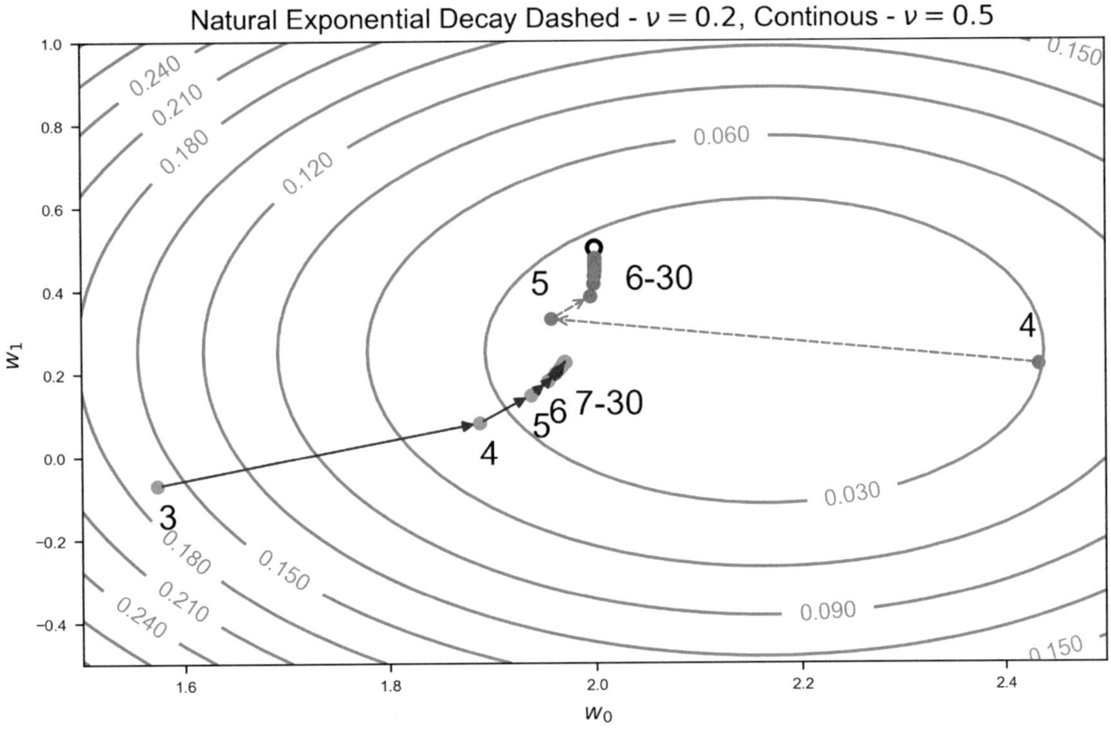

Figure 4-13. *Illustration of the gradient descent algorithm zoomed in around the minimum. The same method and parameters used in Figure 4-12 have been used here.*

Now we see something that makes again sense. The continuous line is for $\nu = 0.5$; therefore, the learning rate decreases much faster and does not manage to reach the minimum. In fact, after only 7 iterations, we have $\gamma = 0.06$, and after 20 iterations, we have $\gamma = 9 \cdot 10^{-5}$, a value so small that the convergence no longer manages to proceed at a reasonable speed! Again, it is very instructive to check the cost function decrease for the two parameters (see Figure 4-14).

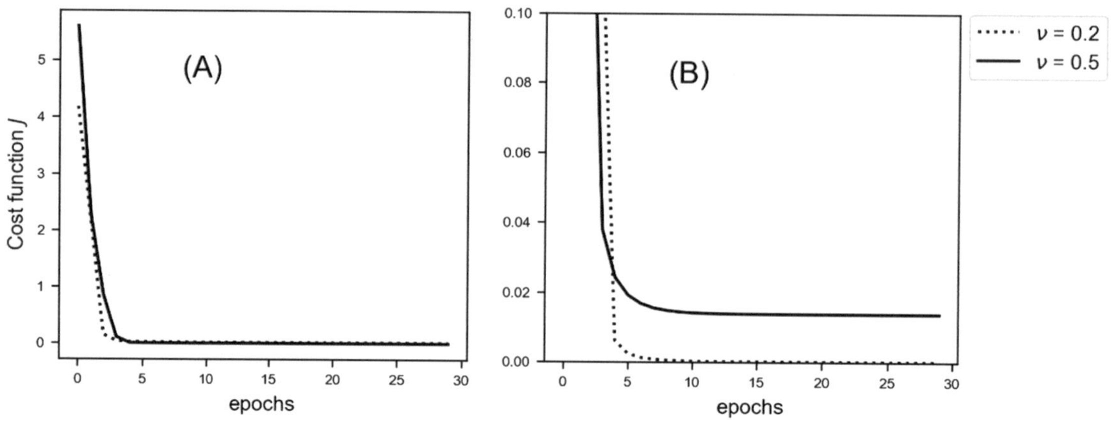

Figure 4-14. *Cost function vs. the number of epochs for natural exponential decay for two values of $\nu = 0.2$ and 0.5. In plot (A), the entire range of values that the cost functions assume are plotted. In plot (B), the area around $J = 0$ has been zoomed in to show how the cost functions decrease much faster for smaller values of ν.*

We see with plot (B) how the cost function for $\nu = 0.5$ does not reach zero and becomes practically constant, because the learning rate is too small. You may think that by using more iterations, the method will eventually converge, but that is not the case. Refer to Figure 4-15 to see that the convergence process actually stops, owing to the learning rate being almost zero after a while. In the figure, the initial learning rate of $\gamma_0 = 2$ has been chosen, and an exponential decay algorithm with $\nu = 0.5$ has been used. The GD does not manage to reach the minimum. The different estimates $\boldsymbol{w}_n$ are indicated with points. The minimum is indicated by the circle approximately in the middle of the image. The algorithm is now able to converge. Each point has been labeled with the iteration number, to make following the weights update easier.

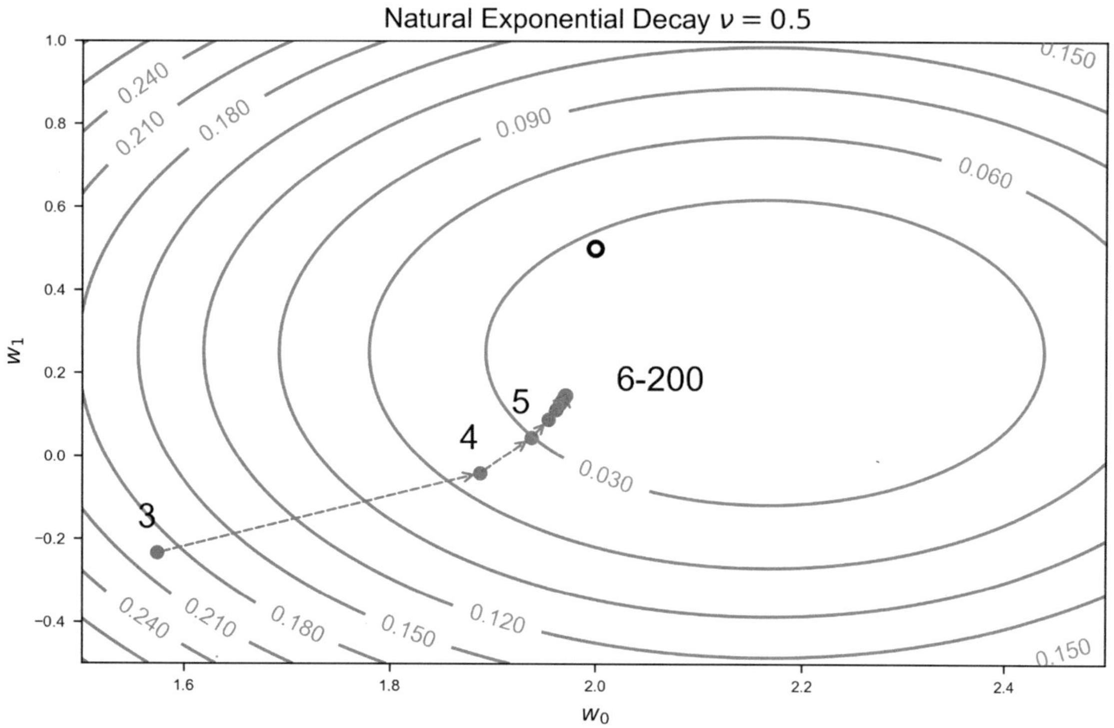

Figure 4-15. *Illustration of the gradient descent algorithm zoomed in around the minimum for 200 iterations*

Let's check the learning rate during this process for $\nu = 0.5$ (see Figure 4-16). Check the values along the y axis. The learning rate reaches 10^{-40} after roughly 175 iterations. For all practical purposes, it is zero. The GD algorithm will not update the weights anymore, regardless of how many iterations you let it run.

Figure 4-16. *Learning rate vs. the number of iterations with natural exponential decay for $\nu = 0.5$. Note that the y axis is in logarithmic scale, to better highlight the change of γ.*

To finish, let's compare the methods by putting them on the same plot, to get an idea of the relative behavior. In Figure 4-17, you can see three plots tracking the learning rate decay for each method with different parameters.

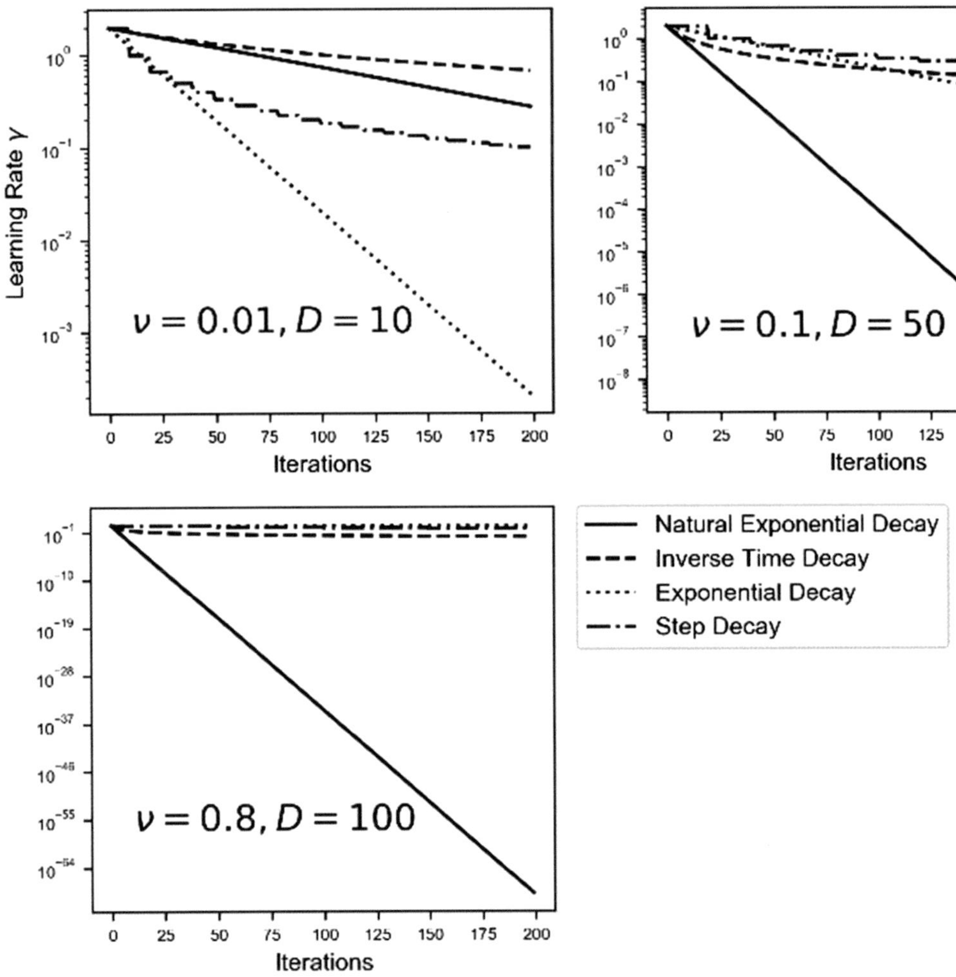

***Figure 4-17.** Comparison of different parameters of the learning rate decay for the algorithm indicated*

Note You should be aware of how fast your learning rate is decreasing, to avoid it becoming practically zero and stopping your convergence altogether.

---

tensorflow Implementation

I should briefly talk about how `tensorflow` implements the methods I just explained, because there are a few details that you should know. In `tensorflow`, you can find the following functions to perform dynamic learning rate decay:[2]

- Exponential decay → `tf.train.exponential_decay` (`https://goo.gl/fiE2ML`)
- Inverse time decay → `tf.train.inverse_time_decay` (`https://goo.gl/GXK6MX`)
- Natural exponential decay → `tf.train.natural_exp_decay` (`https://goo.gl/cGJe52`)
- Step decay → `tf.train.piecewise_constant` (`https://goo.gl/bL47ZD`)
- Polynomial decay → `tf.train.polynomial_decay` (`https://goo.gl/zuJWNo`)

Polynomial decay is a slightly more complex way of decreasing the learning rate. This had not been discussed, because it is rarely used, but you can read the documentation on the TensorFlow web site, to get an idea of how it works.

TensorFlow uses an additional parameter to give you a bit more flexibility. Take, for example, the inverse time decay method. Our equation for the learning rate decay was

$$\gamma = \frac{\gamma_0}{1+\nu j}$$

where we have two parameters: γ_0 and ν. TensorFlow uses three parameters:

$$\gamma = \frac{\gamma_0}{1+\frac{\nu j}{\nu_{ds}}}$$

[2]Check the overview in the official TensorFlow documentation at `https://goo.gl/vpFNp7`.

where ν_{ds} is called in TensorFlow code decay_step. The formula you will find in the TensorFlow official documentation in Python code is

```
decayed_learning_rate = learning_rate / (1 + decay_rate * global_step /
decay_step)
```

to link TensorFlow language with our notation, as follows:

- global_step → j (number of iterations)
- decay_rate → ν
- decay_step → ν_{ds}
- learning_rate → γ_o (initial learning rate)

You may ask yourself why you want to have this additional parameter. The parameter, mathematically speaking, is redundant. We can simply set our ν to the same value of ν/ν_{ds}, and we would get the same result. The problem, practically, is that j (the number of iterations) gets very big very quickly, and, therefore, our ν may need to assume very small values, to be able to get a reasonable learning rate decrease. The goal of the parameter ν_{ds} is to scale the number of iterations. For example, you can set this parameter to $\nu_{ds} = 10^5$, thereby making the decrease of the learning rate occur on a scale of 10^5 iterations, instead of every single iteration. If you have a huge dataset with 10^8 observations, and you use a mini-batch size of 50, you will get $2 \cdot 10^6$ iterations for each epoch. Suppose you then want your learning rate to be 1/5 of the initial value after 100 epochs. For this, you would need a $\nu = 2 \cdot 10^{-8}$, a rather small value that, more important, depends on the size of your dataset and the mini-batch size. If you "normalize," so to speak, the number of iterations, you can choose a value for ν that can remain constant, if you choose to change, for example, the mini-batch size. There is an additional practical reason (more important than that I just discussed), which is the following: the tensorflow function has an additional parameter: staircase, which can assume the values of True or False. If set to True, the following function is used:

$$\gamma = \frac{\gamma_0}{1+\nu\left\lceil \frac{j}{\nu_{ds}} \right\rceil}$$

And, therefore, you get an update only for each ν_{ds} iteration, instead of continuously. In Figure 4-18, you can see the difference for $\nu = 0.5$ and $\nu_{ds} = 20$ for 200 iterations. You may want to keep your learning rate constant for ten epochs before updating it.

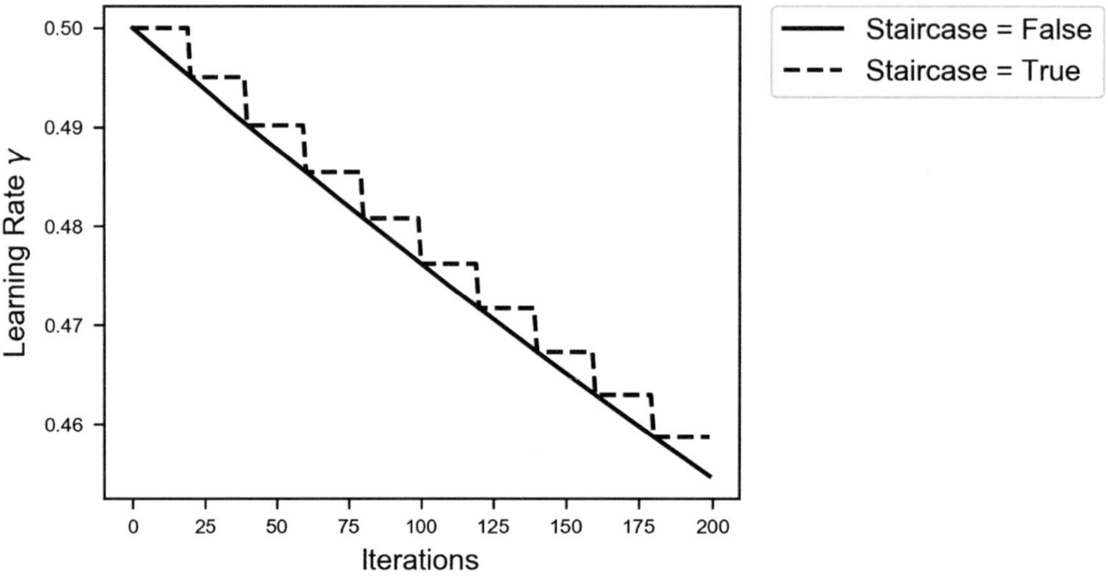

Figure 4-18. *Learning rate decay with the two variations obtained with `tensorflow` with `staircase` = `True` and `False`*

The same parameters are needed by the functions `tf.train.inverse_time_decay`, `tf.train.natural_exp_decay`, and `tf.train.polynomial_decay`. They work in the same way, and the purpose of the additional parameter is what I just described. Don't be confused when implementing the methods in `tensorflow`, if you need this additional parameter. I will show you how to implement it for inverse time decay, but it works in the same exact way for all the other types. You need the following additional lines of code:

```
initial_learning_rate = 0.1
decay_steps = 1000
decay_rate = 0.1
global_step = tf.Variable(0, trainable = False)
learning_rate_decay = tf.train.inverse_time_decay(initial_learning_rate,
global_step, decay_steps, decay_rate)
```

and then you must modify the line of code in which you specify the optimizer you are using with this.

```
optimizer = tf.train.GradientDescentOptimizer(learning_rate_decay).
minimize(cost, global_step = global_step)
```

The only difference is the additional parameter in the `minimize` function: `global_step = global_step`. The `minimize` function will update the `global_step` variable with the iteration number with each update. That's all. It works in the same way for the other functions.

The only difference is for the function `piecewise_constant`, which requires different parameters: `x`, `boundaries`, and `values`. For example (from the TensorFlow documentation):

> *...use a learning rate that's 1.0 for the first 100000 steps, 0.5 for steps 100001 to 110000, and 0.1 for any additional steps*

This would require

```
boundaries = [100000, 110000]
values = [1.0, 0.5, 0.1]
```

The code

```
boundaries = [b1,b2,b3, ..., bn]
values = [l1,l12,l23,l34, ..., ln]
```

will give a learning rate of `l1` before `b1` iterations, `l12` between `b1` and `b2` iterations, `l23` between `b2` and `b3` iterations, and so on. Keep in mind that with this method, you must set manually all the values and boundaries in the code. This will require quite some patience, if you want to test each combination to see whether it is working well. An implementation of the step decay algorithm in TensorFlow would look like this:

```
global_step = tf.Variable(0, trainable=False)
boundaries = [100000, 110000]
values = [1.0, 0.5, 0.1]
learning_rate = tf.train.piecewise_constant(global_step, boundaries,
values)
```

Applying the Methods to the Zalando Dataset

Let's try to apply the methods you just learned to a realistic scenario. For this, we will employ the Zalando dataset used in Chapter 3. Please check Chapter 3 again, to see how to load the dataset and how to prepare the data. At the end of the chapter, we wrote the functions to construct a model with many layers and a function to train it. Let's consider a model with 4 hidden layers, each containing 20 neurons. Let's compare how the model learns with a starting initial learning rate of 0.01, keep that constant, and then apply the inverse time decay algorithm, starting with a $\gamma_0 = 0.1$, $\nu = 0.1$, and $\nu_{ds} = 10^3$ (see Figure 4-19).

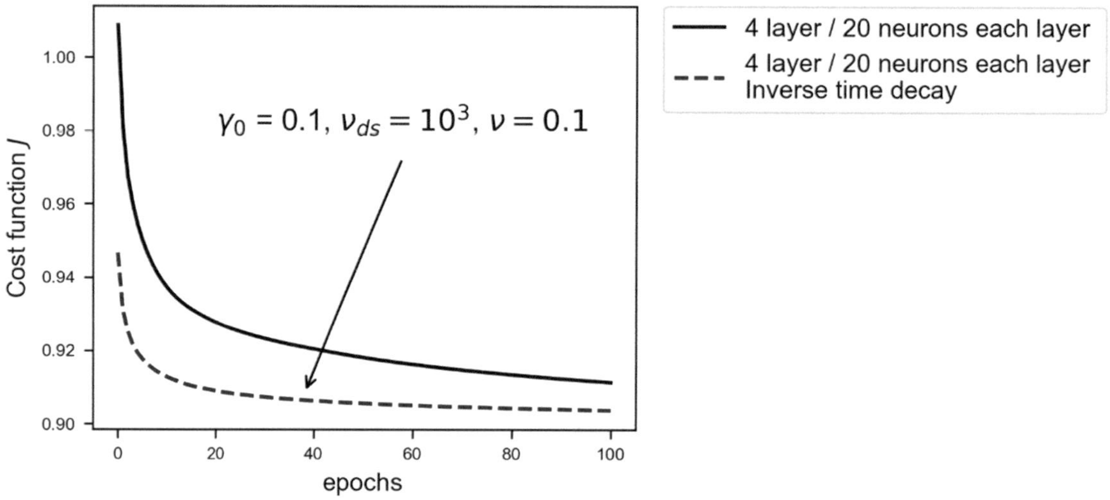

Figure 4-19. *Cost function behavior for a neural network of 4 layers, each having 20 neurons, applied to the Zalando dataset. The continous line is for a model with a constant learning rate of $\gamma = 0.01$. A dashed line is for a network in which we have used the inverse time decay algorithm, with a $\gamma_0 = 0.1$, $\nu = 0.1$, and $\nu_{ds} = 10^3$.*

So, even with a starting learning rate ten times larger, the algorithm is much more efficient. Is has been proven in several research papers that applying a dynamic learning rate makes learning faster and more efficient, as we have noted in this case.

Note Unless you are using optimization algorithms that include a learning rate change during training (you will see them in the next sections), it is generally a good idea to use dynamic learning rate decay. This makes learning stable and usually faster. The downside is that you have more hyperparameters to tune.

Normally, it is a good idea, when using dynamic learning rate decay, to start with an initial learning rate γ_0 bigger than you would normally use. Because γ is decreasing, this won't normally create problems and will make the convergence at the beginning (one hopes) faster. As you should now expect, there are no fixed rules on which method works better. Each case and dataset is different, and some testing is always required, to see which parameter value yields the best results.

Common Optimizers

Until now, we have used gradient descent to minimize our cost function. That is not the most efficient way to proceed, and there are some modifications to the algorithm that can make it much faster and more efficient. This is a very active area of research, and you will find an incredible number of algorithms, based on different ideas, to make the learning faster. I will cover here the most instructive and well-known ones: Momentum, RMSProp, and Adam. Additional material that you can consult to investigate the most exotic algorithms has been written by S. Ruder, in a paper titled *An overview of gradient descent optimization algorithms* (available at `https://goo.gl/KgKVgG`). The paper is not for beginners and requires an extensive mathematical background, but it gives an overview of such unusual algorithms as Adagrad, Adadelta, and Nadam. Additionally, it reviews weights update schemes applicable in distributed in such environments as Hogwild!, Downpour SGD, and many more. Surely, it is a read worth your time.

To understand the basic idea of Momentum (and partially, too, RMSProp and Adam), you first must understand what exponentially weighted averages are.

Exponentially Weighted Averages

Let's suppose that you are measuring a quantity θ (it could be the temperature where you live) over time—once a day, for example. You will have a series of measurements that we can indicate with θ_i, where i goes from 1 to a certain number N. Bear with me, if, at the beginning, this does not make much sense; however, let's define recursively a quantity v_n as

$$
\begin{aligned}
v_0 &= 1 \\
v_1 &= \beta v_0 + (1-\beta)\theta_1 \\
v_2 &= \beta v_1 + (1-\beta)\theta_2
\end{aligned}
$$

and so on, with β, a real number with $0 < \beta < 1$. Generally, we could write the nth term as

$$v_n = \beta v_{n-1} + (1-\beta)\theta_n$$

Now let's write all the terms, v_1, v_2, and so on, just as a function of β and θ_i (so, not recursively). For v_2, we have

$$v_2 = \beta(\beta v_0 + (1-\beta)\theta_1) + (1-\beta)\theta_2 = \beta^2 + (1-\beta)(\beta\theta_1 + \theta_2)$$

for v_3,

$$v_3 = \beta^3 + (1-\beta)\left[\beta^2\theta_1 + \beta\theta_2 + \theta_3\right]$$

Generalizing, we obtain

$$v_n = \beta^n + (1-\beta)\left[\beta^{n-1}\theta_1 + \beta^{n-2}\theta_2 + \ldots + \theta_n\right]$$

Or, more elegantly (without the three dots),

$$v_n = \beta^n + (1-\beta)\sum_{i=1}^{n}\beta^{n-i}\theta_i$$

Now let's try to understand what this formula means. First, note that the term β^n disappears if we choose $v_0 = 0$. Let's do that (we set $v_0 = 0$) and consider now what remains:

$$v_n = (1-\beta)\sum_{i=1}^{n}\beta^{n-i}\theta_i$$

Are you still with me? Now comes the interesting part. Let's define the convolution between two sequences.[3] Consider two sequences: x_n and h_n. The convolution between the two (which we indicate with the symbol $*$) is defined by

$$x_n * h_n = \sum_{k=-\infty}^{\infty} x_k h_{n-k}$$

[3] Generally speaking, a sequence is an enumerated collection of objects.

Now, because we have only a finite number of measurements for our quantity θ_i, we will have

$$\theta_k = 0 \qquad k > n, k \leq 0$$

Therefore, we can write v_n as a convolution as

$$v_n = \theta_n * b_n$$

where we have defined

$$b_n = (1-\beta)\beta^n$$

To get an idea of what that means, let's plot together θ_n, b_n, and v_n. To do this, let's assume that θ_n has a Gaussian shape (the exact form is not relevant, it is only for illustrative purposes), and let's take $\beta = 0.9$ (see Figure 4-20).

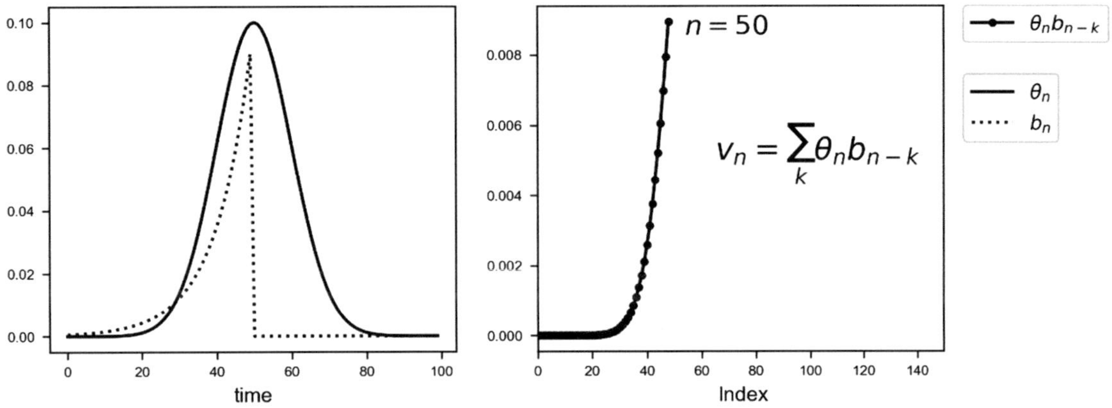

Figure 4-20. *A plot (left) showing θ_n (solid line) and b_n (dotted line) together, and one (right) showing the points that must be summed to obtain v_n for $n = 50$*

Now I'll discuss briefly Figure 4-20. The Gaussian curve (θ_n) will be convoluted with b_n to obtain v_n. The result can be seen in the plot at right. All those terms, $(1 - \beta)\beta^{n-i}\theta_i$ for $i = 1, \ldots, 50$ (plotted at right), will be summed to obtain v_{50}. Intuitively, v_n is the average of all θ_n for $n = 1, \ldots, 50$. Each term is then multiplied by a term (b_n) that is 1 for $n = 50$ and then decreases rapidly for n, decreasing toward 1. Basically, this is a weighted average, with an exponentially decreasing weight (thus the name). The terms farther from $n = 50$ are less and less relevant, while the terms close to $n = 50$ get more weight. This is also a moving average. For each n, all the preceding terms are added, each multiplied by a weight (b_n).

I would like now to show you why there is this factor $1 - \beta$ in b_n. Why not choose only β^n? The reason is very simple. The sum of b_n over all positive n is equal to 1. Let's see why. Consider the following equation:

$$\sum_{k=1}^{\infty} b_k = (1-\beta)\sum_{k=1}^{\infty}\beta^n = (1-\beta)\lim_{N\to\infty}\frac{1-\beta^{N+1}}{1-\beta} = (1-\beta)\frac{1}{1-\beta} = 1$$

where we have used the fact that for $\beta < 1$, we have $\lim_{N\to\infty}\beta^{N+1} = 0$, and that for a geometric series, we have

$$\sum_{k=1}^{n} ar^{k-1} = \frac{a\left(1-r^n\right)}{1-r}$$

The algorithm we described to calculate v_n is nothing else than the convolution of our quantity θ_i, with a series the sum of which is equal to 1 and has the form $(1 - \beta)\beta^i$.

Note The exponentially weighted average v_n of a series of a quantity θ_n is the convolution $v_n = \theta_n * b_n$ of our quantity θ_i, with $b_n = (1 - \beta)\beta^n$, where b_n has the property that its sum over the positive values of n is equal to 1. It has the intuitive meaning of a moving average, in which each term is multiplied by weights given by the sequence b_n.

As you choose β smaller and smaller, the number of points θ_n that have a weight significantly different from zero decreases, as you can see in Figure 4-21, in which the series b_n for different values of β is plotted.

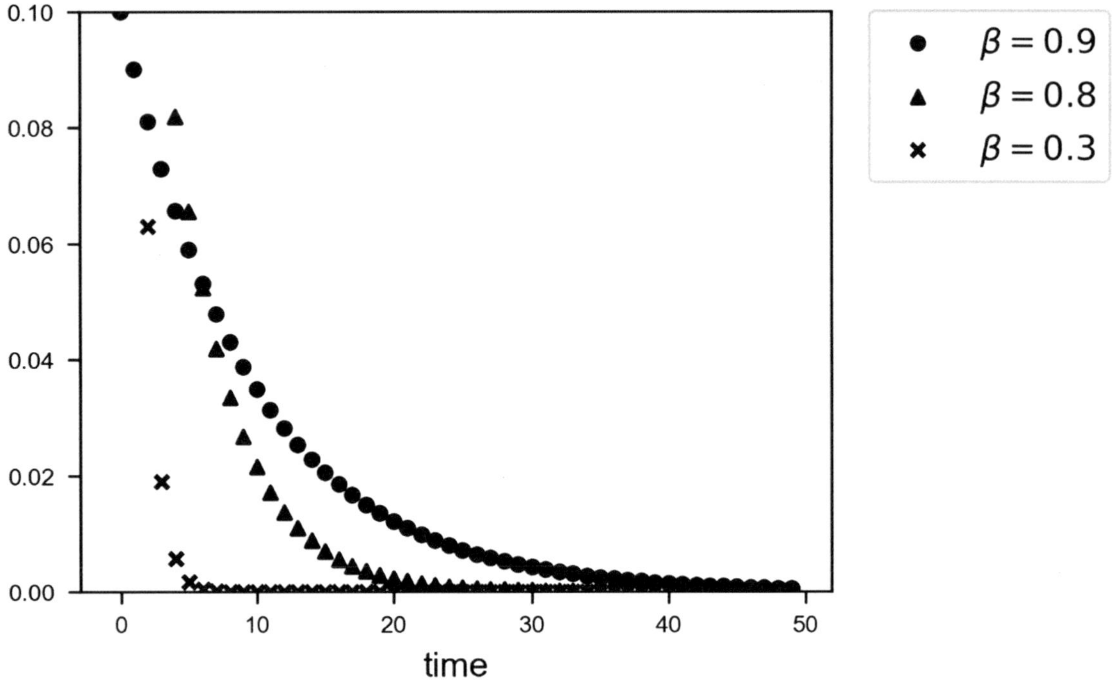

***Figure 4-21.** The series b_n for three values of β: 0.9, 0.8, and 0.3. Note that as β gets smaller, the series is significantly different from zero for an increasingly smaller number of values around $n = 0$.*

This method is at the very core of the Momentum optimizer and more advanced learning algorithms, and you will see in the next sections how it works in practice.

Momentum

You will remember that in plain gradient descent, the weights updates are calculated with the equations

$$\begin{cases} \boldsymbol{w}_{[n+1]} = \boldsymbol{w}_{[n]} - \gamma \nabla_{\mathbf{w}} J\left(\boldsymbol{w}_{[n]}, b_{[n]}\right) \\ b_{[n+1]} = b_{[n]} - \gamma \dfrac{\partial J\left(\boldsymbol{w}_{[n]}, b_{[n]}\right)}{\partial b} \end{cases}$$

The idea behind the Momentum optimizer is to use exponentially weighted averages of the corrections of the gradient and then use them for the weights updates. More mathematically we calculate

$$\begin{cases} \boldsymbol{v}_{w,[n+1]} = \beta \boldsymbol{v}_{w,[n]} + (1-\beta)\nabla_{\mathbf{w}} J\left(\boldsymbol{w}_{[n]}, b_{[n]}\right) \\ v_{b,[n+1]} = \beta v_{b,[n]} + (1-\beta)\dfrac{\partial J\left(\boldsymbol{w}_{[n]}, b_{[n]}\right)}{\partial b} \end{cases}$$

and we will then perform the updates with the equations

$$\begin{cases} \boldsymbol{w}_{[n+1]} = \boldsymbol{w}_{[n]} - \gamma \boldsymbol{v}_{w,[n]} \\ b_{[n+1]} = b_{[n]} - \gamma v_{b,[n]} \end{cases}$$

where usually $\boldsymbol{v}_{w,\,[0]} = \mathbf{0}$ and $v_{b,\,[0]} = 0$ are chosen. That means, as you can now understand from the discussion about exponentially weighted averages from the previous section, that instead of using the derivatives of the cost functions with respect to the weights, we update the weights with a moving average of the derivatives. Usually, experience shows that a bias correction could theoretically be neglected.

Note The Momentum algorithm uses an exponential weighted average of the derivatives of the cost function with respect to the weights for the weights updates. In this way, not only the derivatives at a given iteration are used, but also the past behavior is considered. It may happen that the algorithm oscillates around the minimum, instead of converging directly. This algorithm can escape from plateaus much more efficiently than standard gradient descent.

Sometimes, you find in books or blogs a slightly different formulation (I provide here only the equation for the weights, $\boldsymbol{w}$, for brevity).

$$\boldsymbol{v}_{w,[n+1]} = \gamma \boldsymbol{v}_{w,[n]} + \eta \nabla_{\mathbf{w}} J\left(\boldsymbol{w}_{[n]}, b_{[n]}\right)$$

The idea and meaning remain the same. It is simply a slightly different mathematical formulation. I find that the method I described is easier to understand intuitively with the notion of sequence convolution and of weighted averages than this second formulation. Another formulation that you will find (and one that TensorFlow uses) is

$$v_{w,[n+1]} = \eta^t v_{w,[n]} + \nabla_{\mathbf{w}} J\left(\boldsymbol{w}_{[n]}, b_{[n]}\right)$$

where η^t is called by TensorFlow Momentum (the superscript t indicates that this variable is used by TensorFlow). In this formulation, the weight update assumes the form

$$\boldsymbol{w}_{[n+1]} = \boldsymbol{w}_{[n]} - \gamma^t v_{w,[n+1]} = \boldsymbol{w}_{[n]} - \gamma^t\left(\eta^t v_{w,[n]} + \nabla_{\mathbf{w}} J\left(\boldsymbol{w}_{[n]}, b_{[n]}\right)\right) = \boldsymbol{w}_{[n]} - \gamma^t \eta^t v_{w,[n]} - \gamma^t \nabla_{\mathbf{w}} J\left(\boldsymbol{w}_{[n]}, b_{[n]}\right)$$

where, again, the superscript t indicates that the variable is the one used by TensorFlow. Although it seems different, this formulation is completely equivalent to the formulation I gave you at the beginning of this section.

$$\boldsymbol{w}_{[n+1]} = \boldsymbol{w}_{[n]} - \gamma\beta v_{w,[n]} - \gamma(1-\beta)\nabla_{\mathbf{w}} J\left(\boldsymbol{w}_{[n]}, b_{[n]}\right)$$

The TensorFlow formulation and the one I discussed previously are equivalent, if we choose

$$\begin{cases} \eta = \dfrac{\beta}{1-\beta} \\ \gamma^t = \gamma(1-\beta) \end{cases}$$

That can be seen by simply comparing the two different equations for the weights updates. Typically, values around $\eta = 0.9$ in TensorFlow implementations are used, and they generally work well.

Implementing Momentum in TensorFlow is extraordinarily easy. Just replace the `GradientDescentOptimizer` with `tf.train.MomentumOptimizer(learning_rate = learning_rate, momentum = 0.9)`.

The Momentum almost always converges faster than plain gradient descent.

Note Comparing the different parameters in the different optimizers is wrong. The learning rate, for example, has a different meaning in the different algorithms. What you should compare is the best convergence speed you can achieve with several optimizers, regardless of the choice of parameters. Comparing the GD for a learning rate of 0.01 with Adam (covered later) for the same learning rate does not make much sense. You should compare the optimizers with the parameters that give you the best and fastest convergence, to decide which one to use.

In Figure 4-22, you can see the cost function for the problem discussed in the previous section for plain gradient descent (with $\gamma = 0.05$) and for Momentum (with $\gamma = 0.05$ and $\eta = 0.9$). You can see how the Momentum optimizer oscillates around the minimum. What is difficult to see on the y scale is that with Momentum, J reaches a much lower value.

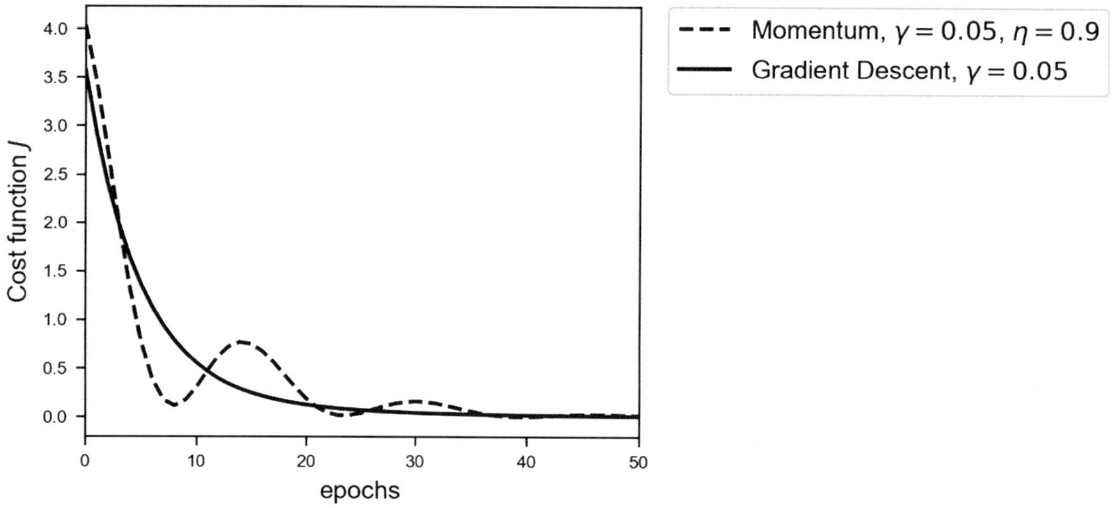

***Figure 4-22.** Cost function vs. the number of epochs for plain gradient descent (with $\gamma = 0.05$) and for Momentum (with $\gamma = 0.05$ and $\eta = 0.9$). You can see how the Momentum optimizer oscillates a bit around the minimum.*

More interesting is to check how the Momentum optimizer chooses its path along the cost function surface. In Figure 4-23, you can see a 3D surface plot of the cost function. The continuous line is the path that the gradient descent optimizer chooses, along the maximum steepness, as expected. The dashed line is the one that the Momentum optimizer chooses as it oscillates around the minimum.

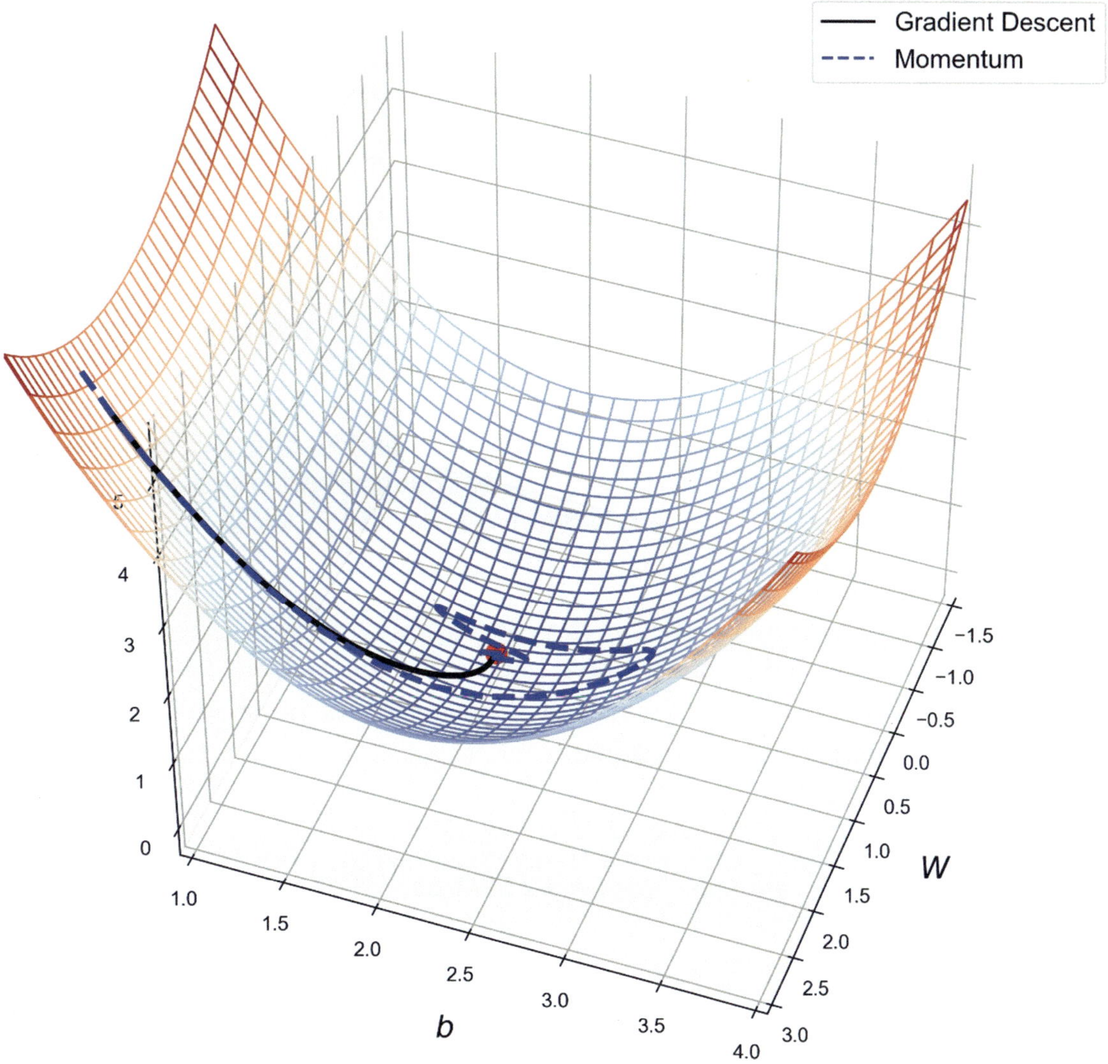

Figure 4-23. *3D surface plot of the cost function J. The continuous line is the path that the gradient descent optimizer chooses—along the maximum steepness, as expected. The dashed line is the one that the Momentum optimizer chooses as it oscillates around the minimum.*

I want to convince you that Momentum is faster and better at converging. To do that, let's check in the weights plane how the two optimizers behave. In Figure 4-24, you can see the path that the two optimizers have chosen. On the right plot, you can see a zoom around the minimum. You can see how gradient descent after 100 epochs does not manage to reach the minimum, although it seems to choose a more direct path toward the minimum. It gets very close, but not close enough. The Momentum optimizer oscillates around the minimum and reaches it very efficiently.

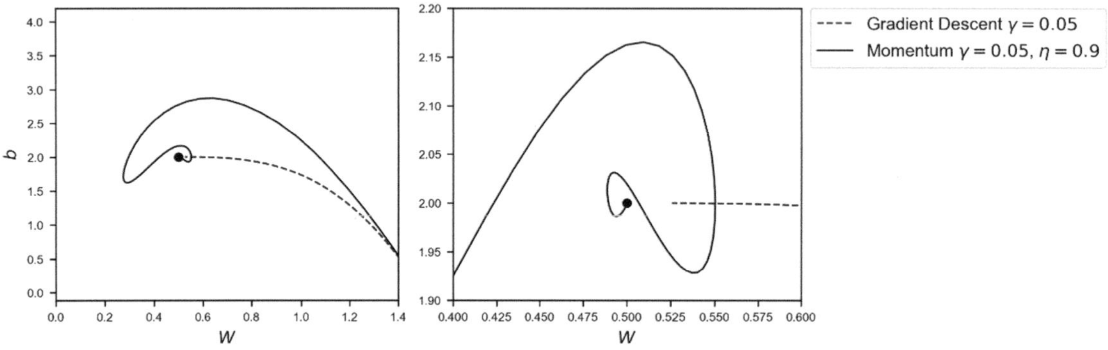

Figure 4-24. *Path that the two optimizers have chosen. The right plot shows a zoom around the minimum. You can see how Momentum reaches the minimum after oscillating around it, while GD does not manage to reach it in 100 epochs.*

RMSProp

Let's move to something a bit more complex, but usually more efficient. Let me give you the mathematical equations, and then we will compare them to the others we have seen so far. At each iteration, we need to calculate

$$\begin{cases} \boldsymbol{S}_{\boldsymbol{w},[n+1]} = \beta_2 \boldsymbol{S}_{\boldsymbol{w},[n]} + (1-\beta_2)\nabla_{\boldsymbol{w}} J(\boldsymbol{w}, b) \circ \nabla_{\boldsymbol{w}} J(\boldsymbol{w}, b) \\ S_{b,[n+1]} = \beta_2 S_{b,[n]} + (1-\beta_2)\dfrac{\partial J(w,b)}{\partial b} \circ \dfrac{\partial J(w,b)}{\partial b} \end{cases}$$

where the symbol ∘ indicates an element-wise product. Then we will do the update of our weights with the equations

$$\begin{cases} \boldsymbol{w}_{[n+1]} = \boldsymbol{w}_{[n]} - \dfrac{\gamma \nabla_{\boldsymbol{w}} J(\boldsymbol{w}, b)}{\sqrt{\boldsymbol{S}_{\boldsymbol{w},[n+1]}} + \epsilon} \\ b_{[n+1]} = b_{[n]} - \gamma \dfrac{\partial J(w,b)}{\partial b} \dfrac{1}{\sqrt{S_{b,[n]}} + \epsilon} \end{cases}$$

So, first you determine an exponential weighted average of the quantities $\boldsymbol{S}_{\boldsymbol{w},[n+1]}$ and $S_{b,[n+1]}$ and then use them to modify the derivatives that you use to do your weights updates. The ϵ, usually $\epsilon = 10^{-8}$, is there to avoid the denominator going to zero in case the quantities $\boldsymbol{S}_{\boldsymbol{w},[n+1]}$ and $S_{b,[n+1]}$ go to zero. The intuitive idea is that if the derivative is big, then the S quantities are big; therefore, the factors $1/\sqrt{\boldsymbol{S}_{\boldsymbol{w},[n+1]}+\epsilon}$ or $1/\sqrt{S_{b,[n]}+\epsilon}$ will be smaller and the learning will slow down. The reverse is also true, so if the derivatives are small, the learning will be faster. This algorithm will make the learning faster for the parameters that are slowing it down. In TensorFlow, it is again particularly easy to use it simply with the following code:

```
optimizer = tf.train.RMSPropOptimizer(learning_rate, momentum = 0.9).
minimize(cost)
```

Let's check what path this optimizer chooses. In Figure 4-25, you can see that RMSProp oscillates around the minimum. While the GD does not reach it, the RMSProp algorithm has time to do several loops around it before reaching it.

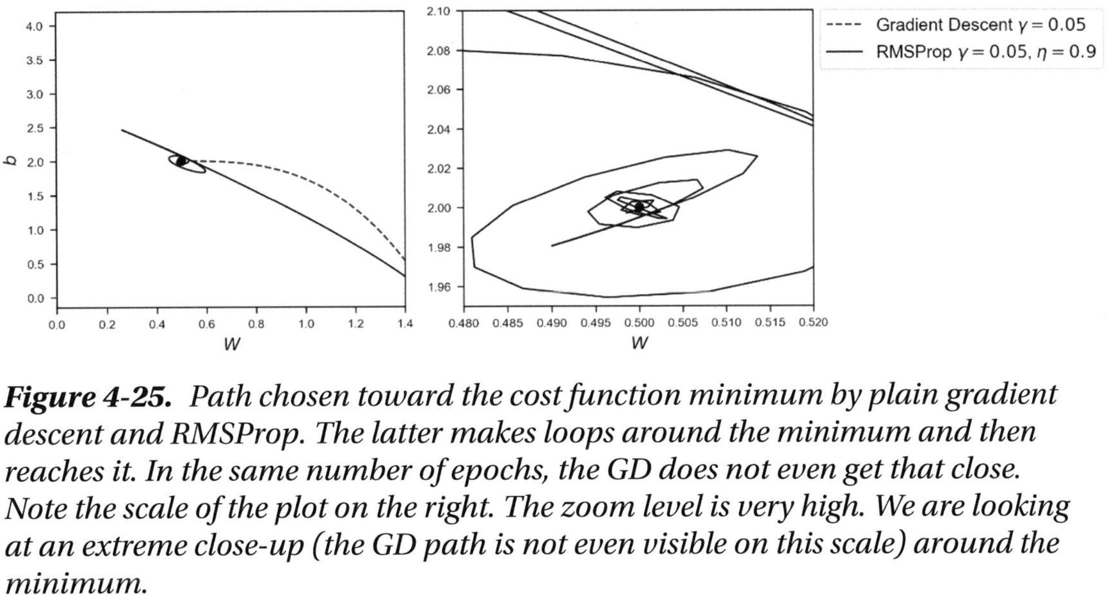

***Figure 4-25.** Path chosen toward the cost function minimum by plain gradient descent and RMSProp. The latter makes loops around the minimum and then reaches it. In the same number of epochs, the GD does not even get that close. Note the scale of the plot on the right. The zoom level is very high. We are looking at an extreme close-up (the GD path is not even visible on this scale) around the minimum.*

In Figure 4-26, you can see in 3D the same path along the cost function surface.

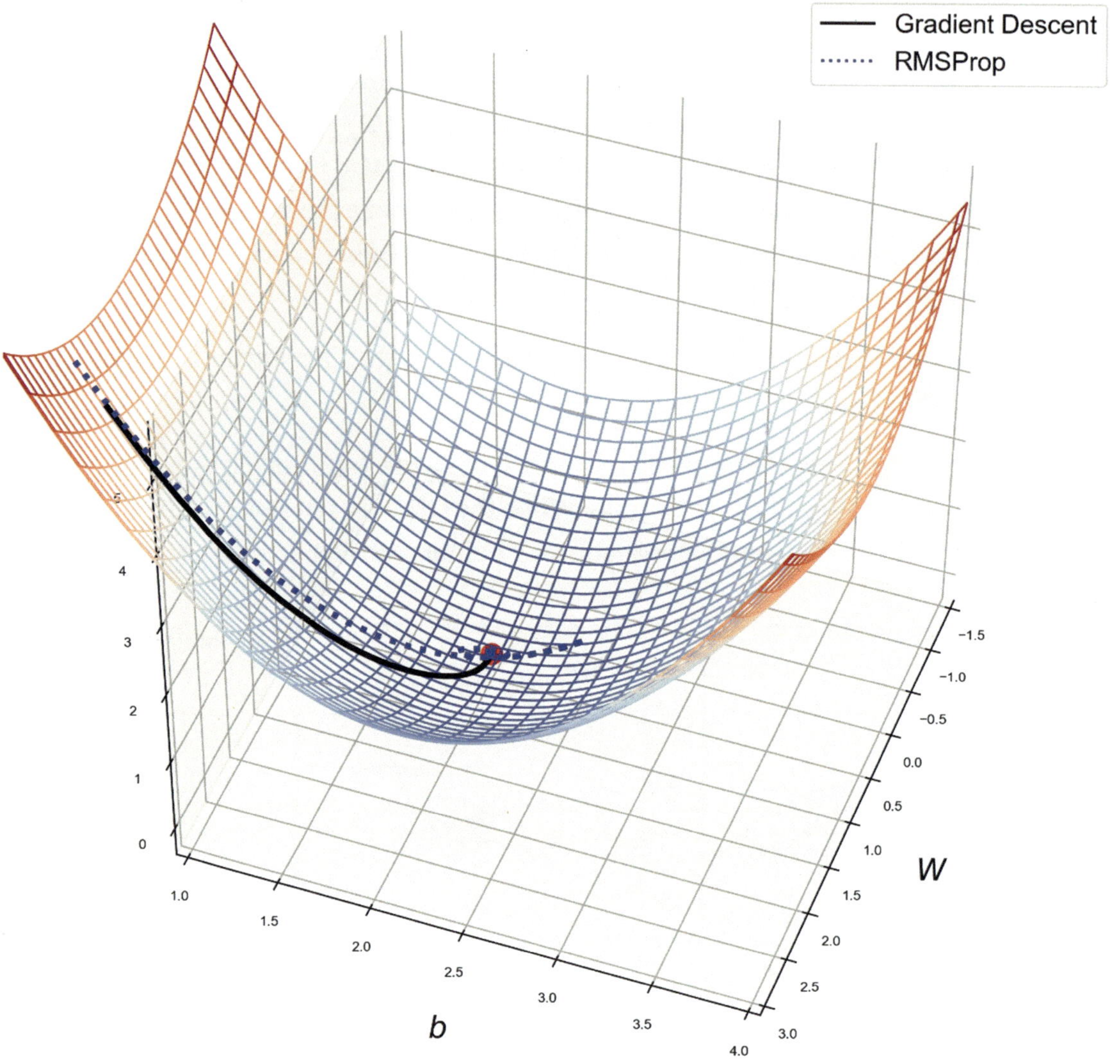

***Figure 4-26.** Path choosen by the GD ($\gamma = 0.05$) and RMSProp ($\gamma = 0.05$, $\eta = 0.9$, $\epsilon = 10^{-10}$) along the surface of the cost function. The red dot indicates the minimum. RMSProp, especially at the beginnig, chooses a more direct path toward the minimum than GD.*

In Figure 4-27, you can see GD, RMSProp and Momentum paths. You can see how the RMSProp path is much more direct toward the minimum. It gets close to it very quickly and then oscillates closer and closer. It overshoots a bit at the beginning but then corrects itself quickly and comes back.

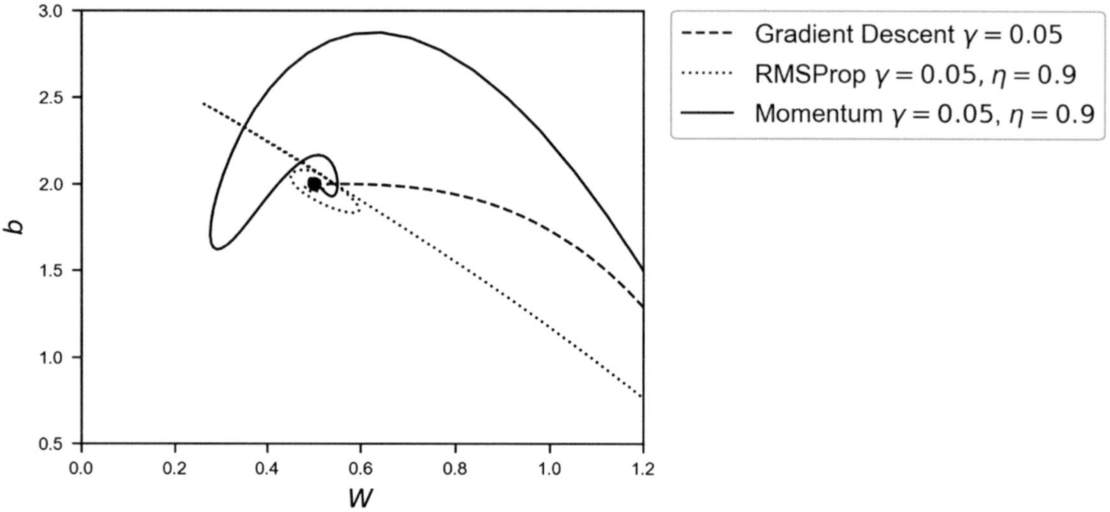

***Figure 4-27.** Path toward the minimum choosen by GD, RMSProp, and Momentum. You can see how the RMSProp path toward the minimum is much more direct. It gets around it very quickly and then oscillates closer and closer.*

Adam

The last algorithm we will look at is called Adam (Adaptive Moment estimation). It combines the ideas of RMSProp and Momentum in one optimizer. Like Momentum, it uses an exponential weighted averages of past derivatives, and like RMSProp, it uses the exponentially weighted averages of past squared derivatives.

You will have to calculate the same quantities that you need for Momentum and for RMSProp, and then you must calculate the following quantities:

$$\boldsymbol{v}_{\boldsymbol{w},[n]}^{corrected} = \frac{\boldsymbol{v}_{\boldsymbol{w},[n]}}{1-\beta_1^n}$$

$$v_{b,[n]}^{corrected} = \frac{v_{b,[n]}}{1-\beta_1^n}$$

Similarly, you must calculate

$$\boldsymbol{S}_{\boldsymbol{w},[n]}^{corrected} = \frac{\boldsymbol{S}_{\boldsymbol{w},[n]}}{1-\beta_2^n}$$

$$S_{b,[n]}^{corrected} = \frac{S_{b,[n]}}{1-\beta_2^n}$$

Where we have used β_1 for the hyperparameter, we will use it in Momentum and β_2 for the one we used in RMSProp. Then, as we did in RMSProp, we will update our weights with the equations

$$\begin{cases} \boldsymbol{w}_{[n+1]} = \boldsymbol{w}_{[n]} - \dfrac{\gamma \boldsymbol{v}_{\boldsymbol{w},[n]}^{corrected}}{\sqrt{\boldsymbol{S}_{\boldsymbol{w},[n+1]}^{corrected}} + \epsilon} \\ b_{[n+1]} = b_{[n]} - \gamma \dfrac{v_{b,[n]}^{corrected}}{\sqrt{S_{b,[n]}^{corrected}} + \epsilon} \end{cases}$$

TensorFlow does everything for us, if we simply use the following line:

```
optimizer = tf.train.AdamOptimizer(learning_rate = learning_rate, beta1 =
0.9, beta2 = 0.999, epsilon = 1e-8).minimize(cost)
```

where, in this case, the typical values for the parameters have been chosen: $\gamma = 0.3$, $\beta_1 = 0.9$, $\beta_2 = 0.999$, and $\epsilon = 10^{-8}$. Note that because this algorithm adapts the learning rate to the situation, we can start with a bigger learning rate, to speed up the convergence.

In Figure 4-28, you can see the path around the minimum chosen by GD and the Adam optimizer. Adam, too, oscillates around the minimum, but it reaches it without problems. On the right plot (a zoom around the minimum), you can see how the algorithm gets very close to the minimum. To give you an idea of how good the optimizer is, after just 200 epochs, the weights and bias get to 0.499983, 2.000047, which is really close to the minimum (remember that the minimum is at $w = 0.5$ and $b = 2.0$).

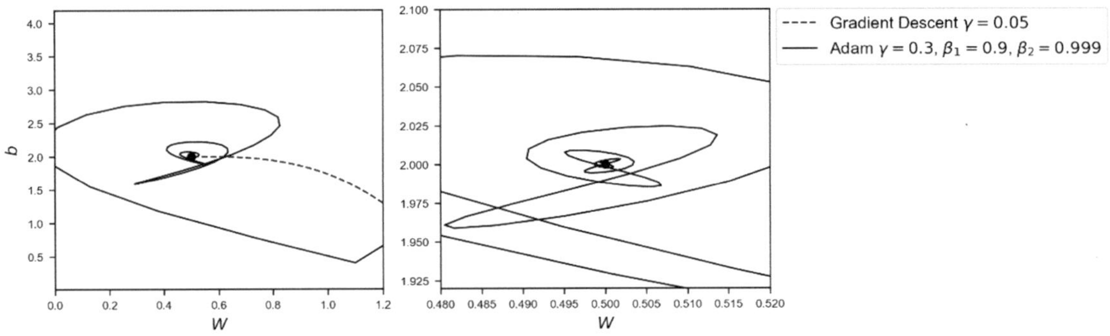

Figure 4-28. *Path that GD and Adam optimizers choose after 200 epochs. Note the amount of loops that Adam takes around the minimum. Regardless, the opimizer is really efficient compared to the plain GD.*

I haven't shown you all the optimizers together, since you would see a lot of loops, and that would not really teach you anything.

Which Optimizer Should I Use?

In short, you should use *Adam*. It is generally considered faster and better than other methods. This does not mean that is always the case. There are recent research papers that indicate how these optimizers could generalize poorly on new datasets (see, for example, Ashia C. Wilson, Rebecca Roelofs, Mitchell Stern, Nathan Srebro, and Benjamin Recht, "The Marginal Value of Adaptive Gradient Methods in Machine Learning," at `https://goo.gl/Nzc8bQ`). And there are other papers that endorse use of GD with a dynamical learning rate decay. It mostly depends on your problem. But, generally, Adam is a very good starting point.

Note If you are unsure about which optimizer to start with, use Adam. It is generally considered faster and better than other methods.

To give you an idea of how good Adam can be, let's apply it to the Zalando dataset. We will use a network with 4 hidden layers, each with 20 neurons. The model we will use is the one discussed at the very end of Chapter 3. Figure 4-29 shows how the cost function converges faster when using Adam optimization, compared to GD. Additionally, in 100 epochs, GD reaches an accuracy of 86%, while Adam reaches 90%. Note that I have not changed anything in the model, except the optimizer! For Adam, I have used the following code:

```
optimizer = tf.train.AdamOptimizer(learning_rate = learning_rate,
beta1 = 0.9, beta2 = 0.999, epsilon = 1e-8).minimize(cost)
```

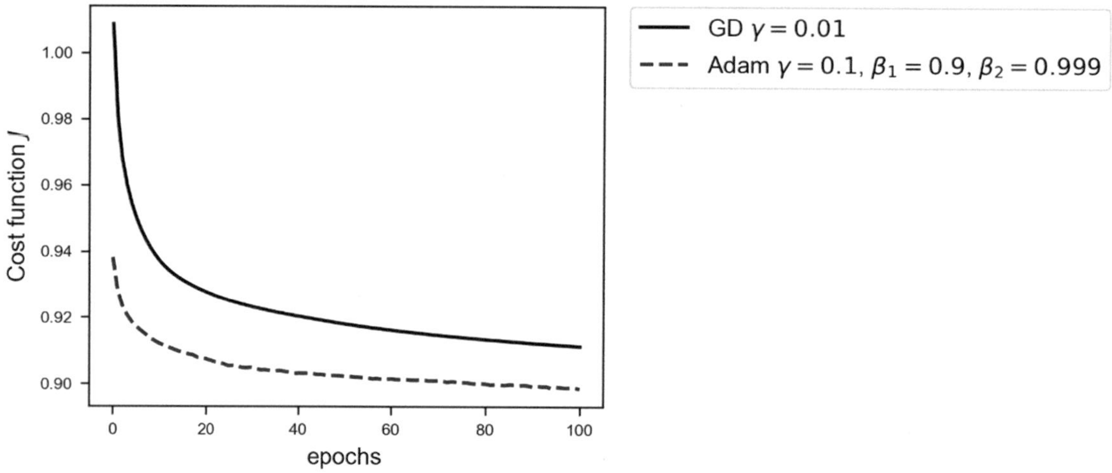

Figure 4-29. *Cost function of the Zalando dataset for a network with 4 hidden layers, each with 20 neurons. The continous line is plain GD, with a learning rate of $\gamma = 0.01$, and the dashed line is Adam optimization, with $\gamma = 0.1$, $\beta_1 = 0.9$, $\beta_2 = 0.999$, and $\epsilon = 10^{-8}$.*

As I suggested, when testing complex networks on big datasets, the Adam optimizer is a good place to start. But you should not limit your tests only to this optimizer. A test of other methods is always worthwhile. Perhaps another approach will work better.

Example of Self-Developed Optimizer

Before completing this chapter, I want to show you how to develop your own optimizer, using TensorFlow. This is very useful when you want to use an optimizer that is not directly available. Take, for example, the paper from Neelakantan et al.[4] In their research, they show how adding random noise to the gradients when training complex networks allows plain gradient descent to become very effective. They show how a 20-layer deep network can be trained efficiently with standard GD, even starting with poor weight initialization.

If you want to test this method, for example, you cannot use the `tf.GradientDescentOptimizer` function, because this implements a plain GD, without the noise described in the paper. To test it, you must have access to the gradients in the code, add the noise to them, and then update the weights with the modified gradients. We will not test their method here; that would require too much time and would go beyond the scope of this book, but is instructive to see how to develop plain gradient descent without using the `tf.GradientDescentOptimizer` and without calculating any derivative manually.

Before constructing our network, we must know the dataset we want to use and what problem (regression, classification, etc.) we want to solve. Let's make something new with a known dataset. Let's use the MNIST dataset we used in Chapter 2, but this time, lets perform multiclass classification using the `softmax` function, as we did on the Zalando dataset in Chapter 3. In Chapter 2, I discussed at length how to load the MNIST dataset with sklearn, so let's do it in a different (and more efficient) way here. TensorFlow has a method to download the MNIST dataset, including labels already one-hot encoded. This can be done simply with the following lines:

```
from tensorflow.examples.tutorials.mnist import input_data
mnist = input_data.read_data_sets("/tmp/data/", one_hot=True)
```

[4] A. Neelakantan et al., "Adding Gradient Noise Improves Learning for Very Deep Learning," conference paper presented at ICLR 2016, available at `https://arxiv.org/abs/1511.06807`.

This gives you the output

```
Successfully downloaded train-images-idx3-ubyte.gz 9912422 bytes.
Extracting /tmp/data/train-images-idx3-ubyte.gz
Successfully downloaded train-labels-idx1-ubyte.gz 28881 bytes.
Extracting /tmp/data/train-labels-idx1-ubyte.gz
Successfully downloaded t10k-images-idx3-ubyte.gz 1648877 bytes.
Extracting /tmp/data/t10k-images-idx3-ubyte.gz
Successfully downloaded t10k-labels-idx1-ubyte.gz 4542 bytes.
Extracting /tmp/data/t10k-labels-idx1-ubyte.gz
```

You will find the files in the folder (if you are using Windows) `c:\tmp\data`. If you want to change the location where the files are stored, you must change the `"/tmp/data"` parameter of the function `read_data_sets`. Now, as you probably remember from Chapter 2, the MNIST images are 28 × 28 pixels (784 pixels in total) images, in grayscale, so each pixel can assume a value from 0 to 254. Having this information, we can now construct our network.

```
X = tf.placeholder(tf.float32, [784, None]) # mnist data image of shape
28*28=784
Y = tf.placeholder(tf.float32, [10, None]) # 0-9 digits recognition => 10
classes
learning_rate_ = tf.placeholder(tf.float32, shape=())
W = tf.Variable(tf.zeros([10, 784]), dtype=tf.float32)
b = tf.Variable(tf.zeros([10,1]), dtype=tf.float32)

y_ = tf.nn.softmax(tf.matmul(W,X)+b)
cost = - tf.reduce_mean(Y * tf.log(y_)+(1-Y) * tf.log(1-y_))

grad_W, grad_b = tf.gradients(xs=[W, b], ys=cost)

new_W = W.assign(W - learning_rate_ * grad_W)
new_b = b.assign(b - learning_rate_ * grad_b)
```

The line

```
grad_W, grad_b = tf.gradients(xs=[W, b], ys=cost)
```

The preceding code gives you the tensors that contain the gradients of the `cost` node with respect to `W` and `b`, respectively. `TensorFlow` calculates them for you automatically! If you are interested to know how, check the official documentation of the `tf.gradients` function at https://goo.gl/XAjRkX. Now we must add nodes to the computational graph that updates the weights, and that is what we do with the lines

```
new_W = W.assign(W - learning_rate_ * grad_W)
new_b = b.assign(b - learning_rate_ * grad_b)
```

When we ask `TensorFlow` to evaluate the nodes `new_W` and `new_b` during our session, the weights and bias get updated. Finally, we must modify the function that evaluates the graph, using (for the mini-batch GD) the line

```
_, _, cost_ = sess.run([new_W, new_b , cost], feed_dict = {X: X_train_mini,
Y: y_train_mini, learning_rate_: learning_r})
```

In this way, the new nodes `new_W` and `new_b` get evaluated, and, in doing so, `TensorFlow` updates the weights and bias. The following lines are no longer required:

```
sess.run(optimizer, feed_dict = {X: X_train_mini, Y: y_train_mini,
learning_rate_: learning_r})
```

because we don't have the `optimizer` node anymore. The entire function you require is the following:

```
def run_model_mb(minibatch_size, training_epochs, features, classes,
logging_step = 100, learning_r = 0.001):
    sess = tf.Session()
    sess.run(tf.global_variables_initializer())

    total_batch = int(mnist.train.num_examples/minibatch_size)

    cost_history = []
    accuracy_history = []

    for epoch in range(training_epochs+1):
        for i in range(total_batch):
            batch_xs, batch_ys = mnist.train.next_batch(minibatch_size)
            batch_xs_t = batch_xs.T
            batch_ys_t = batch_ys.T
```

```
            _, _, cost_ = sess.run([new_W, new_b ,
                                    cost], feed_dict = {X: batch_xs_t,
                                    Y: batch_ys_t, learning_rate_:
                                    learning_r})

        cost_ = sess.run(cost, feed_dict={ X:features, Y: classes})
        accuracy_ = sess.run(accuracy, feed_dict={ X:features, Y: classes})
        cost_history = np.append(cost_history, cost_)
        accuracy_history = np.append(accuracy_history, accuracy_)

        if (epoch % logging_step == 0):
                print("Reached epoch",epoch,"cost J =", cost_)
                print ("Accuracy:", accuracy_)

    return sess, cost_history, accuracy_history
```

This function is slightly different than those we have used before, because here, I used some features of TensorFlow to make our life a bit easier. In particular, the line

```
total_batch = int(mnist.train.num_examples/minibatch_size)
```

calculates the total number of mini-batches that we have, because the variable `mnist.train.num_examples` contains the number of observations we have at our disposal. Then to get the batches, we use

```
batch_xs, batch_ys = mnist.train.next_batch(minibatch_size)
```

This returns two tensors, containing the training input data (`batch_xs`) and the one-hot encoded labels (`batch_ys`). We then simply have to transpose them, because `TensorFlow` returns the array with observations as rows. We do that with the lines

```
batch_xs_t = batch_xs.T
batch_ys_t = batch_ys.T
```

I also added to the function the accuracy calculation, to make it easier to see how well we are doing. Letting the model run with the python call

```
sess, cost_history, accuracy_history = run_model (100, 50, X_train_tr,
labels_, logging_step = 10, learning_r = 0.01)
```

will give you the following output:

```
Reached epoch 0 cost J = 1.06549
Accuracy: 0.773786
Reached epoch 10 cost J = 0.972171
Accuracy: 0.853371
Reached epoch 20 cost J = 0.961519
Accuracy: 0.869357
Reached epoch 30 cost J = 0.956766
Accuracy: 0.877814
Reached epoch 40 cost J = 0.953982
Accuracy: 0.883143
Reached epoch 50 cost J = 0.952118
Accuracy: 0.886386
```

This model will work exactly as the one with the gradient descent optimizer provided by TensorFlow. But now, you have access to the gradients, and you can modify them, add noise to them (if you want to try), and so on. In Figure 4-30, you can see the cost function behavior (on the right side) and the accuracy vs. the epochs (on the left side) that we get with this model.

Note TensorFlow is a great library, because it gives you the flexibility to build your models basically from scratch. But it is important to understand how the different methods work, to be able to use the library to its fullest. You need to have a very good understanding of the mathematics behind the algorithms, to be able to tune them or to develop variations.

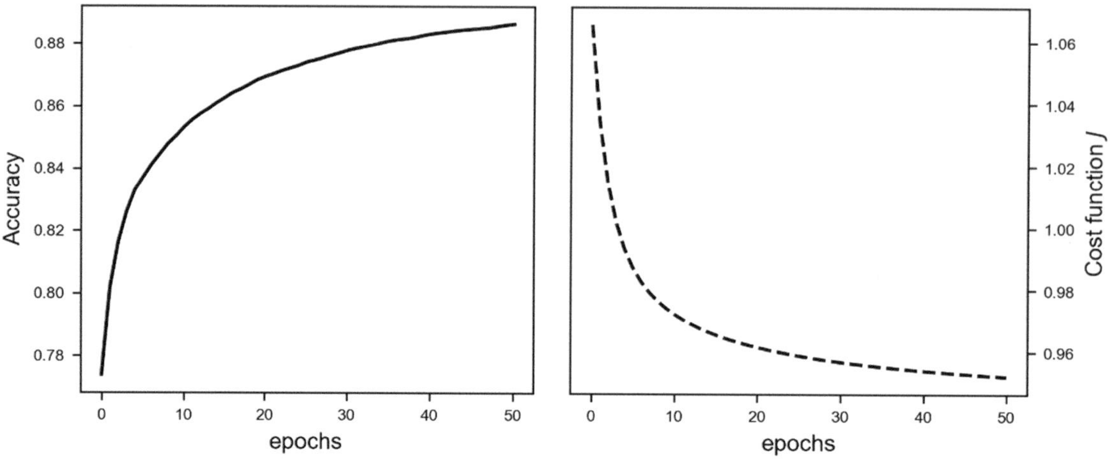

***Figure 4-30.** Cost function behavior (right) and the accuracy vs. epochs (left) for the neural network with one neuron and with the gradient descent developed with the `tf.gradients` function*

CHAPTER 5

Regularization

In this chapter, you will look at a very important technique often used when training deep networks: regularization. You will look at techniques such as the ℓ_2 and ℓ_1 methods, dropout, and early stopping. You will see how these methods help avoid the problem of overfitting and achieve much better results from your models, when applied correctly. You will look at the mathematics behind the methods and at how to implement it in Python and TensorFlow correctly.

Complex Networks and Overfitting

In the previous chapters, you have learned how to build and train complex networks. One of the most common problems you will encounter when using complex networks is overfitting. Review Chapter 3 for an overview of what overfitting is. In this chapter, you will face an extreme case of overfitting, and I will discuss a few strategies to avoid it. A perfect dataset to study this problem is the Boston housing price dataset discussed in Chapter 2. Let's review how to get the data (for a more detailed discussion, please refer to Chapter 2). Start with the packages we need.

```
import matplotlib.pyplot as plt
%matplotlib inline

import tensorflow as tf
import numpy as np

from sklearn.datasets import load_boston
import sklearn.linear_model as sk
```


U. Michelucci, *Applied Deep Learning*, https://doi.org/10.1007/978-1-4842-3790-8_5

Then import the dataset.

```
boston = load_boston()
features = np.array(boston.data)
target = np.array(boston.target)
```

The dataset has 13 features (contained in the `features` `NumPy` array) and the house price contained in the `target` `NumPy` array. As in Chapter 2, to normalize the features, we will use the function

```
def normalize(dataset):
    mu = np.mean(dataset, axis = 0)
    sigma = np.std(dataset, axis = 0)
    return (dataset-mu)/sigma
```

To conclude our dataset preparation, let's normalize it and then create training and a dev dataset.

```
features_norm = normalize(features)
np.random.seed(42)
rnd = np.random.rand(len(features_norm)) < 0.8

train_x = np.transpose(features_norm[rnd])
train_y = np.transpose(target[rnd])
dev_x = np.transpose(features_norm[~rnd])
dev_y = np.transpose(target[~rnd])
```

The `np.random.seed(42)` is there so that you will always get the same `training` and dev dataset (this way, your results will be reproducible). Now, let's reshape the arrays we need.

```
train_y = train_y.reshape(1,len(train_y))
dev_y = dev_y.reshape(1,len(dev_y))
```

Next, let's build a complex neural network with 4 layers and 20 neurons for each layer. Define the following function to build each layer:

```
def create_layer (X, n, activation):
    ndim = int(X.shape[0])
    stddev = 2.0 / np.sqrt(ndim)
    initialization = tf.truncated_normal((n, ndim), stddev = stddev)
```

```
    W = tf.Variable(initialization)
    b = tf.Variable(tf.zeros([n,1]))
    Z = tf.matmul(W,X)+b
    return activation(Z), W, b
```

Note that this time, we return the weights tensor W and the bias b. We will need them when implementing regularization. You have already seen this function at the end of Chapter 3, so you should understand what it does. We use the He initialization here, because we will use ReLU activation functions. The network can be created with the following code:

```
tf.reset_default_graph()

n_dim = 13
n1 = 20
n2 = 20
n3 = 20
n4 = 20
n_outputs = 1

tf.set_random_seed(5)

X = tf.placeholder(tf.float32, [n_dim, None])
Y = tf.placeholder(tf.float32, [1, None])

learning_rate = tf.placeholder(tf.float32, shape=())

hidden1, W1, b1 = create_layer (X, n1, activation = tf.nn.relu)
hidden2, W2, b2 = create_layer (hidden1, n2, activation = tf.nn.relu)
hidden3, W3, b3 = create_layer (hidden2, n3, activation = tf.nn.relu)
hidden4, W4, b4 = create_layer (hidden3, n4, activation = tf.nn.relu)
y_, W5, b5 = create_layer (hidden4, n_outputs, activation = tf.identity)

cost = tf.reduce_mean(tf.square(y_-Y))

optimizer = tf.train.AdamOptimizer(learning_rate = learning_rate, beta1 =
0.9, beta2 = 0.999, epsilon = 1e-8).minimize(cost)
```

In our output layer, we have one neuron with the identity activation function for regression. Additionally, we use the Adam optimizer, as suggested in Chapter 4. Now let's run the model with this code:

```
sess = tf.Session()
sess.run(tf.global_variables_initializer())

cost_train_history = []
cost_dev_history = []
for epoch in range(10000+1):

    sess.run(optimizer, feed_dict = {X: train_x, Y: train_y, learning_rate:
    0.001})
    cost_train_ = sess.run(cost, feed_dict={ X:train_x, Y: train_y,
    learning_rate: 0.001})
    cost_dev_ = sess.run(cost, feed_dict={ X:dev_x, Y: dev_y, learning_
    rate: 0.001})
    cost_train_history = np.append(cost_train_history, cost_train_)
    cost_dev_history = np.append(cost_test_history, cost_test_)

    if (epoch % 1000 == 0):
        print("Reached epoch",epoch,"cost J(train) =", cost_train_)
        print("Reached epoch",epoch,"cost J(test) =", cost_test_)
```

As you may have noticed, there are a few differences from what we did before. To make things simpler, I avoided writing a function and simply hard-coded all the values in the code, because, in this case, we don't need to tune the parameters much. I am not using mini-batches here, because we have only a few hundred observations, and I am calculating the MSE (mean squared error) for both training and dev datasets with the following lines:

```
cost_train_ = sess.run(cost, feed_dict={ X:train_x, Y: train_y, learning_
rate: 0.001})
cost_dev_ = sess.run(cost, feed_dict={ X:dev_x, Y: dev_y, learning_rate:
0.001})
```

In this way, we can check what is happening on both datasets at the same time. Now if you let the code run and plot the two MSEs, one for the training, which we will indicate by MSE_{train}, and one for the dev dataset, indicated by MSE_{dev}, we get Figure 5-1.

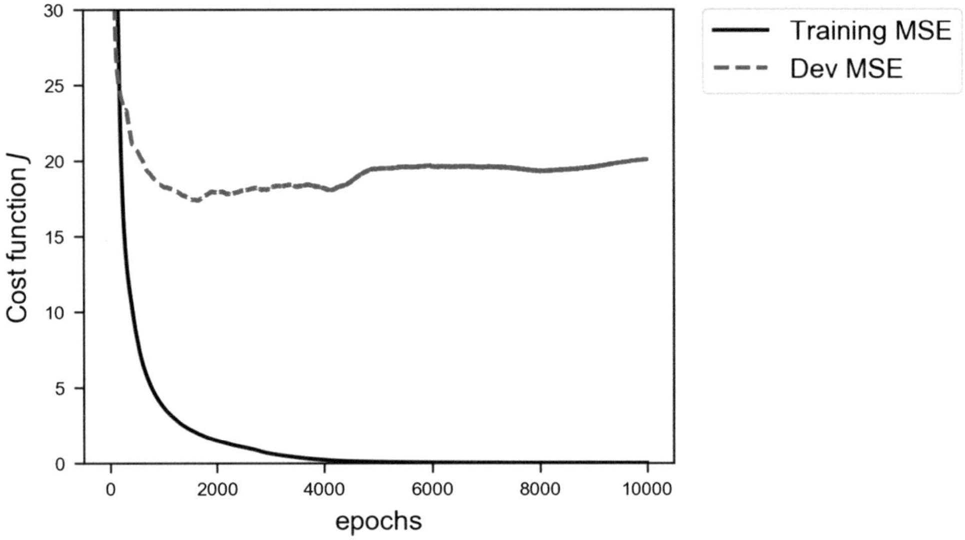

Figure 5-1. *MSE for the training (continuous line) and the dev dataset (dashed line) for the neural network with 4 layers, each having 20 neurons*

You will notice how the training error goes down to zero, while the dev error remains constant at around a value of roughly 20, after dropping rapidly at the beginning. If you remember the introduction to basic error analysis, you should know that this means that we are in a regime of extreme overfitting (when $MSE_{train} \ll MSE_{dev}$). The error on the training dataset is practically zero, while the one for the dev dataset is not. The model cannot generalize at all when applied to new data. In Figure 5-2, you can see the predicted value plotted vs. the real value. You will notice how in the plot at the left, for the training data, the prediction is almost perfect, while the plot on the right, for the dev dataset, is not that good. You will remember that a perfect model would give you predicted values exactly equal to the measured ones. So, while plotting one vs. the other, they would all lie on the 45 degree line of the plot, as in Figure 5-2, on the left.

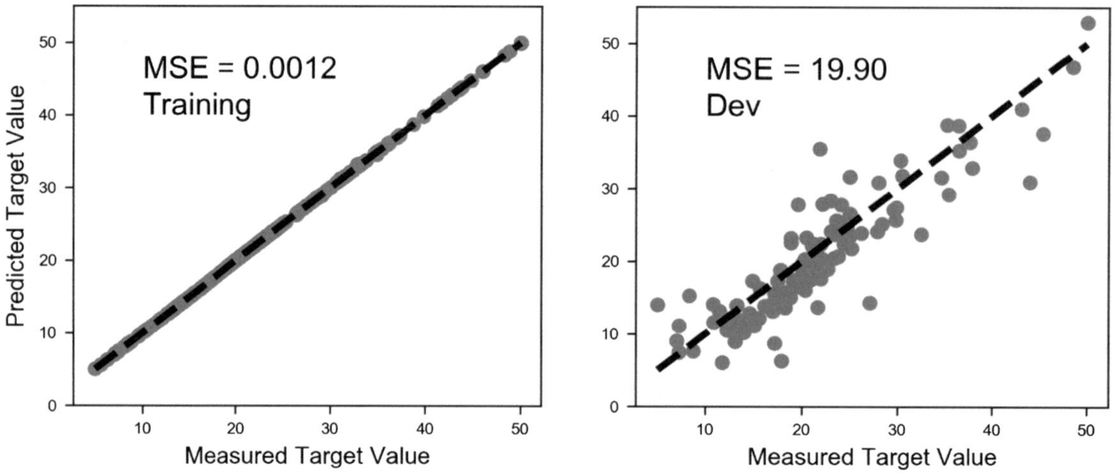

Figure 5-2. *Predicted value vs. the real value for the target variable (the house price). You will notice how in the left-hand plot, for the training data, the prediction is almost perfect, while on the plot on the right, for the dev dataset, the predictions are more spread.*

What can we do in this case to avoid the problem of overfitting? One solution, of course, would be to reduce the complexity of the network, that is, reducing the number of layers and/or the number of neurons in each layer. But, as you can imagine, this strategy is very time-consuming. You must try several network architectures to see how the training error and the dev error behave. In this case, this is still a viable solution, but if you are working on a problem for which the training phase takes several days, this can be quite difficult and extremely time-consuming. Several strategies have been developed to deal with this problem. The most common is called regularization, the focus of this chapter.

What Is Regularization?

Before going into the different methods, I would like to quickly discuss what the deep-learning community understands by the term *regularization*. The term has deeply (pun intended) evolved over time. For example, in the traditional sense (from the '90s), the term is reserved only to as a penalty term in the loss function (Christopher M. Bishop, *Neural Networks for Pattern Recognition*, New York: Oxford University Press, 1995). Lately the term has gained a much more broader meaning. For example, Ian Goodfellow et al. (*Deep Learning*, Cambridge, MA, MIT Press, 2016) define it as "any modification we make to a learning algorithm that is intended to reduce its test error but not its training error." Jan Kukačka et al. ("Regularization for deep learning: a taxonomy," arXiv:1710.10686v1, available at `https://goo.gl/wNkjXz`) generalize the term even further and offer the following definition: "Regularization is any supplementary technique that aims at making the model generalize better, i.e., produce better results on the test set." So, be aware when using the term, and always be precise about what you mean.

You may also have heard or read the claim that regularization has been developed to fight overfitting. This is also a way of understanding it. Remember: A model that is overfitting the training dataset is not generalizing well to new data. This definition can also be found online, along with all the others. Although merely definitions, it is important to have a familiarity with them, so that you may better understand what is meant when reading papers or books. This is a very active research area, and to give you an idea, Kukačka et al., in their review paper referenced above, list 58 different regularization methods. Yes, 58; that is not a typo. But it is important to understand that in their general definition, SGD (stochastic gradient descent) also is considered a regularization method, something not everyone agrees on. So be warned, when reading research material, check what is understood by the term *regularization*.

In this chapter, you will look at the three most common and well-known methods: ℓ_1, ℓ_2, and dropout, and I will briefly discuss early stopping, although this method does not, technically speaking, fight overfitting. ℓ_1 and ℓ_2 achieve a so-called weight decay, by adding a so-called regularization term to the cost function, while dropout simply removes, in a random fashion, nodes from the network during the training phase. To understand the three methods properly, we must study them in detail. Let's start with probably the most instructive one: ℓ_2 regularization.

At the end of the chapter, we will explore a few other ideas about how to fight overfitting and get the model to generalize better. Instead of changing or modifying the model or the learning algorithm, we will consider strategies with the idea of modifying the training data, to make learning more effective.

About Network Complexity

I would like to spend a few moments discussing briefly a term I've used very often: network complexity. You have read here, as you can almost anywhere, that with regularization, you want to reduce network complexity. But what does that really mean? Actually, it is relatively difficult to give a definition of network complexity, so much so that no one does it. You can find several research papers on the problem of model complexity (note that I did not say *network* complexity), with roots in information theory. You will see in this chapter how, for example, the number of weights that is different than zero will change dramatically with the number of epochs, with the optimization algorithm, and so on, therefore making this vaguely intuitive concept of complexity dependent also on how long you train your model. To make a long story short, the term *network complexity* should be used only on an intuitive level, because, theoretically, it is a very complex concept to define. A complete discussion of the subject would be way beyond the scope of this book.

ℓ_p Norm

Before we start studying what ℓ_1 and ℓ_2 regularization are, I must introduce the ℓ_p norm notation. We define the ℓ_p norm of a vector $\boldsymbol{x}$ with x_i components as

$$\|\boldsymbol{x}_p\| = \sqrt[p]{\sum_i |x_i|^p} \qquad p \in \mathbb{R}$$

where the sum is performed over all components of the vector $\boldsymbol{x}$.

Let's begin with the most instructive norm: the ℓ_2.

ℓ_2 Regularization

One of the most common regularization methods, ℓ_2 regularization consists of adding a term to the cost function that has the goal of effectively reducing the capacity of the network to adapt to complex datasets. Let's first have a look at the mathematics behind the method.

Theory of ℓ_2 Regularization

When doing plain regression, you will remember from Chapter 2, our cost function is simply the MSE

$$J(\boldsymbol{w}) = \frac{1}{m}\sum_{i=1}^{m}(y_i - \hat{y}_i)^2$$

where y_i is our measured target variable, $\hat{y}_i$ is the predicted value, $\boldsymbol{w}$ is the vector of all the weights of our network, including the bias, and m is the number of observations. Now let's define a new cost function $\tilde{J}(\boldsymbol{w}, b)$.

$$\tilde{J}(\boldsymbol{w}) = J(\boldsymbol{w}) + \frac{\lambda}{2m}|\boldsymbol{w}|^2{}_2$$

This additional term,

$$\frac{\lambda}{2m}\|\boldsymbol{w}\|^2{}_2$$

is called a regularization term and is nothing else than the ℓ_2-norm squared of $\boldsymbol{w}$ multiplied by a constant factor $\lambda/2m$. λ is called the regularization parameter.

Note The new regularization parameter, λ, is a new hyperparameter that you must tune to find the optimal value.

Now let's try to get an intuitive understanding of what the effect of this term on the GD (gradient descent) algorithm is. Let's consider the updated equation for the weight w_j

$$w_{j,[n+1]} = w_{j,[n]} - \gamma \frac{\partial \tilde{J}(\boldsymbol{w}_{[n]})}{\partial w_j} = w_{j,[n]} - \gamma \frac{\partial J(\boldsymbol{w}_{[n]})}{\partial w_j} - \frac{\gamma\lambda}{m} w_{j,[n]}$$

Since

$$\frac{\partial}{\partial w_j}\|\boldsymbol{w}\|^2{}_2 = 2w_j$$

this gives us

$$w_{j,[n+1]} = w_{j,[n]}\left(1 - \frac{\gamma\lambda}{m}\right) - \lambda \frac{\partial J(\boldsymbol{w}_{[n]})}{\partial w_j}$$

This is the equation that we must use for the weights update. The difference with the one we already know from plain GD is that, now, the weight $w_{j,[n]}$ is multiplied with a constant $1-\frac{\gamma\lambda}{m}<1$, and, therefore, this has the effect of effectively shifting the weight values during the update toward zero, making the network less complex (intuitively), thus fighting overfitting. Let's try to see what is really happening to the weights, by applying the method to the Boston housing dataset.

tensorflow Implementation

The implementation in `tensorflow` is quite easy. Remember: We must calculate the additional term $\|\boldsymbol{w}\|_2^2$, then add it to the cost function. The model construction remains almost the same. We can do it with the following code:

```
tf.reset_default_graph()

n_dim = 13
n1 = 20
n2 = 20
n3 = 20
n4 = 20
n_outputs = 1

tf.set_random_seed(5)

X = tf.placeholder(tf.float32, [n_dim, None])
Y = tf.placeholder(tf.float32, [1, None])

learning_rate = tf.placeholder(tf.float32, shape=())

hidden1, W1, b1 = create_layer (X, n1, activation = tf.nn.relu)
hidden2, W2, b2 = create_layer (hidden1, n2, activation = tf.nn.relu)
hidden3, W3, b3 = create_layer (hidden2, n3, activation = tf.nn.relu)
hidden4, W4, b4 = create_layer (hidden3, n4, activation = tf.nn.relu)
y_, W5, b5 = create_layer (hidden4, n_outputs, activation = tf.identity)

lambd = tf.placeholder(tf.float32, shape=())
reg = tf.nn.l2_loss(W1) + tf.nn.l2_loss(W2) + tf.nn.l2_loss(W3) + \
          tf.nn.l2_loss(W4) + tf.nn.l2_loss(W5)

cost_mse = tf.reduce_mean(tf.square(y_-Y))
cost = tf.reduce_mean(cost_mse + lambd*reg)
```

```
optimizer = tf.train.AdamOptimizer(learning_rate = learning_rate, beta1 =
0.9, beta2 = 0.999, epsilon = 1e-8).minimize(cost)
```

For our new regularization parameter λ, we create a placeholder.

```
lambd = tf.placeholder(tf.float32, shape=())
```

Remember that in Python, lambda is a reserved word, so we cannot use it. This is the reason we use lambd. Then we calculate our regularization term $\|\boldsymbol{w}\|_2^2$.

```
reg = tf.nn.l2_loss(W1) + tf.nn.l2_loss(W2) + tf.nn.l2_loss(W3) + \
        tf.nn.l2_loss(W4) + tf.nn.l2_loss(W5)
```

with the useful TensorFlow function `tf.nn.l2_loss()`, and then we add it to the MSE function `cost_mse`.

```
cost_mse = tf.reduce_mean(tf.square(y_-Y))
cost = tf.reduce_mean(cost_mse + lambd*reg)
```

Now our `cost` tensor will contain the MSE plus the regularization term. Then we simply need to train the network and observe what happens. To train the network, we use this function:

```
def model(training_epochs, features, target, logging_step = 100, learning_r
= 0.001, lambd_val = 0.1):
    sess = tf.Session()
    sess.run(tf.global_variables_initializer())

    cost_history = []
    for epoch in range(training_epochs+1):

        sess.run(optimizer, feed_dict = {X: features, Y: target, learning_
        rate: learning_r, lambd: lambd_val})
        cost_ = sess.run(cost_mse, feed_dict={ X:features, Y: target,
        learning_rate: learning_r, lambd: lambd_val})
        cost_history = np.append(cost_history, cost_)

        if (epoch % logging_step == 0):
                pred_y_test = sess.run(y_, feed_dict = {X: test_x, Y:
                test_y})
                print("Reached epoch",epoch,"cost J =", cost_)
```

```
            print("Training MSE = ", cost_)
            print("Dev MSE      = ", sess.run(cost_mse, feed_dict = {X:
            test_x, Y: test_y}))

    return sess, cost_history
```

This time, I printed the MSE coming from the training (MSE_{train}) and dev (MSE_{dev}) datasets, to check what is going on. As mentioned, applying this method makes many weights go to zero, effectively reducing the complexity of the network and, therefore, fighting overfitting. Let's run the model for $\lambda = 0$, without regularization, and for $\lambda = 10.0$. We can run our model with the following code:

```
sess, cost_history = model(learning_r = 0.01,
                                training_epochs = 5000,
                                features = train_x,
                                target = train_y,
                                logging_step = 5000,
                                lambd_val = 0.0)
```

which gives us

```
Reached epoch 0 cost J = 238.378
Training MSE = 238.378
Dev MSE = 205.561
Reached epoch 5000 cost J = 0.00527479
Training MSE = 0.00527479
Dev MSE = 28.401
```

As expected, we are in an extreme overfitting regime ($MSE_{train} \ll MSE_{dev}$) after 5000 epochs. Now let's try it with $\lambda = 10$.

```
sess, cost_history = model(learning_r = 0.01,
                                training_epochs = 5000,
                                features = train_x,
                                target = train_y,
                                logging_step = 5000,
                                lambd_val = 10.0)
```

This gives the result

```
Reached epoch 0 cost J = 248.026
Training MSE = 248.026
Dev MSE = 214.921
Reached epoch 5000 cost J = 23.795
Training MSE = 23.795
Dev MSE = 21.6406
```

Now we are no more in an overfitting regime, because the two MSE values are of the same order of magnitude. The best way of checking what is going on is to study the weights distribution for each layer. In Figure 5-3, the weights distribution for the first 4 layers are plotted. The light gray histogram is for the weights without regularization, and the darker (and much more concentrated around zero) area is for the weights with regularization. I neglected layer 5, since it is the output layer.

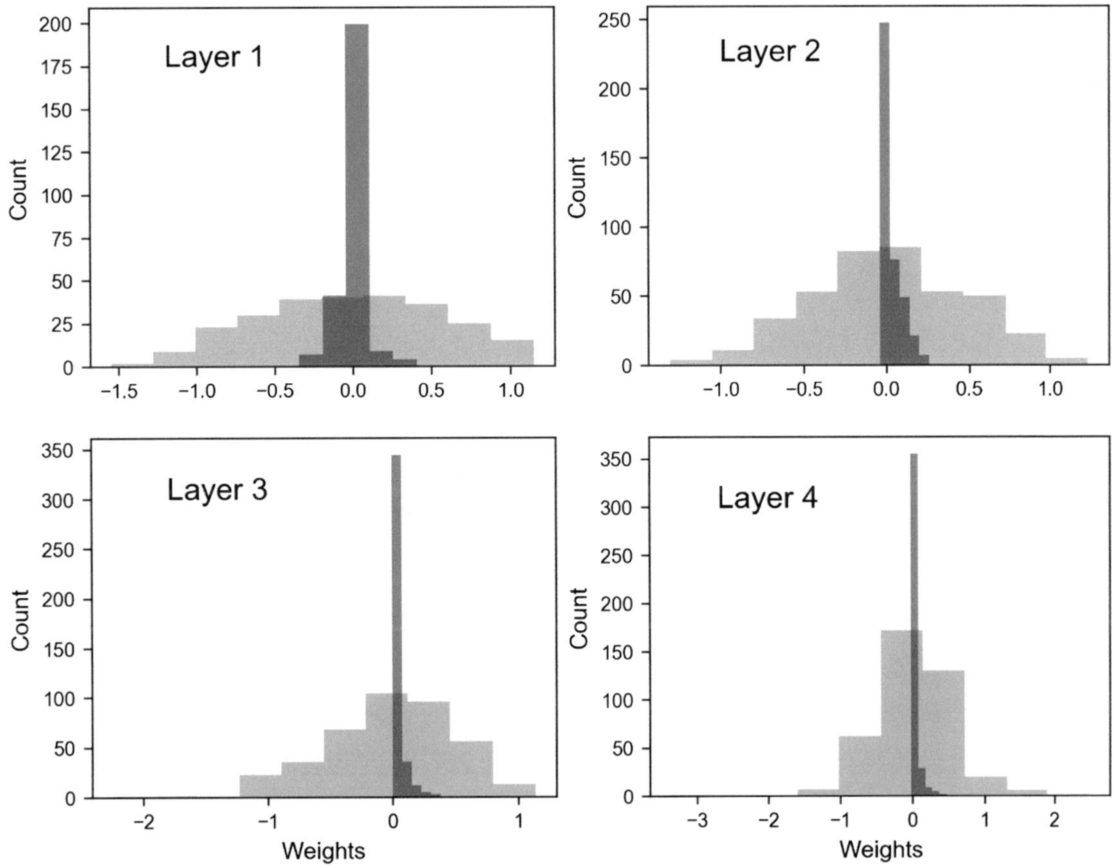

Figure 5-3. *Weights distribution for each layer*

You can clearly see how the weights, when we apply regularization, are much more concentrated around zero, meaning they are much smaller than without regularization. This makes the weight decay effect of regularization very evident. I would like to briefly take the chance to make another brief digression on network complexity. I said that this method reduces the network complexity. I told you in Chapter 3 that you can consider the number of learnable parameters an indication of the complexity of a network, but I also warned you that this can be very misleading. Now I would like to show you why. You will remember from Chapter 3 that the total number of learnable parameters we have in a network like the one we are using here is determined by the formula

$$Q = \sum_{j=1}^{L} n_l \left(n_{l-1} + 1 \right)$$

where n_l is the number of neurons in layer l, and L is the total number of layers, including the output layer. In our case, we have an input layer with 13 features, then 4 layers, each with 20 neurons, and then an output layer with 1 neuron. Therefore, Q is given by

$$Q = 20 \times (13+1) + 20 \times (20+1) + 20 \times (20+1) + 20 \times (20+1) + 1 \times (20+1) = 1561$$

Q is quite a big number. But already, without regularization, it is interesting to note that we have roughly 48% of the weights that after 10,000 epochs are less than 10^{-10}, so, effectively, zero. This is the reason I warned you about talking about complexity in terms of numbers of learnable parameters. Additionally, using regularization will change the scenario completely. Complexity is a difficult concept to define: it depends on many things, among others, architecture, optimization algorithm, cost function, and number of epochs trained.

Note Defining the complexity of a network only in terms of number of weights is not completely correct. The total number of weights gives an idea, but it can be quite misleading, because many may be zero after the training, effectively disappearing from the network, and making it less complex. It is more correct to talk about "Model Complexity," instead of network complexity, because many more aspects are involved than simply how many neurons or layers the network has.

Incredibly enough, only half of the weights play a role in the predictions in the end. This is the reason I told you in Chapter 3 that defining the network complexity only with the parameter Q is misleading. Given your problem, your loss function, and optimizer, you may well end up with a network that when trained is much simpler than it was at construction phase. So be very careful when using the term *complexity* in the deep learning world. Be aware of the subtleties involved.

To give you an idea of how effective regularization is in reducing the weights, see Table 5-1, in which the percentage of weights less than 1e-3 is compared with and without regularization after 1000 epochs in each layer.

Table 5-1. *Percentage of Weights Less Than 1e-3 with and Without Regularization After 1000 Epochs*

Layer	% of Weights Less Than 1e-3 for $\lambda = 0$	% of Weights Less Than 1e-3 for $\lambda = 3$
1	0.0	20.0
2	0.25	41.5
3	0.75	60.5
4	0.25	66.0
5	0.0	35.0

But how should we choose λ? To get an idea (repeat after me: "In the deep learning world, there is no universal rule."), it is useful to see what is happening when varying the parameter λ to your optimizing metric (in this case, the MSE). In Figure 5-4, you can see the behavior of MSE_{train} (continuous line) and MSE_{dev} (dashed) datasets for our network varying λ after 1000 epochs.

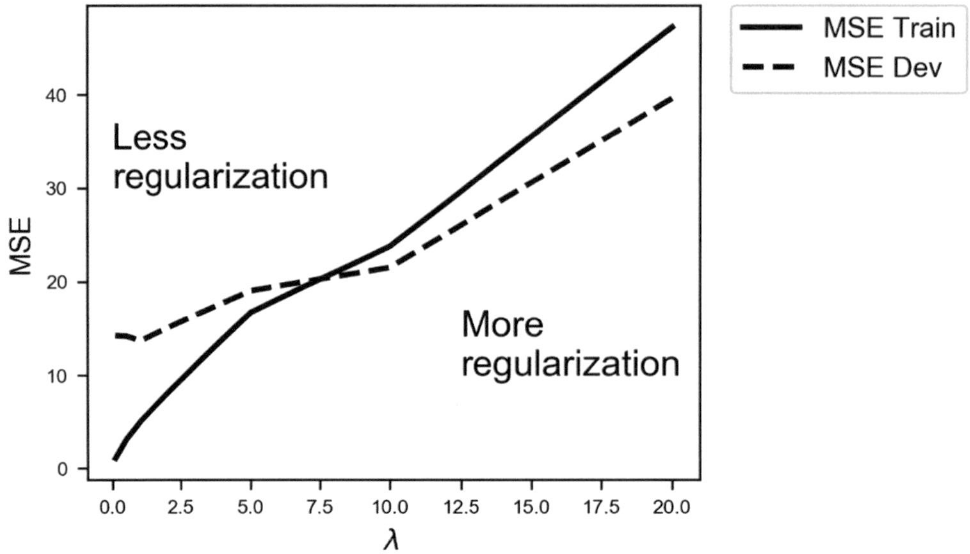

***Figure 5-4.** Behavior of the MSE for the training (continuous line) dataset and for the dev (dashed) dataset for our network varying λ.*

As you can see with small values of λ (effectively without regularization), we are in an overfitting regime ($MSE_{train} \ll MSE_{dev}$): slowly the MSE_{train} increases, while the MSE_{dev} remains roughly constant. Until $\lambda \approx 7.5$, the model overfits the training data, then the two values cross, and the overfitting finishes. After that, they grow together, at which point the model cannot capture the fine data structures anymore. After the crossing of the lines, the model becomes too simple to capture the features of the problem, and, therefore, the errors grow together, and the error on the training dataset gets bigger, because the model doesn't even fit the training data well. In this specific case, a good value to choose for λ would be about 7.5, nearly the value when the two lines cross, because there, you are no longer in an overfitting region, as $MSE_{train} \approx MSE_{dev}$. Remember: The main goal of having the regularization term is to get a model that generalizes in the best way possible when applied to new data. You can look at it in an even different way: a value of $\lambda \approx 7.5$ gives you the minimum of MSE_{dev} outside the overfitting region (for $\lambda \lesssim 7.5$); therefore, it would be a good choice. Note that you may observe for your problems a very different behavior for your optimizing metric, so you will have to decide on a case-by-case basis what the best value for λ is that works for you.

Note A good way to estimate the optimal value of the regularization parameter λ is to plot your optimizing metric (in this example, the MSE) for the training and dev datasets and observe how they behave for various values of λ. Then choose the value that gives the minimum of your optimizing metric on the dev dataset and, at the same time, gives you a model that no longer overfits your training data.

I would like now to show you the effects of ℓ_2 regularization in an even more visual way. Let's consider a dataset generated with the following code:

```
nobs = 30

np.random.seed(42)

xx1 = np.array([np.random.normal(0.3,0.15) for i in range (0,nobs)])
yy1 = np.array([np.random.normal(0.3,0.15) for i in range (0,nobs)])
xx2 = np.array([np.random.normal(0.1,0.1) for i in range (0,nobs)])
yy2 = np.array([np.random.normal(0.3,0.1) for i in range (0,nobs)])

c1_ = np.c_[xx1.ravel(), yy1.ravel()]
c2_ = np.c_[xx2.ravel(), yy2.ravel()]

c = np.concatenate([c1_,c2_])

yy1_ = np.full(nobs, 0, dtype=int)
yy2_ = np.full(nobs, 1, dtype=int)
yyL = np.concatenate((yy1_, yy2_), axis = 0)

train_x = c.T
train_y = yyL.reshape(1,60)
```

Our dataset has two features: *x* and *y*. We generate two groups of points, `xx1,yy1` and `xx2,yy2`, from a normal distribution. To the first group, we assign the label 0 (contained in the array `yy1_`), and to the second, the label 1 (in the array `yy2_`). Now let's use a network such as that described before (with 4 layers, each having 20 neurons) to do some binary classification on this dataset. We can take the same code given before, modifying the output layer and the cost function. You will remember that for binary classification, we need one neuron in the output layer with the sigmoid activation function

```
y_, W5, b5 = create_layer (hidden4, n_outputs, activation = tf.sigmoid)
```

and the following cost function:

```
cost_class = - tf.reduce_mean(Y * tf.log(y_)+(1-Y) * tf.log(1-y_))
cost = tf.reduce_mean(cost_class + lambd*reg)
```

All the rest remains the same as was described earlier. Let's plot the decision boundary[1] for this problem. This means that we will run our network on our dataset with the code

```
sess, cost_history = model(learning_r = 0.005,
                            training_epochs = 100,
                            features = train_x,
                            target = train_y,
                            logging_step = 10,
                            lambd_val = 0.0)
```

In Figure 5-5, you can see our datasets where the white points are of the first class and the black of the second. The gray area is the zone that the network classifies as being of one class, and the white of the other. You can see that the network is able to capture the complex structure of our data in a flexible way.

[1]In a statistical-classification problem with two classes, a decision boundary, or decision surface, is a surface that partitions the underlying space into two sets, one for each class. (Source: Wikipedia, `https://goo.gl/E5nELL`).

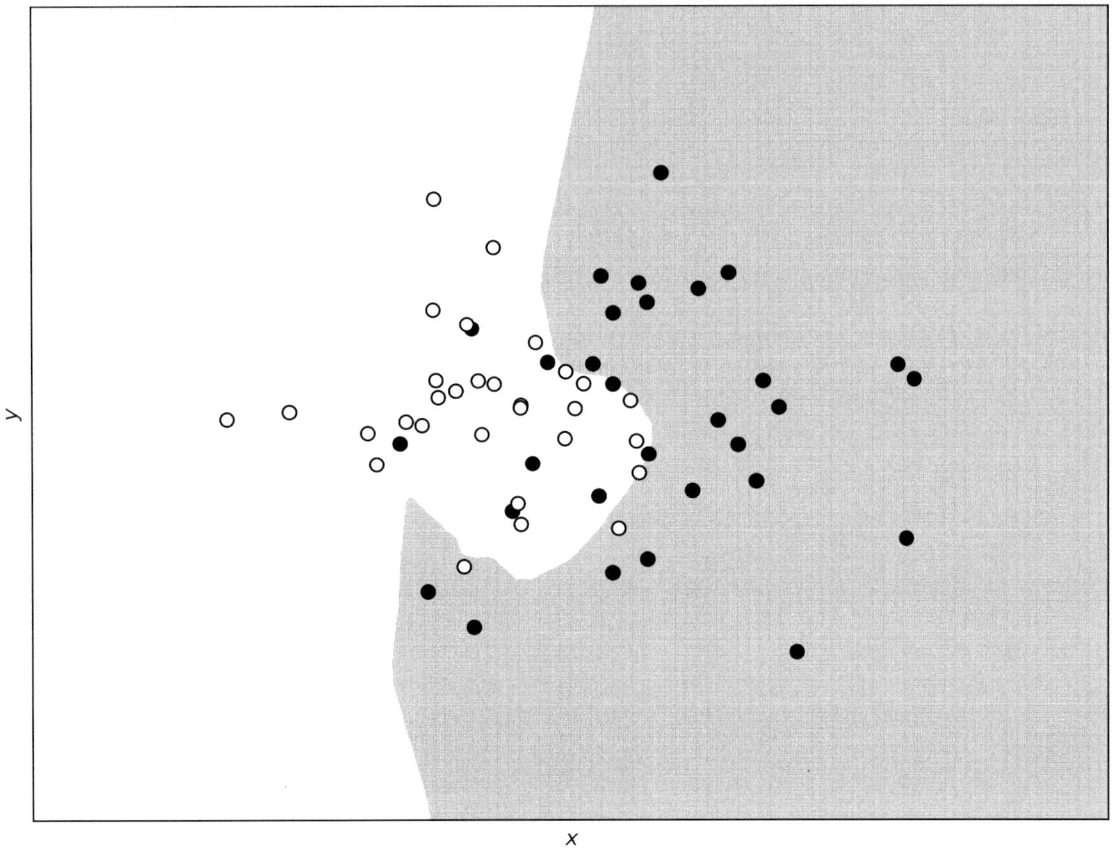

Figure 5-5. *Decision boundary without regularization. White points are of the first class, and the black of the second.*

Now let's apply regularization to the network, exactly as we did before, and see how the decision boundary is modified. Here, we will use a regularization parameter $\lambda = 0.1$.

You can clearly see how in Figure 5-6 the decision boundary is almost linear and not able to capture the complex structure of our data anymore. Exactly what we expected: the regularization term makes the model simpler and, therefore, less able to capture the fine structures.

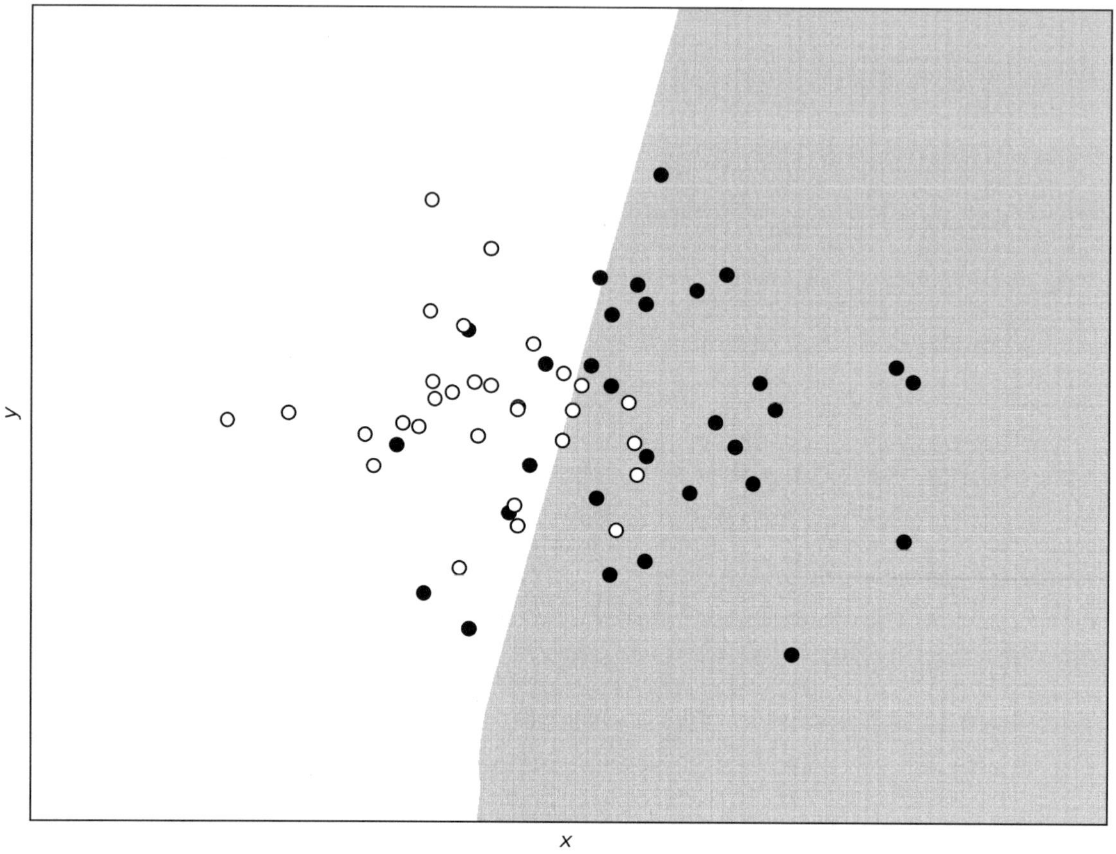

Figure 5-6. *Decision boundary, as predicted by the network with ℓ_2 regularization and with a regularization parameter $\lambda = 0.1$*

It is interesting to compare the decision boundary of our network with the result of logistic regression with just one neuron. I will not put the code here, for space considerations, but if you compare the two decision boundaries in Figure 5-7 (the one coming from the network with one neuron is linear), you can see that they are almost the same. A regularization term of $\lambda = 0.1$ gives effectively the same results as a network with just one neuron.

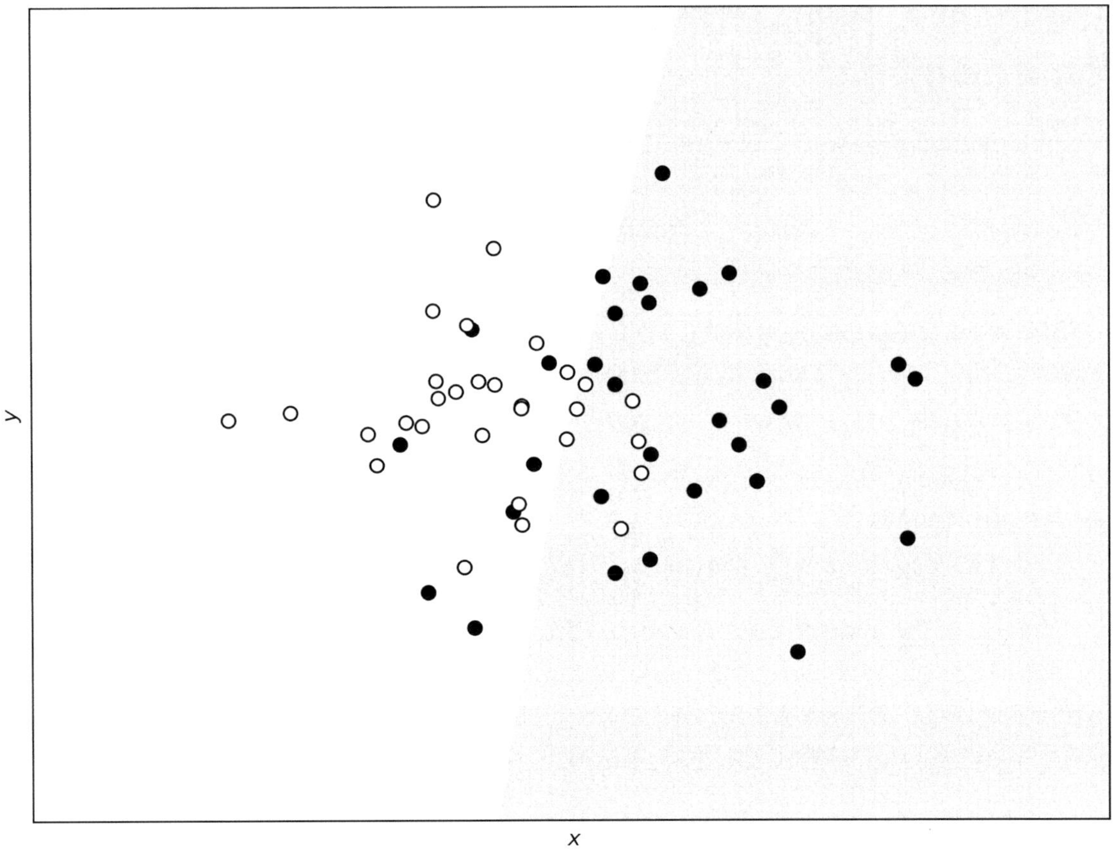

Figure 5-7. *Decision boundaries for a complex network with $\lambda = 0.1$ and for one with just one neuron. The two boundaries almost overlap completely.*

ℓ_1 Regularization

Now we will look at a regularization technique that is very similar to ℓ_2 regularization. It is based on the same principle, adding a term to the cost function. This time, the mathematical form of the added term is different, but the method works very similarly to what I explained in the previous sections. Let's again first have a look at the mathematics behind the algorithm.

Theory of ℓ_1 Regularization and tensorflow Implementation

ℓ_1 regularization also works when adding an additional term to the cost function

$$\tilde{J}(\boldsymbol{w}) = J(\boldsymbol{w}) + \frac{\lambda}{m}\|\boldsymbol{w}\|_1$$

The effect it has on the learning is effectively the same as was described with ℓ_2 regularization. TensorFlow does not have, as for ℓ_2, a function ready to be used. We must code it manually, using the following code:

```
reg = tf.reduce_sum(tf.abs(W1))+tf.reduce_sum(tf.abs(W2))+tf.reduce_
sum(tf.abs(W3))+\
        tf.reduce_sum(tf.abs(W4))+tf.reduce_sum(tf.abs(W5))
```

The rest of the code discussed remains the same. We can again compare the weights distribution between the model without a regularization term ($\lambda = 0$) and with regularization ($\lambda = 3$, Figure 5-8). We have used the Boston dataset for the calculation. We have trained the model with the following call:

```
sess, cost_history = model(learning_r = 0.01,
                                training_epochs = 1000,
                                features = train_x,
                                target = train_y,
                                logging_step = 1000,
                                lambd_val = 3.0)
```

once with $\lambda = 0$, and once with $\lambda = 3$.

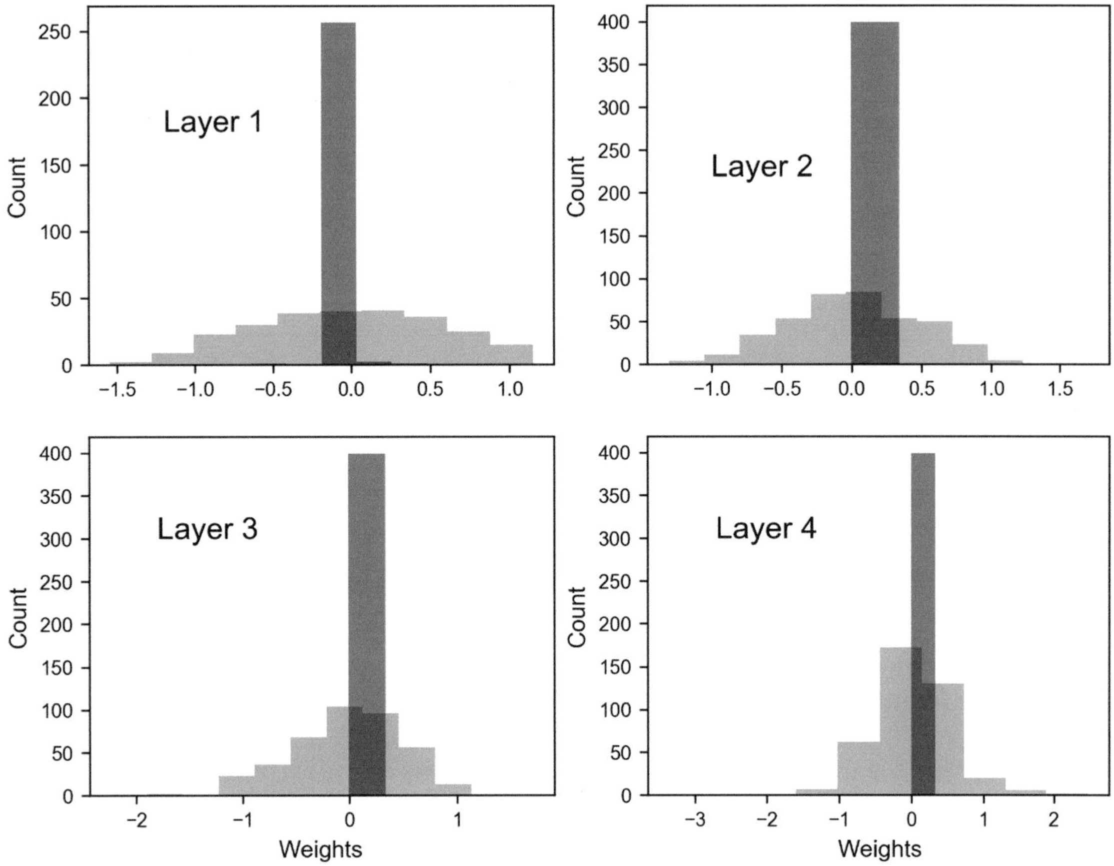

***Figure 5-8.** Weights distribution comparison between the model without the ℓ_1 regularization term ($\lambda = 0$, light gray) and with ℓ_1 regularization ($\lambda = 3$, dark gray)*

As you can see, ℓ_1 regularization has the same effect as ℓ_2. It reduces the effective complexity of the network, reducing many weights to zero.

To give you an idea of how effective regularization is in reducing the weights, see Table 5-2, which compares the percentage of weights less than 1e-3 with and without regularization after 1000 epochs.

Table 5-2. *Comparison of Percentage of Weights Less Than 1e-3 with and Without Regularization*

Layer	% of Weights Less Than 1e-3 for $\lambda = 0$	% of Weights Less Than 1e-3 for $\lambda = 3$
1	0.0	52.7
2	0.25	53.8
3	0.75	46.3
4	0.25	45.3
5	0.0	60.0

Are Weights Really Going to Zero?

It is very instructive to see how weights are going to zero. In Figure 5-9, you can see weight $w_{12,5}^{[3]}$ (from layer 3) plotted vs. the number of epochs for our artificial dataset with two features, ℓ_2 regularization, $\gamma = 10^{-3}$, $\lambda = 0.1$, after 1000 epochs. You can see how it quickly decreases to zero. The value after 1000 epochs is $2 \cdot 10^{-21}$, so, for all purposes, zero.

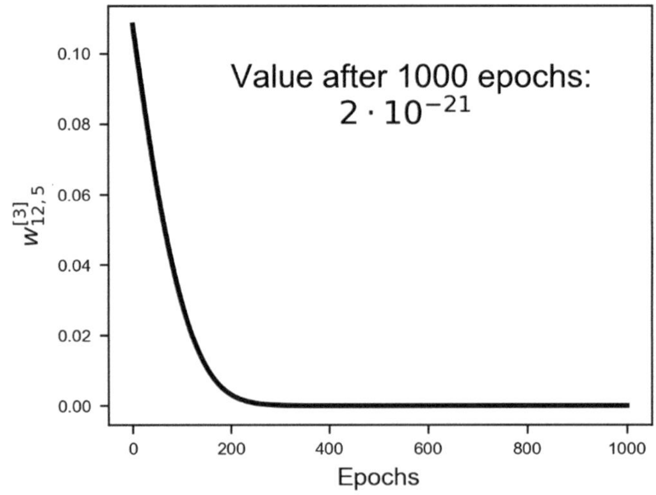

Figure 5-9. *Weight $w_{12,5}^{[3]}$ plotted vs. the epochs for our artificial dataset with two features, ℓ_2 regularization, $\gamma = 10^{-3}$, $\lambda = 0.1$, trained for 1000 epochs*

In case you are wondering, the weight goes to zero almost exponentially. A way of understanding why this is the case is the following. Let's consider the weight update equation for one weight.

$$w_{j,[n+1]} = w_{j,[n]}\left(1-\frac{\gamma\lambda}{m}\right) - \frac{\gamma\partial J\left(\boldsymbol{w}_{[n]}\right)}{\partial w_j}$$

Let's now suppose that we find ourselves close to the minimum, in a region where the derivative of the cost function *J* is almost zero, so that we can neglect it. In other words, let's suppose

$$\frac{\partial J\left(\boldsymbol{w}_{[n]}\right)}{\partial w_j} \approx 0$$

We can rewrite the weight update equation as

$$w_{j,[n+1]} - w_{j,[n]} = -w_{j,[n]}\frac{\gamma\lambda}{m}$$

Now the equation can be read as follows: the rate of variation of the weight with respect to the iteration number is proportional to the weight itself. For those of you with knowledge of differential equations, you may realize that we can draw a parallel to the following equation:

$$\frac{dx(t)}{dt} = -\frac{\gamma\lambda}{m}x(t)$$

This can be read as the rate of variation of $x(t)$ with respect to time is proportional to the function itself. For those of you who know how to solve this equation, you may know that a generic solution is

$$x(t) = Ae^{-\frac{\gamma\lambda}{m}(t-t_0)}$$

You can now see why the weight decay will have a decay similar to that of an exponential function, by drawing a parallel between the two equations. In Figure 5-10, you can see the weight decay already discussed, with a pure exponential decay. The two curves are not identical, as expected, because, especially at the beginning, the gradient of the cost function is surely not zero. But the similarity is remarkable and gives us an idea of how fast the weights can go to zero (read: really fast).

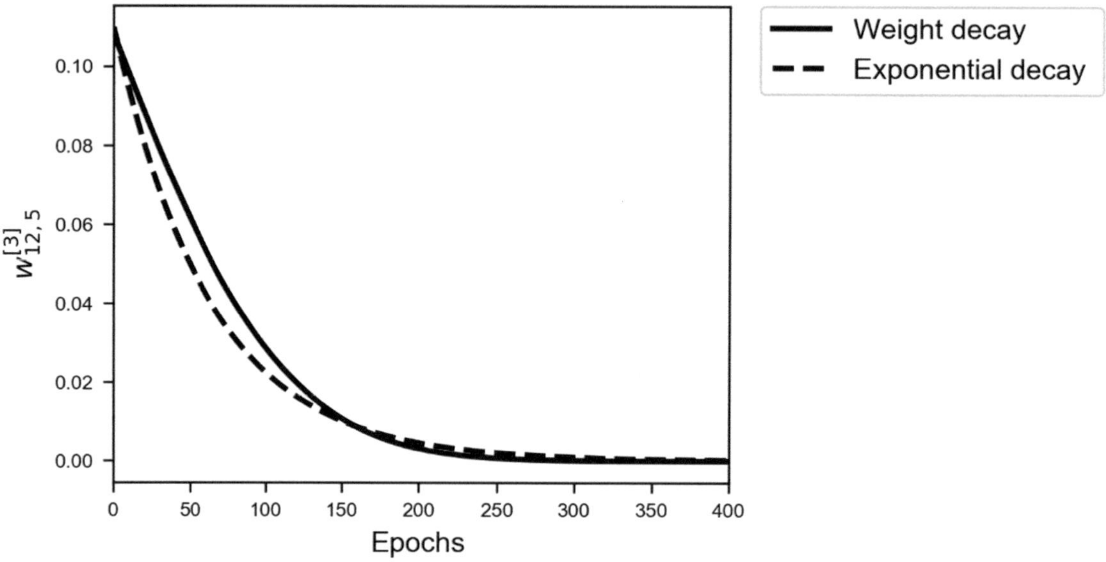

***Figure 5-10.** Weight $w^{[3]}_{12,5}$ plotted vs. the epochs for our artificial dataset with two features, ℓ_2 regularization, $\gamma = 10^{-3}$, $\lambda = 0.1$, trained for 1000 epochs (continuous line) together with a pure exponential decay (dashed line), provided for illustrative purposes*

Note that when using regularization, you end up having tensors with a lot of zero elements, called sparse tensors. You can then profit from special routines that are extremely efficient with sparse tensors. This is something to keep in mind when you start moving toward more complex models, but a subject too advanced for this book and that would require too much space.

Dropout

The basic idea of dropout is different: during the training phase, you remove nodes from layer *l* randomly with a probability $p^{[l]}$. In each iteration, you remove different nodes, effectively training at each iteration a different network (when using mini-batches, you train a different network for each batch, for example). Usually, the probability (often called keep_prob in Python) is set the same for all the network (but, technically speaking, it can be layer-specific). Intuitively, let's consider the output tensor Z of a layer *l*. In Python, we can define a vector such as

```
d = np.random.rand(Z.shape[0], Z.shape[1]) < keep_prob
```

and then simply multiply the layer output Z by d, as follows:

```
Z = np.multiply(Z, d)
```

This effectively removes all elements that have a probability less than keep_prob. Of much importance when doing predictions on a dev dataset is that no dropout be used!

Note During training, dropout removes nodes randomly each iteration. But when doing predictions on a dev dataset, the entire network without dropout must be used. In other words, you must set keep_prob=1.

Dropout can be layer-specific. For example, for layers with many neurons, keep_prob can be small. For layers with a few neurons, one can set keep_prob = 1.0, effectively keeping all neurons in such layers.

The implementation in TensorFlow is easy. First, you define a placeholder that will contain the value of the keep_prob parameter

```
keep_prob = tf.placeholder(tf.float32, shape=())
```

and then for each layer, you add a regularization operation in this way:

```
hidden1, W1, b1 = create_layer (X, n1, activation = tf.nn.relu)
hidden1_drop = tf.nn.dropout(hidden1, keep_prob)
```

Then, when creating the next layer, instead of using hidden1, you use hidden1_drop. The entire construction code looks like this:

```
tf.reset_default_graph()

n_dim = 13
n1 = 20
n2 = 20
n3 = 20
n4 = 20
n_outputs = 1

tf.set_random_seed(5)

X = tf.placeholder(tf.float32, [n_dim, None])
Y = tf.placeholder(tf.float32, [1, None])

learning_rate = tf.placeholder(tf.float32, shape=())
keep_prob = tf.placeholder(tf.float32, shape=())

hidden1, W1, b1 = create_layer (X, n1, activation = tf.nn.relu)
hidden1_drop = tf.nn.dropout(hidden1, keep_prob)
hidden2, W2, b2 = create_layer (hidden1_drop, n2, activation = tf.nn.relu)
hidden2_drop = tf.nn.dropout(hidden2, keep_prob)
hidden3, W3, b3 = create_layer (hidden2, n3, activation = tf.nn.relu)
hidden3_drop = tf.nn.dropout(hidden3, keep_prob)
hidden4, W4, b4 = create_layer (hidden3, n4, activation = tf.nn.relu)
hidden4_drop = tf.nn.dropout(hidden4, keep_prob)
y_, W5, b5 = create_layer (hidden4_drop, n_outputs, activation =
tf.identity)

cost = tf.reduce_mean(tf.square(y_-Y))

optimizer = tf.train.AdamOptimizer(learning_rate = learning_rate, beta1 =
0.9, beta2 = 0.999, epsilon = 1e-8).minimize(cost)
```

Now let's analyze what happens to the cost function when using dropout. Let's run our model applied to the Boston dataset for two values of the keep_prob variable: 1.0 (without dropout) and 0.5. In Figure 5-11, you can see that when applying dropout, the cost function is very irregular. It oscillates wildly. The two models have been evaluated with the calls

```
sess, cost_history05 = model(learning_r = 0.01,
                             training_epochs = 5000,
                             features = train_x,
                             target = train_y,
                             logging_step = 1000,
                             keep_prob_val = 1.0)
```

for keep_prob_val = 1.0 and for 0.5.

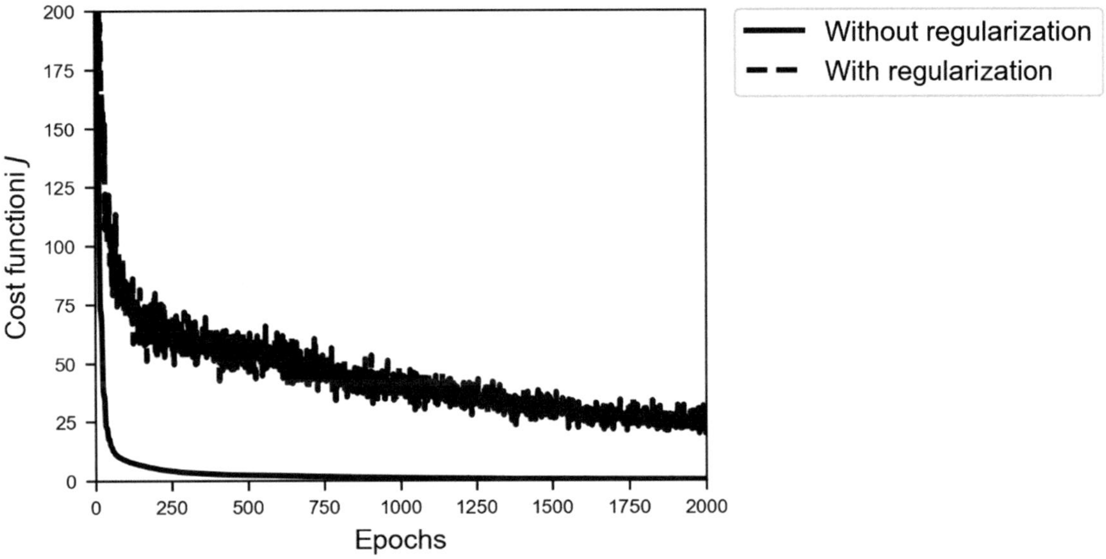

Figure 5-11. *Cost function for the training dataset for our model with two values of the keep_prob variable: 1.0 (no dropout) and 0.5. The other parameters are: $\gamma = 0.01$. The models have been trained for 5000 epochs. No mini-batch has been used. The oscillating line is the one evaluated with regularization.*

In Figure 5-12, you can see the evolution of the MSE for the training and the dev dataset in the case of dropout (`keep_prob=0.4`).

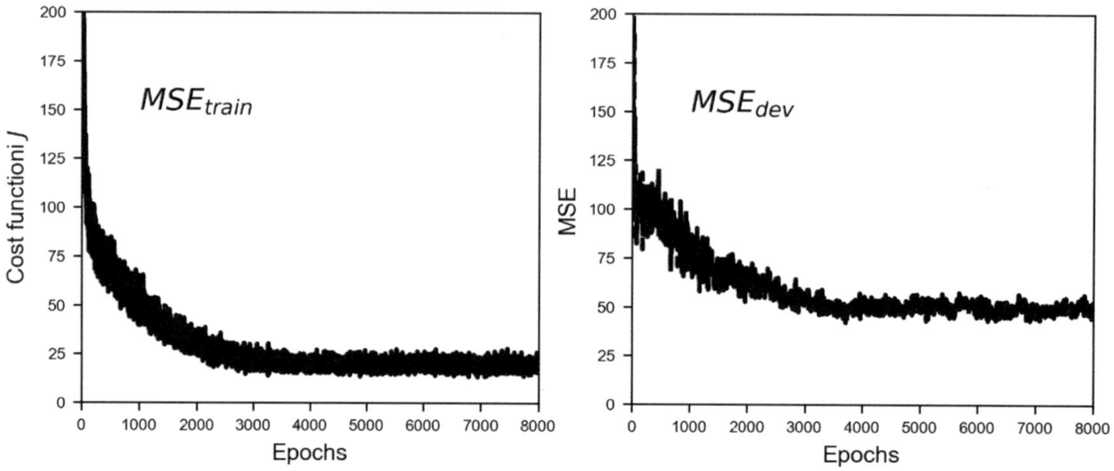

***Figure 5-12.** MSE for the training and dev datasets with dropout (`keep_prob=0.4`)*

In Figure 5-13, you can see the same plot but without dropout. The difference is quite striking. Very interesting is the fact that without dropout, MSE_{dev} grows with epochs, while using dropout, it is rather stable.

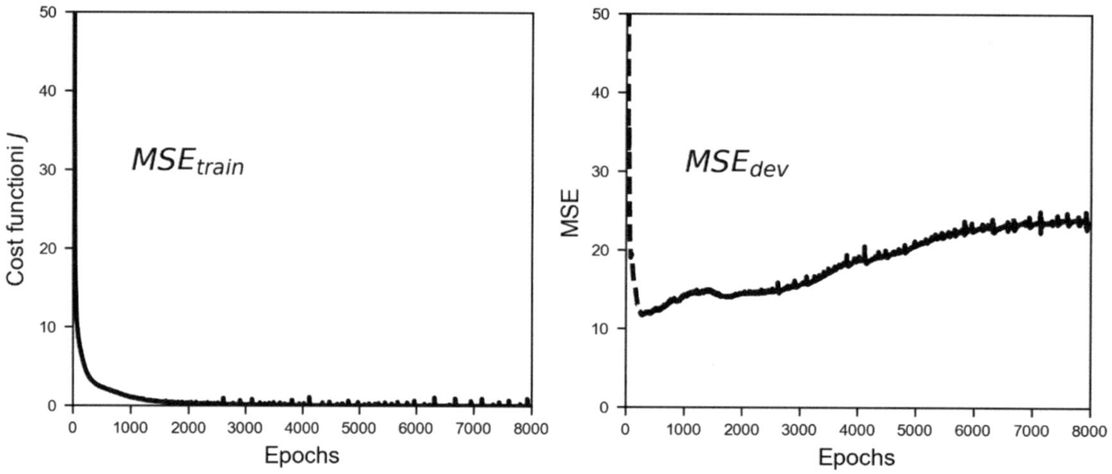

***Figure 5-13.** MSE for the training and dev datasets without dropout (`keep_prob=1.0`)*

In Figure 5-13, the MSE_{dev} grows after dropping at the beginning. The model is in clear extreme overfitting regime ($MSE_{train} \ll MSE_{dev}$), and it generalizes worse and worse when applied to the new data. In Figure 5-12, you can see how MSE_{train} and MSE_{dev} are of the same order of magnitude, and the MSE_{dev} does not continue to grow. So, we have a model that is a lot better at generalizing than the one whose results are shown in Figure 5-13.

Note When applying dropout, your metric (in this case, the MSE) will oscillate, so don't be surprised when trying to find the best hyperparameters, if you see your optimizing metric oscillating.

Early Stopping

There is another technique that is sometimes used to fight overfitting. Strictly speaking, this method does nothing to avoid overfitting; it simply stops the learning before the overfitting problem becomes too bad. Consider the example in last section. In Figure 5-14, you can see MSE_{train} and MSE_{dev} plotted on the same plot.

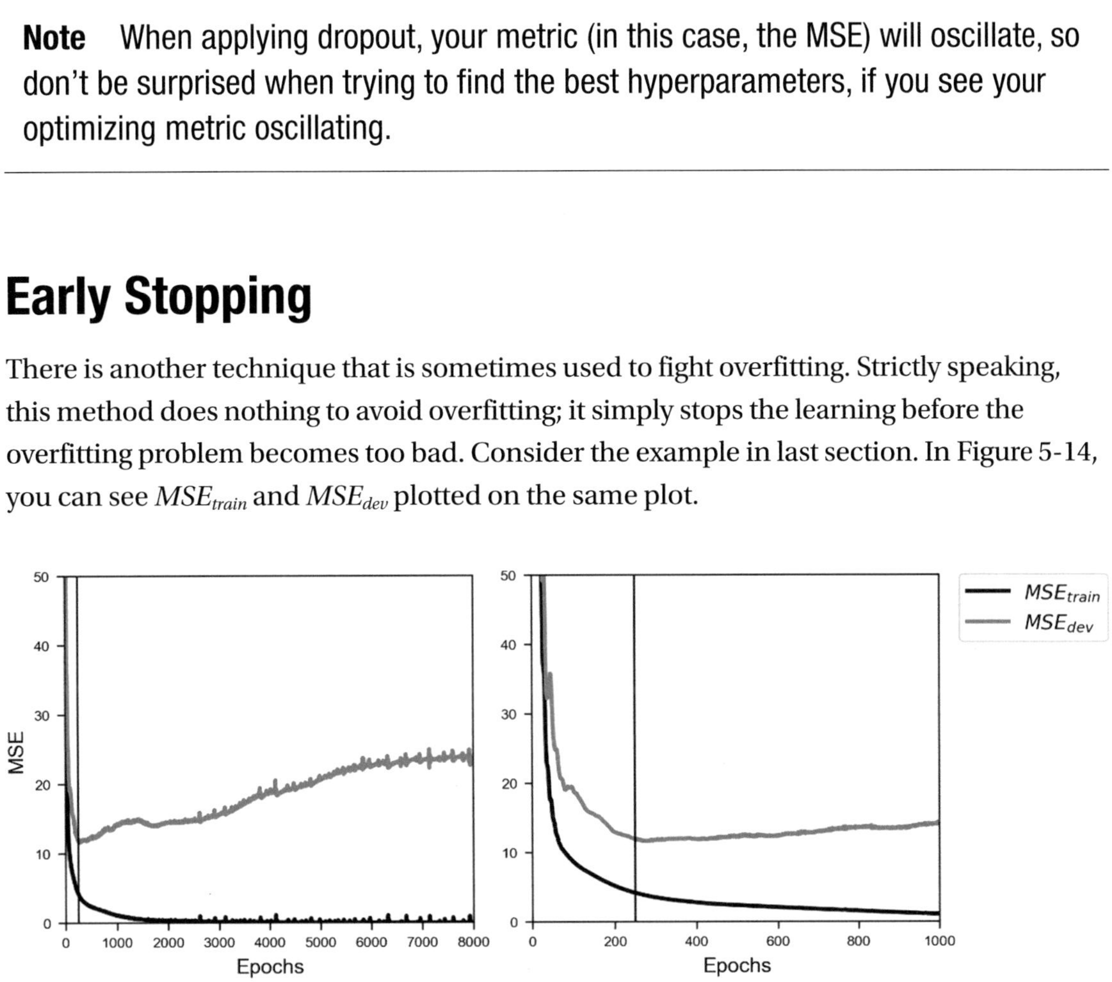

Figure 5-14. *MSE for the training and the dev datasets without dropout (*`keep_prob=1.0`*). Early stopping consists in stopping the learning phase at the iteration when the MSE_{dev} is minimum (indicated with a vertical line in the plot). At right, you can see a zoom of the left plot for the first 1000 epochs.*

Early stopping simply consists of stopping the training at the point at which the MSE_{dev} has its minimum (see Figure 5-14, the minimum is indicated by a vertical line in the figure). Note that this is not an ideal way to solve the overfitting problem. Your model will still most probably generalize very badly to new data. I usually prefer to use other techniques. Additionally, this is also time-consuming and a manual process that is very error-prone. You can get a good overview of the different application contexts by checking the Wikipedia page for early stopping: `https://goo.gl/xnKo2s`.

Additional Methods

All the methods I discussed so far consist, in some form or another, in making the model less complex. You keep the data as it is and modify your model. But we can try to do the opposite: leave the model as it is and work on the data. Here are two common strategies that work for fighting overfitting (but not very easily applicable):

- *Get more data*. This is the simplest way of fighting overfitting. Unfortunately, very often in real life, this is not possible. Keep in mind that this is a complicated matter that I will discuss at length in the next chapter. If you are classifying cat pictures taken with a smartphone, you may think of getting more data from the Web. Although this may seem a perfectly good idea, you may discover that the images have varying quality, that possibly not all the images are really of cats (what about cat toys?). Also, you may find only images of young white cats, and so on. Basically, your additional observations may probably come from a very different distribution than your original data, and that will be a problem, as you will see. So, when getting additional data, consider the potential problems well before proceeding.
- *Augment your data*. For example, if you are working with images, you can generate additional ones by rotating, stretching, shifting, etc., your images. That is a very common technique that may really be useful.

Resolving the problem of making the model generalize better on new data is one of machine learning's biggest goals. It is a complicated problem that requires experience and tests. Lots of tests. Much research is going on that tries to solve these kinds of bugs when working on very complex problems. I will discuss additional techniques in the next chapter.

CHAPTER 6

Metric Analysis

Let's consider the problem we analyzed in Chapter 3 for which we performed classification on the Zalando dataset. While doing all our work, we made a strong assumption without explicitly saying it: we assumed that all the observations were correctly labeled. We cannot say that with certainty. To perform the labelling, some manual intervention was needed, and, therefore, a certain number of images were surely wrongly classified, as humans are not perfect. This is an important revelation. Consider the following scenario: in Chapter 3, we achieved roughly 90% accuracy with our model. One could try to get better and better accuracy, but when is it sensible to stop trying? If your labels are wrong in 10% of cases, your model, as sophisticated as it may be, will never be able to generalize to new data with very high accuracy, because it will have learned wrong classes for many images. We spent quite some time checking and preparing the training data, normalizing it, for example, but we never spent any time checking the labels themselves. We also assumed that all classes have similar characteristics. (I will discuss later in this chapter what this exactly means, for the moment, an intuitive understanding of the concept will suffice.) What if the quality of the images for specific classes is worse than for others? What if the number of pixels whose gray value differs from zero is dramatically different for different classes? We also did not check if some images are completely blank. What happens in that case? As you can imagine, we cannot check all images manually, attempting to detect such issues. Suppose we have millions of images, a manual analysis is surely not possible.

We need a new weapon in our arsenal to be able to spot such cases and to be able to tell how a model is doing. This new weapon is the focus of this chapter, and it is what I call "metric analysis." Very often, people in the field refer to this array of methods as "error analysis." I find that this name is very confusing, especially for beginners. *Error* may refer to too many things: Python code bugs, errors in the methods, in algorithms, errors in the choice of optimizers, and so on. You will see in this chapter how to obtain fundamental information on how your model is doing and how good your data is. We will do this by evaluating your optimizing metric on a set of different datasets that you can derive from your data.

U. Michelucci, *Applied Deep Learning*, https://doi.org/10.1007/978-1-4842-3790-8_6

You have already seen a basic example previously. You will remember that we discussed, with regard to regression, how in the case of $MSE_{train} \ll MSE_{dev}$, we are in a regime of overfitting. Our metric is the MSE (mean squared error), and evaluating it on two datasets, training and dev, and comparing the two values, can inform you whether the model is overfitting. I will expand on this methodology in this chapter, to allow you to extract much more information from your data and model.

Human-Level Performance and Bayes Error

In most of the datasets that we use for supervised learning, someone must have labeled the observations. Take, for example, a dataset in which we have images that are classified. If we ask people to classify all images (imagine this being possible, regardless of the number of images), the accuracy obtained will never be 100%. Some images may be too blurry to be classified correctly, and people make mistakes. If, for example, 5% of the images are not classifiable correctly, owing, for example, to how blurry they are, we must expect that the maximum accuracy people can reach will always be less than 95%.

Let's consider a classification problem. First, let's define what we mean by the word *error*. In this chapter, the word *error* will be used to indicate the following quantity, represented by ϵ:

$$\epsilon \equiv 1 - Accuracy$$

For example, if, with a model, we achieve an accuracy of 95%, we will have $\epsilon = 1 - 0.95 = 0.05$ or, expressed as a percent, $\epsilon = 5\%$.

A useful concept to understand is human-level performance, which can be defined as follows:

Human-level performance (definition 1): The lowest value for the error ϵ that can be achieved by a person performing the classification task. We will indicate it with ϵ_{hlp}.

Let's devise a concrete example. Suppose we have a set of 100 images. Now let's suppose we ask three people to classify the 100 images. Imagine that they obtain 95%, 93%, and 94% accuracy. In this case, human-level performance accuracy will be $\epsilon_{hlp} = 5\%$. Note that someone else may be much better at this task, and, therefore, it is always important to consider that the value of ϵ_{hlp} we get is always an estimate and should only serve as a guideline.

Now let's complicate things a bit. Suppose we are working on a problem in which doctors classify MRI scans in two classes: with signs of cancer and without. Now let's suppose we calculate ϵ_{hlp} from the results of untrained students obtaining 15%, from doctors with a few years of experience obtaining 8%, from experienced doctors obtaining 2%, and from experienced *groups* of doctors obtaining 0.5%. What then is ϵ_{hlp}? You should always choose the lowest value you can get, for reasons I will discuss later.

We can now expand the definition of ϵ_{hlp} with a second definition.

Human level performance (definition 2): The lowest value for the error ϵ that can be achieved by people or *groups* of people performing the classification task

---

Note You don't have to decide which definition is right. Just use the one that gives you the lowest value of ϵ_{hlp}.

Now I'll talk a bit about why we must choose the lowest value we can get for ϵ_{hlp}. Suppose that of the 100 images, 9 are too blurry to be correctly classified. This means that the lowest error any classifier will be able to reach is 9%. The *lowest error that can be reached by any classifier* is called the Bayes error. We will indicate this with ϵ_{Bayes}. In this example, $\epsilon_{Bayes} = 9\%$. Usually, ϵ_{hlp} is very close to ϵ_{Bayes}, at least in tasks at which humans excel, such as image recognition. It is commonly said that human-level performance error is a proxy for the Bayes error. Normally it is impossible or very hard to know ϵ_{Bayes}, and, therefore, practitioners use ϵ_{hlp} assuming the two are close, because the latter is easier (relatively) to estimate.

Keep in mind that it makes sense to compare the two values and assume that ϵ_{hlp} is a proxy for ϵ_{Bayes} only if persons (or groups of persons) perform classification in the same way as the classifier. For example, it is OK if both use the same images to do classification. But, in our cancer example, if the doctors use additional scans and analysis to diagnose cancer, the comparison is no longer fair, because human-level performance will not be a proxy for a Bayes error anymore. Doctors, having more data at their disposal, clearly will be more accurate than the model that has as input only the images at its disposal.

Note ϵ_{hlp} and ϵ_{Bayes} are close to each other only in cases in which the classification is done in the same way by humans and from the model. So, always check if that is the case, before assuming that human-level performance is a proxy for the Bayes error.

Something else that you will notice when working on models is that with relatively little effort, you can achieve a quite low rate of error and often (almost) reach ϵ_{hlp}. After passing human-level performance (and, in several cases, that is possible), progress tends to be very, very slow, as is illustrated in Figure 6-1.

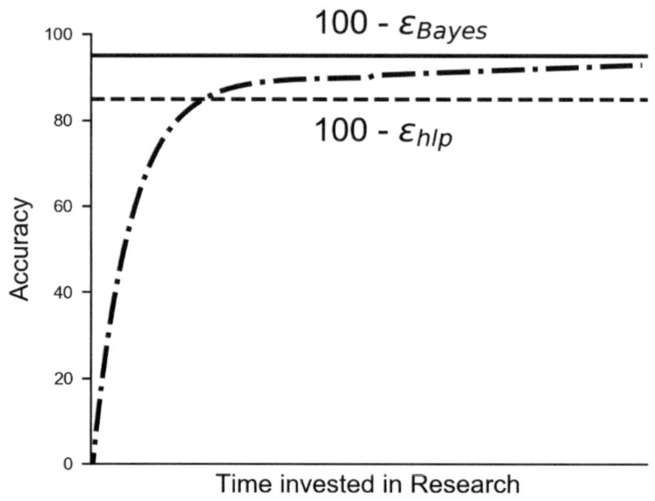

Figure 6-1. *Typical values of accuracy that can be achieved vs. amount of time invested. At the beginning, it is very easy to achieve quite a good accuracy with machine learning often reaching ϵ_{hlp}. This is intuitively indicated by the line in the plot. After that point, the progress tends to be very slow.*

As long as the error of your algorithm is bigger than ϵ_{hlp}, you can use the following techniques to get better results:

- Get better labels from humans or groups, for example, from groups of doctors, as in the case of medical data in our example.
- Get more labeled data from humans or groups.
- Do a good metric analysis to determine the best strategy for getting better results. You will learn how to do this in this chapter.

As soon as your algorithm exceeds human-level performance, you cannot rely on those techniques anymore. So, it is important to get an idea of those numbers, to decide what to do to obtain better results. Taking our example of MRI scans, we could get better labels by relying on sources that are not related to humans, for example, checking diagnoses a few years after the date of the MRI, when it is usually clear whether a patient has developed cancer. Or, for example, in the case of image classification, you may decide yourself to take a few thousands of images of specific classes. This is not usually possible, but I wanted to make the concept clear: you can get labels by means other than by asking humans to perform the same kind of task that your algorithm is performing.

Note Human-level performance is a good proxy for Bayes error for tasks at which humans excel, such as image recognition. For tasks that humans are very bad at, performance can be very far from the Bayes error.

A Short Story About Human-Level Performance

I want to tell you a story about the work that Andrej Karpathy has done while trying to estimate human-level performance in a specific case. You can read the entire story on his blog post (a long post, but one that I suggest you read) at `https://goo.gl/iqCbCO`. Let me summarize what he did, since it is extremely instructive concerning what human-level performance really is. Karpathy was involved in the ILSVRC (ImageNet Large Scale Visual Recognition Challenge) in 2014 (`https://goo.gl/PCHWMJ`). The task was made up of 1.2 million images (training set) classified in 1000 categories, including such objects as animals, abstract objects such as a spiral, scenes, and many more. Results were evaluated on a dev dataset. GoogleLeNet (a model developed by Google) reached an astounding 6.7% error. Karpathy wondered how humans would compare.

The question is a lot more complicated than it may seem at first sight. Because the images were all classified by humans, shouldn't $\epsilon_{hlp} = 0\%$? Well, actually, no. In fact, the images were first obtained with a web search, then they were filtered and labeled by asking people *binary* questions, for example, Is this a hook or not? The images were collected, as Karpathy mentions in his blog post, in a binary way. People were not asked to assign to each image a class, choosing from the 1000 available, as the algorithms were doing. You may think that this is a technicality, but the difference in how the labeling occurs makes the correct evaluation of a ϵ_{hlp} quite a complicated matter. So, Karpathy set to work and developed a web interface that consisted of an image on the left, and the 1000 classes with examples on the right. You can see an example of the interface in Figure 6-2. You can try the interface (and I suggest you do so) at `https://goo.gl/Rh8S6g`, to understand how complicated such a task is. People trying the interface kept missing classes and making mistakes. The best error that was reached was about 15%.

So, Karpathy did what every scientist at some point in his/her career must do: he bored himself to death and did a careful annotation himself, sometimes requiring 20 minutes for a single image. As he states in his blog post, he did it only `#forscience`. He was able to reach a stunning $\epsilon_{hlp} = 5.1\%$, 1.7% better than the best algorithm at the time. He listed sources of errors to which GoogLeNet is more susceptible than humans, such as problems with multiple objects in an image, and sources of errors to which humans are more susceptible than GoogLeNet, such as problems with classes with a huge granularity (dogs are classified in 120 different subclasses, for example).

***Figure 6-2.** Web interface developed by Karpathy. Not everyone would find it amusing to look at 120 breeds of dogs, to try to classify the dog on the left (which, by the way, is a Tibetan mastiff).*

If you have a few hours to spare, I suggest you try. You will gain a whole new appreciation of the difficulties of evaluating human-level performance. Defining and evaluating human-level performance is a very tricky task. It is important to understand that ϵ_{hlp} is dependent on how humans approach the classification task, which is dependent on the time invested, the patience of the persons performing the task, and on many factors that are difficult to quantify. The main reason for it being so important, apart from the philosophical aspect of knowing when a machine becomes better than humans, is that it is often taken as a proxy for the Bayes error, which gives a lower limit of our possibilities.

Human-Level Performance on MNIST

Before moving on to the next subject, I would like to give you another example of human-level performance on a dataset we have analyzed together: the MNIST dataset. Human-level performance has been widely analyzed, and it has been found that $\epsilon_{hlp} = 0.2\%$. (You can read a good review on the subject by Dan Cireşan: "Multi-column Deep Neural Networks for Image Classification," Technical Report No. IDSIA-04-12, Dalle Molle Institute for Artificial Intelligence, `https://goo.gl/pEHZVB`.) Now you may wonder why a human cannot achieve 100% accuracy classifying simple digits, but see Figure 6-3, and attempt to identify which digits are in the images. I surely cannot. You may, therefore, better understand why $\epsilon_{hlp} = 0\%$ is not possible, and why a person cannot achieve 100% accuracy. Other reasons may be related to which culture people come from. In some countries, the digit representing seven is written in a very similar way to that for ones, for example, and in some cases, mistakes can be made. In other countries, the digit seven has a small dash along the vertical bar, making it easier to distinguish from a one.

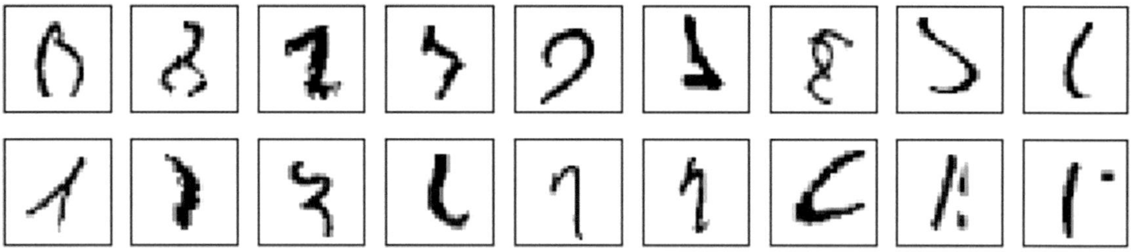

Figure 6-3. *A set of digits from the MNIST dataset that are almost impossible to recognize. Such examples are one of the reasons why ϵ_{hlp} cannot be zero.*

Bias

Now let's start with a metric analysis: a set of procedures that will give you information on how your model is doing and how good or bad your data is, by evaluating your optimizing metric on different datasets.

Note Metric analysis consists of a set of procedures that will give you information on how your model is doing and how good or bad your data is, by looking at your evaluating your optimizing metric on different datasets.

To start, we must first define a third error: the one evaluated on the training dataset, indicated with ϵ_{train}.

The first question we want to answer is if our model is not as flexible or complex as needed to reach human-level performance. Or, in other words, we want to know if our model has a high bias, with respect to human-level performance.

To answer the previous question, we can do the following: calculate the error from our model from our training dataset ϵ_{train} and then calculate $|\epsilon_{train} - \epsilon_{hlp}|$. If the number is not small (bigger than a few percent), we are in the presence of bias (sometimes called avoidable bias), that is, our model is too simple to capture the real subtleties of our data.

Let's define the following quantity

$$\Delta\epsilon_{Bias} = \left|\epsilon_{train} - \epsilon_{hlp}\right|$$

The bigger $\Delta\epsilon_{Bias}$ is, the more bias our model has. In this case, you want to do better on the training set, because you know you can do better on your training data. (We will look at the problem of overfitting in a moment.) The following techniques work to reduce bias:

- Bigger networks (more layers or neurons)
- More complex architectures (convolutional neural networks, for example)
- Training your model longer (for more epochs)
- Using better optimizers (such as Adam)
- Doing a better hyperparameter search (covered in Chapter 7)

There is something else you need to understand. Knowing ϵ_{hlp} and reducing the bias to reach it are two very different things. Suppose you know the ϵ_{hlp} for your problem. This does not mean that you have to reach it. It may well be that you are using the wrong architecture, but you may not have the skills required to develop a more sophisticated network. It may even be that the effort required to achieve the desired error level would be prohibitive (in terms of hardware or infrastructure). Always keep in mind what your problem requirements are. Always try to understand what is good enough. For an application that recognizes cancer, you may want to invest as much as possible to achieve the highest accuracy possible: you don't want to send someone home only to discover the presence of cancer months later. On the other hand, if you build a system to recognize cats from web images, you may find a higher error than ϵ_{hlp} completely acceptable.

Metric Analysis Diagram

In this chapter, we look at different problems that you will encounter when developing your models and how to spot them. We have looked at the first one: bias, sometimes also called avoidable bias. We have seen how this can be spotted by calculating $\Delta\epsilon_{Bias}$. At the end of this chapter, you will have a few of those quantities that you can calculate to spot problems. To make understanding them easier, I use what I like to call the metric analysis diagram (MAD). It is simply a bar diagram, in which each bar represents a problem. Let's start to build one with (for the moment) the only quantity we have discussed: bias. You can see it in Figure 6-4. At the moment, it is a pretty dumb diagram, but you will see how useful it is to keep things under control when you have several problems at the same time.

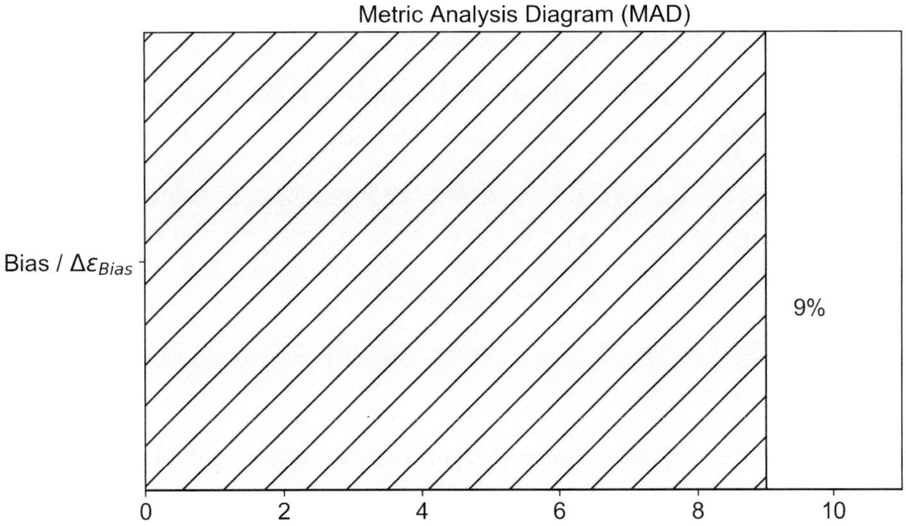

Figure 6-4. *Metric analysis diagram (MAD) with only one of the quantities we will encounter in this chapter:* $\Delta\epsilon_{Bias}$

Training Set Overfitting

Another problem we have discussed at length in the previous chapters is overfitting of training data. You will remember in Chapter 5, while executing regression, we saw an extreme case of overfitting, in which $MSE_{train} \ll MSE_{dev}$. The same applies in classification problems. Let's indicate with ϵ_{train} the error our model has on our training dataset and with ϵ_{dev} the one on the dev dataset. We can then say we are overfitting the training set if $\epsilon_{train} \ll \epsilon_{dev}$. Let's define a new quantity

$$\Delta\epsilon_{overfitting\ train} = |\epsilon_{train} - \epsilon_{dev}|$$

With this quantity, we can say that we are overfitting the training dataset if $\Delta\epsilon_{overfitting\ train}$ is bigger than a few percent.

Let's summarize what we have defined and discussed so far. We have three errors:

- ϵ_{train}: The error of our classifier on the training dataset
- ϵ_{hlp}: Human-level performance (as discussed in the previous sections)
- ϵ_{dev}: The error of our classifier on the dev dataset

With those three quantities, we have defined

- $\Delta\epsilon_{Bias} = |\epsilon_{train} - \epsilon_{hlp}|$: Measuring how much "bias" we have between the training dataset and human-level performance
- $\Delta\epsilon_{overfitting\ train} = |\epsilon_{train} - \epsilon_{dev}|$: Measuring the amount of overfitting of the training dataset

In addition, up to now, we have used two datasets

- *Training dataset*: The dataset that we use to train our model (you should know it by now)
- *Dev dataset*: A second dataset that we use to check the overfitting on the training dataset

Now let's suppose our model has bias and is slightly overfitting the training dataset, meaning we have $\Delta\epsilon_{Bias} = 6\%$ and $\Delta\epsilon_{overfitting\ train} = 4\%$. Our MAD now becomes what is depicted in Figure 6-5.

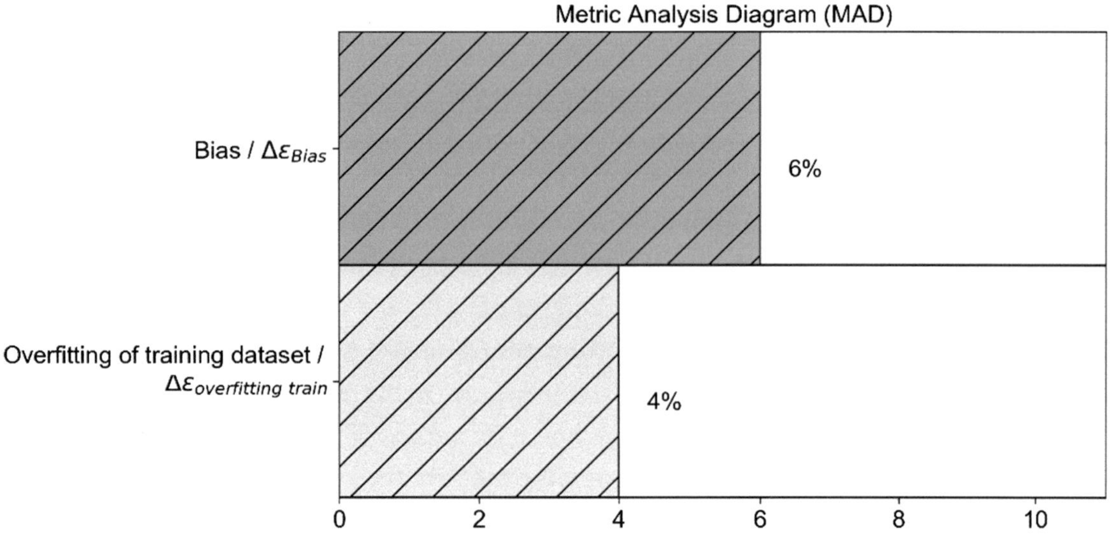

Figure 6-5. *MAD diagram for our two problems: bias and overfitting of training dataset*

As you can see in Figure 6-5, you can have a quick overview of the relative gravity of the problems we have, and you may decide which one you want to address first.

Usually when you are overfitting the training dataset, it is commonly known as a variance problem. When this happens, you can try the following techniques to minimize this problem:

- Get more data for your training set
- Use regularization (review Chapter 5 for a complete discussion of the subject)
- Try data augmentation (for example, if you are working with images, you can try rotating them, shifting them, etc.)
- Try "simpler" network architectures

As usual, there are no fixed rules, and you must test which techniques work best on your problem.

Test Set

I would like to quickly mention another problem you may encounter. We will look at it in detail in Chapter 7, because it is related to hyperparameter search. Recall how you choose the best model in a machine-learning project (this is not specific to deep learning, by the way)? Let's suppose we are working on a classification problem. First, we decide which optimizing metric we want, let's suppose we decide to use accuracy. Then we build an initial system, feed it with training data, and see how it is doing on the dev dataset, to check if we are overfitting our training data. You will remember that in previous chapters, we have talked often about hyperparameters—parameters that are not influenced by the learning process. Examples of hyperparameters are the learning rate, regularization parameter, etc. We have seen many of them in the previous chapters. Let's say you are working with a specific neural network architecture. You need to search the best values for the hyperparameters, to see how good your model can get. To do this, you train several models with different values of the hyperparameters and check their performance on the dev dataset. What can happen is that your models work well on the dev dataset but don't generalize at all, because you select the best values using only the dev dataset. You incur the risk of overfitting the dev dataset by choosing specific values for your hyperparameters. To check if this is the case, you create a third dataset, called the test dataset, cutting a portion of the observations from your starting dataset, which you use to check the performance of your models.

We must define a new quantity

$$\Delta\epsilon_{overfitting\ dev} = |\epsilon_{dev} - \epsilon_{test}|$$

where ϵ_{test} is the error evaluated on the test set. We can add it to our MAD diagram (Figure 6-6).

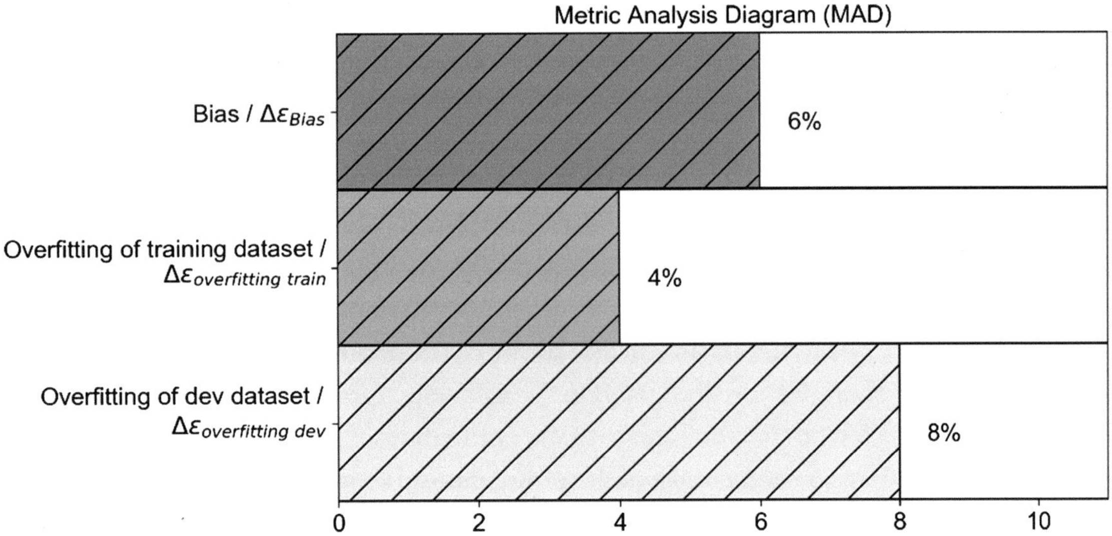

***Figure 6-6.** The MAD diagram for the three problems we may encounter: bias, overfitting of training data, overfitting of dev data*

Note that if you are not doing any hyperparameter search, you will not need a test dataset. It is only useful when you are doing extensive searches; otherwise, in most cases, it is useless and takes away observations that you may use for training. What we discussed so far assumes that your dev and test set observations have the same characteristics. For example, if you are working on an image recognition problem and you decide to use images from a smartphone with high resolution for training and the dev dataset, and images from the Web in low resolution for your test dataset, you may see a big $|\epsilon_{dev} - \epsilon_{test}|$, but that will probably be owing to the differences in the images and not to an overfitting problem. I will discuss later in the chapter what can happen when different sets come from different distributions (another way of saying that the observations have different characteristics), what exactly this means, and what you can do about it.

How to Split Your Dataset

Now I would like to discuss briefly how to split your data in both a general and deep-learning context.

But what exactly does "split" mean? Well, as discussed in the previous section, you will require a set of observations to make the model learn, which you call your training set. You also will need a set of observations that will constitute your dev set, and a final set called the test set. Typically, you would see splits such as 60% of observations for the training set, 20% of observations for the dev set, and 20% of observations for the test set. Usually, these kinds of splits are indicated in the following form: 60/20/20, where the first number (60) refers to the percentage of the entire dataset that makes up the training set, the second (20) to the percentage of the entire dataset that makes up the dev set, and the last (20) to the percentage that makes up the test set. In books, blogs, or articles, you may encounter sentences such as "We will split our dataset 80/10/10." You now have an explanation of what this means.

Usually, in the deep-learning field, you will deal with big datasets. For example, if we have $m = 10^6$, we could use a split such as 98/1/1. Keep in mind that 1% of 10^6 is 10^4—a big number! Remember that the dev/test set must be big enough to give high confidence to the performance of the model, but not unnecessarily big. Additionally, you will want to save as many observations as possible for your training set.

Note When deciding on how to split your dataset, if you have a big number of observations (for example, 10^6 or even more), you can split your dataset 98/1/1 or 90/5/5. So, as soon as your dev and test dataset reach a reasonable size (depending on your problem), you can stop. When deciding how to split your dataset, keep in mind how big your dev/test sets must be.

Now remember that, as you may know, size is not everything. Your dev and test datasets should be representative of your training dataset and problem. Let's create an example. Let's consider the ImageNet challenge described earlier. There, you want to classify images in 1000 different classes. To know how your model is performing in your dev and test datasets, you will require enough images for each class in each set. If you decide to take only 1000 observations for the dev or test dataset, you are not going to get any reasonable result, because, in case all classes are represented in the dev set, you will only have one observation for each class. You should decide to build your dev and test dataset choosing, for example, 100 images for each class at least, building two datasets (dev and test), each containing 10^5 observations in total (remember we have 1000 classes). In this case, it would not be sensible to go below this number. This is not only relevant in a deep-learning context but in machine learning in general. You should always try to build a dev/test dataset reflecting the same distribution of observations you have in your training set. To understand what I mean, take the MNIST dataset, for example. Let's load the dataset (as we have done before) with the following code:

```
import numpy as np
from sklearn.datasets import fetch_mldata
mnist = fetch_mldata('MNIST original')
X,y = mnist["data"], mnist["target"]
total = 0
```

then we can check how often (in %) each digit appears in the dataset.

```
for i in range(10):
    print ("digit", i, "makes", np.around(np.count_nonzero
(y == i)/70000.0*100.0, decimals=1), "% of the 70000 observations")
```

This gives us the result

```
digit 0 makes 9.9 % of the 70000 observations
digit 1 makes 11.3 % of the 70000 observations
digit 2 makes 10.0 % of the 70000 observations
digit 3 makes 10.2 % of the 70000 observations
digit 4 makes 9.7 % of the 70000 observations
digit 5 makes 9.0 % of the 70000 observations
digit 6 makes 9.8 % of the 70000 observations
digit 7 makes 10.4 % of the 70000 observations
digit 8 makes 9.8 % of the 70000 observations
digit 9 makes 9.9 % of the 70000 observations
```

Not every digit appears the same number of times in the dataset. When building our dev and test datasets, we should check that our distributions reflect this one; otherwise, when applying our model to the dev or test dataset, we could get a result that does not make much sense, because the model has learned from a different class distribution. You may remember that in Chapter 5, we created a dev dataset with a code like this one:

```
np.random.seed(42)
rnd = np.random.rand(len(y)) < 0.8

train_y = y[rnd]
dev_y = y[~rnd]
```

In this case, for the sake of clarity, I just split the labels, to see how the algorithm is working. In real life, you also would have to split the features, of course. Because our original distribution is almost uniform, you should expect a result that is very similar to the original one. Let's check it with the following code:

```
for i in range(10):
    print ("digit", i, "makes", np.around(np.count_nonzero
    (train_y == i)/56056.0*100.0, decimals=1), "% of the 56056
    observations")
```

This gives us the result

```
digit 0 makes 9.9 % of the 56056 observations
digit 1 makes 11.3 % of the 56056 observations
digit 2 makes 9.9 % of the 56056 observations
digit 3 makes 10.1 % of the 56056 observations
digit 4 makes 9.8 % of the 56056 observations
digit 5 makes 9.0 % of the 56056 observations
digit 6 makes 9.8 % of the 56056 observations
digit 7 makes 10.4 % of the 56056 observations
digit 8 makes 9.8 % of the 56056 observations
digit 9 makes 9.9 % of the 56056 observations
```

You can compare these results with those from the entire dataset. You will notice that they are very close—not the same (compare, for example, digit 2), but close enough. In this case, I would simply proceed without worries. But let's create a slightly different example. Suppose that instead of choosing randomly the observations to create your training and dev datasets, you decide to take the first 80% of the observations and assign it to the training set and the last 20% and assign it to the dev set, because you assume that your observations are randomly distributed in your original NumPy arrays. Let's try and see what happens. First, let's build our train and dev datasets, using the first 56,000 (0.8*70000) observations for the training set and the rest for the dev set.

```
srt = np.zeros_like(y,  dtype=bool)

np.random.seed(42)
srt[0:56000] = True

train_y = y[srt]
dev_y = y[~srt]
```

We can again check how many digits we have with the following code:

```
 total = 0
for i in range(10):
    print ("class", i, "makes", np.around(np.count_nonzero
    (train_y == i)/56000.0*100.0, decimals=1), "% of the 56000
    observations")
```

This gives us the result

```
class 0 makes 8.5 % of the 56000 observations
class 1 makes 9.6 % of the 56000 observations
class 2 makes 8.5 % of the 56000 observations
class 3 makes 8.8 % of the 56000 observations
class 4 makes 8.3 % of the 56000 observations
class 5 makes 7.7 % of the 56000 observations
class 6 makes 8.5 % of the 56000 observations
class 7 makes 9.0 % of the 56000 observations
class 8 makes 8.4 % of the 56000 observations
class 9 makes 2.8 % of the 56000 observations
```

Do you notice anything different? The biggest difference is that now, class 9 is only appearing in 2.8% of the cases. Before, it was appearing in 9.9% of the cases. Apparently, our hypothesis that the classes are distributed according to a random uniform distribution was not right. This can be quite dangerous when checking how the model is doing or because your model may end up learning from a so-called *unbalanced class distribution*.

Note Usually, an unbalanced class distribution in a dataset refers to a classification problem in which one or more classes appear a different number of times than others. Generally, this becomes a problem in the learning process when the difference is significant. A few percent difference is often not an issue.

If you have a dataset with three classes, for example, where you have 1000 observations in each class, then the dataset has a perfectly balanced class distribution, but if you have in class 1 only 100 observations, in class 2 10,000 observations, and in class 3 5000, then we talk about an unbalanced class distribution. You should not think that this is a rare occurrence. Suppose you have to build a model that recognizes fraudulent credit card transactions. It is safe to assume that those transactions are a very small percent of the entire amount of transactions that you will have at your disposal.

Note When splitting your dataset, you must pay great attention not only to the number of observations you have in each dataset but also to which observations go in each dataset. Note that this problem is not specific to deep learning but is important generally in machine learning.

To go into details on how to deal with unbalanced datasets would be beyond the scope of this book, but it is important to understand what kind of consequences they may have. In the next section, I will show you what can happen if you feed an unbalanced dataset to a neural network, so that you gain a concrete understanding of the possibility. At the end of the section, I will offer a few hints on what to do in such a case.

Unbalanced Class Distribution: What Can Happen

Because we are talking about how to split our dataset to perform metric analysis, it is important to grasp the concept of unbalanced class distribution and how to deal with it. In deep learning, you will find yourself very often splitting datasets, and you should be aware of the problems you may encounter if you do this in the wrong way. Let me give you a concrete example of how bad things can go if you do it wrongly.

We will use the MNIST dataset, and we will do basic logistic regression (as we did in Chapter 2) with a single neuron. Let's look very quickly again at how to load and prepare the data. We will do it in a similar way as in Chapter 2, apart from some modifications that I will point out to you. First, we load the data

```
import numpy as np
from sklearn.datasets import fetch_mldata
from sklearn.metrics import confusion_matrix
import tensorflow as tf

mnist = fetch_mldata('MNIST original')
Xinput,yinput = mnist["data"], mnist["target"]
```

Here comes the important part. We create a new label in this way: we assign to all observations for the digit zero the label 0, and to all other digits (1, 2, 3 ,4, 5, 6, 7, 8, and 9) the label 1, with the code

```
y_ = np.zeros_like(yinput)
y_[np.any([yinput == 0], axis = 0)] = 0
y_[np.any([yinput > 0], axis = 0)] = 1
```

Now the array y_ will contain the new labels. Note that now the dataset is heavily unbalanced. Label 0 appears roughly in 10% of the cases, while label 1 appears in 90% of the cases. Let's split the data randomly in a train and a dev dataset.

```
np.random.seed(42)
rnd = np.random.rand(len(y_)) < 0.8

X_train = Xinput[rnd,:]
y_train = y_[rnd]
X_dev = Xinput[~rnd,:]
y_dev = y_[~rnd]
```

We then normalize the training data.

```
X_train_normalised = X_train/255.0
```

We then transpose and prepare the tensors.

```
X_train_tr = X_train_normalised.transpose()
y_train_tr = y_train.reshape(1,y_train.shape[0])
```

Then we assign proper names to the variables.

```
Xtrain = X_train_tr
ytrain = y_train_tr
```

Then we build our network with one single neuron, exactly as we did in Chapter 2.

```
tf.reset_default_graph()

X = tf.placeholder(tf.float32, [n_dim, None])
Y = tf.placeholder(tf.float32, [1, None])
learning_rate = tf.placeholder(tf.float32, shape=())

W = tf.Variable(tf.zeros([1, n_dim]))
b = tf.Variable(tf.zeros(1))

init = tf.global_variables_initializer()y_ = tf.sigmoid(tf.matmul(W,X)+b)
cost = - tf.reduce_mean(Y * tf.log(y_)+(1-Y) * tf.log(1-y_))
training_step = tf.train.GradientDescentOptimizer(learning_rate).
minimize(cost)
```

If you don't understand the code, review Chapter 2 for more details. I expect that you now understand this simple model well, as we have seen it several times. Next, we define the function to run the model (you have seen it several times in the previous chapters).

```
def run_logistic_model(learning_r, training_epochs, train_obs, train_
labels, debug = False):
    sess = tf.Session()
    sess.run(init)

    cost_history = np.empty(shape=[0], dtype = float)

    for epoch in range(training_epochs+1):

        sess.run(training_step, feed_dict = {X: train_obs, Y: train_labels,
        learning_rate: learning_r})

        cost_ = sess.run(cost, feed_dict={ X:train_obs, Y: train_labels,
        learning_rate: learning_r})
        cost_history = np.append(cost_history, cost_)
```

```
        if (epoch % 10 == 0) & debug:
            print("Reached epoch",epoch,"cost J =", str.format
            ('{0:.6f}', cost_))

    return sess, cost_history
```

Let's run the model with the code

```
sess, cost_history = run_logistic_model(learning_r = 0.01,
                                training_epochs = 100,
                                train_obs = Xtrain,
                                train_labels = ytrain,
                                debug = True)
```

and check the accuracy with the following code (explained at length in Chapter 2, if you don't remember):

```
correct_prediction=tf.equal(tf.greater(y_, 0.5), tf.equal(Y,1))
accuracy = tf.reduce_mean(tf.cast(correct_prediction, tf.float32))
print(sess.run(accuracy, feed_dict={X:Xtrain, Y: ytrain, learning_rate:
0.05}))
```

We get an incredible 91.2% accuracy. Not bad, right? But are we sure that the result is that good? Now let's check the confusion matrix[1] for our labels with the code

```
ypred = sess.run(tf.greater(y_, 0.5), feed_dict={X:Xtrain, Y: ytrain,
learning_rate: 0.05}).flatten().astype(int)
confusion_matrix(ytrain.flatten(), ypred)
```

When you run the code, you get the following result:

```
array([[ 659, 4888],
       [ 6, 50503]], dtype=int64)
```

[1]In machine learning classification, the confusion matrix is one in which each column of the matrix represents the number of instances in a predicted class, while each row represents the number of instances in an actual class.

Slightly more nicely formatted and with some explanatory information, the matrix looks like Table 6-1.

Table 6-1. *Confusion Matrix for the model described in the text*

	Predicted Class 0	Predicated Class 1
Real class 0	659	4888
Real class 1	6	50503

How should we read the table? In the column "Predicted Class 0," you will see the number of observations that our model predicts as being of class 0 for each real class. 659 is the number of observations our model predicts as being of class 0 that are really in class 0. 6 is the number of observations that our model predicts in class 0 that are really in class 1.

It should be easy to see now that our model predicts effectively almost all observations to be in class 1 (a total of 4888 + 50,503 = 55,391). The number of correct classified observations is 659 (for class 0) and 50,503 (for class 1), for a total of 51,162 observations. Because we have a total of 56,056 observations in our training set, we get an accuracy of 51162/56056 = 0.912, as our TensorFlow code above told us. This is not because our model is good; it is simply because it has classified effectively all observations in class 1. In this case, we don't need a neural network to achieve this accuracy. What happens is that our model sees observations belonging to class 0 so rarely that it almost doesn't influence the learning, which is dominated by the observations in class 1.

What at the beginning seemed a nice result turns out to be a really bad one. This is an example of how bad things can go, if you don't pay attention to the distributions of your classes. This, of course, applies not only when splitting your dataset, but in general, when you approach a classification problem, regardless of the classifier you want to train (it does not apply only to neural networks).

Note When splitting your dataset in complex problems, you must pay special attention not only to the number of observations you have in your datasets but also to what observations you choose and to the distribution of the classes.

To conclude this section, let me give you a few hints on how to deal with unbalanced datasets.

- *Change your metric*: In the preceding example, you may want to use something else instead of accuracy, because it can be misleading. You could try using the confusion matrix, for example, or other metrics, such as precision, recall, or F1. Another important way of checking how your model is doing, and one that I strongly suggest you learn, is the ROC curve, which will help you tremendously.
- *Work with an undersampled dataset*. If, for example, you have 1000 observations in class 1 and 100 in class 2, you may create a new dataset with 100 random observations in class 1 and the 100 you have in class 2. The problem with this method, however, is that you usually will have a lot less data to feed to your model to train it.
- *Work with an oversampled dataset*. You may try to do the opposite. You may take the 100 observations in class 2 mentioned above and simply replicate them 10 times, to end up with 1000 observations in class 2 (sometimes called sampling with replacement).
- *Try to get more data in the class with less observations*: This is not always possible. In the case of fraudulent credit card transactions, you cannot go around and generate new data, unless you want to go to jail...

Precision, Recall, and F1 Metrics

Let's look at some other metrics that are very useful when dealing with unbalanced datasets. Consider the following example. Suppose we are doing some tests to determine if a subject has a certain disease or not. Imagine that we have 250 test results. Consider the following confusion matrix (you should know what that is from our previous discussion):

	Prediction : NO	*Prediction : YES*
True value : NO	75	15
True value : YES	10	150

We will indicate with N the total number of test results, in this case $N = 250$. We will use the following terminology:

- *True positives (tp)*: Tests that predicted yes, and the subjects really have the disease
- *True negatives (tn)*: Tests that predicted no, and the subjects do not have the disease
- *False positives (fp)*: Tests that predicted yes, and the subjects do not have the disease
- *False negatives (fn)*: Tests that predicted no, but the subjects do have the disease

This translates visually to the following:

	Prediction: *NO*	*Prediction*: *YES*
True value: *NO*	***TRUE NEGATIVES***	***FALSE POSITIVES***
True value: *YES*	***FALSE NEGATIVES***	***TRUE POSITIVES***

Let's also indicate with *ty* the number of patients who really have a disease, in this example, *ty* = 10 + 150 = 160, and with *tno*, the number of patients who don't have a disease, in this example, *tno* = 75 + 15 = 90. In the examples we would have

$$tp = 150$$

$$tn = 75$$

$$fp = 15$$

$$fn = 10$$

We can express several metrics as functions of the previously discussed terms. For example:

- **Accuracy**: $(tp + tn)/N$, how often our test is right
- **Misclassification rate**: $(fp + fn)/N$, how often our test is wrong. Note that this is equal to 1 − *accuracy*.
- **Sensitivity/Recall**: tp/ty, how often the test really predicts yes when the subjects have the disease

- **Specificity**: tn/tno, when the subjects have no disease, how often our test predicts no
- **Precision**: $tp/(tp+fp)$, the portion of tests predicting correctly the subject having the disease with respect to all positive results obtained

All those quantities can be used as metrics, depending on your problem. Let's create an example. Suppose your test should predict if a person has cancer or not. In this case, what you want is the highest sensitivity possible, because it is important to detect the disease. But at the same time, you also want the specificity to be high, because there is nothing worse than sending someone home without treatment when it is needed.

Let's look a bit closer at precision and recall. Having a high precision means that when you say someone is sick, you are right. But you don't know how many people really have the sickness, since the quantity is defined only by the result of your test. Precision is a measure of how your test is doing. Having a high recall means that you can identify all the sick people in your sample. Let me give you another example, to make the point even clearer. Suppose we have 1000 people. Only 10 are sick and 990 are healthy. Let's suppose we want to identify healthy people (this is important), and we build a test that returns yes if someone is healthy and **always** predicts that people are healthy. The confusion matrix would look like this:

	$Prediction: NO\,(Sick)$	$Prediction: YES\,(Healthy)$
$True: NO\,(Sick)$	0	10
$True: YES\,(Healthy)$	0	990

We would have

$$tp = 990$$

$$tn = 0$$

$$fp = 10$$

$$fn = 0$$

That means that

- Accuracy would be 99%.
- The misclassification rate would be 10/1000 or, in other words, 1%.
- Recall would be 990/990 or 100%.
- Specificity would be 0%.
- Precision would be 99%.

This looks good, right? If want to find healthy people, this test would be great. The only problem is that it is a lot more important to identify sick people! Let's recalculate the preceding quantities, but this time, considering that a positive result is when someone is sick. In this case, the confusion matrix would like this:

	$Prediction: NO(Healthy)$	$Prediction: YES(Sick)$
$True: NO(Healthy)$	990	0
$True: YES(Sick)$	10	0

because this time, a yes result means that someone is sick and not, as before, that someone is healthy. Let's calculate the quantities above again.

$$tp = 0$$

$$tn = 990$$

$$fp = 0$$

$$fn = 10$$

Therefore,

- Accuracy would still be 99%.
- The misclassification rate would still be 10/1000 or, in other words, 1%.
- Recall would now be 0/10 or 0%.
- Specificity would be 990/990 or 100%.
- Precision would be (0 + 0)/1000 or 0%.

Note how the accuracy remains the same. If you look only at that, you would not be able to understand how your model is doing. We have simply changed what we want to predict and use only accuracy. We cannot say anything about the performance of our model. But look at how recall and precision changed. See the matrix below for a comparison.

	Predicting healthy people	*Predicting sick people*
Recall	100%	0%
Precision	99%	0%

Now we have something that changes that can give us enough information, depending on the question we pose. Note that changing what we want to predict will change how the confusion matrix will look. We can immediately say, looking at the preceding matrix, that our model that predicts that everyone is healthy works very well when predicting healthy people (not very useful) but fails miserably when trying to predict sick people.

There is another metric that is important to know, and that is the F1 score. It is defined as

$$F1 = \frac{2}{\frac{1}{Precision} + \frac{1}{Recall}} = 2\frac{Precision \cdot Recall}{Precision + Recall}$$

An intuitive understanding is difficult to get, but it is basically the harmonic average of precision and recall. The example we created was a bit extreme and, having 0% for recall or precision, would not allow us to calculate $F1$. Let's suppose that our model is bad at predicting sick people, but not that bad. Let's suppose we have the following confusion matrix:

	Prediction: NO (Healthy)	*Prediction: YES (Sick)*
True: NO (Healthy)	985	5
True: YES (Sick)	9	1

In this case, we would have (I leave the calculation to you)

- Precision: 54.5%
- Recall: 10%

We would have

$$F1 = 2 \cdot \frac{0.545 * 0.1}{0.545 + 0.1} = 2 \frac{0.0545}{0.645} = 0.16.9 \rightarrow 16.9\%$$

This quantity will give you information keeping precision (the portion of tests predicting correctly the subject having the disease with respect to all positive results obtained) and recall (how often the test really predicts yes when the subjects have the disease) in consideration. For some problems, you want to maximize precision, and for others, you want to maximize recall. If that is the case, simply choose the right metric. The $F1$ score will be the same for two cases in which you have $Precision = 32\%$ and $Recall = 45\%$ and one with $Precision = 45\%$ and $Recall = 32\%$. Be aware of this fact. Use $F1$ score, if you want to find a balance between *Precision* and *Recall.*

Note The $F1$ score is used when you want to maximize the harmonic average of *Precision* and *Recall*, or, in other words, when you don't want to maximize either *Precision* or *Recall* alone, but you want to find the best balance between the two.

If we calculate $F1$ when predicting healthy people, as we did at first, we would have

$$F1 = 2 \frac{1.0 \cdot 0.99}{1.0 + 0.99} = 2 \frac{0.99}{1.99} = 0.995 \rightarrow 99.5\%$$

This tells us that the model is quite good at predicting healthy people.

The $F1$ score is usually useful, because, normally, as a metric, you want one single number, and in this way, you don't have to decide between precision or recall, as both are useful. Remember that the values of the metrics discussed will always be dependent on the question you are asking (what is yes and no for you). Be aware that an interpretation is *always* dependent on the question you want to answer.

Note Remember that when calculating your metric, whatever it may be, changing your question will change the results. You must be very clear at the beginning of what you want to predict and then choose the right metric. In the case of highly unbalanced datasets, it is always a good idea to use not accuracy but other metrics as recall, precision, or, even better, *F*1, it being an average of precision and recall.

Datasets with Different Distributions

Now I would like to discuss another terminology issue, which will lead you to understand a common problem in the deep-learning world. Very often, you will hear sentences such as "The sets come from different distributions." This sentence is not always easy to understand. Take, for example, two datasets formed by images taken with a professional DSLR, and a second one made up of images taken with a dodgy smartphone. In the deep-learning world, we would characterize those two sets as coming from different distributions. But what is the real meaning of the sentence? The two datasets differ for various reasons: resolution of images, blurriness resulting from different quality lenses, amount of colors, quality of the focus, and possibly more. All these differences are what is usually meant by *distributions*. Let's look at another example. We could consider two datasets: one made of images of white cats and one made of images of black cats. Also, in this case, we are talking about different distributions. This becomes a problem when you train a model on one set and want to apply it to the other. For example, if you train a model on a set of images of white cats, you probably are not going to do very well on the dataset of black cats, because your model has never seen black cats during training.

Note When talking about datasets coming from different distributions, it is usually meant that the observations have different characteristics in the two datasets: black and white cats, high and low-resolution images, speech recorded in Italian and German, and so on.

Because data is so precious, people often try to create different datasets (train, dev, etc.) from different sources. For example, you may decide to train your model on a set made of images taken from the Web and check how good it is with a set made of images you've taken with your smartphone. It may seem like a good idea to be able to use as much data as possible, but this may give you many headaches. Let's see what happens in a real case, so that you may get a feeling of the consequences of doing something similar.

Let's consider the subset of the MNIST dataset that we have used in Chapter 2, made of the two digits: 1 and 2. We will build a dev dataset coming from a different distribution, shifting a subset of the images 10 pixels to the right. We will train our model on the images as they are in the original dataset and apply the model to images shifted 10 pixels to the right and see what happens. Let's first load the data (you can check for more details Chapter 2).

```
import numpy as np
from sklearn.datasets import fetch_mldata
%matplotlib inline

import matplotlib
import matplotlib.pyplot as plt
from random import *

mnist = fetch_mldata('MNIST original')
Xinput,yinput = mnist["data"], mnist["target"]
```

We will do the data preparation exactly as in Chapter 2. First, let's select only digit 1 and 2.

```
X_ = Xinput[np.any([y == 1,y == 2], axis = 0)]
y_ = yinput[np.any([y == 1,y == 2], axis = 0)]
```

We have 14,867 observations in our dataset. Now let's create a train and a dev dataset with our random selection (as we have done before), as in this case, we have roughly the same number of ones and twos.

```
np.random.seed(42)
rnd_train = np.random.rand(len(y_)) < 0.8

X_train = X_[rnd_train,:]
y_train = y_[rnd_train]
```

```
X_dev = X_[~rnd_train,:]
y_dev = y_[~rnd_train]
```

Then we normalize the features.

```
X_train_normalized = X_train/255.0
X_dev_normalized = X_dev/255.0
```

And then we transform the matrices to have them with the right dimensions.

```
X_train_tr = X_train_normalized.transpose()
y_train_tr = y_train.reshape(1,y_train.shape[0])

n_dim = X_train_tr.shape[0]
dim_train = X_train_tr.shape[1]

X_dev_tr = X_dev_normalized.transpose()
y_dev_tr = y_dev.reshape(1,y_dev.shape[0])
```

Finally, we shift the labels to have 0 and 1 (if you don't remember why, you can quickly review Chapter 2).

```
y_train_shifted = y_train_tr - 1
y_dev_shifted = y_dev_tr - 1
```

Now let's give the arrays reasonable names.

```
Xtrain = X_train_tr
ytrain = y_train_shifted

Xdev = X_dev_tr
ydev = y_dev_shifted
```

We can check the sizes of the arrays with the code

```
print(Xtrain.shape)
print(Xdev.shape)
```

This gives us

```
(784, 11893)
(784, 2974)
```

We have 11,893 observations in our training set and 2974 in the dev set. Now let's duplicate the dev dataset and shift each image to the right by 10 pixels. We can do it quickly with the following code:

```
Xtraindev = np.zeros_like(Xdev)
for i in range(Xdev.shape[1]):
    tmp = Xdev[:,i].reshape(28,28)
    tmp_shifted = np.zeros_like(tmp)
    tmp_shifted[:,10:28] = tmp[:,0:18]
    Xtraindev[:,i] = tmp_shifted.reshape(784)

ytraindev = ydev
```

To make the shift easy, I first reshaped the images in a 28 × 28 matrix, then simply shifted the columns with `tmp_shifted[:,10:28] = tmp[:,0:18]`, and then I simply reshaped the images in a one-dimensional array of 784 elements. The labels remain the same. In Figure 6-7, you can see a random image from the dev dataset on the left and its shifted version on the right.

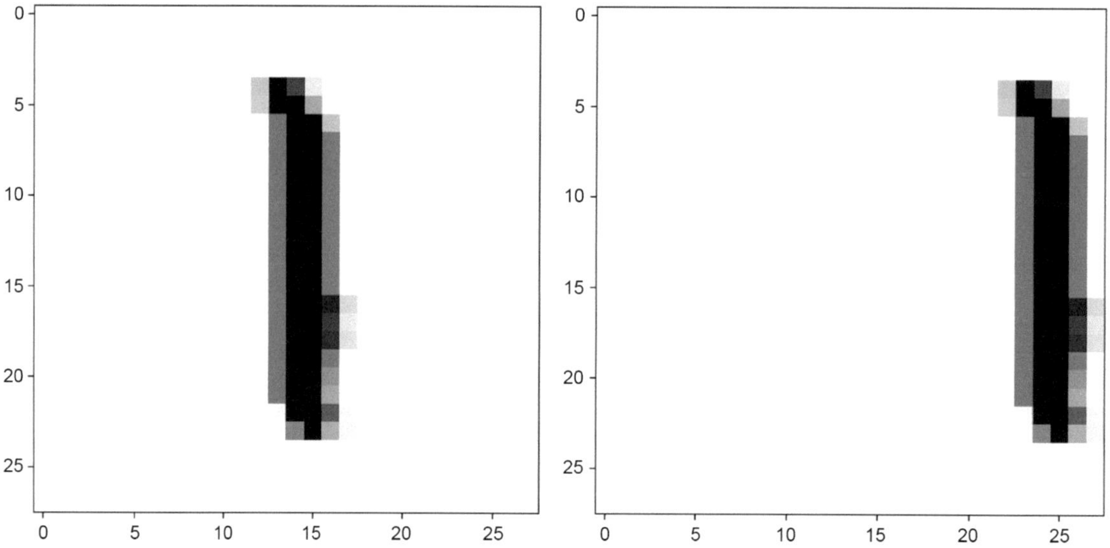

***Figure 6-7.** One random image from the dataset (left) and its shifted version (right)*

Now let's build a network with a single neuron and see what happens. We build the model as we have in Chapter 2.

```
tf.reset_default_graph()

X = tf.placeholder(tf.float32, [n_dim, None])
Y = tf.placeholder(tf.float32, [1, None])
learning_rate = tf.placeholder(tf.float32, shape=())

W = tf.Variable(tf.zeros([1, n_dim]))
b = tf.Variable(tf.zeros(1))

init = tf.global_variables_initializer()
y_ = tf.sigmoid(tf.matmul(W,X)+b)
cost = - tf.reduce_mean(Y * tf.log(y_)+(1-Y) * tf.log(1-y_))
training_step = tf.train.GradientDescentOptimizer(learning_rate).
minimize(cost)
```

To train the model, we will use the same function you have already seen

```
def run_logistic_model(learning_r, training_epochs, train_obs, train_
labels, debug = False):
    sess = tf.Session()
    sess.run(init)

    cost_history = np.empty(shape=[0], dtype = float)

    for epoch in range(training_epochs+1):

        sess.run(training_step, feed_dict = {X: train_obs, Y: train_labels,
        learning_rate: learning_r})

        cost_ = sess.run(cost, feed_dict={ X:train_obs, Y: train_labels,
        learning_rate: learning_r})
        cost_history = np.append(cost_history, cost_)

        if (epoch % 10 == 0) & debug:
            print("Reached epoch",epoch,"cost J =", str.format('{0:.6f}',
            cost_))

    return sess, cost_history
```

and we will train the model with the code

```
sess, cost_history = run_logistic_model(learning_r = 0.01,
                                        training_epochs = 100,
                                        train_obs = Xtrain,
                                        train_labels = ytrain,
                                        debug = True)
```

This gives us the output

```
Reached epoch 0 cost J = 0.678501
Reached epoch 10 cost J = 0.562412
Reached epoch 20 cost J = 0.482372
Reached epoch 30 cost J = 0.424058
Reached epoch 40 cost J = 0.380005
Reached epoch 50 cost J = 0.345703
Reached epoch 60 cost J = 0.318287
Reached epoch 70 cost J = 0.295878
Reached epoch 80 cost J = 0.277208
Reached epoch 90 cost J = 0.261400
Reached epoch 100 cost J = 0.247827
```

Next, let's calculate the accuracy of the three datasets: Xtrain, Xdev, and Xtraindev, with the code

```
correct_prediction=tf.equal(tf.greater(y_, 0.5), tf.equal(Y,1))
accuracy = tf.reduce_mean(tf.cast(correct_prediction, tf.float32))
print(sess.run(accuracy, feed_dict={X:Xtrain, Y: ytrain, learning_rate:
0.05}))
```

simply using the right `feed_dict` for the three datasets. We get the following results after 100 epochs:

- For the training dataset, we get 96.8%.
- For the dev dataset, we get 96.7%.
- For the train-dev (you will see later why it is called like this), the one with the shifted images, we get 46.7%. A very bad result.

What has happened is that the model has learned from a dataset where all images are centered in the box and, therefore, could not generalize well to images shifted and no longer centered.

When training a model on a dataset, usually you will get good results for observations that are like the ones in the training set. But how can you find out if you have such a problem? There is a relatively easy way of doing that: expanding our MAD diagram. Let's see how to do it.

Suppose you have a training dataset and a dev dataset in which the observations have different characteristics (come from different distributions). What you do is create a small subset from the training set, called the train-dev dataset, ending up with three datasets: a training and a train-dev from the same distribution (the observations have the same characteristics) and a dev set, for which the observations are somehow different, as I have discussed previously. What you do now is train your model on your training set and then evaluate your error ϵ on the three datasets: ϵ_{train}, ϵ_{dev}, and $\epsilon_{train-dev}$. If your train and dev sets come from the same distributions, so does the train-dev set. In this case, you should expect $\epsilon_{dev} \approx \epsilon_{train-dev}$. If we define

$$\Delta\epsilon_{train-dev} = \epsilon_{train-dev}$$

we should expect $\Delta\epsilon_{train-dev} \approx 0$. If the train (and train-dev) and the dev set come from different distributions (the observations have different characteristics), we should expect $\Delta\epsilon_{trian-dev}$ to be big. If we consider the MNIST example we have created before, we have, in fact, $\Delta\epsilon_{train-dev} = 0.437$, or 43.7%, which is a huge difference. Let's recap what you should do to determine if your training and your dev (or test) dataset have observations with different characteristics (come from different observations).

1. Split your training set in two—one that you will use for training and one we will call the train set—and a smaller one that you will call train-dev set.
2. Train your model on the train set.
3. Evaluate your error ϵ on the three sets: train, dev, and train-dev.
4. Calculate the quantity $\Delta\epsilon_{train-dev}$. If it is big, this will provide strong evidence that the original training and dev sets come from different distributions.

In Figure 6-8, you can see an example of the MAD diagram with the added problem just discussed. Don't look at the numbers; they are there only for illustrative purposes (read: I just put them there).

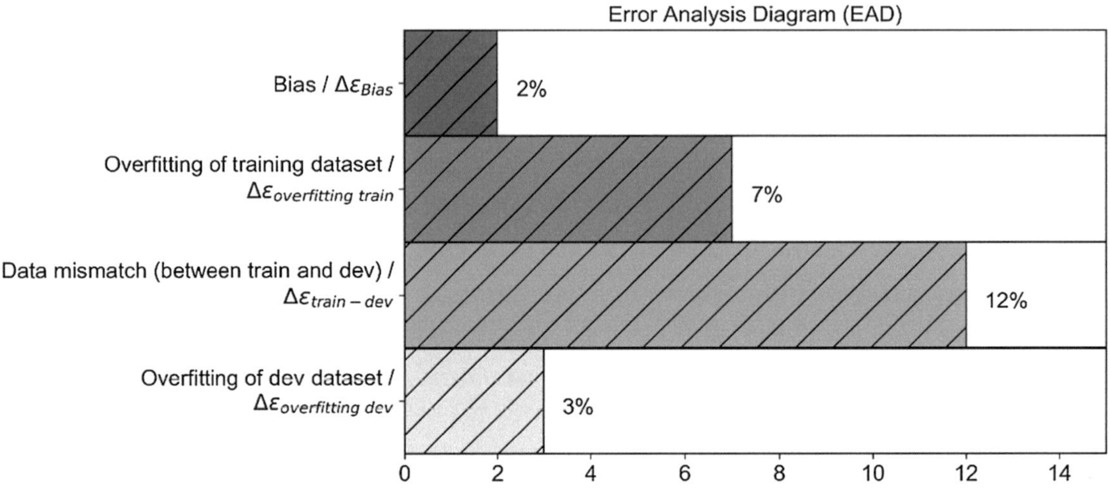

Figure 6-8. *Example of the MAD diagram with the data mismatch problem added. Don't look at the numbers; they are there strictly for illustrative purposes.*

The MAD diagram in Figure 6-8 can tell us the following things. (I highlight in the bulleted list only a few items. For a more complete list, review the previous sections.)

- The bias (between training and human-level performance) is quite small, so we are not that far from the best we can achieve (let's assume here that human-level performance is a proxy for the Bayes error). Here, you could try bigger networks, better optimizers, and so on.
- We are overfitting the datasets, so we could try regularization or get more data.
- We have a strong problem with data mismatch (sets coming from different distributions) between train and dev. At the end of this section, I suggest what you could do to solve this problem.
- We are also slightly overfitting the dev dataset, during our hyperparameter search.

Note that you don't need to create the bar plot, as I have done here. Technically, you require only the four numbers, to draw the same conclusions.

Note Once you have your MAD diagram (or simply the numbers), interpreting it will give you hints on what you should try to get better results, for example, higher accuracy.

You can try the following techniques to address data mismatch between sets:

- You can conduct manual error analysis, to understand the difference between the sets, and then decide what to do (in the last section of the chapter, I will give you an example). This is time-consuming and usually quite difficult, because once you know what the difference is, it may be very difficult to find a solution.
- You could try to make the training set more like your dev/test sets. For example, if you are working with images and the test/dev sets have a lower resolution, you may decide to lower the resolution of the images in the training set.

As usual, there are no fixed rules. Just be aware of the problem and think about the following: your model will learn the characteristics from your training data, so when applied to completely different data, it (usually) won't do well. Always get training data that reflect the data you want your model to work on, not vice versa.

K-Fold Cross-Validation

Now I would like to finish this chapter with another technique that is very powerful and should be known by any machine-learning practitioner (not only in the deep-learning world): k-fold cross-validation. The technique is a way of finding a solution to the following two problems:

- What to do when your dataset is too small to split it in a train and dev/test set
- How to get information on the variance of your metric

Let's describe the idea with pseudo-code.

1. Partition your complete dataset in k equally big subsets: $f_1, f_2, \ldots, f_k$. The subsets are also called folds. Normally the subsets are not overlapping, that means that each observation appears in one and only one fold.
2. For `i` going from 1 to k:
   - Train your model on all the folds except f_i
   - Evaluate your metric on the fold f_i. The fold f_i will be the dev set in iteration i
3. Evaluate the average and variance of your metric on the k results

A typical value for k is 10, but that depends on the size of your dataset and the characteristic of your problem.

Remember that the discussion we did on how to split a dataset applies here also.

Note When you are creating your folds, you must take care that they reflect the structure of your original dataset. For example, if your original dataset has 10 classes, you must make sure that each of your folds has all the 10 classes, with the same proportions.

Although this may seem a very attractive technique to deal generally with datasets with less than optimal size, it may be quite complex to implement. But, as you will see shortly, checking your metric on the different folds will give you important information on possible overfitting of your training dataset.

Let's try it on a real dataset and see how to implement it. Note that you can implement k-fold cross-validation easily in with the sklearn library, but I will develop it from scratch, to show you what is happening in the background. Everyone (well, almost) can copy code from the Web to implement k-fold cross-validation in sklearn, but not many can explain how it works or understand it, therefore being able to choose the right sklearn method or parameters. As a dataset, we will use the same we used in Chapter 2: the reduced MNIST dataset containing only digits 1 and 2. We will perform a simple logistic regression with one neuron, to make the code easy to understand and to let us concentrate on the cross-validation part and not on other implementation details that are not relevant here. The goal of this section is to let you understand how k-fold cross-validation works and why it is useful, not on how to implement it with the smallest number of lines of code possible.

Let's import the necessary libraries, as usual.

```
import numpy as np
from sklearn.datasets import fetch_mldata

%matplotlib inline

import matplotlib
import matplotlib.pyplot as plt

from random import *
```

Then let's import the MNIST dataset.

```
mnist = fetch_mldata('MNIST original')
Xinput_,yinput_ = mnist["data"], mnist["target"]
```

Remember that the dataset has 70,000 observations and is made of grayscale images, each 28 × 28 pixels in size. You can again check Chapter 2 for a detailed discussion. Then let's select only digits 1 and 2 and rescale the labels, to make sure that digit 1 has label 0 and digit 2 has label 1. You will remember from Chapter 2 that the cost function we will use for logistic regression expects the two labels to be 0 and 1.

```
Xinput = Xinput_[np.any([yinput_ == 1,yinput_ == 2], axis = 0)]
yinput = yinput_[np.any([yinput_ == 1,yinput_ == 2], axis = 0)]
yinput = yinput - 1
```

We can check the number of observations with the code

```
Xinput.shape[0]
```

We have 14,867 observations (images). Now we perform a small trick. To keep the code simple, we want each fold to have the same number of observations. Technically speaking, this is not required, and you will often end up with the last fold having a number of observations that is smaller than the others. In this case, if we want 10 folds, we cannot have in each fold the same number of observations, because 14,867 is not a multiple of 10. To make things easier, let's simply remove the last seven images from the dataset. (From an aesthetic point of view, this is horrible, but it will make our code much easier to understand and write.)

```
Xinput = Xinput[:-7,:]
yinput = yinput[:-7]
```

Now let's create 10 arrays, each containing a list of indexes that we will use to select images.

```
foldnumber = 10
idx = np.arange(0,Xinput.shape[0])
np.random.shuffle(idx)
al = np.array_split(idx,foldnumber)
```

In each fold, we will have, as expected, 1486 images. Now let's create the arrays containing the images.

```
Xinputfold = []
yinputfold = []
for i in range(foldnumber):
    tmp = Xinput[al[i],:]
    Xinputfold.append(tmp)
    ytmp = yinput[al[i]]
    yinputfold.append(ytmp)

Xinputfold = np.asarray(Xinputfold)
yinputfold = np.asarray(yinputfold)
```

if you think this code is convoluted, you are right. There are faster ways of doing it with the sklearn library, but it is very instructive to see how to do it manually, step by step. I am convinced that the preceding code, in which each step is isolated, makes understanding it easier. We first create empty lists: `Xinputfold` and `yinputfold`. Each element of the list will be a fold, that is, an array of images or labels. So, if we want to get all images in fold 2, we will simply use `Xinputfold[1]`. (Remember: In Python, indexes start from zero.). Those listed, converted with the last two lines in numpy arrays, will have three dimensions, as you can easily see with the statements

```
print(Xinputfold.shape)
print(yinputfold.shape)
```

This gives us

```
(10, 1486, 784)
(10, 1486)
```

In `Xinputfold`, the first dimension indicates the fold number, the second the observation, and the third the gray values of the pixels. In `yinputfold`, the first dimension indicates the fold number and the second the label. For example, to get an image with index 1234 from fold 0, you would have to use the following code:

```
Xinputfold[0][1234,:]
```

Remember: You should check that you still have a balanced dataset in each fold or, in other words, that you have as many ones as twos. Let's check for fold 0 (you can do the same check for the others).

```
for i in range(0,2,1):
    print ("label", i, "makes", np.around(np.count_nonzero(yinputfold[0] ==
i)/1486.0*100.0, decimals=1), "% of the 1486 observations")
```

This gives us

```
label 0 makes 51.2 % of the 1486 observations
label 1 makes 48.8 % of the 1486 observations
```

That, for our purposes, is balanced enough. Now we need to normalize the features (as we did in Chapter 2).

```
Xinputfold_normalized = np.zeros_like(Xinputfold, dtype = float)
for i in range (foldnumber):
    Xinputfold_normalized[i] = Xinputfold[i]/255.0
```

You could normalize the data in one shot, but I would like to make it evident that we are dealing with folds, to make it clear for the reader. Now let's reshape the arrays as we need them.

```
X_train = []
y_train = []
for i in range(foldnumber):
```

```
    tmp = Xinputfold_normalized[i].transpose()
    ytmp = yinputfold[i].reshape(1,yinputfold[i].shape[0])
    X_train.append(tmp)
    y_train.append(ytmp)

X_train = np.asarray(X_train)
y_train = np.asarray(y_train)
```

The code is written in the easiest way possible, for instructive purposes, not in the most optimized way. Now we can check the dimensions of the final arrays with

```
print(X_train.shape)
print(y_train.shape)
```

This gives us

```
(10, 784, 1486)
(10, 1, 1486)
```

Exactly what we need. Now we are ready to build our network. We will use a one-neuron network for logistic regression, with the sigmoid activation function.

```
import tensorflow as tf
tf.reset_default_graph()

X = tf.placeholder(tf.float32, [n_dim, None])
Y = tf.placeholder(tf.float32, [1, None])
learning_rate = tf.placeholder(tf.float32, shape=())

#W = tf.Variable(tf.zeros([1, n_dim]))
W = tf.Variable(tf.random_normal([1, n_dim], stddev= 2.0 / np.sqrt(2.0*n_
dim)))
b = tf.Variable(tf.zeros(1))
y_ = tf.sigmoid(tf.matmul(W,X)+b)
cost = - tf.reduce_mean(Y * tf.log(y_)+(1-Y) * tf.log(1-y_))
training_step = tf.train.AdamOptimizer(learning_rate = learning_rate, beta1
= 0.9, beta2 = 0.999, epsilon = 1e-8).minimize(cost)

init = tf.global_variables_initializer()
```

Here, we have used the Adam optimizer, but the gradient descent would work as well. This is a very easy case. We will use our well-known function to train the model.

```
def run_logistic_model(learning_r, training_epochs, train_obs, train_
labels, debug = False):
    sess = tf.Session()
    sess.run(init)

    cost_history = np.empty(shape=[0], dtype = float)

    for epoch in range(training_epochs+1):

        sess.run(training_step, feed_dict = {X: train_obs, Y: train_labels,
        learning_rate: learning_r})


        cost_ = sess.run(cost, feed_dict={ X:train_obs, Y: train_labels,
        learning_rate: learning_r})
        cost_history = np.append(cost_history, cost_)

        if (epoch % 200 == 0) & debug:
            print("Reached epoch",epoch,"cost J =", str.format('{0:.6f}',
            cost_))

    return sess, cost_history
```

At this point, we will have to iterate through the folds. Remember our pseudo code at the beginning? Select one fold as the dev set and train the model on all other folds concatenated. Proceed in this way for all the folds. The code could look like that following. (It is a bit long, so take a few minutes to understand it.) In the code, I have added comments indicating which step we are talking about, since you will find following a corresponding numbered list of explanatory steps.

```
train_acc = []
dev_acc = []

for i in range (foldnumber): # Step 1

    # Prepare the folds - Step 2
    lis = []
    ylis = []
```

```
    for k in np.delete(np.arange(foldnumber), i):
        lis.append(X_train[k])
        ylis.append(y_train[k])
        X_train_ = np.concatenate(lis, axis = 1)
        y_train_ = np.concatenate(ylis, axis = 1)

    X_train_ = np.asarray(X_train_)
    y_train_ = np.asarray(y_train_)

    X_dev_ = X_train[i]
    y_dev_ = y_train[i]


    # Step 3
    print('Dev fold is', i)
    sess, cost_history = run_logistic_model(learning_r = 5e-4,
                                 training_epochs = 600,
                                 train_obs = X_train_,
                                 train_labels = y_train_,
                                 debug = True)

    # Step 4
    correct_prediction=tf.equal(tf.greater(y_, 0.5), tf.equal(Y,1))
    accuracy = tf.reduce_mean(tf.cast(correct_prediction, tf.float32))
    print('Train accuracy:',sess.run(accuracy, feed_dict={X:X_train_, Y:
    y_train_, learning_rate: 5e-4}))
    train_acc = np.append( train_acc, sess.run(accuracy, feed_dict={X:X_
    train_, Y: y_train_, learning_rate: 5e-4}))

    correct_prediction=tf.equal(tf.greater(y_, 0.5), tf.equal(Y,1))
    accuracy = tf.reduce_mean(tf.cast(correct_prediction, tf.float32))
    print('Dev accuracy:',sess.run(accuracy, feed_dict={X:X_dev_, Y: y_
    dev_, learning_rate: 5e-4}))
    dev_acc = np.append( dev_acc, sess.run(accuracy, feed_dict={X:X_dev_,
    Y: y_dev_, learning_rate: 5e-4}))

    sess.close()
```

The code follows these steps:

1. Do a loop over all the folds (in this case, from 1 to 10), iterating with the variable i from 0 to 9.
2. For each i, use the fold i as the dev set, and concatenate all other folds and use the result as train set.
3. For each i, train the model.
4. For each i, evaluate the accuracy on the two datasets (train and dev) and save the values in the two lists: `train_acc` and `dev_acc`.

If you run this code, you will get an output that will look like the following, for each fold (you will get 10 times the following output, once for each fold):

```
Dev fold is 0
Reached epoch 0 cost J = 0.766134
Reached epoch 200 cost J = 0.169536
Reached epoch 400 cost J = 0.100431
Reached epoch 600 cost J = 0.074989
Train accuracy: 0.987289
Dev accuracy: 0.984522
```

You will notice that you will get for each fold slightly different accuracy values. It is very instructive to study how the accuracy values are distributed. Because we have 10 folds, we have 10 values to study. In Figure 6-9, you can see the distribution of the values for the train set (left) and for the dev set (right).

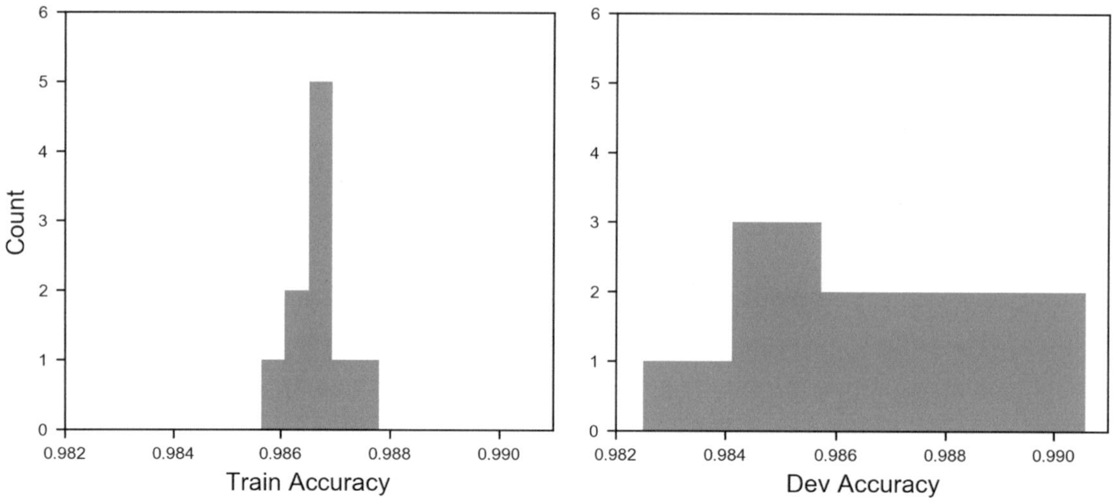

***Figure 6-9.** Distribution of the accuracy values for the train set (left) and for the dev set (right). Note that the two plots use the same scale on both axes.*

The image is quite instructive. You can see that the accuracy values for the training set are quite concentrated around the average, while the ones evaluated on the dev set are much more spread. This shows how the model on new data behaves less well than on the data it has trained on. The standard deviation for the training data is $5.4 \cdot 10^{-4}$ and for the dev set $2.4 \cdot 10^{-3}$, 4.5 times larger than the value on the train set. In this way, you also get an estimate of the variance of your metric when applied on new data, and on how it generalizes. If you are interested in learning how to do this quickly with sklearn, you can check the official documentation for the `KFold` method here: `https://goo.gl/Gq1Ce4`. When you are dealing with datasets with many classes (remember the discussion on how to split your sets?), you must pay attention and do what is called stratified sampling.[2] sklearn provides a method to do that too: `stratifiedKFold`, which can be accessed here: `https://goo.gl/ZBKrdt`.

You can now easily find averages and standard deviations. For the training set, we have an average accuracy of 98.7% and a standard deviation of 0.054%, while for the dev set, we have an average of 98.6% with a standard deviation of 0.24%. So, now you can even give an estimate of the variance of your metric. Pretty cool!

[2]Wikipedia, "Stratified sampling," `https://goo.gl/Wd8fuD`,2018. "In statistical surveys, when subpopulations within an overall population vary, it is advantageous to sample each subpopulation (stratum) independently. Stratification is the process of dividing members of the population into homogeneous subgroups before sampling."

Manual Metric Analysis: An Example

I mentioned earlier that sometimes it is useful to do a manual analysis of your data, to check if the results (or the errors) you are getting are plausible. I would like to give you a basic example here, to give you a concrete idea of what is involved and how complicated it can be. Let's consider the following: our very simple model (remember, we are using only one neuron) can get 98% of accuracy. Is the problem of recognizing digits that easy? Let's try to see if that is the case. First, note that our training set does not even have the two-dimensional information of the images. If you remember, each image is converted in a one-dimensional array of values: the gray values of each pixel, starting on the top left and going row by row from top to bottom. Are the ones and the twos so easy to recognize? Let's check how the real input for our model might look. Let's start analyzing the digit 1. Let's take an example from fold 0. In Figure 6-10, you can see the image on the left and a bar plot of the gray values of 784 pixels, as they are seen from our model. Remember that as observations, we have a one-dimensional array of the 784 gray values of the pixels of the image.

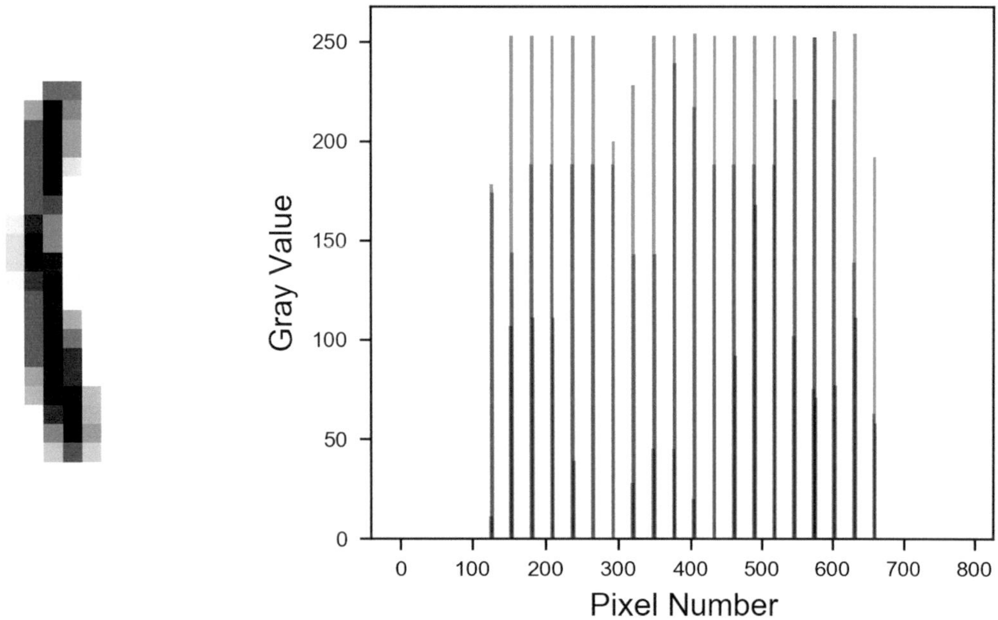

Figure 6-10. *Example from fold 0 for the digit 1. The image on the left is a bar plot of the gray values of the 784 pixels, as they are seen in our model on the right. Remember that as inputs, we have a one-dimensional array of the 784 gray values of the pixels of the image.*

Remember that we reshape our 28 × 28 pixels image in a one-dimensional array, so when reshaping the digit 1 in Figure 6-10, we will find black points roughly each 28 pixels, because the 1 is almost a vertical column of black points. In Figure 6-11, you can see other ones, and you will notice how, when reshaped as one dimensional, they all look the same: several bars roughly equally spaced. Now that you know what to look for, you can easily say that all the images in Figure 6-11 are all of digit 1.

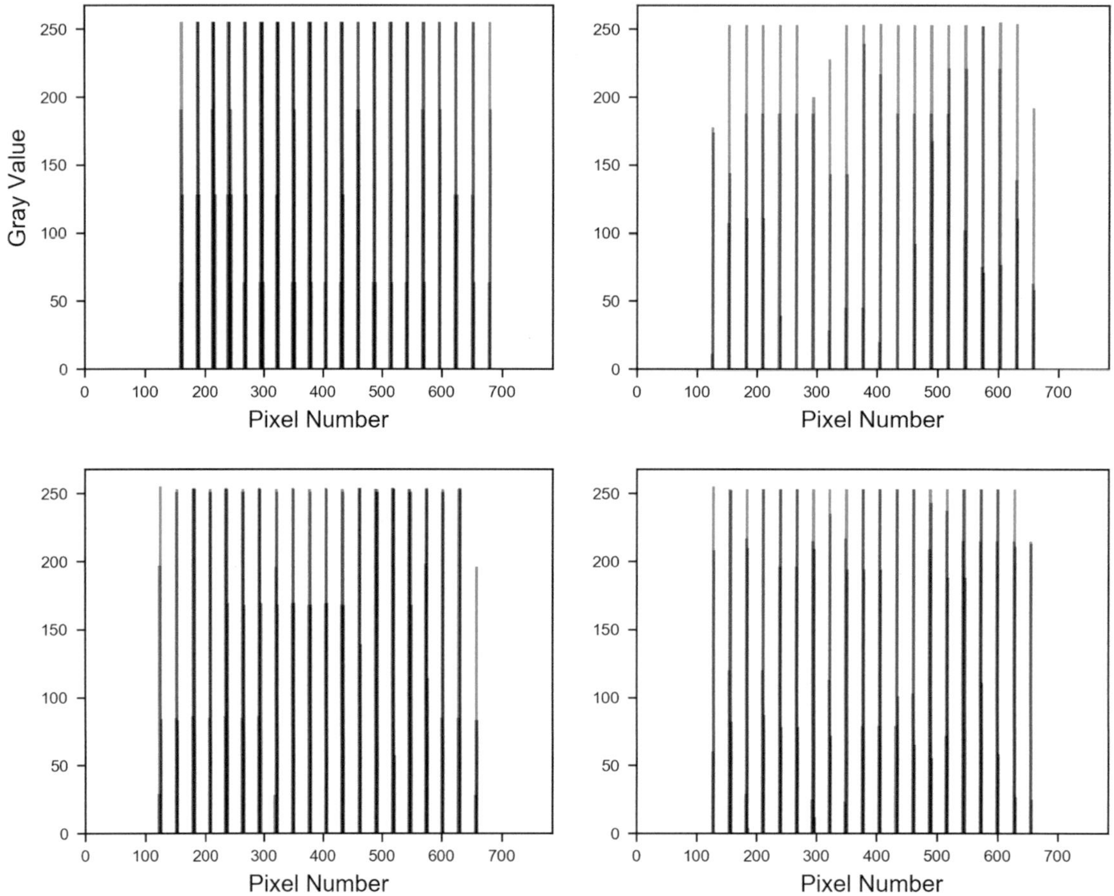

Figure 6-11. *Four examples of the digit 1 reshaped as one-dimensional arrays. All look the same: a number of bars roughly equally spaced.*

Now let's look at the digit 2. In Figure 6-12, you can see an example, similar to what we had in Figure 6-10.

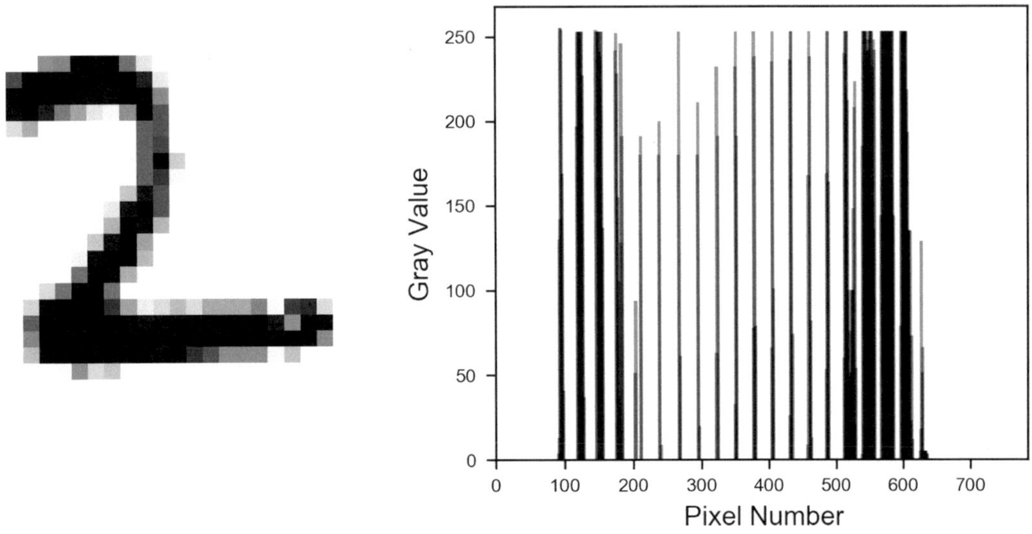

***Figure 6-12.** Example from fold 0 for the digit 2. The image on the left is a bar plot of the gray values of the 784 pixels, as they are seen in our model. Remember that as observations, we have a one-dimensional array of the 784 gray values of the pixels of the image.*

Now things look different. We have two regions in which the bars are much denser, seen in the plot on the right in Figure 6-12. This is the case between pixels 100 and 200 and especially after pixel 500. Why? Well, the two areas correspond to the two horizontal parts of the image. In Figure 6-13, I have highlighted how different parts look when reshaped as one-dimensional arrays.

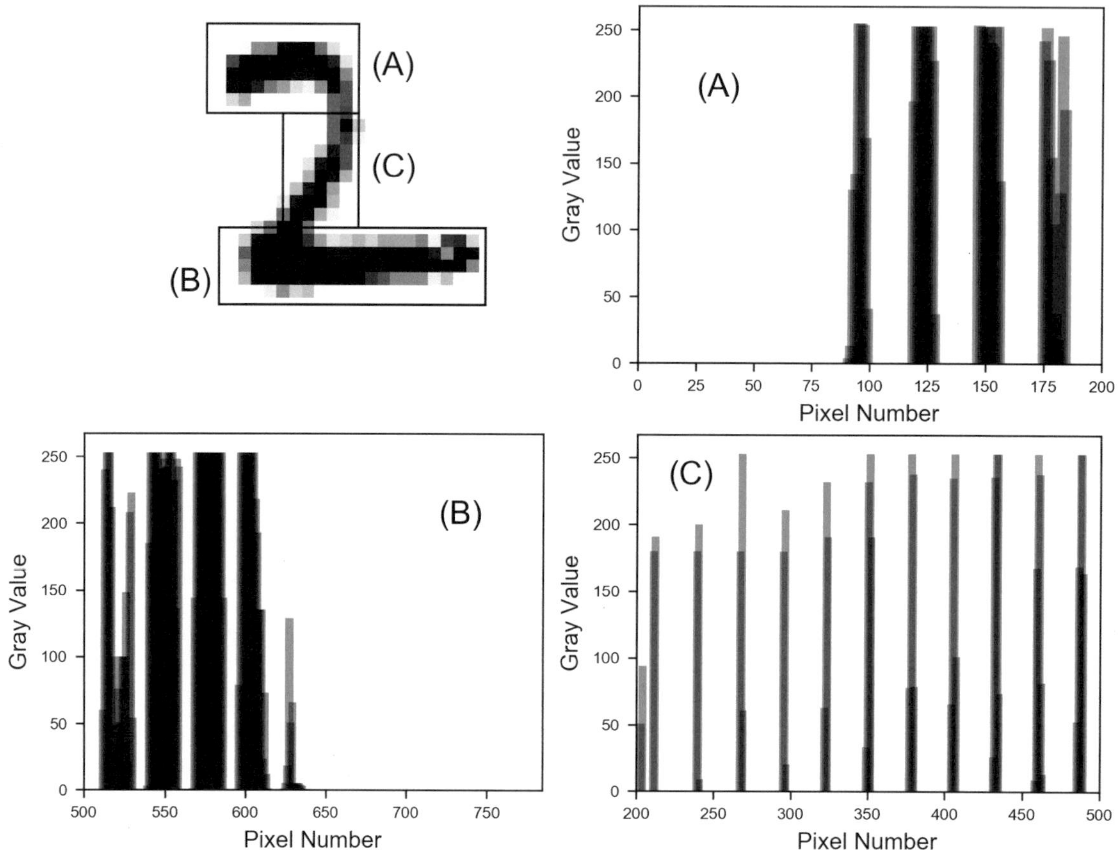

***Figure 6-13.** How different parts of the images look when reshaped as one-dimensional arrays. Horizontal parts are labeled (A) and (B), and the more vertical part is labeled (C).*

Horizontal parts (A) and (B) are clearly different from part (C) when reshaped as a one-dimensional array. The vertical part (C) looks like the digit 1, with many equally spaced bars, as you can see in the lower right bar plot labeled (C), while the more horizontal parts appear as many bars clustered in groups, as can be seen in the upper right and lower left bar plots labeled (A) and (B). So, when reshaped, if you find those clusters of bars, you are looking at a 2. If you see only equally spaced small groups of bars, as in the plot (C) in Figure 6-13, you are looking at a 1. You don't even have to see the two-dimensional image, if you know what to look for. Note that this pattern is very constant. In Figure 6-14, you can see four examples of the digit 2, and you can clearly see the wider clusters of bars.

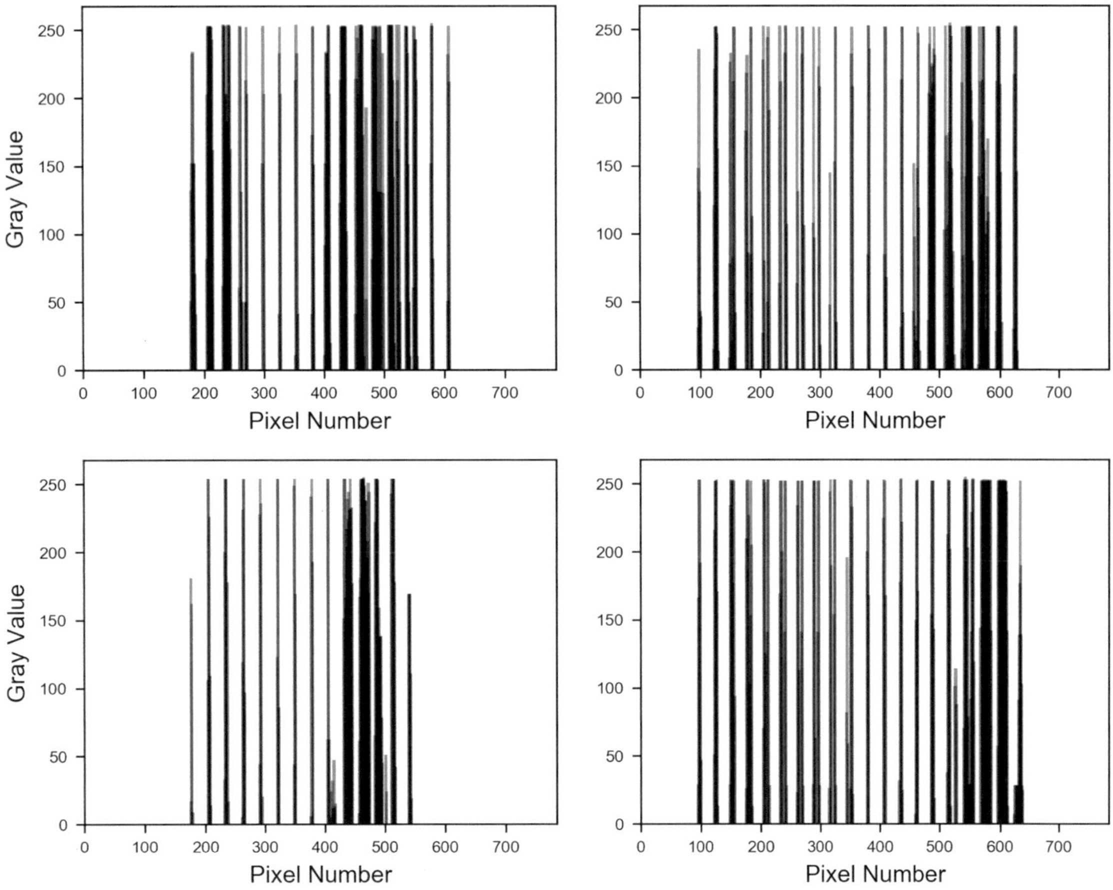

Figure 6-14. *Four examples of the digit 2, reshaped as one-dimensional arrays. The wider clusters of bars can be seen clearly.*

As you can imagine, this is an easy pattern to spot for an algorithm, and so it is to be expected that our model works well. Even a human can spot the images, even when reshaped, without any effort. Such a detailed analysis would not be necessary in a real-life project, but it is instructive to see what you can learn from your data. Understanding the characteristics of your data may help you in designing your model or understanding why it is not working. Advanced architectures, such as convolutional networks, will be able to learn those two-dimensional features exactly in a very efficient way.

Let's also check how the network learned to recognize digits. You will remember that the output of our neuron is

$$\hat{y} = \sigma(z) = \sigma\left(w_1 x_1 + w_2 x_2 + \ldots + w_{n_x} x_{n_x} + b\right)$$

where σ is the sigmoid function, x_i for $i = 1, \ldots, 784$ are the gray values of the pixel of the image, w_i for $i = 1, \ldots, 784$ are the weights, and b is the bias. Remember that when $\hat{y} > 0.5$, we classify the image in class 1 (so, digit 2), and if $\hat{y} < 0.5$, we classify the image in class 0 (so, digit 1). Now from the discussion of the sigmoid function in Chapter 2, you will remember that $\sigma(z) \geq 0.5$ when $z \geq 0$ and $\sigma(z) < 0.5$ for $z < 0$. This means that our network should learn the weights in such a way that for all the ones, we have $z < 0$, and for all the twos, $z \geq 0$. Let's see if that is really the case. In Figure 6-15, you can see a plot for a digit 1, from which you can find the weights w_i (solid line) of our trained network after 600 epochs (and after reaching an accuracy of 98%) and the gray value of the pixel x_i rescaled to have a maximum of 0.5 (dashed line). Note how each time x_i is big, w_i is negative. And when $w_i > 0$, the x_i are almost zero. Clearly, the result $w_1x_1 + w_2x_2 + \ldots + w_{n_x}x_{n_x} + b$ will be negative, and, therefore, $\sigma(z) < 0.5$, and the network will identify the image as a 1. In the image, I zoomed in to make this behavior more evident.

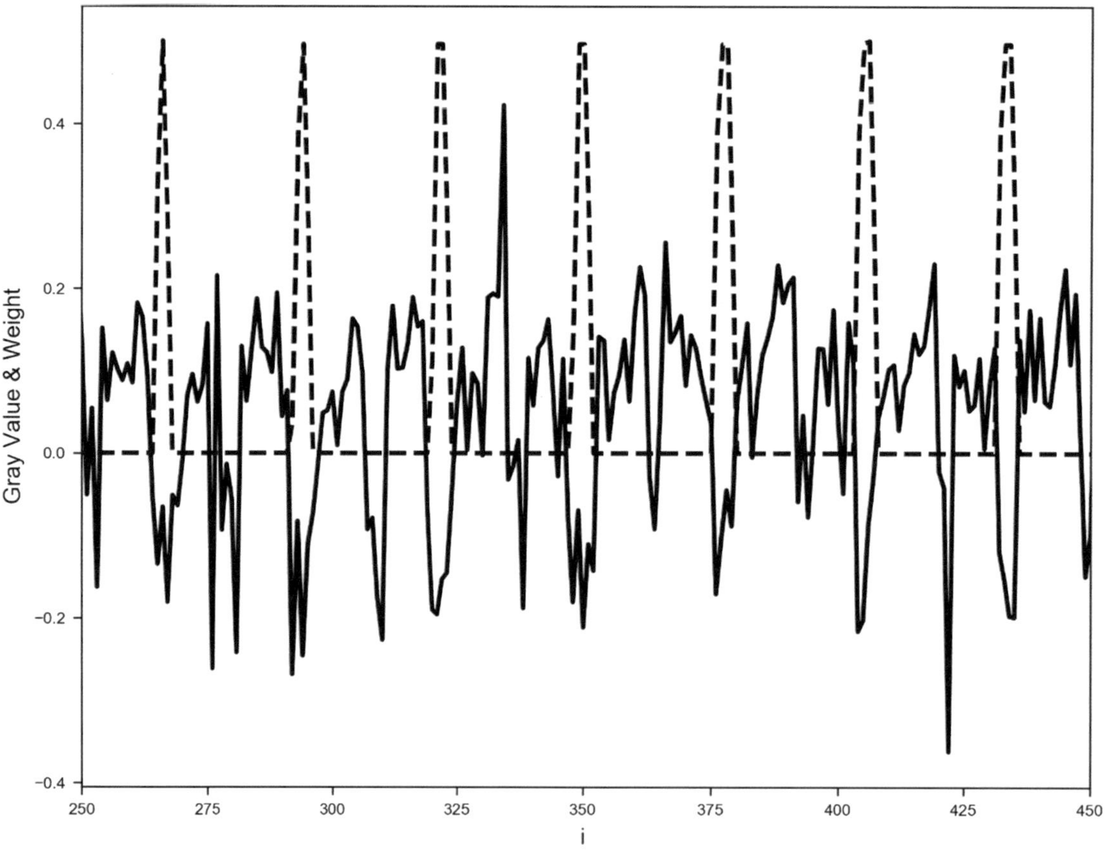

***Figure 6-15.** Plot for a digit 1, from which you can find the weights w_i (solid line) of our trained network after 600 epochs (and after reaching an accuracy of 98%) and the gray value of the pixel x_i rescaled to have a maximum of 0.5 (dashed line)*

In Figure 6-16, you can see the same plot for a digit 2. You will remember from the previous discussion that for a 2, we can see many bars clustered together in groups up to pixel 250 (roughly). Let's check how the weights in that region are. Now you will see that where the pixel gray values are big, the weights are positive, giving, then, a positive value of z and, therefore, $\sigma(z) \geq 0.5$, and so the image would be classified as a 2.

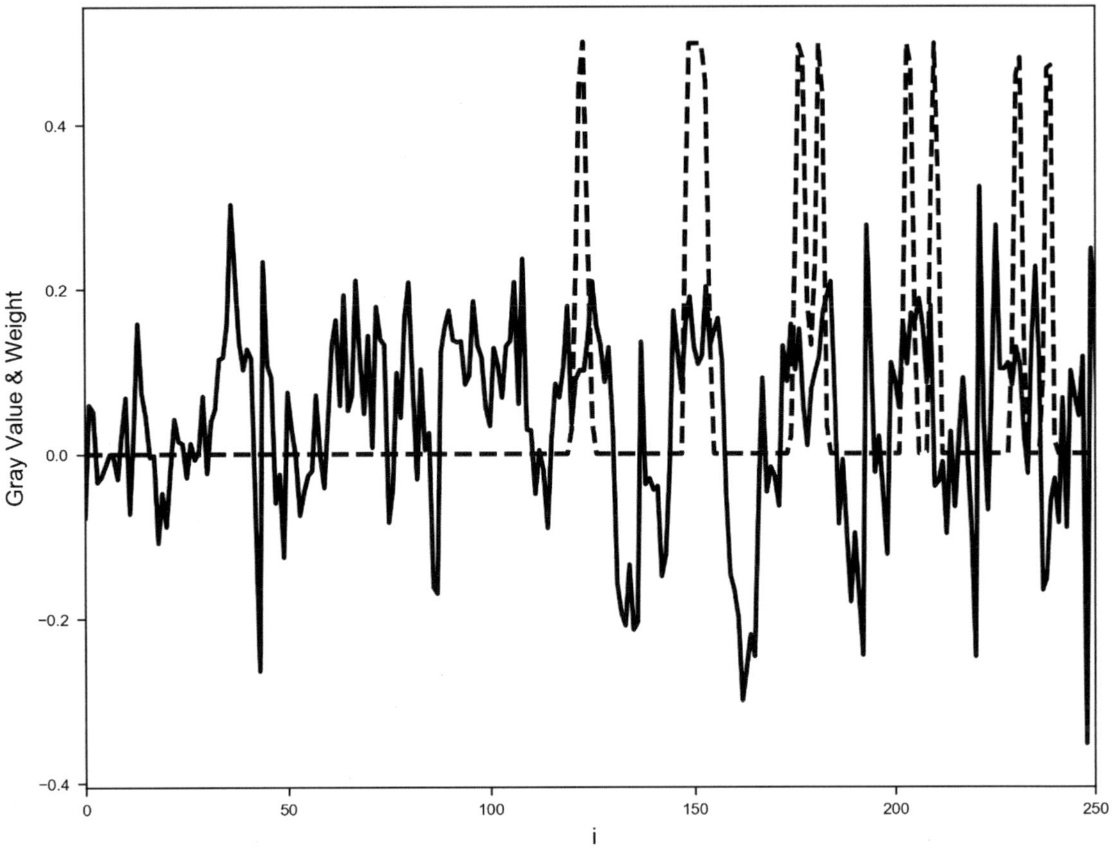

***Figure 6-16.** Plot for a digit 2, from which you can find the weights w_i (solid line) of our trained network after 600 epochs (and after reaching an accuracy of 98%) and the gray value of the pixel x_i rescaled to have a maximum of 0.5 (dashed line)*

As an additional check, I plotted $w_i \cdot x_i$ for all values of i for a digit 1, shown in Figure 6-17. You can see how almost all points lie below zero. Note also that $b = -0.16$, in this case.

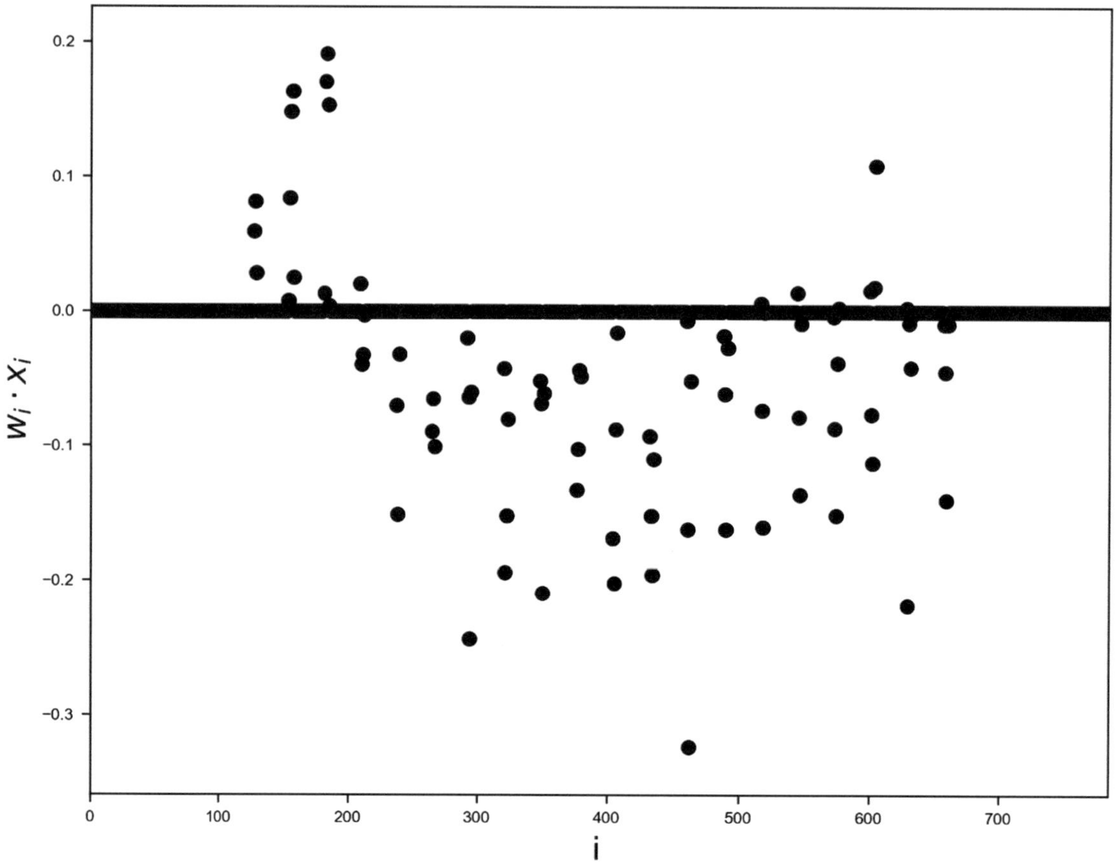

Figure 6-17. *$w_i \cdot x_i$ for $i = 1, \ldots, 784$ for a digit 1. You can see how almost all values lie below zero. The thick line at zero is made of all the points i, such that $w_i \cdot x_i = 0$.*

As you can see, in very easy cases, it is possible to understand how a network learns and, therefore, it is much easier to debug strange behaviors. But don't expect this to be possible when dealing with much more complex cases. The analysis we have done would not be so easy, for example, if you tried to do the same with digits 3 and 8, instead of 1 and 2.

CHAPTER 7

Hyperparameter Tuning

In this chapter, you will look at the problem of finding the best hyperparameters to get the best results from your models. First, I will describe what a black-box optimization problem is, and how that class of problems relate to hyperparameter tuning. You will see the three best-known methods to tackle these kind of problems: grid search, random search, and Bayesian optimization. I will show you, with examples, which one works under which conditions, and I will give you a few tricks that are very helpful for improving optimization and sampling on a logarithmic scale. At the end of the chapter, I will show you how you can use those techniques to tune a deep model, using the Zalando dataset.

Black-Box Optimization

The problem of hyperparameter tuning is just a subclass of a much more general type of problem: black-box optimization. A black-box function $f(x)$

$$f(x):\mathbb{R}^n \rightarrow \mathbb{R}$$

is a function whose analytic form is unknown. A black-box function can be evaluated to obtain its value for all values of x that are defined, but no other information (such as its gradient) can be obtained. Generally, by the term *global optimization of a black-box function* (sometimes called a black-box problem), we mean that we are trying to find the maximum or minimum of $f(x)$, sometimes under certain constraints. Here are some examples of this kind of problem:

- Finding the hyperparameter for a given machine-learning model that maximizes the chosen optimizing metric

U. Michelucci, *Applied Deep Learning*, https://doi.org/10.1007/978-1-4842-3790-8_7

- Finding the maximum or minimum of a function that can only be evaluated numerically or with code that we cannot look at. In some industry contexts, there can be legacy code that is very complicated, and there are some functions that must be maximized, based on its outcome.
- Finding the best place to drill for oil. In this case, your function would be how much oil you can find and x your location.
- Finding the best combination of parameters for situations that are too complex to model, for example, when launching a rocket in space, how to optimize the amount of fuel, diameter of each stage of the rocket, precise trajectory, etc.

This is a very fascinating class of problems, which has produced smart solutions. You will see three of them: grid search, random search, and Bayesian optimization. If you are curious about the subject, you can check out the black-box optimization competition at `https://goo.gl/LY7huY`. The rules of the competition mirror real-life problems. A problem is set up for which you must optimize a function (find the maximum or minimum) through a black-box interface. You can get the value of the function for all values of x, but you cannot get any other information, as its gradients, for example.

Why does finding the best hyperparameters for neural networks constitute a black-box problem? Because we cannot calculate information, such as the gradients of our network output, with respect to the hyperparameters, especially when using complex optimizers or custom functions, we require other approaches, to be able to find the best hyperparameters that maximize the chosen optimizing metric. Note that if we could have the gradients, we could use an algorithm as the gradient descent to find the maximum or minimum.

Note Our black-box function f will be our neural network model (including things such as the optimizer, cost function form, etc.) that gives as output our optimizing metric, given the hyperparameters as input, and x will be the array containing the hyperparameters.

The problem may seem quite trivial. Why not try all the possibilities? Well, this may be possible in the examples you have looked at in previous chapters, but if you are working on a problem and training your model takes a week, this may present a challenge. Because, typically, you will have several hyperparameters, trying all possibilities will not be feasible. Let's consider an example to understand this better. Suppose we are training a model of a neural network with several layers. We may decide to consider the following hyperparameters, to see which combination works better:

- *Learning rate*: Suppose we want to try the values $n \cdot 10^{-4}$ for $n = 1, \ldots, 10^2$. (100 values)
- *Regularization parameter*: 0, 0.1, 0.2, 0.3, 0.4, and 0.5 (6 values)
- *Choice of optimizer*: GD, RMSProp, or Adam (3 values)
- *Number of hidden layers*: 1, 2, 3, 5, and 10 (5 values)
- *Number of neurons in the hidden layers*: 100, 200, and 300 (3 values)

Consider that you will need to train your network

$$100 \times 6 \times 3 \times 5 \times 3 = 27000$$

times, if you want to test all possible combinations. If your training takes 5 minutes, you will require 13.4 weeks of computing time. If the training takes hours or days, you will not have any chance. If the training takes one day, for example, you will require 73.9 years to try all possibilities. Most of the hyperparameter choices will come from experience. For example, you can always use Adam safely, because it is the better optimizer available (in almost all cases). But you will not be able to avoid trying to tune other parameters, such as the number of hidden layers or learning rate. You can reduce the number of combinations you need with experience (as with the optimizer), or with some smart algorithm, as you will see later in this chapter.

Notes on Black-Box Functions

Black-box functions are usually classified into two main classes:

- *Cheap functions*: Functions that can be evaluated thousands of times
- *Costly functions*: Functions that can only be evaluated a few times, usually less than 100 times

If the black-box function is cheap, the choice of the optimization method is not critical. For example, we can evaluate the gradient with respect to the x numerically, or simply search the maximum evaluating the functions on a high number of points. If the function is costly, we need much smarter approaches. One of these is Bayesian optimization, which I will discuss later in this chapter, to give you an idea of how these methods work and how complex they are.

Note Especially in the deep-learning world, neural networks are almost always costly functions.

For costly functions, we must find methods that solve our problem with the smallest number of evaluations possible.

The Problem of Hyperparameter Tuning

Before looking at how we can find the best hyperparameters, I would like to quickly go back to neural networks and discuss what can we tune in deep models. Typically, when talking about hyperparameters, beginners think only of numerical parameters, such as the learning rate or regularization parameter, for example. Remember that the following also can be varied, to see if you can get better results:

- *Number of epochs*: Sometimes, simply training your network longer will give you better results.
- *Choice of optimizer*: You can try choosing a different optimizer. If you are using plain gradient descent, you may try Adam and see if you get better results.
- *Varying the regularization method*: As discussed previously, there are several ways of applying regularization. Varying the method may well be worth trying.
- *Choice of activation function*: Although the activation function always used in the previous chapters for neurons in hidden layers was ReLU, others may work a lot better. Trying sigmoid or Swish, for example, may help you get better results.

- *Number of layers and number of neurons in each layer: try different configurations*: Try layers with different numbers of neurons, for example.
- *Learning rate decay methods*: Try (if you are not using optimizers that do this already) different learning rate decay methods.
- *Mini-batch size*: Vary the size of mini-batches. When you have little data, you can use batch gradient descent. When you have a lot of data, mini-batches are more efficient.
- *Weight initialization methods*

Let's classify the parameters we can tune in our models in the following three categories:

- Parameters that are continuous real numbers or, in other words, that can assume any value. Example: learning rate, regularization parameter
- Parameters that are discrete but can theoretically assume an infinite number of values. Example: number of hidden layers, number of neurons in each layer, or number of epochs
- Parameters that are discrete and can only assume a finite number of possibilities. Example: optimizer, activation function, learning rate decay method.

For category 3, there is not much to do except try all possibilities. Typically, these parameters will completely change the model itself, and, therefore, it is impossible to model their effects, making a test the only possibility. This is also the category for which experience may help the most. It is widely known that the Adam optimizer is almost always the best choice, for example, so you may concentrate your efforts somewhere else at the beginning. For categories 1 and 2, this is a bit more difficult, and we will have to come up with some smart ideas to find the best values.

Sample Black-Box Problem

To try our hands at solving a black-box problem, let's create a "fake" black-box problem. The problem is the following: find the maximum of the function $f(x)$ given by the formula

$$g(x) = \cos\frac{x}{4} - \sin\frac{x}{4} - \frac{5}{2}\cos\frac{x}{2} + \frac{1}{2}\sin\frac{x}{2}$$

$$h(x) = -\cos\frac{x}{3} - \sin\frac{x}{3} - \frac{5}{2}\cos\frac{2}{3}x + \frac{1}{2}\sin\frac{2}{3}x$$

$$f(x) = 10 + g(x) + \frac{1}{2}h(x)$$

pretending not to know the formula itself. The formula will allow us to check our results, but we will pretend they are unknown. You may wonder why we use such a complicated formula. I wanted to have something with a few maxima and minima, to give you an idea of how the methods work on a non-trivial example. $f(x)$ can be implemented in Python with the code

```
def f(x):
    tmp1 = -np.cos(x/4.0)-np.sin(x/4.0)-2.5*np.cos(2.0*x/4.0)+0.5*np.
sin(2.0*x/4.0)
    tmp2 = -np.cos(x/3.0)-np.sin(x/3.0)-2.5*np.cos(2.0*x/3.0)+0.5*np.
sin(2.0*x/3.0)
    return 10.0+tmp1+0.5*tmp2
```

In Figure 7-1, you can see how $f(x)$ looks.

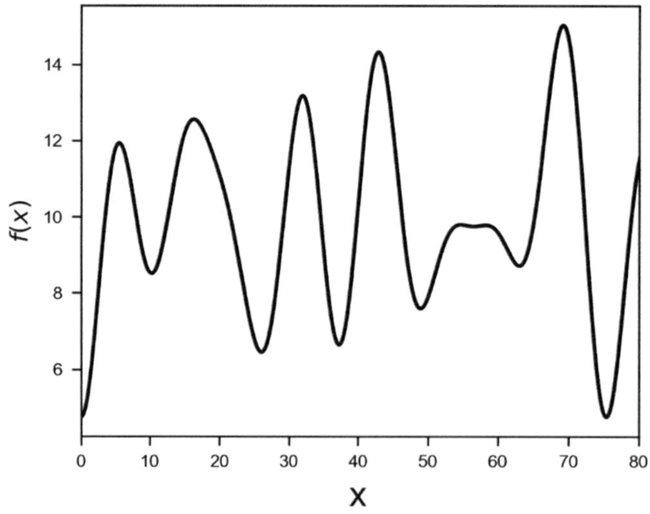

Figure 7-1. *Plot of the function f(x), as described in the text*

The maximum is at an approximate value $x = 69.18$ and has a value of 15.027. Our challenge is to find this maximum in the most efficient way possible, without knowing anything about $f(x)$, except its value at any point we want. When we say "efficient," we mean, of course, with the smallest number of evaluations possible.

Grid Search

The first method we look at, grid search, is also the least "intelligent." Grid search entails simply trying the function at regular intervals and seeing for which x the function $f(x)$ assumes the highest value. In this example, we want to find the maximum of the function $f(x)$ between two x values x_{min} and x_{max}. What we will do is simply take n points equally spaced between x_{min} and x_{max} and evaluate the function at these points. We will define a vector of points

$$\boldsymbol{x} = \left(x_{min}, x_{min} + \frac{\Delta x}{n}, \ldots, x_{min} + (n-1)\frac{\Delta x}{n} \right)$$

where we defined $\Delta x = x_{max} - x_{min}$. Then we evaluate the function $f(x)$ at those points, obtaining a vector $\boldsymbol{f}$ of values

$$\boldsymbol{f} = \left(f(x_{min}), f\left(x_{min} + \frac{\Delta x}{n} \right), \ldots, f\left(x_{min} + (n-1)\frac{\Delta x}{n} \right) \right)$$

The estimate of the maximum $(\tilde{x}, \tilde{f})$ will then be

$$\tilde{f} = \max_{0 \le i \le n-1} f_i$$

and, assuming the maximum is found at $i = \tilde{i}$, we will also have

$$\tilde{x} = x_{\min} + \frac{\tilde{i}\Delta x}{n}$$

Now, as you may imagine, the more points you use, the more accurate your maximum estimation will be. The problem is that, if the evaluation of $f(x)$ is costly, you will not be able to take as many points as you might like. You will need to find a balance between number of points and accuracy. Let's explore an example with the function

$f(x)$ that I described earlier. Let's consider $x_{max} = 80$ and $x_{min} = 0$, and let's take $n = 40$ points. We will have $\frac{\Delta x}{n} = 2$. We can create the vector $\boldsymbol{x}$ easily in Python with the following code:

```
gridsearch = np.arange(0,80,2)
```

The array `gridsearch` will look like this:

```
array([ 0, 2, 4, 6, 8, 10, 12, 14, 16, 18, 20, 22, 24, 26, 28, 30, 32,
34, 36, 38, 40, 42, 44, 46, 48, 50, 52, 54, 56, 58, 60, 62, 64, 66, 68,
70, 72, 74, 76, 78])
```

In Figure 7-2, you can see the function $f(x)$ as a continuous line; the crosses mark the points we sample in the grid search; and the black square marks the precise maximum of the function. The right plot shows a zoom around the maximum.

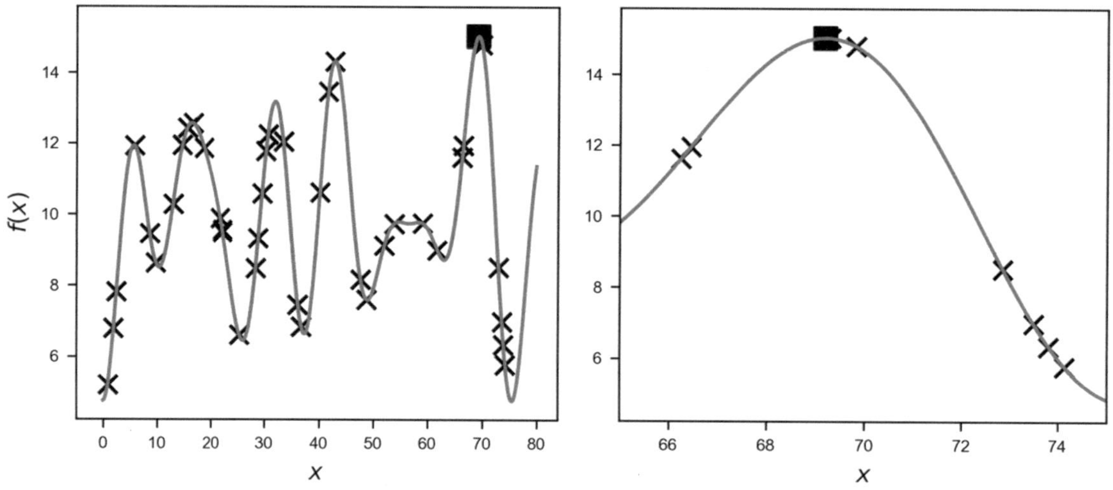

***Figure 7-2.** Function f(x) on the range [0, 80]. The crosses mark the point we sample in the grid search, and the black square marks the maximum.*

You can see how the points we sample in Figure 7-2 get close to the maximum but don't get it exactly. Of course, sampling more points would get us closer to the maximum but would cost us more evaluations of $f(x)$. We can find the maximum $\left(\tilde{x}, \tilde{f}\right)$ easily with the trivial code

```
x = 0
m = 0.0
for i, val in np.ndenumerate(f(gridsearch)):
    if (val > m):
        m = val
        x = gridsearch[i]

print(x)
print(m)
```

This gives us

```
70
14.6335957578
```

This is close to the actual maximum (69.18, 15.027) but not quite right. Let's try the previous example, varying the number of points we sample, and then see what results we get. We will vary the number of points sampled *n* from 4 to 160. For each case, we will find the maximum and its location, as described earlier. We can do it with the code

```
xlistg = []
flistg = []

for step in np.arange(1,20,0.5):
    gridsearch = np.arange(0,80,step)

    x = 0
    m = 0.0
    for i, val in np.ndenumerate(maxim(gridsearch)):
        if (val > m):
            m = val
            x = gridsearch[i]

    xlistg.append(x)
    flistg.append(m)
```

In the lists `xlistg` and `flistg`, we will find the position of the maximum found and the value of the maximum for the various values of *n*.

In Figure 7-3, we plot the distributions of the results. The black vertical line is the correct value of the maximum.

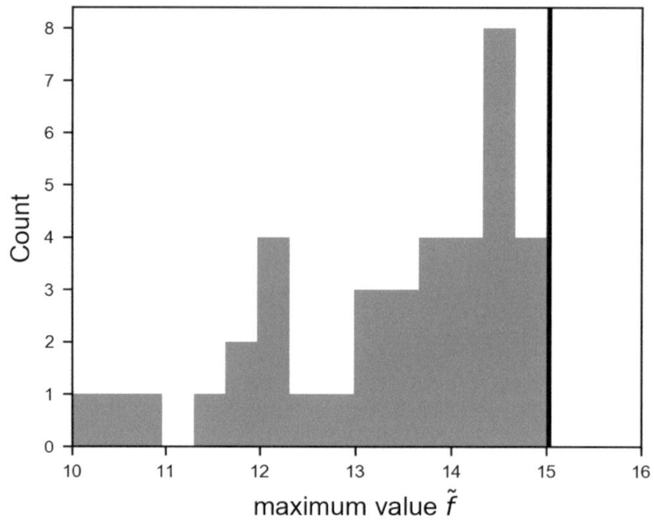

***Figure 7-3.** Distribution of the results for $\tilde{f}$ obtained by varying the number of points n sampled in the grid search. The black vertical line indicates the real maximum of f(x).*

As you can see, the results vary quite a lot and can be very far from the correct value, as far as 10. This tells us that using the wrong number of points can yield very wrong results. As you can imagine, the best results are the ones with the smallest step Δx, because it is more probable to get closer to the maximum. In Figure 7-4, you can see how the value of the found maximum varies with the step Δx.

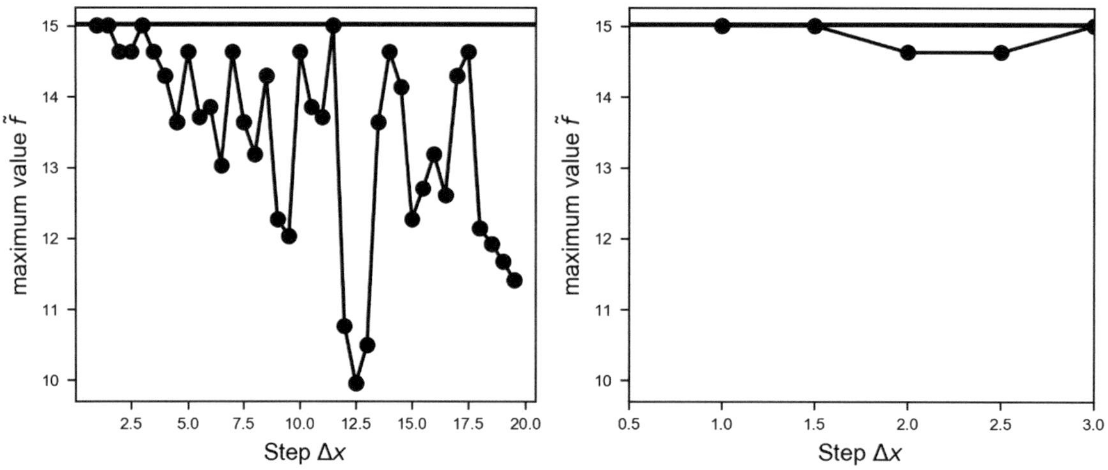

***Figure 7-4.** Behavior of the found value of the maximum vs. the x step Δx*

In the zoom in the right plot in Figure 7-4, it is evident how smaller values of Δx get you better values of $\tilde{f}$. Note that a step of 1.0 means sampling 80 values of $f(x)$. If, for example, the evaluation takes 1 day, you will have to wait 80 days to get all the measurements you require.

Note Grid search is a method that is efficient only when the black-box function is cheap. To get good results, a big number of sampling points is usually needed.

To make sure you are really getting the maximum, you should decrease the step Δx, or increase the number of sampling points, until the maximum value you find does not change appreciably anymore. In the preceding example, as you see from the right plot in Figure 7-4, we are sure we are close to the maximum when our step Δx gets smaller than roughly 2.0, or, in other words, when the number of sampled points is greater or roughly equal to 40. Remember: 40 may seem quite a small number at first sight, but if $f(x)$ evaluates the metric of your deep-learning model, and the training takes 2 hours, for example, you are looking at 3.3 days of computer time. Normally, in the deep-learning world, 2 hours is not much for training a model, so make a quick calculation before starting a long grid search. Additionally, keep in mind that when doing hyperparameter tuning, you are moving in a multidimensional space (you are not optimizing only one parameter, but many), so the number of evaluations needed gets big very fast.

Let's create a quick example. Suppose you decide you can afford 50 evaluations of your black-box function. If you decide you want to try the following hyperparameters:

- Optimizer (RMSProp, Adam, or plain GD) (3 values)
- Number of epochs (1000, 5000, or 10,000) (3 values)

you are already looking at nine evaluations. How many values of the learning rate can you then afford to try? Only five! And with five values, it is not probable to get close to the optimal value. This example has the goal of helping you to understand how grid search is viable only for cheap black-box functions. Remember that often time is not the only problem. For example, if you are using the Google cloud platform to train your network, you are paying for the hardware you use by the second. Maybe you have lots of time at your disposal, but costs may exceed your budget very quickly.

Random Search

A strategy that is as "dumb" as grid search but works amazingly a lot better is random search. Instead of sampling x points regularly in the range (x_{min}, x_{max}), you sample the points randomly. We can do it with the code

```
Import numpy as np
randomsearch = np.random.random([40])*80.0
```

The array randomsearch will look like this:

```
array([ 0.84639256, 66.45122608, 74.12903502, 36.68827838, 61.71538757,
69.29592273, 48.76918387, 69.81017465, 1.91224209, 21.72761762,
22.17756662, 9.65059426, 72.85707634, 2.43514133, 53.80488236, 5.70717498,
28.8624395 , 33.44796341, 14.51234312, 41.68112826, 42.79934087,
25.36351055, 58.96704476, 12.81619285, 15.40065752, 28.36088144,
30.27009067, 16.50286852, 73.49673641, 66.24748556, 8.55013954,
29.55887325, 18.61368765, 36.08628824, 22.1053749 , 40.14455129,
73.80825225, 30.60089111, 52.01026629, 47.64968904])
```

Depending on the seed you used, the actual numbers you get may be different. As we have done for grid search, you can see in Figure 7-5 the plot of $f(x)$, where the crosses mark the sampled points, and the black square the maximum. On the right plot, you see a zoom around the maximum.

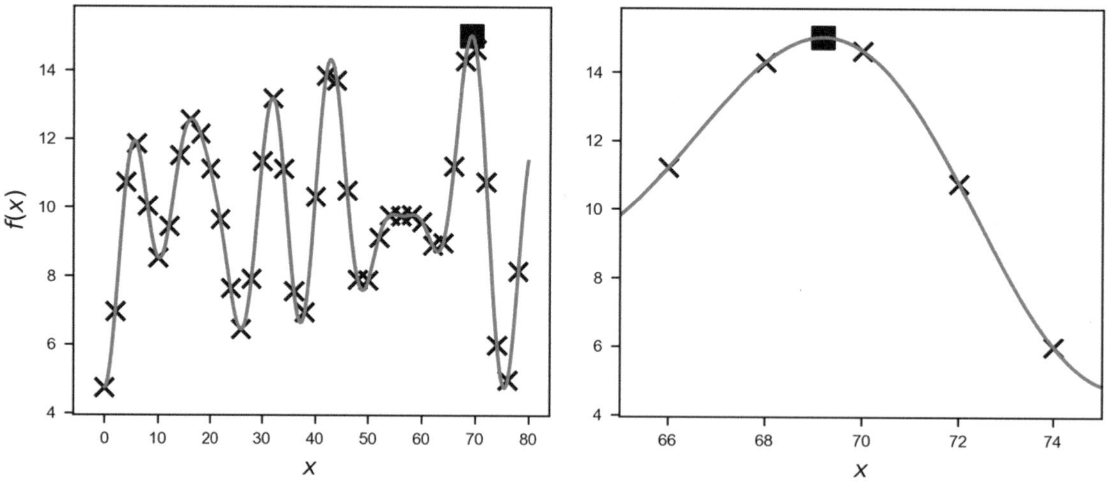

***Figure 7-5.** Function f(x) on the range [0, 80]. The crosses mark the point we sampled with random search, and the black square marks the maximum.*

The risk with this method is that if you are very unlucky, your random chosen points are nowhere close to the real maximum. But that probability is quite low. Note that if you take a constant probability distribution for your random points, you have the same probability of getting the points everywhere. It is interesting to see how this method performs. Let's consider 200 different random sets of 40 points, obtained by varying the random seed used in the code. The distributions of the maximum found $\tilde{f}$ is plotted in Figure 7-6.

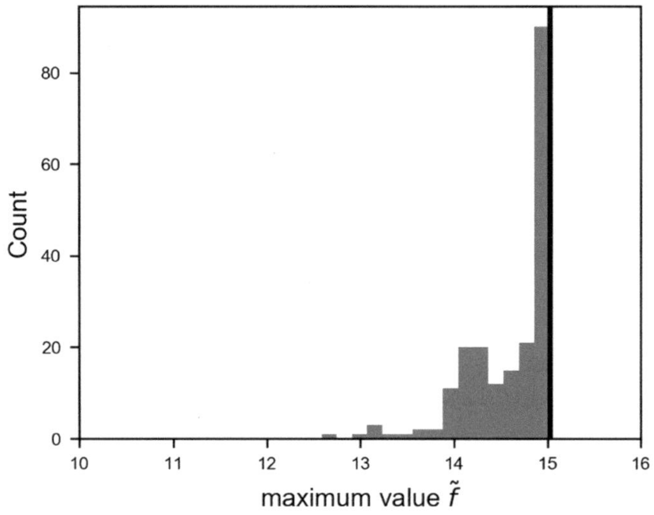

Figure 7-6. *Distribution of the results for* $\tilde{f}$ *obtained by 200 different random sets of 40 points sampled in the random search. The black vertical line indicates the real maximum of f(x).*

As you can see, regardless of the random sets used, you get, in the most cases, very close to the real maximum. In Figure 7-7, you can see the distributions of the maximum found with random search varying the number of points sampled, from 10 to 80.

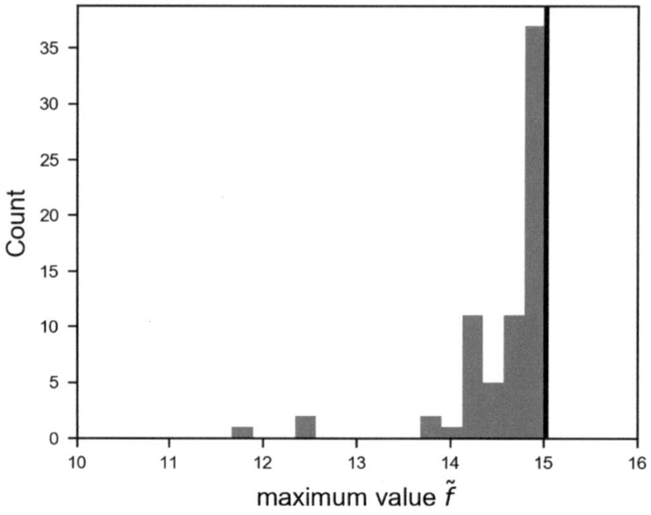

Figure 7-7. *Distribution of the results for $\tilde{f}$ obtained by varying the number of points n sampled in the random search, from 10 to 80. The black vertical line indicates the real maximum of f(x).*

If you compare it with grid search, you can see that random search is consistently better at getting results closer to the real maximum. In Figure 7-8, you can see a comparison between the distribution you get for your maximum $\tilde{f}$ when using a different number of sampling points *n* with random and grid searches. In both cases, the plots were generated with 38 different sets, so that the total count is the same.

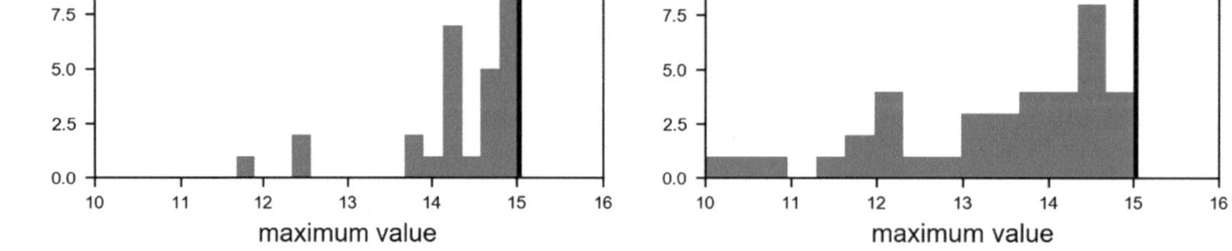

Figure 7-8. *Comparison of the distribution of $\tilde{f}$ between grid (right) and random (left) searches, while varying the number of sampling points n. Both plots count sums to 38, the number of different numbers of sampling points used. The correct value of the maximum is marked by the vertical black line in both plots.*

It is easy to see how on average random search is better than grid search. The values you get are consistently closer to the right maximum.

Note Random search is consistently better than grid search, and you should use it whenever possible. The difference between random search and grid search becomes even more marked when dealing with a multidimensional space for your variable *x*. Hyperparameter tuning is practically always a multidimensional optimization problem.

If you are interested in a very good paper on how random search scales for high dimensional problems, read James Bergstra and Yoshua Bengio, *Random Search for Hyper-Parameter Optimization,* available at `https://goo.gl/efc8Qv`.

Coarse-to-Fine Optimization

There is still an optimization trick that helps with grid or random search. It is called coarse-to-fine optimization. Suppose we want to find the maximum of $f(x)$ between x_{min} and x_{max}. I will explain the concept behind random search, but it works the same way for grid search. The following steps give you the algorithm you require to follow for this optimization.

1. Do a random search in the region $R_1 = (x_{min}, x_{max})$. Let's indicate the maximum found with (x_1, f_1).

2. Consider now a smaller region around x_1, $R_2 = (x_1 - \delta x_1, x_1 + \delta x_1)$, for some δx_1, which I will discuss later, and again do a random search in this region. The hypothesis is, of course, that the real maximum lies in this region. We will indicate the maximum you find here with (x_2, f_2).

3. Repeat step 2 around x_2, in the region we will indicate with R_3, with a δx_2 smaller than δx_1, and indicate the maximum you find in this step with (x_3, f_3).

4. Now repeat step 2 around x_3, in the region we will indicate with R_4, with a δx_3 smaller than δx_2.

5. Continue in the same way as often as you require, until the maximum (x_i, f_i) in the region R_{i+1} no longer changes.

Usually, just one or two iterations are used, but, theoretically, you could go on for a large number of iterations. The problem with this method is that you cannot be really sure that your real maximum lies in your regions R_i. But this optimization has a big advantage, if it does. Let's consider the case in which we do a standard random search. If we want to have on average a distance between the sampled points of 1% of $x_{max} - x_{min}$, we would need about 100 points, if we decided to perform only one random search, and, consequently, we had to perform 100 evaluations. Now let's consider the algorithm I just described. We could start with just 10 points in region $R_1 = (x_{min}, \ x_{max})$. Here, we will indicate the maximum we find with (x_1, f_1). Then let's take $2\delta x = \frac{x_{max} - x_{min}}{10}$ and take again 10 points in region $R_2 = (x_1 - \delta x, x_1 + \delta x)$. In the interval $(x_1 - \delta x, x_1 + \delta x)$, we will have on average a distance between the points of 1% of $x_{max} - x_{min}$, but we just sampled our functions only 20 times, instead of 100, so by a factor 5 fewer! For example, let's just sample the function we used previously between $x_{min} = 0$ and $x_{max} = 80$ with 10 points, with the code

```
np.random.seed(5)
randomsearch = np.random.random([10])*80

x = 0
m = 0.0
for i, val in np.ndenumerate(f(randomsearch)):
    if (val > m):
        m = val
        x = randomsearch[i]
```

This gives us the maximum location and value of $x_1 = 69.65$ and $f_1 = 14.89$, not bad, but not yet as precise as the real ones: 69.18 and 15.027. Now let's again sample 10 points around the maximum we have found in the regions $R_2 = (x_1 - 4, x_1 + 4)$.

```
randomsearch = x + (np.random.random([10])-0.5)*8

x = 0
m = 0.0
for i, val in np.ndenumerate(maxim(randomsearch)):
    if (val > m):
        m = val
        x = randomsearch[i]
```

This gives us the result 69.189 and 15.027. Quite a precise result, with only 20 evaluations of the function. If we do a plain random search with *500* (25 times more than what we just did) sampling points, we get $x_1 = 69.08$ and $f_1 = 15.022$. This result shows how this trick can be really helpful. But remember the risk: If your maximum is not in your regions R_i, you will never be able to find it, since you are still dealing with random numbers. So, it is always a good idea to choose the regions $(x_i - \delta x_i, x_i + \delta x_i)$, which are relatively big, to make sure that they contain your maximum. How big depends, as almost everything in the deep-learning world, on your dataset and problem, and these may be impossible to know in advance. Unfortunately, testing is required. In Figure 7-9, you can see the sampled points on the function $f(x)$. In the plot on the left, you see the first 10 points, and on the right, the region R_2 with the additional 10 points. The small rectangle on the left plot marks the x region R_2.

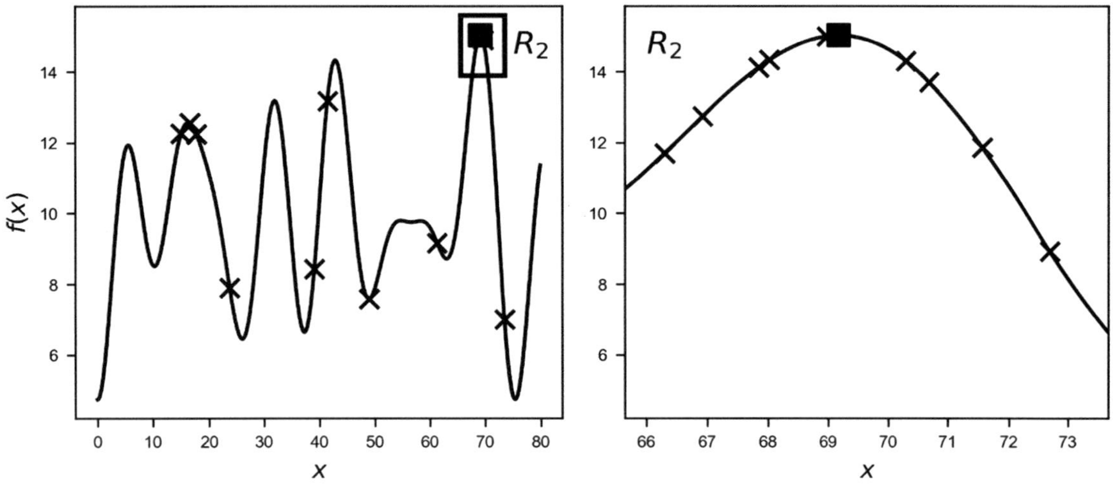

***Figure 7-9.** Function f(x). The crosses mark the sampled points: on the left, the 10 points sampled in the regions R_1 (entire range), on the right, the 10 points sampled in R_2. The black square marks the real maximum. The plot on the right is a zoom of the region R_2.*

Now the choice of how many points you should sample at the beginning is crucial. We had luck here. Let's consider a different seed when choosing our initial 10 random points and then see what can happen (see Figure 7-10). Choosing the wrong initial points leads to disaster!

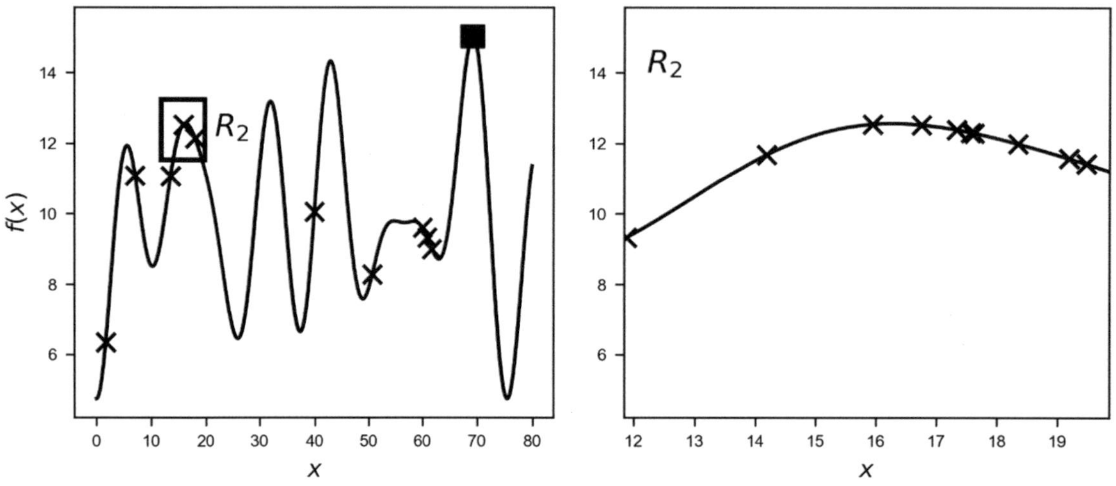

***Figure 7-10.** Function f(x). The crosses mark the sampled points: on the left, the 10 points sampled in the regions R_1 (entire range), on the right, the 10 points sampled in R_2. The black square marks the real maximum. The algorithm finds a maximum very well around 16, simply not the absolute maximum. The small rectangle on the left marks the region R_2. The plot on the right is a zoom of the region R_2.*

Note, in Figure 7-10, how the algorithm finds the maximum at around 16, because in the initial sampled points, the maximum value is about $x = 16$, as you can see on the plot at the left in Figure 7-10. No points are close to the real maximum, about $x = 69$. The algorithm finds a maximum very well, simply not the absolute maximum. That is the danger you face when using this trick. Things can even be worse than that. Consider Figure 7-11, in which only one single point is sampled at the beginning. You can see on the plot at the left in Figure 7-11 how the algorithm completely misses any maximum. It simply gives as a result the highest values of the points marked by crosses on the points on the right plot: (58.4, 9.78).

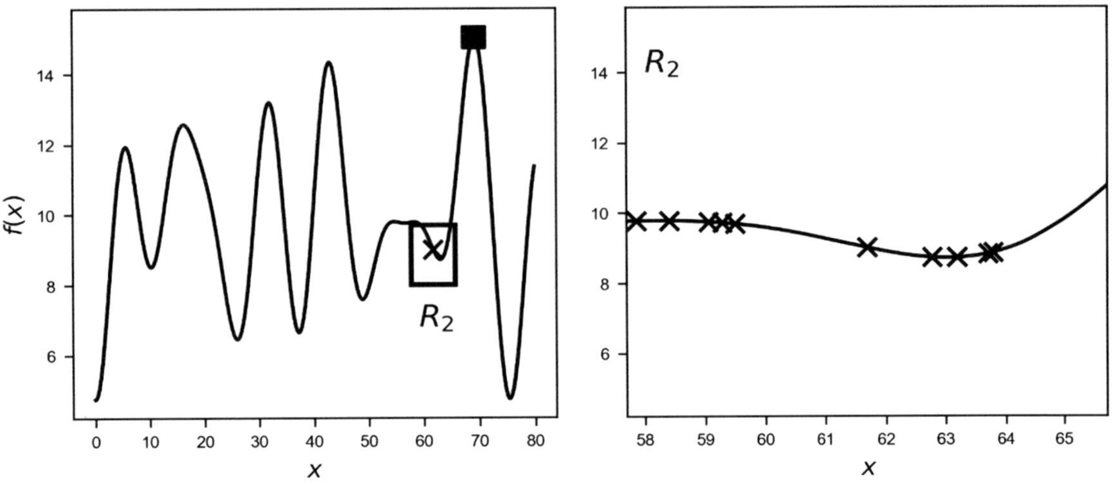

Figure 7-11. *Function f(x). The crosses mark the sampled points: on the left, the 1 point is sampled in the regions R_1 (entire range), on the right, the 10 points are sampled in R_2. The black square marks the real maximum. The algorithm does not find any maximum, because none is present in the region R_2. The plot on the right is the zoom of the region R_2.*

If you decide to use this method, keep in mind that you will still require a good number of points at the beginning, to get close to the maximum, before refining your search. After you are relatively sure to have points around your maximum, you can use this technique to refine your search.

Bayesian Optimization

In this section, we will look at a specific and efficient technique for finding the minimum (or maximum) of a black-box function. This is a rather clever algorithm that basically consists of choosing the sampling points from which to evaluate the function in a much more intelligent way than simply choosing them randomly or on a grid. To understand how this works, you must first look at a few new mathematical concepts, because the method is not trivial and requires some understanding of more advanced concepts. Let's start with the Nadaraya-Watson regression.

Nadaraya-Watson Regression

This method was developed in 1964 by Èlizbar Akakevič (E. A.) Nadaraya in "On Estimating Regression," published in the Russian journal *Theory of Probability and Its Applications*. The basic idea is quite simple. Given an unknown function $y(x)$, and given N points $x_i = 1, \ldots, N$, we indicate with $y_i = f(x_i)$, with $i = 1, \ldots, N$, the value of the function calculated at the different x_i. The idea of the Nadaraya-Watson regression is that we can evaluate the unknown function at an unknown point x using the formula

$$y(x) = \sum_{i=1}^{N} w_i(x) y_i$$

where $w_i(x)$ are weights that are calculated according to the formula

$$w_i(x) = \frac{K(x, x_i)}{\sum_{j=1}^{N} K(x, x_j)}$$

where $K(x, x_i)$ is called a kernel. Note that given how the weights are defined we have

$$\sum_{i=1}^{N} w_i(x) = 1$$

In the literature, you can find several kernels, but the one we are interested in is the Gaussian one, often called the *radial basis function* (RBF)

$$K(x, x_i) = \sigma^2 e^{-\frac{1}{2l^2}\|x - x_i\|^2}$$

The parameter l makes the Gaussian shape wider or narrower. The σ is typically the variance of your data, but, in this case, it plays no role, because the weights are normalized to one. This is at the basis of Bayesian optimization, as you will see later.

Gaussian Process

Before talking about Gaussian processes, first I must define what a random process is. A *random process* refers to any point $x \in R^d$ to which we assign a random variable $f(x) \in R$. A random process is Gaussian, if for any finite number of points, their joint distribution is normal. This means that $\forall n \in N$, and for $\forall x_1, \ldots x_n \in R^d$, the vector is

$$\boldsymbol{f} \equiv \begin{pmatrix} f(x_1) \\ \vdots \\ f(x_n) \end{pmatrix} \sim \mathcal{N}$$

where with the notation we intend that the vector components follow a normal distribution, indicated with $\mathcal{N}$. Remember that a random variable with a Gaussian distribution is said to be normally distributed. From this comes the name Gaussian process. The probability distribution of the normal distribution is given by the function

$$g(x \mid \mu, \sigma^2) = \frac{1}{\sqrt{2\pi\sigma^2}} e^{\frac{(x-\mu)^2}{2\sigma^2}}$$

where μ is the mean or expectation of the distribution, and σ is the standard deviation. I will use the following notation from here on:

$$Mean\ value\ of\ f:\ m$$

and the covariance of the random values will be indicated here by K.

$$cov\left[f(x_1), f(x_2)\right] = K(x_1, x_2)$$

The choice of the letter K has a reason. We will assume in what follows that the covariance will have a Gaussian shape, and we will use for K the RBF function defined previously.

Stationary Process

For simplicity, we will consider here only stationary processes. A random process is stationary if its joint probability distribution does not change with time. That means also that mean and variance will not change when shifted in time. We will also consider a process whose distribution depends only on the relative position of the points. This leads to the conditions

$$K(x_1, x_2) = \tilde{K}(x_1 - x_2)$$
$$Var\left[f(x)\right] = \tilde{K}(0)$$

Note that to apply the method we are describing, first you must convert your data to be stationary, if that is not already the case, eliminating seasonality or trends in time, for example.

Prediction with Gaussian Processes

Now we have reached the interesting part: given the vector $\boldsymbol{f}$, how can we estimate $f(x)$ at an arbitrary point x? Because we are dealing with random processes, what we will estimate is the probability that the unknown function assumes a given value $f(x)$. Mathematically, we will predict the following quantity:

$$p(f(x)|\boldsymbol{f})$$

Or, in other words, the probability of getting the value $f(x)$, given the vector $\boldsymbol{f}$, composed by all the points $f(x_1), \ldots, f(x_n)$.

Assuming that $f(x)$ is a stationary Gaussian process with $m = 0$, the prediction can be shown to be given by

$$p(f(x)|\boldsymbol{f}) = \frac{p(f(x), f(x_1), \ldots, f(x_n))}{p(f(x_1), \ldots, f(x_n))} = \frac{\mathcal{N}(f(x), f(x_1), \ldots, f(x_n)|0, \tilde{C})}{\mathcal{N}(f(x_1), \ldots, f(x_n)|0, C)}$$

Where, with $\mathcal{N}(f(x), f(x_1), \ldots, f(x_n)|0, \tilde{C})$, we have indicated the normal distribution calculated on the points with average 0 and covariance matrix $\tilde{C}$ of dimensions $n + 1 \times n + 1$, because we have $n + 1$ points in the numerator. The derivation is somewhat involved and is based on several theorems, such as Bayes' theorem.

For more information, you can refer to the (advanced) explanation by Chuong B. Do in "Gaussian Processes" (2007), available at `https://goo.gl/cEPYwX`, in which everything is explained in elaborate detail. To understand what Bayesian optimization is, we can simply use the formula without derivation. C will have dimensions $n \times n$, because we have only n points in the denominator.

We have

$$C = \begin{pmatrix} K(0) & K(x_1 - x_2) & \cdots \\ K(x_2 - x_1) & \ddots & \vdots \\ \vdots & \cdots & K(0) \end{pmatrix}$$

and

$$\tilde{C} = \begin{pmatrix} K(0) & \boldsymbol{k}^T \\ \boldsymbol{k} & C \end{pmatrix}$$

where we have defined

$$\boldsymbol{k} = \begin{pmatrix} K(x - x_1) \\ \vdots \\ K(x - x_n) \end{pmatrix}$$

It can be shown[1] that the ratio of two normal distributions is again a normal distribution, so that we can write

$$p(f(x) \mid \boldsymbol{f}) = \mathcal{N}(f(x) \mid \mu, \sigma^2)$$

with

$$\mu = \boldsymbol{k}^T C^{-1} \boldsymbol{f}$$
$$\sigma^2 = K(0) - \boldsymbol{k}^T C^{-1} \boldsymbol{k}$$

The derivation of the exact form for μ and σ is quite long and would be beyond the scope of the book. Basically, we know now that, on average, our unknown function will assume the value μ in x, with a variance σ. Let's now see how this method really works in practice in Python. Let's first define our kernel $K(x)$.

```
def K(x, l, sigm = 1):
    return sigm**2*np.exp(-1.0/2.0/l**2*(x**2))
```

[1]Remember that a normal distribution has an exponential form, and the ratio of two exponentials is still an exponential.

Let's simulate our unknown function with an easy one

$$f(x) = x^2 - x^3 + 3 + 10x + 0.07x^4$$

which can be implemented as

```
def f(x):
    return x**2-x**3+3+10*x+0.07*x**4
```

Let's consider the function in the range (0, 12). In Figure 7-12, you can see how the function looks.

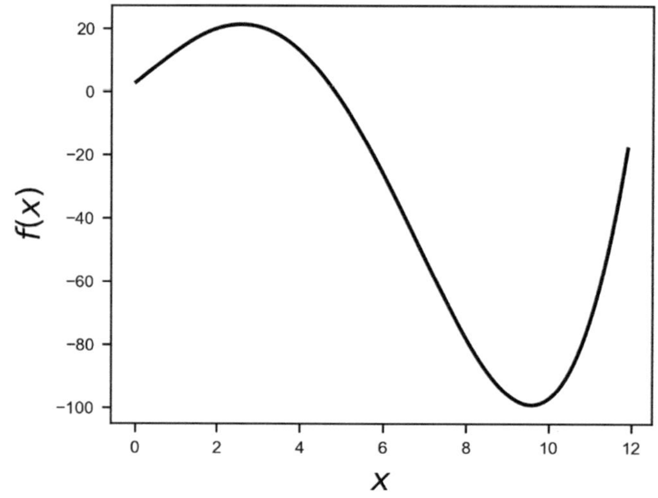

Figure 7-12. *Plot of our unknown test function, as described in the text*

Let's build first our ***f*** vector with five points, as follows:

```
randompoints = np.random.random([5])*12.0
f_ = f(randompoints)
```

where we have used the seed 42 for the random numbers: `np.random.seed(42)`. In Figure 7-13, you can see the random points marked with crosses on the plot.

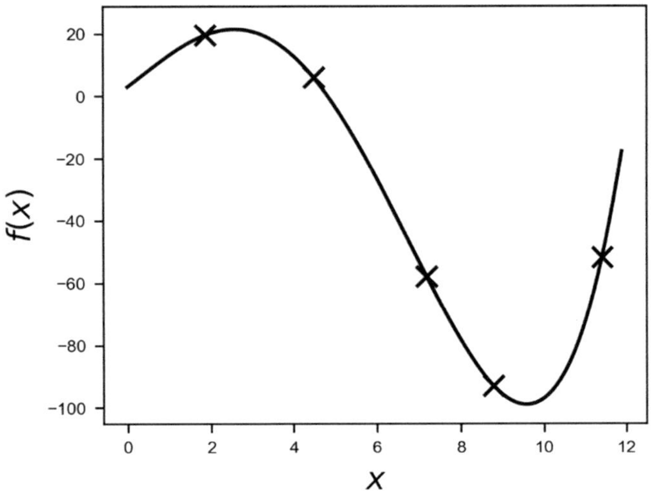

Figure 7-13. *Plot of the unknown function. The crosses mark the random point chosen in the text.*

We can apply the method described earlier with the following code:

```
xsampling = np.arange(0,14,0.2)

ybayes_ = []
sigmabayes_ = []
for x in xsampling:

    f1 = f(randompoints)
    sigm_ = np.std(f1)**2
    f_ = (f1-np.average(f1))

    k = K(x-randompoints, 2 , sigm_)


    C = np.zeros([randompoints.shape[0], randompoints.shape[0]])
    Ctilde = np.zeros([randompoints.shape[0]+1, randompoints.shape[0]+1])
    for i1,x1_ in np.ndenumerate(randompoints):
        for i2,x2_ in np.ndenumerate(randompoints):
            C[i1,i2] = K(x1_-x2_, 2.0, sigm_)

    Ctilde[0,0] = K(0, 2.0, sigm_)
    Ctilde[0,1:randompoints.shape[0]+1] = k.T
    Ctilde[1:,1:] = C
    Ctilde[1:randompoints.shape[0]+1,0] = k
```

```
    mu = np.dot(np.dot(np.transpose(k), np.linalg.inv(C)), f_)
    sigma2 = K(0, 2.0,sigm_)- np.dot(np.dot(np.transpose(k), np.linalg.
    inv(C)), k)
    ybayes.append(mu)
    sigmabayes_.append(np.abs(sigma2))

ybayes = np.asarray(ybayes_)+np.average(f1)
sigmabayes = np.asarray(sigmabayes_)
```

Now please take some time to understand it. In the list `ybayes`, we will find the values of $\mu(x)$ evaluated on the values contained in the array `xsampling`. Here are some hints that will help you to understand the code:

- We do a loop over a range of x points, where we want to evaluate our function, with the code `for x in xsampling:`.
- We build our $\boldsymbol{k}$ and $\boldsymbol{f}$ vectors with the code for each element of the vectors: `k = K(x-randompoints, 2 , sigm_)` and `f1 = f(randompoints)`. For the kernel, we have chosen a value for the parameter `l`, as defined in the function of 2. We have subtracted, in the vector $\boldsymbol{f}$, the average to obtain $m(x) = 0$, to be able to apply the formulas as derived.
- We build the matrices C and $\tilde{C}$.
- We calculate μ with `mu = np.dot(np.dot(np.transpose(k), np.linalg.inv(C)), f_)` and the standard deviation.
- At the end, we reapply all the transformation that we have done to make our process stationary in the opposite order, simply adding the average of $f(x)$ again to the evaluated surrogate function `ybayes = np.asarray(ybayes_)+np.average(f1)`.

In Figure 7-14, you can see how this method works. The dashed line is the predicted function obtained by plotting $\mu(x)$, as calculated in the code, when we have five points at our disposal ($n = 5$). The gray area is the region between the estimated function and +/- σ.

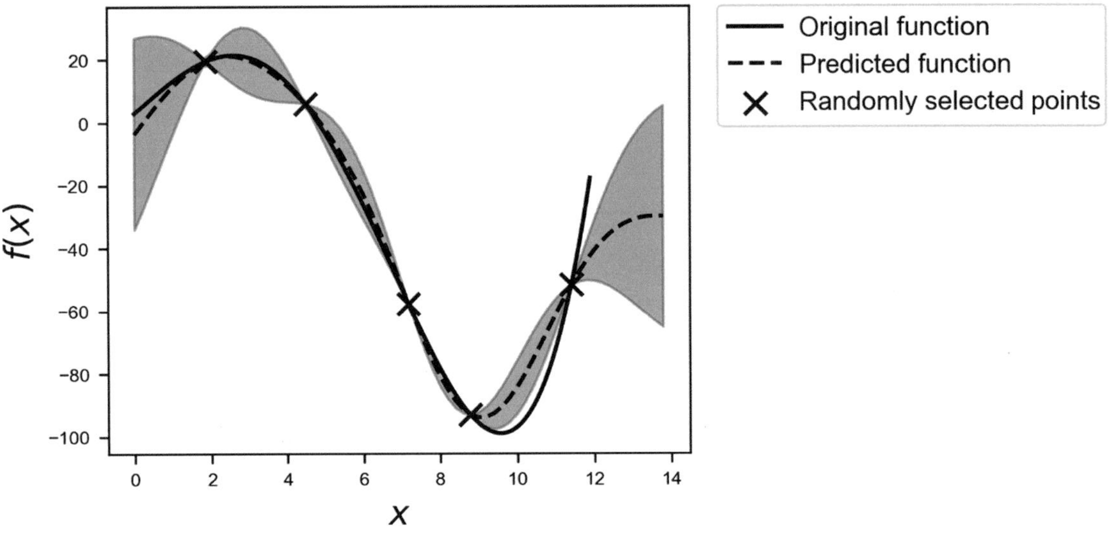

***Figure 7-14.** Predicted function (dashed line), calculated by evaluating $\mu(x)$. The gray area is the region between the estimated function and +/- σ.*

Given the few points we have, it is not a bad result. Now keep in mind that you still need a few points, to be able to get a reasonable approximation. In Figure 7-15, you can see the result, if we have only two points at our disposal. The result is not as good. The gray area is the region around the estimated function and +/- σ. You can see how, as far as we are from the points we have, the higher the uncertainty, or the variance, of the predicted function.

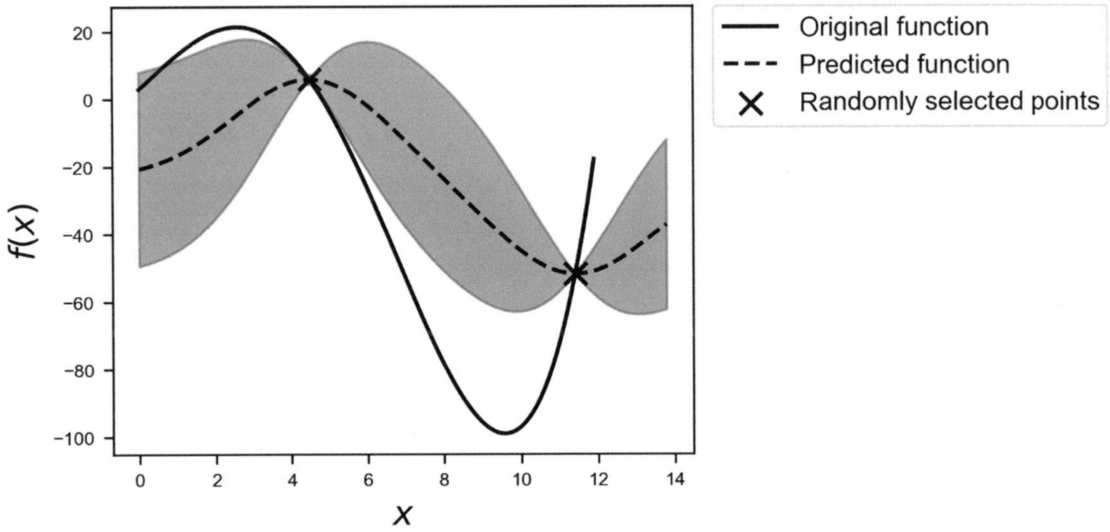

***Figure 7-15.** Predicted function (dashed line), when we have only two points at our disposal. The gray area is the region between the estimated function +/- σ.*

Let's stop for a second and think about why we do all this. The idea is to find a so-called surrogate function $\tilde{f}$ that approximates our function f and has the property

$$\max \tilde{f} \approx \max f$$

This surrogate function must have another very important property: it must be cheap to evaluate. In this way, we can find easily the maximum of $\tilde{f}$, and, using the previous property, we will have the maximum of f, which, by hypothesis, is costly.

But as you have seen, it may be very difficult to know if we have enough points to find the right value of the maximum. After all, by definition, we don't have any idea how our black-box function looks. So, how to solve this problem?

The main idea behind the method can be described by the following algorithm:

1. We start with a small number of sample points randomly chosen (how small it should be will depend on your problem).
2. We use this set of points to get a surrogate function, as described.
3. We add an additional point to our set, with a specific method that I will discuss later, and reevaluate the surrogate function.
4. If the maximum we find with the surrogate function continues to change, we will continue adding points, as in step 3, until the maximum does not change anymore, or we run out of time or budget and cannot perform any further evaluation.

If the method I hinted at in step 3 is smart enough, we will be able to find our maximum relatively quickly and accurately.

Acquisition Function

But how to choose the additional points I mentioned in step 3 in the previous section? The idea is to use a so-called acquisition function. The algorithm works in this way:

1. We choose a function (and we will see a few possibilities in a moment) called an acquisition function.
2. Then we choose, as additional point x, the one at which the acquisition function has a maximum.

There are several acquisition functions we can use. I will describe here only one that we will use to see how this method works, but there are several that you may want to check out, such as entropy search, probability of improvement, expected improvement, and upper confidence bound.

Upper Confidence Bound (UCB)

In the literature, you find two variations of this acquisition function. We can write the function as

$$a_{UCB}(x) = \mathbb{E}\tilde{f}(x) + \eta\sigma(x)$$

where we have indicated with $\mathbb{E}\tilde{f}(x)$ the "expected" value of the surrogate function on the x-range we have in our problem. The expected value is nothing other than the average of the function over the given x range. $\sigma(x)$ is the variance of the surrogate function that we calculate with our method at point x. The new point we select is the one in which $a_{UCB}(x)$ is maximum. $\eta > 0$ is a trade-off parameter. This acquisition function basically selects the points where the variance is biggest. Review Figure 7-15. The method selects the points at which the variance is greater, so, points as far as possible from the points we have already. In this way, the approximation tends to get better and better.

Another variation of the UCB acquisition function is the following:

$$\tilde{a}_{UCB}(x) = \tilde{f}(\mathrm{x}) + \eta\sigma(x)$$

This time, the acquisition function will make a trade-off between choosing points around the surrogate function maximum and points where its variance is biggest. This second method works best to find quickly good approximation of the maximum of f, while the first tends to give good approximation of f over the entire x range. In the next section, we will see how these methods works.

Example

Let's start with the complex trigonometric function, as described at the beginning of the chapter, and consider the x range $[0, 40]$. Our goal is to find its maximum and approximate the function. To facilitate our coding, let's define two functions: one to evaluate the surrogate function and one to evaluate the new point. To evaluate the surrogate function, we can use the following function:

```
def get_surrogate(randompoints):
    ybayes_ = []
    sigmabayes_ = []
    for x in xsampling:

        f1 = f(randompoints)
        sigm_ = np.std(f_)**2
        f_ = (f1-np.average(f1))
        k = K(x-randompoints, 2.0, sigm_ )

        C = np.zeros([randompoints.shape[0], randompoints.shape[0]])
        Ctilde = np.zeros([randompoints.shape[0]+1, randompoints.shape[0]+1])
        for i1,x1_ in np.ndenumerate(randompoints):
            for i2,x2_ in np.ndenumerate(randompoints):
                C[i1,i2] = K(x1_-x2_, 2.0, sigm_)

        Ctilde[0,0] = K(0, 2.0)
        Ctilde[0,1:randompoints.shape[0]+1] = k.T
        Ctilde[1:,1:] = C
        Ctilde[1:randompoints.shape[0]+1,0] = k

        mu = np.dot(np.dot(np.transpose(k), np.linalg.inv(C)), f_)
        sigma2 = K(0, 2.0, sigm_)- np.dot(np.dot(np.transpose(k),
        np.linalg.inv(C)), k)
        ybayes_.append(mu)
        sigmabayes_.append(np.abs(sigma2))

    ybayes = np.asarray(ybayes_)+np.average(f1)
    sigmabayes = np.asarray(sigmabayes_)

    return ybayes, sigmabayes
```

This function has the same code I have already discussed in our example in the previous sections, but it is packed in a function that returns the surrogate function, contained in the array ybayes, and the σ^2, contained in the array sigmabayes. Additionally, we require a function that evaluates the new points, using the acquisition function $a_{UCB}(x)$. We can get it easily with the function

```
def get_new_point(ybayes, sigmabayes, eta):

    idxmax = np.argmax(np.average(ybayes)+eta*np.sqrt(sigmabayes))
    newpoint = xsampling[idxmax]

    return newpoint
```

To make things simpler, I decided to define the array that contains all the x values we want at the beginning outside the functions. Let's start with just six randomly selected points. To check how our method is doing, let's start with some definitions.

```
xmax = 40.0
numpoints = 6
xsampling = np.arange(0,xmax,0.2)
eta = 1.0

np.random.seed(8)
randompoints1 = np.random.random([numpoints])*xmax
```

In the array randompoints1, we will have our first six selected random points. We can easily get the surrogate function of our function with

```
ybayes1, sigmabayes1 = get_surrogate(randompoints1)
```

In Figure 7-16, you can see the result. The dotted line is the acquisition function $a_{UCB}(x)$, normalized to fit in the plot.

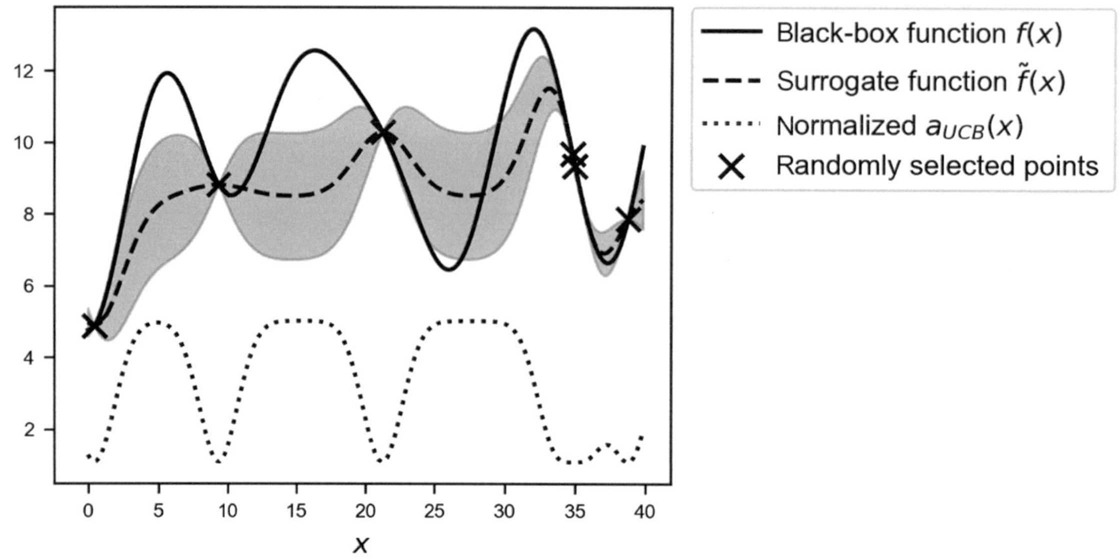

***Figure 7-16.** Overview of the black-box function f(x) (solid line), the randomly selected points (marked by crosses), the surrogate function (dashed line), and the acquisition function $a_{UCB}(x)$ (dotted line), shifted to fit in the plot. The gray area is the region contained between the lines $\tilde{f}(x)+\sigma(x)$ and $\tilde{f}(x)-\sigma(x)$.*

The surrogate function is not yet very good, because we don't have enough points, and the big variance (the gray area) makes this evident. The only region that is well approximated is the region $x \gtrsim 35$. You can see how the acquisition function is big when the surrogate function is not approximating the black-box function well and small when it does, as, for example, for $x \gtrsim 35$. So, intuitively choosing as a new point the one where $a_{UCB}(x)$ is maximum is equivalent to choosing the points where the function is less well approximated, or, in more mathematical terms, where the variance is bigger. By comparison, in Figure 7-17, you can see the same plot as in Figure 7-16, but with the acquisition function $\tilde{a}_{UCB}(x)$ and with $\eta = 3.0$.

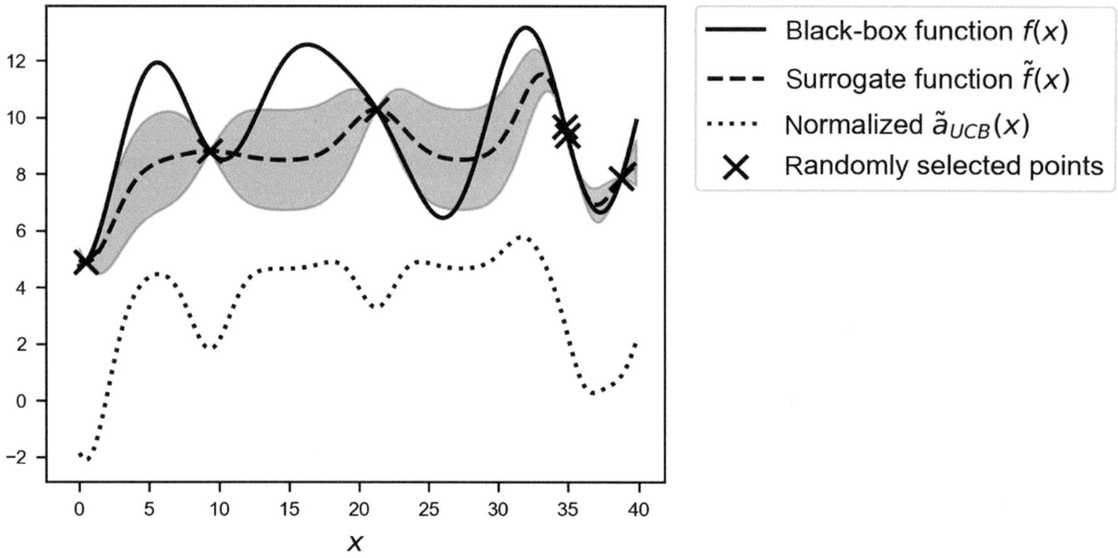

***Figure 7-17.** Overview of the black-box function f(x) (solid line), the randomly selected points (marked by crosses), the surrogate function (dashed line), and the acquisition function $\tilde{a}_{UCB}(x)$ (dotted line), shifted to fit in the plot. The gray area is the region contained between the lines $\tilde{f}(x)+\sigma(x)$ and $\tilde{f}(x)-\sigma(x)$.*

As you can see, $\tilde{a}_{UCB}(x)$ tends to have a maximum around the maximum of the surrogate function. Keep in mind that if η is big, the maximum of the acquisition function will shift toward regions with high variance. But this acquisition function tends to find "a" maximum slightly faster. I said "a," because it depends on where the maximum of the surrogate function is, and not where the maximum of the black-box function is.

Let's see now what happens while using $a_{UCB}(x)$ with $\eta = 1.0$. For the first additional point, we must simply run the following three lines of code:

```
newpoint = get_new_point(ybayes1, sigmabayes1, eta)
randompoints2 = np.append(randompoints1, newpoint)
ybayes2, sigmabayes2 = get_surrogate(randompoints2)
```

For the sake of simplicity, I named each array for each step differently, instead of creating a list. But, typically, you should make these iterations automatic. In Figure 7-18, you can see the result with the additional point, marked with a black circle.

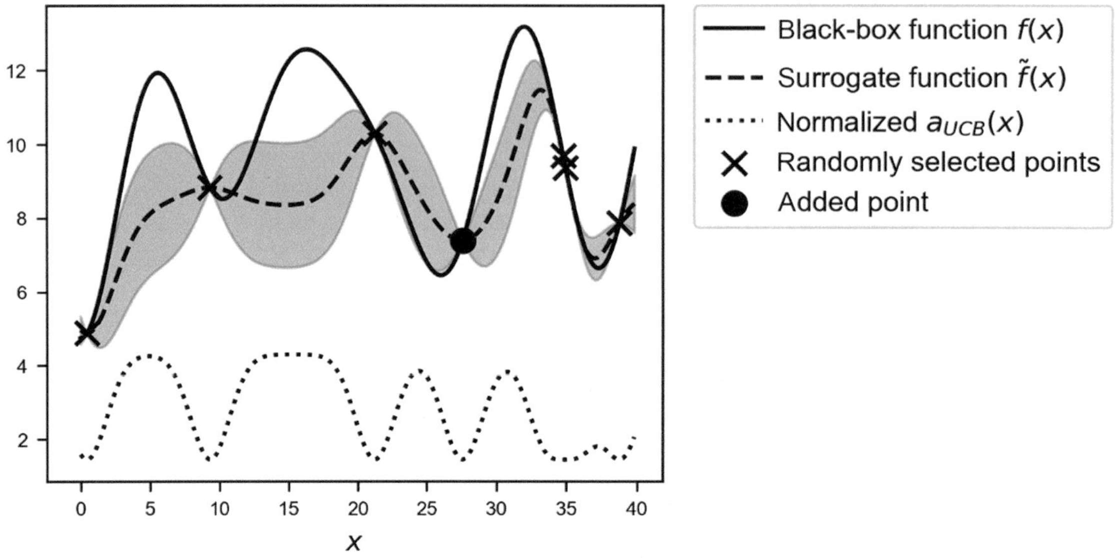

Figure 7-18. *Overview of the black-box function f(x) (solid line), the randomly selected points (marked with crosses), and with the new selected point around $x \approx 27$ (marked by a circle), the surrogate function (dashed line), and the acquisition function $a_{UCB}(x)$ (dotted line), shifted to fit in the plot. The gray area is the region contained between the lines $\tilde{f}(x)+\sigma(x)$ and $\tilde{f}(x)-\sigma(x)$.*

The new point is around $x \approx 27$. Let's continue to add points. In Figure 7-19, you can see the results after adding five points.

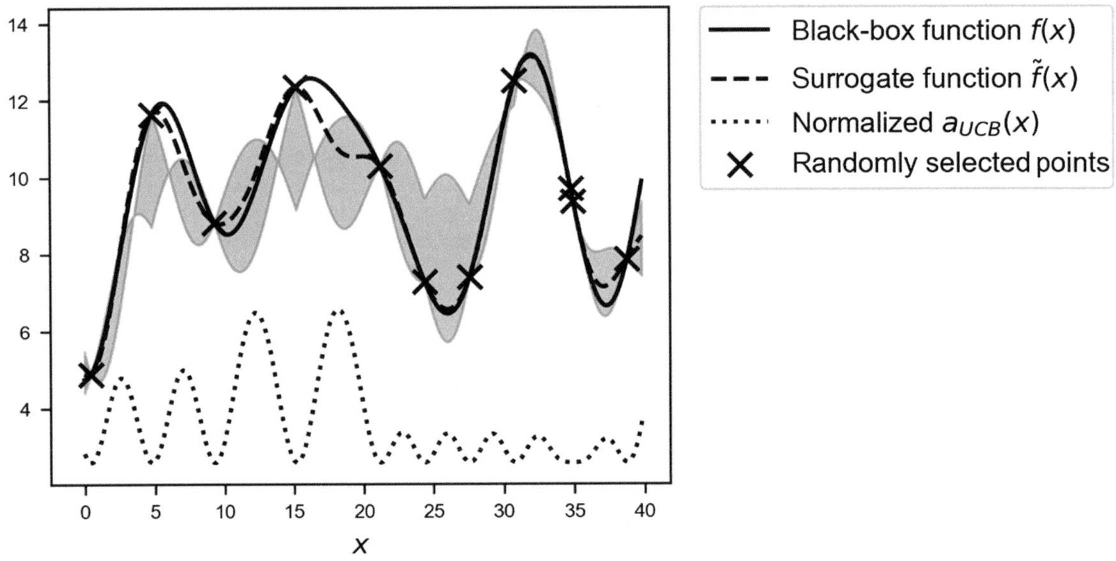

Figure 7-19. *Overview of the black-box function f(x) (solid line), the randomly selected points with the six selected new points (marked by crosses), the surrogate function (dashed line), and the acquisition function* $\tilde{a}_{UCB}(x)$ *(dotted line), shifted to fit in the plot. The gray area is the region contained between the lines* $\tilde{f}(x)+\sigma(x)$ *and* $\tilde{f}(x)-\sigma(x)$.

Note the dashed line. Now our surrogate function approximates the black-box function quite well, especially around the real maximum. Using this surrogate function, we can find a very good approximation of our original function with just 11 evaluations in total! Keep in mind that we don't have any additional information about *f*, except the 11 evaluations.

Now let's see what happens with the acquisition function $\tilde{a}_{UCB}(x)$, and let's check how fast we can find the maximum. In this case, we'll use $\eta = 3.0$, to get a better balance between the maximum of the surrogate function and its variance. In Figure 7-20, you can see the result after just adding one single additional point, marked by a black circle. We have already a quite good approximation of the real maximum!

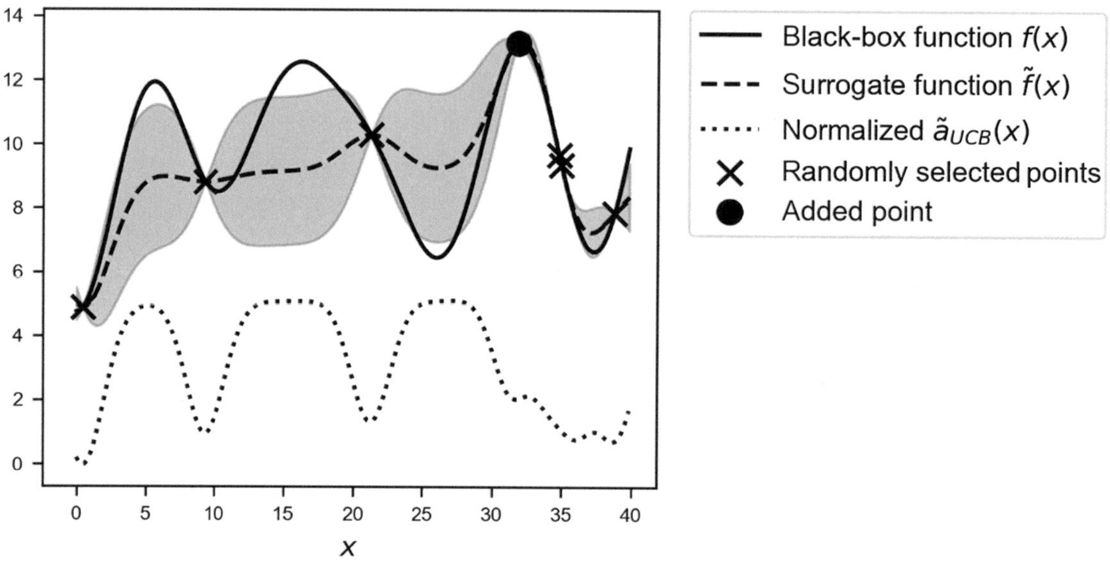

Figure 7-20. *Overview of the black-box function f(x) (solid line), the randomly selected points with the additional selected points (marked by crosses), the surrogate function (dashed line), and the acquisition function $\tilde{a}_{UCB}(x)$ (dotted line), shifted to fit in the plot. The gray area is the region contained between the lines $\tilde{f}(x)+\sigma(x)$ and $\tilde{f}(x)-\sigma(x)$.*

Now let's add an additional point. You can see in Figure 7-21 that the additional point is now still close to the maximum but shifted in the direction of the area with a high variance around 30.

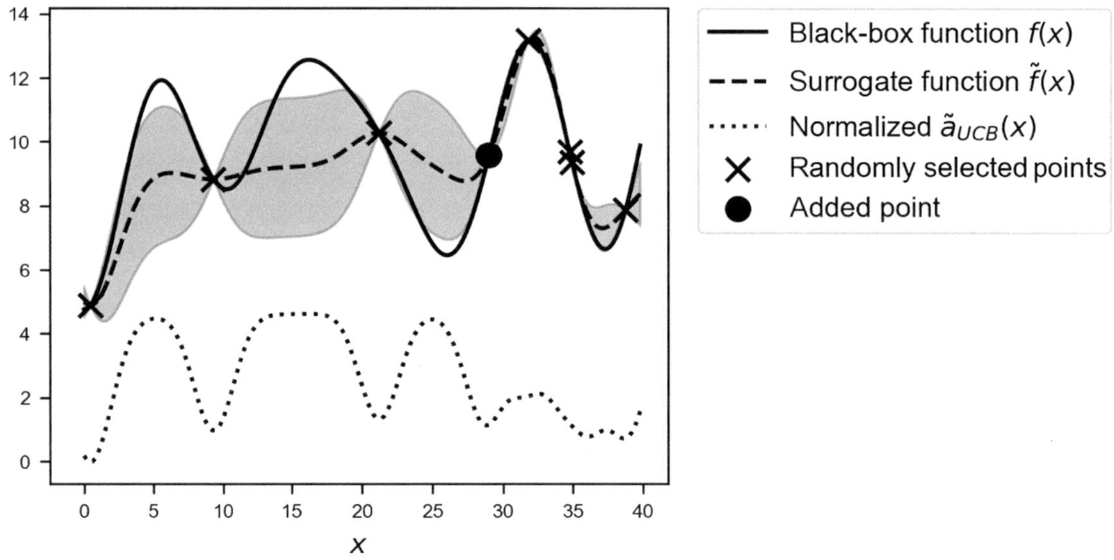

Figure 7-21. *Overview of the black-box function f(x) (solid line), the randomly selected points with the additional selected points (marked by crosses), the surrogate function (dashed line), and the acquisition function* $\tilde{a}_{UCB}(x)$ *(dotted line), shifted to fit in the plot. The gray area is the region contained between the lines* $\tilde{f}(x)+\sigma(x)$ *and* $\tilde{f}(x)-\sigma(x)$.

If we choose to make η smaller, the point would be closer to the maximum, and if we choose to make it bigger, the point would be closer to the point with the highest variance, between 25 and roughly 32. Now let's add an additional point and see what happens. In Figure 7-22, you can see how the method now chooses a point close to another region with high variance, between 10 and roughly 22, again, marked by a black circle.

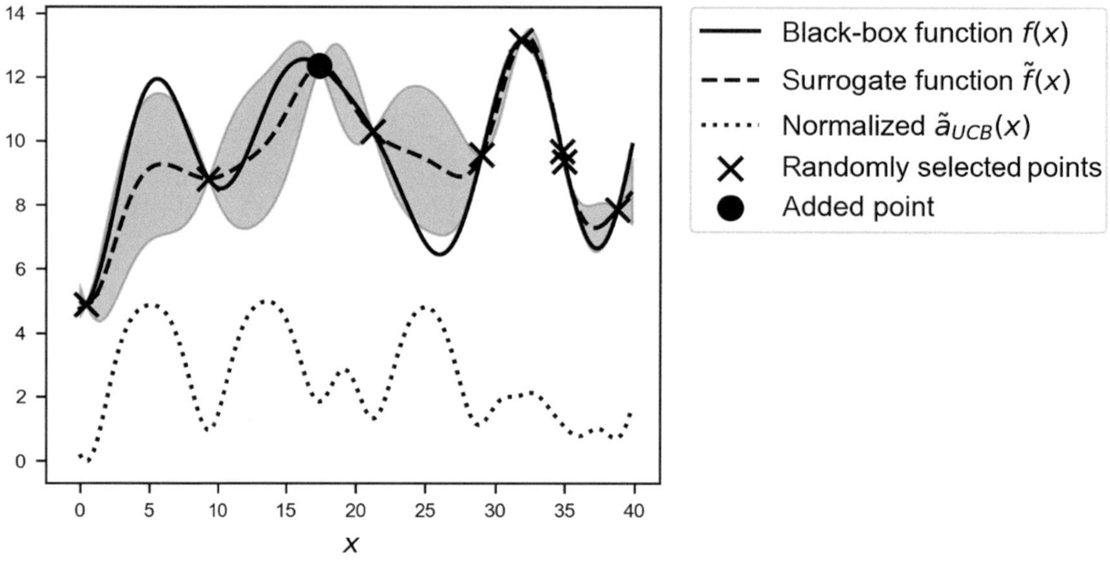

***Figure 7-22.** Overview of the black-box function f(x) (solid line), the randomly selected points (marked by crosses), and the additional selected point (marked by a black circle), the surrogate function (dashed line), and the acquisition function $\tilde{a}_{UCB}(x)$ (dotted line), shifted to fit in the plot. The gray area is the region contained between the lines $\tilde{f}(x)+\sigma(x)$ and $\tilde{f}(x)-\sigma(x)$.*

And, finally, the method refines the maximum area around 15, as you can see in Figure 7-23, adding a point around 14, marked by the black circle.

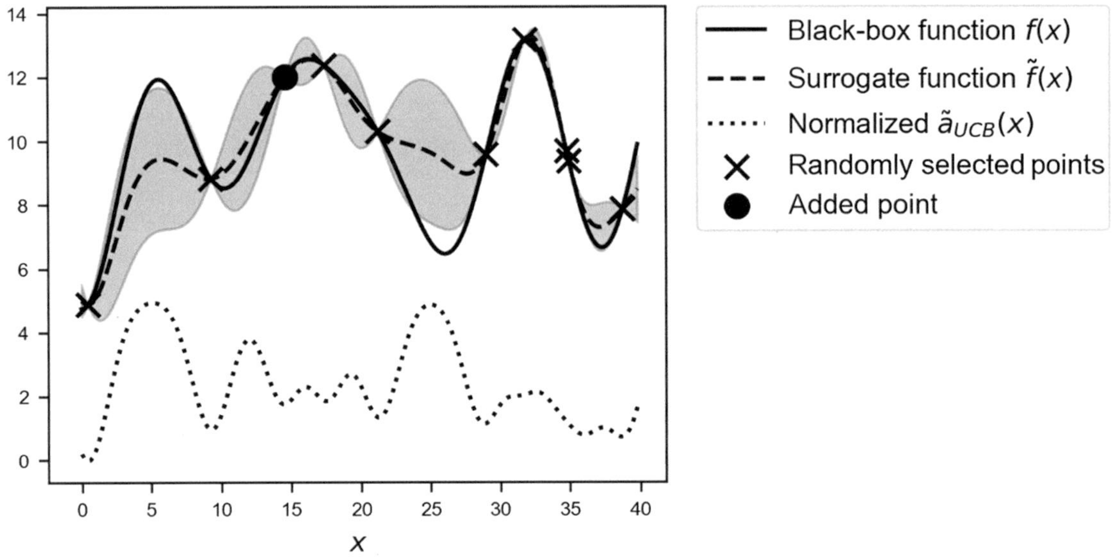

Figure 7-23. *Overview of the black-box function f(x) (solid line), the randomly selected points with the additional selected points (marked by crosses), the surrogate function (dashed line), and the acquisition function* $\tilde{a}_{UCB}(x)$ *(dotted line), shifted to fit in the plot. The gray area is the region contained between the lines* $\tilde{f}(x)+\sigma(x)$ *and* $\tilde{f}(x)-\sigma(x)$*.*

The previous discussion and comparison of the behavior of the two types of acquisition functions should have made clear how, depending on what strategy you want to apply to approximate your black-box function, you should choose the right acquisition function.

Note Different types of acquisition functions will give different strategies in approximating the black-box function. For example, $a_{UCB}(x)$ will add points in regions with the highest variance, while $\tilde{a}_{UCB}(x)$ will add points finding a balance, regulated by η, between the maximum of the surrogate function and areas with high variance.

An analysis of all the different types of acquisition functions would exceed the scope of this book. A good deal of research and reading of published papers is required to gain sufficient experience and understand how different acquisition functions work and behave.

If you want to use Bayesian optimization with your TensorFlow model, you don't have to develop the method completely from scratch. You can try the library GPflowOpt that is described in a paper by Nicolas Knudde et al., "GPflowOpt: A Bayesian Optimization Library using TensorFlow," available at `https://goo.gl/um4LSy` or `arXiv.org`.

Sampling on a Logarithmic Scale

There is a last small subtlety that I would like to discuss. Sometimes, you will find yourself in a situation in which you want to try a big range of possible values for a parameter, but you know from experience that the best value of it is probably in a specific range. Suppose you want to find the best value for the learning rate for your model, and you decide to test values from 10^{-4} to 1, but you know, or at least suspect, that your best value probably lies between 10^{-3} and 10^{-4}. Now let's suppose you are working with grid search, and you sample 1000 points. You may think you have enough points, but you will get

- 0 points between 10^{-4} and 10^{-3}
- 8 points between 10^{-3} and 10^{-2}
- 89 points between 10^{-1} and 10^{-2}
- 899 points between 1 and 10^{-1}

You get a lot more points in the less interesting ranges, and zero where you want them. In Figure 7-24, you can see the distribution of the points. Note that on the *x* axis, I am using a logarithmic scale. You can clearly see how you get much more points for bigger values of the learning rate.

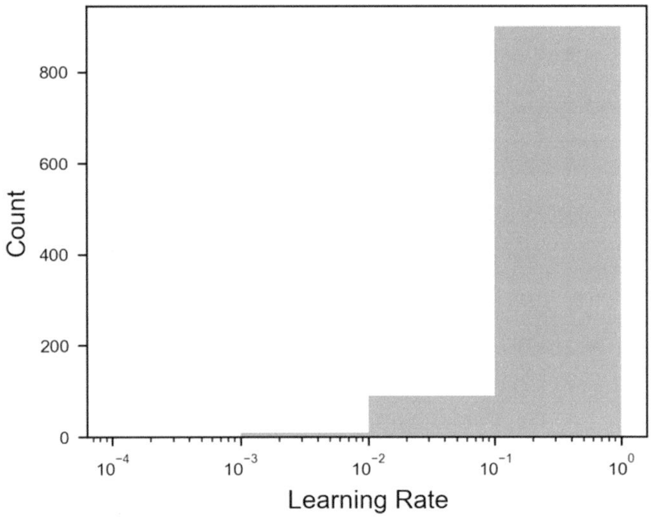

***Figure 7-24.** Distribution of 1000 points selected with grid search on a logarithmic x scale*

You probably want to sample in a much finer way for smaller values of the learning rate than for bigger ones. What you should do is sample your points on a logarithmic scale. Let me explain. The basic idea is that you want to sample the same number of points between 10^{-4} and 10^{-3}, 10^{-3} and 10^{-2}, 10^{-1} and 10^{-2}, and 10^{-1} and 1. To do this, you can use the following Python code. First, select a random number between 0 and subtract the absolute value of the highest number of the power of 10 you have, in this case -4.

```
r = - np.arange(0,1,0.001)*4.0
```

Then your array with the selected points can be created with

```
points2 = 10**r
```

In Figure 7-25, you can see now how the distributions of the points contained in the array `points2` is completely flat, as we wanted.

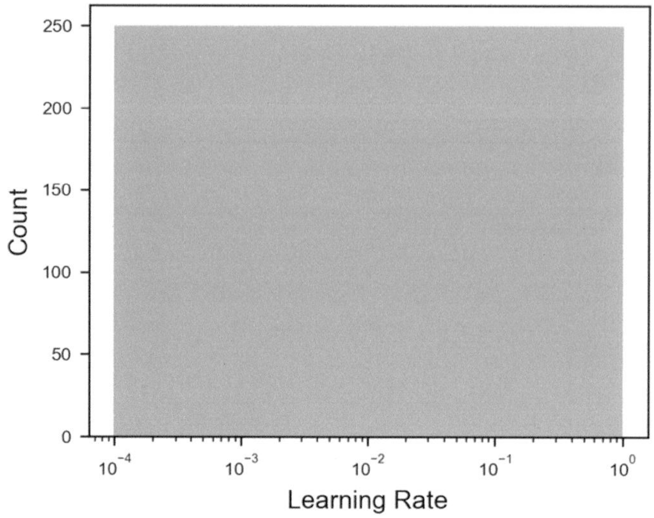

Figure 7-25. *Distribution of 1000 points selected with grid search on a logarithmic x scale, with the modified selection method*

You get 250 points in each region, as you can easily check with this code for the range 10^{-3} and 10^{-4} (for the other ranges simply change the numbers in the code):

```
print(np.sum((alpha <= 1e-3) & (alpha > 1e-4)))
```

Now you can see how you have the same number of points between the different powers of 10. With this simple trick, you can ensure that you also get enough points in the region of your chosen range, where, otherwise, you would get almost no points. Remember that in this example, with 1000 points, with the standard method, we get zero points between 10^{-3} and 10^{-4}. This range is the most interesting for the learning rate, so you want to have enough points in this range to optimize your model. Note that the same applies to random search. It works in the exact same way.

Hyperparameter Tuning with the Zalando Dataset

To give you a concrete example of how hyperparameter tuning works, let's apply what we have learned in a simple case. Let's start with the data, as usual. We'll use the Zalando dataset from Chapter 3. For a complete discussion, please refer to that chapter. Let's quickly load and prepare the data and then discuss tuning.

First, as usual, load the necessary libraries.

```
import pandas as pd
import numpy as np
import tensorflow as tf

%matplotlib inline

import matplotlib
import matplotlib.pyplot as plt

from random import *
```

You will require the necessary CSV files in the folder in which your Jupyter notebook is. To get them, refer again to Chapter 3. Once you have the files in the same folder as your notebook, you can simply load the data with

```
data_train = pd.read_csv('fashion-mnist_train.csv', header = 0)
data_dev = pd.read_csv('fashion-mnist_test.csv', header = 0)
```

Remember: We have 60,000 observations in the train dataset and 10,000 in the dev dataset. For example, printing the shape of the `data_train` array with

```
print(data_train.shape)
```

will give you (60000, 785). Remember that one of the columns in the `data_train` array contains the labels, and 784 are the gray values of the image pixels (that have a size of 28 × 28 pixels). We must separate the labels from the features (the gray values of the pixels), then we need to reshape the arrays.

```
labels = data_train['label'].values.reshape(1, 60000)
labels_ = np.zeros((60000, 10))
labels_[np.arange(60000), labels] = 1
labels_ = labels_.transpose()
train = data_train.drop('label', axis=1).transpose()
```

Checking the dimensions with

```
print(labels_.shape)
print(train.shape)
```

will give us

```
(10, 60000)
(784, 60000)
```

as desired. (For a detailed discussion on data preparation for this dataset, refer to Chapter 3.) We must, of course, do the same for the dev dataset.

```
labels_dev = data_test['label'].values.reshape(1, 10000)
labels_dev_ = np.zeros((10000, 10))
labels_dev_[np.arange(10000), labels_test] = 1
labels_dev_ = labels_test_.transpose()
dev = data_dev.drop('label', axis=1).transpose()
```

Now let's normalize the features and transform everything in a numpy array.

```
train = np.array(train / 255.0)
dev = np.array(dev / 255.0)
labels_ = np.array(labels_)
labels_dev_ = np.array(labels_dev_)
```

We have prepared the data as required. Now let's move on to the model. Let's start with something easy. As the metric, we'll use accuracy for this example, because the dataset is balanced. Let's consider a network with just one layer and see what number of neurons gives us the best accuracy. Our hyperparameter in this example will be the number of neurons in the hidden layer. Basically, we will have to build a new network for each value of the hyperparameter (the number of neurons in the hidden layer) and train it. We will require two functions: one to build the network and one to train it. To build the model, we can define the following function:

```
def build_model(number_neurons):
    n_dim = 784
    tf.reset_default_graph()

    # Number of neurons in the layers
    n1 = number_neurons # Number of neurons in the hidden layer
    n2 = 10 # Number of neurons in output layer

    cost_history = np.empty(shape=[1], dtype = float)
```

```
    learning_rate = tf.placeholder(tf.float32, shape=())

    X = tf.placeholder(tf.float32, [n_dim, None])
    Y = tf.placeholder(tf.float32, [10, None])
    W1 = tf.Variable(tf.truncated_normal([n1, n_dim], stddev=.1))
    b1 = tf.Variable(tf.constant(0.1, shape = [n1,1]) )
    W2 = tf.Variable(tf.truncated_normal([n2, n1], stddev=.1))
    b2 = tf.Variable(tf.constant(0.1, shape = [n2,1]))

    # Let's build our network...
    Z1 = tf.nn.relu(tf.matmul(W1, X) + b1) # n1 x n_dim * n_dim x n_obs =
    n1 x n_obs
    Z2 = tf.matmul(W2, Z1) + b2 # n2 x n1 * n1 * n_obs = n2 x n_obs
    y_ = tf.nn.softmax(Z2,0) # n2 x n_obs (10 x None)

    cost = - tf.reduce_mean(Y * tf.log(y_)+(1-Y) * tf.log(1-y_))
    optimizer = tf.train.GradientDescentOptimizer(learning_rate).
    minimize(cost)

    init = tf.global_variables_initializer()


    return optimizer, cost, y_, X, Y, learning_rate
```

You should understand this function, since we have used the code several times in the book already. This function has an input parameter: `number_neurons`, that will contain, as the name indicates, the number of neurons in the hidden layer. But there is a small difference: the functions return the tensors we must refer to during the training, for example, when we want to evaluate the `cost` tensor during training. If we don't return them to the caller, they will be visible only inside this function, and we will not be able to train this model. The function to train the model will look like this:

```
def model(minibatch_size, training_epochs, features, classes, logging_step
= 100, learning_r = 0.001, number_neurons = 15):

    opt, c, y_, X, Y, learning_rate = build_model(number_neurons)

    sess = tf.Session()
    sess.run(tf.global_variables_initializer())

    cost_history = []
```

```
    for epoch in range(training_epochs+1):
        for i in range(0, features.shape[1], minibatch_size):
            X_train_mini = features[:,i:i + minibatch_size]
            y_train_mini = classes[:,i:i + minibatch_size]

            sess.run(opt, feed_dict = {X: X_train_mini, Y: y_train_mini,
            learning_rate: learning_r})
        cost_ = sess.run(c, feed_dict={ X:features, Y: classes, learning_
        rate: learning_r})
        cost_history = np.append(cost_history, cost_)

        if (epoch % logging_step == 0):
                print("Reached epoch",epoch,"cost J =", cost_)

    correct_predictions = tf.equal(tf.argmax(y_,0), tf.argmax(Y,0))
    accuracy = tf.reduce_mean(tf.cast(correct_predictions, "float"))
    accuracy_train = accuracy.eval({X: train, Y: labels_, learning_rate:
    learning_r}, session = sess)
    accuracy_dev = accuracy.eval({X: dev, Y: labels_dev_, learning_rate:
    learning_r}, session = sess)

    return accuracy_train, accuracy_dev, sess, cost_history
```

You have already seen a function very similar to this one several times. The main parts should be clear. You will find a few things that are new. First, we build the model in the function itself with

```
opt, c, y_, X, Y, learning_rate = build_model(number_neurons)
```

and, additionally, we evaluate the accuracy on the train dataset and on the dev dataset and return the values to the caller. In this way, we can run a loop for several values of the number of neurons in the hidden layer and get the accuracies. Note, this time, that the function has an additional input parameter: `number_neurons`. We must pass this number to the function that builds the model.

Let's suppose we choose the following parameters: minibatch size = 50, we train for 100 epochs, the learning rate =0.00 , and we build our model with 15 neurons in the hidden layer.

We then run the model.

```
acc_train, acc_test, sess, cost_history = model(minibatch_size = 50,
                                 training_epochs = 100,
                                 features = train,
                                 classes = labels_,
                                 logging_step = 10,
                                 learning_r = 0.001,
                                 number_neurons = 15)

print(acc_train)
print(acc_test)
```

For the train dataset, we get 0.75755 accuracy and for the dev dataset 0.754 accuracy. Can we do better? Well, we can surely do a grid search to start with.

```
nn = [1,5,10,15,25,30, 50, 150, 300, 1000, 3000]
for nn_ in nn:
    acc_train, acc_test, sess, cost_history = model(minibatch_size = 50,
                                 training_epochs = 50,
                                 features = train,
                                 classes = labels_,
                                 logging_step = 50,
                                 learning_r = 0.001,
                                 number_neurons = nn_)
    print('Number of neurons:',nn_,'Acc. Train:', acc_train, 'Acc. Test',
    acc_test)
```

Keep in mind that this will take quite some time. Three thousand neurons is quite a high number, so be warned, in case you want to attempt this. We get the results, as found in Table 7-1.

Table 7-1. *Overview of the Accuaracy on the Train and Test Datasets for a Different Number of Neurons*

Number of Neurons	Accuracy on the Train Dataset	Accuracy on the Test Dataset
1	0.201383	0.2042
5	0.639417	0.6377
10	0.639183	0.6348
15	0.687183	0.6815
25	0.690917	0.6917
30	0.6965	0.6887
50	0.73665	0.7369
150	0.78545	0.7848
300	0.806267	0.8067
1000	0.828117	0.8316
3000	0.8468	0.8416

Not surprisingly, more neurons deliver better accuracy, with no signs of overfitting of the train dataset, because the accuracy on the dev dataset is almost equal to that of the train dataset. In Figure 7-26, you can see a plot of the accuracy on the test dataset vs. the number of neurons in the hidden layer. Note that the x axis uses a logarithmic scale, to make the changes more evident.

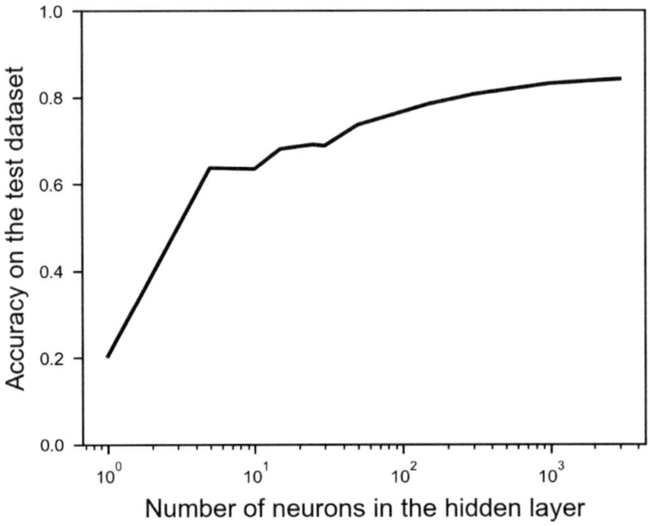

Figure 7-26. *Accuracy on the test dataset vs. the number of neurons in the hidden layer*

If your goal was to reach 80% accuracy, you could well stop here. But there are a few things to consider. First, we may be able to do better, and, second, training the network with 3000 neurons takes quite some time—on my laptop, roughly 35 minutes. We should see if we can get the same result in a fraction of the time. We want a model that trains as fast as we can. Let's try a slightly different approach. Because we want to be faster, let's consider a model with four layers. Actually, we could also tune the number of layers, but let's stick to four for this example and tune the other parameters. We will try to find the optimal value for learning rate, mini-batch size, number of neurons in each layer, and number of epochs. We will use random search. For each parameter, we will select randomly 10 values.

- *Number of neurons*: Between 35 and 60
- *Learning rate*: We will use the search on the logarithmic scale between 10^{-1} and 10^{-3}.
- *Mini-batch size*: Between 20 and 80
- *Number of epochs*: Between 40 and 100

We can create arrays with the possible values with this code:

```
neurons_ = np.random.randint(low=35, high=60.0, size=(10))
r = -np.random.random([10])*3.0-1
learning_ = 10**r
mb_size_ = np.random.randint(low=20, high=80, size = 10)
epochs_ = np.random.randint(low = 40, high = 100, size = (10))
```

Note that we will not try all possible combinations, but we will consider only ten possible combinations: the first value of each array, the second value of each array, and so on. I want to show you how efficient random search can be with just ten evaluations! We can test our model with the following loop:

```
for i in range(len(neurons_)):
    acc_train, acc_test, sess, cost_history = model_layers(minibatch_size =
mb_size_[i],
                                training_epochs = epochs_[i],
                                features = train,
                                classes = labels_,
                                logging_step = 50,
                                learning_r = learning_[i],
                                number_neurons = neurons_[i], debug = False)
    print('Epochs:', epochs_[i], 'Number of neurons:',neurons_[i],'learning
rate:', learning_[i], 'mb size',mb_size_[i],
          'Acc. Train:', acc_train, 'Acc. Test', acc_test)
```

If you run this code, you will get a few combinations that end up in nan, and, therefore, it gets you an accuracy of 0.1 (basically random, because we have ten classes) and a few good combinations. You will find that the combinations with 41 epochs, 41 neurons in each layer, a learning rate of 0.0286, and a mini-batch size of 61 gives you an accuracy on the dev dataset of 0.86. Not bad, considering that this run took 2.5 minutes, so 14 times faster than the model with 1 layer and 3000 neurons and 6% better. Our naive initial test gave us an accuracy of 0.75, so with hyperparameter tuning, we got 11% better than our initial guess. Eleven percent increased accuracy in deep learning is an incredible result. Even 1% or 2% better is considered a great result, normally. What we did should give you an idea of how powerful hyperparameter tuning can be, if done properly. Keep in mind that you should spend quite some time doing it, thinking especially about *how* to do it.

Note Always think about *how* you want to do your hyperparameter tuning, and use your experience, or ask for help from someone with experience. It is useless to invest time and resources to try combinations of parameters that you know will not work. For example, it is better to spend time testing learning rates that are very small than to test learning rates around one. Remember that every training round of your network will cost time, even if the results are not useful!

The point of this last section is not to get the best model possible but to give you an idea of how the tuning process may work. You could continue, trying different optimizers (for example Adam), considering wider ranges for the parameters, more parameter combinations, and so on.

A Quick Note on the Radial Basis Function

Before completing this chapter, I would like to discuss a minor point about the radial basis function

$$K(x, x_i) = \sigma^2 e^{-\frac{1}{2l^2}\|x - x_i\|^2}$$

It is important that you understand what the role of the parameter l is. In the examples, I have chosen $l = 2$, but I have not discussed why. The reason is the following. Choosing l too small will make the acquisition function develop very narrow peaks around the points we already have, as you can see in the left plot in Figure 7-27. Big values for l will have a smoothing effect on the acquisition function, as you can see in the center and right plots in Figure 7-27.

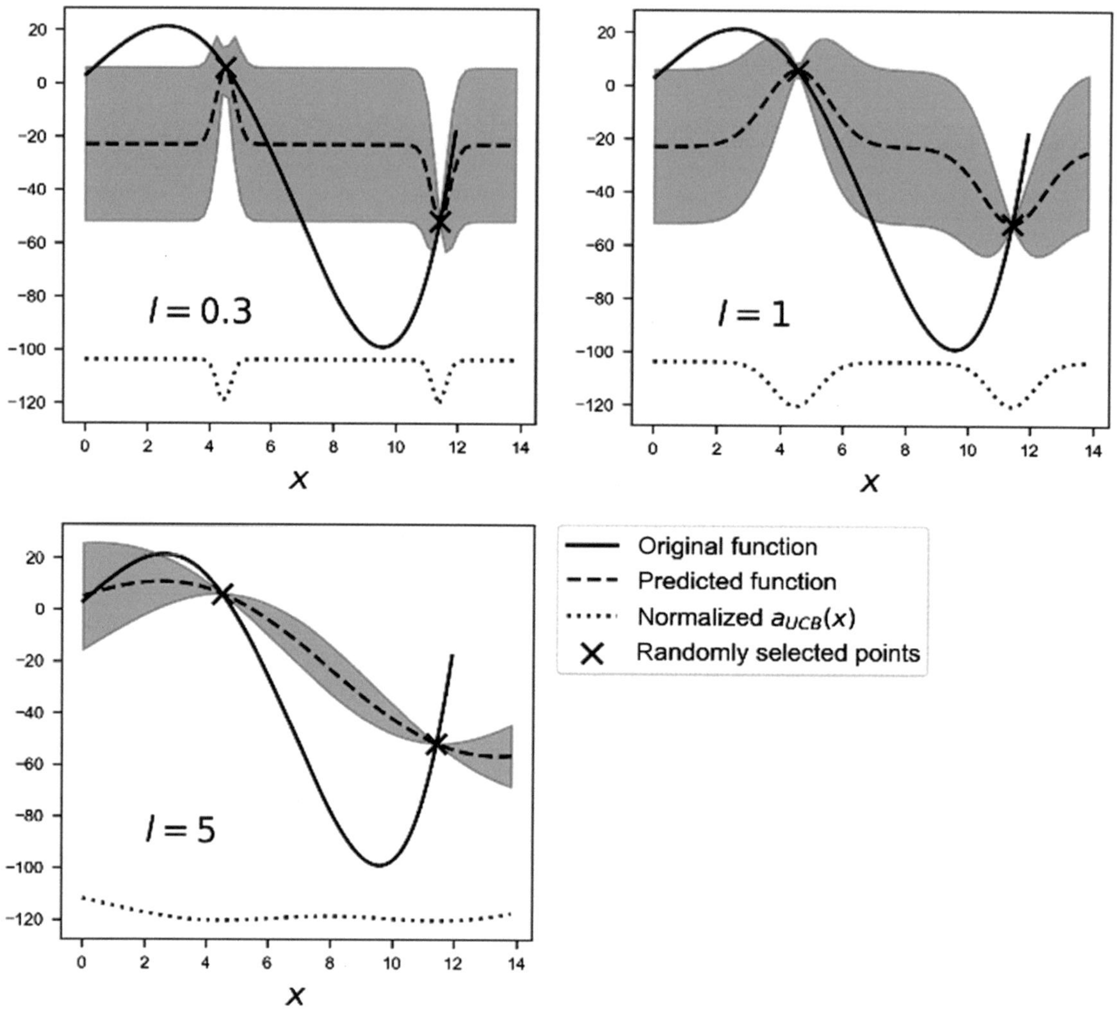

Figure 7-27. *Effect of changing the parameter l in the radial basis function*

Usually, it is good practice to avoid values for l that are too small or too big, to be able to have a variance that varies in a smooth way between known points, as in Figure 7-27, for $l = 1$. Having a very small l will make the variance between points almost constant and, therefore, make the algorithm almost always choose the middle point between points, as you can see from the acquisition function. Choosing a big l will make the variance small and, therefore, with some acquisition functions, difficult to use. As you can see for $l = 5$ in Figure 7-27, the acquisition function is almost constant. Typical values that are used are around 1 or 2.

CHAPTER 8

Convolutional and Recurrent Neural Networks

In the previous chapters, you have looked at fully connected networks and all the problems encountered while training them. The network architecture we have used, one in which each neuron in a layer is connected to all neurons in the previous and following layer, is not really good at many fundamental tasks, such as image recognition, speech recognition, time series prediction, and many more. Convolutional neural networks (CNNs) and recurrent neural networks (RNNs) are the advanced architectures most often used today. In this chapter, you will look at convolution and pooling, the basic building blocks of CNNs. Then you will check how RNNs work on a high level, and you will look at a select number of examples of applications. I will also discuss a complete, although basic, implementation of CNNs and RNNs in TensorFlow. The topic of CNNs and RNNs is much too vast to cover in a single chapter. Therefore, I will cover here only the fundamental concepts, to show you how those architectures work, but a complete treatment would require a separate book.

Kernels and Filters

One of the main components of CNNs are filters—square matrices that have dimensions $n_K \times n_K$, where, usually, n_K is a small number, such as 3 or 5. Sometimes, filters are also called kernels. Let's define four different filters and check their effect later in the chapter,

U. Michelucci, *Applied Deep Learning*, https://doi.org/10.1007/978-1-4842-3790-8_8

when they are used in convolution operations. For these examples, we will work with 3 × 3 filters. For the moment, consider the following definitions just for reference; you will see how to use them later in the chapter.

- The following kernel will allow the detection of horizontal edges:

$$\mathfrak{I}_H = \begin{pmatrix} 1 & 1 & 1 \\ 0 & 0 & 0 \\ -1 & -1 & -1 \end{pmatrix}$$

- The following kernel will allow the detection of vertical edges:

$$\mathfrak{I}_V = \begin{pmatrix} 1 & 0 & -1 \\ 1 & 0 & -1 \\ 1 & 0 & -1 \end{pmatrix}$$

- The following kernel will allow the detection of edges when luminosity changes drastically:

$$\mathfrak{I}_L = \begin{pmatrix} -1 & -1 & -1 \\ -1 & 8 & -1 \\ -1 & -1 & -1 \end{pmatrix}$$

- The following kernel will blur edges in an image:

$$\mathfrak{I}_B = -\frac{1}{9}\begin{pmatrix} 1 & 1 & 1 \\ 1 & 1 & 1 \\ 1 & 1 & 1 \end{pmatrix}$$

In the next sections, we will apply convolution to a test image with the filters, and you will see what its effect is.

Convolution

The first step toward understanding CNNs is to understand convolution. The easiest way to see it in action is in a few simple cases. First, in the context of neural networks, convolution is done between tensors. The operation gets two tensors as input and produces a tensor as output. The operation is usually indicated with the operator $*$. Let's see how it works. Let's get two tensors, both with dimensions 3 × 3. The convolution operation is performed by applying the following formula:

$$\begin{pmatrix} a_1 & a_2 & a_3 \\ a_4 & a_5 & a_6 \\ a_7 & a_8 & a_9 \end{pmatrix} * \begin{pmatrix} k_1 & k_2 & k_3 \\ k_4 & k_5 & k_6 \\ k_7 & k_8 & k_9 \end{pmatrix} = \sum_{i=1}^{9} a_i k_i$$

In this case, the result is simply the sum of each element a_i, multiplied by the respective element k_i. In a more typical matrix formalism, this formula could be written with a double sum as

$$\begin{pmatrix} a_{11} & a_{12} & a_{13} \\ a_{21} & a_{22} & a_{23} \\ a_{31} & a_{32} & a_{33} \end{pmatrix} * \begin{pmatrix} k_{11} & k_{12} & k_{13} \\ k_{21} & k_{22} & k_{23} \\ k_{31} & k_{32} & k_{33} \end{pmatrix} = \sum_{i=1}^{3}\sum_{j=1}^{3} a_{ij} k_{ij}$$

But the first version has the advantage of making the fundamental idea very clear: each element from one tensor is multiplied by the corresponding element (the element in the same position) of the second tensor, and then all the values are summed to get the result.

In the previous section, I mentioned kernels, and the reason is that convolution is usually done between a tensor, which we may indicate here with A, and a kernel. Typically, kernels are small, 3 × 3 or 5 × 5, while the input tensors A are normally bigger. In image recognition, for example, the input tensors A are the images that may have dimensions as high as 1024 × 1024 × 3, where 1024 × 1024 is the resolution, and the last dimension (3) is the number of the color channels, the RGB (red, green, blue) values. In advanced applications, the images may have even higher resolution. How do we apply convolution when we have matrices with different dimensions? To understand how, let's consider a matrix A that is 4 × 4.

$$A = \begin{pmatrix} a_1 & a_2 & a_3 & a_4 \\ a_5 & a_6 & a_7 & a_8 \\ a_9 & a_{10} & a_{11} & a_{12} \\ a_{13} & a_{14} & a_{15} & a_{16} \end{pmatrix}$$

And let's see how to do convolution with a kernel K, which, for this example, we will take to be 3 × 3.

$$K = \begin{pmatrix} k_1 & k_2 & k_3 \\ k_4 & k_5 & k_6 \\ k_7 & k_8 & k_9 \end{pmatrix}$$

The idea is to start at the top-left corner of matrix A and select a 3 × 3 region. In our example, that would be

$$A_1 = \begin{pmatrix} a_1 & a_2 & a_3 \\ a_5 & a_6 & a_7 \\ a_9 & a_{10} & a_{11} \end{pmatrix}$$

or the elements marked in boldface following.

$$A = \begin{pmatrix} \boldsymbol{a_1} & \boldsymbol{a_2} & \boldsymbol{a_3} & a_4 \\ \boldsymbol{a_5} & \boldsymbol{a_6} & \boldsymbol{a_7} & a_8 \\ \boldsymbol{a_9} & \boldsymbol{a_{10}} & \boldsymbol{a_{11}} & a_{12} \\ a_{13} & a_{14} & a_{15} & a_{16} \end{pmatrix}$$

Then we perform the convolution, as explained at the beginning, between this smaller matrix A_1 and K, getting (we will indicate the result with B_1)

$$B_1 = A_1 * K = a_1k_1 + a_2k_2 + a_3k_3 + k_4a_5 + k_5a_5 + k_6a_7 + k_7a_9 + k_8a_{10} + k_9a_{11}$$

Then we must shift the selected 3 × 3 region in matrix A by one column to the right and select the elements marked in boldface following.

$$A = \begin{pmatrix} a_1 & \mathbf{a_2} & \mathbf{a_3} & \mathbf{a_4} \\ a_5 & \mathbf{a_6} & \mathbf{a_7} & \mathbf{a_8} \\ a_9 & \mathbf{a_{10}} & \mathbf{a_{11}} & \mathbf{a_{12}} \\ a_{13} & a_{14} & a_{15} & a_{16} \end{pmatrix}$$

That will give us the second sub-matrix A_2

$$A_2 = \begin{pmatrix} a_2 & a_3 & a_4 \\ a_6 & a_7 & a_8 \\ a_{10} & a_{11} & a_{12} \end{pmatrix}$$

and we perform again the convolution between this smaller matrix A_2 and K

$$B_2 = A_2 * K = a_2k_1 + a_3k_2 + a_4k_3 + a_6k_4 + a_7k_5 + a_8k_6 + a_{10}k_7 + a_{11}k_8 + a_{12}k_9$$

Now we cannot shift our 3 × 3 region any more to the right, because we have reached the end of matrix A, so what we do is shift it one row down and start again from the left side. The next selected region would be

$$A_3 = \begin{pmatrix} a_5 & a_6 & a_7 \\ a_9 & a_{10} & a_{11} \\ a_{13} & a_{14} & a_{15} \end{pmatrix}$$

Again, we perform the convolution of A_3 with K

$$B_3 = A_3 * K = a_5k_1 + a_6k_2 + a_7k_3 + a_9k_4 + a_{10}k_5 + a_{11}k_6 + a_{13}k_7 + a_{14}k_8 + a_{15}k_9$$

As you may have guessed by this point, the last step is to shift our 3 × 3 selected region to the right by one column and perform the convolution again. Our selected region will now be

$$A_4 = \begin{pmatrix} a_6 & a_7 & a_8 \\ a_{10} & a_{11} & a_{12} \\ a_{14} & a_{15} & a_{16} \end{pmatrix}$$

and the convolution will give the result

$$B_4 = A_4 * K = a_6k_1 + a_7k_2 + a_8k_3 + a_{10}k_4 + a_{11}k_5 + a_{12}k_6 + a_{14}k_7 + a_{15}k_8 + a_{16}k_9$$

Now we cannot shift our 3 × 3 region any more, neither right nor down. We have calculated 4 values: B_1, B_2, B_3, and B_4. Those elements will form the resulting tensor of the convolution operation, giving us the tensor B.

$$B = \begin{pmatrix} B_1 & B_2 \\ B_3 & B_4 \end{pmatrix}$$

The same process can be applied when the tensor A is bigger. You will simply get a bigger resulting B tensor, but the algorithm to get the elements B_i is the same. Before moving on, there is still a small detail that I must discuss, and that is the concept of stride. In the preceding process, we always have moved our 3 × 3 region one column to the right and one row down. The number of rows and columns, in this example 1, is called stride and is often indicated with s. Stride $s = 2$ means simply that we would shift our 3 × 3 region two columns to the right and two rows down. Something else that I must discuss is the size of the selected region in the input matrix A. The dimensions of the selected region that we shifted around in the process must be the same as that of the kernel used. If you use a 5 × 5 kernel, then you must select a 5 × 5 region in A. In general, given a $n_K \times n_K$ kernel, you will select a $n_K \times n_K$ region in A.

A more formal definition is that convolution with stride s, in the neural network context, is a process that takes a tensor A of dimensions $n_A \times n_A$ and a kernel K of dimensions $n_K \times n_K$ and gives as output a matrix B of dimensions $n_B \times n_B$ with

$$n_B = \left\lfloor \frac{n_A - n_K}{s} + 1 \right\rfloor$$

where we have indicated with $\lfloor x \rfloor$ the integer part of x (in the programming world, this is often called the floor of x). A proof of this formula would take too long to discuss, but it is easy to see why it is true (try to derive it). To make things a bit easier, we will suppose that n_K is odd. You will see soon why this is important (although not fundamental).

Let me begin explaining formally the case with a stride $s = 1$. The algorithm generates a new tensor B from an input tensor A and a kernel K, according to the formula

$$B_{ij} = (A * K)_{ij} = \sum_{f=0}^{n_K - 1} \sum_{h=0}^{n_K - 1} A_{i+f,j+h} K_{i+f,j+h}$$

The formula is cryptic and very difficult to understand. Let's see some more examples, to grasp the meaning better. In Figure 8-1, you can see a visual explanation of how convolution works. Suppose you have a 3 × 3 filter. Then, in the figure, you can see that the top left nine elements of the matrix A, marked by a square drawn with a black continuous line, are the ones used to generate the first element of the matrix B_1, according to the preceding formula. The elements marked by the square drawn with a dotted line are the ones used to generate the second element B_2, and so on. To reiterate what I discussed in the example at the beginning, the basic idea is that each element of the 3 × 3 square from matrix A is multiplied by the corresponding element of the kernel K, and all the numbers are summed. The sum is then the element of the new matrix B. After having calculated the value for B_1, you shift the region you are considering in the original matrix by one column to the right (the square indicated in Figure 8-1 with a dotted line) and repeat the operation. You continue to shift your region to the right, until you reach the border, and then you move one element down and start again from the left and continue in this fashion until reaching the lower right angle of the matrix. The same kernel is used for all the regions in the original matrix.

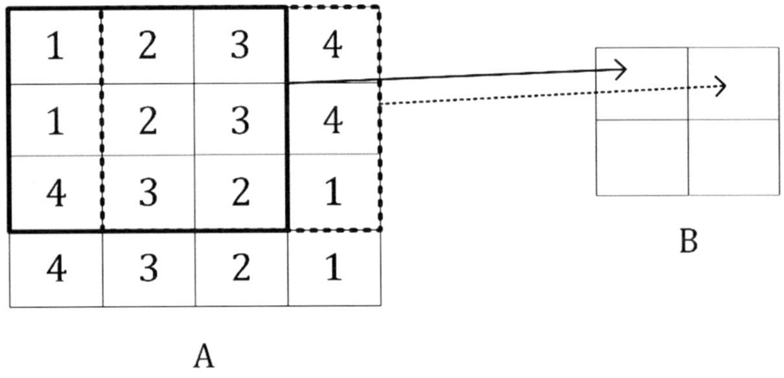

***Figure 8-1.** Visual explanation of convolution*

Given the kernel $\Im_H$, for example, you can see in Figure 8-2 which element of A gets multiplied by which element in $\Im_H$ and the result for the element B_1, that is nothing else as the sum of all the multiplications

$$B_{11} = 1\times1 + 2\times1 + 3\times1 + 1\times0 + 2\times0 + 3\times0 + 4\times(-1) + 3\times(-1) + 2\times(-1) = -3$$

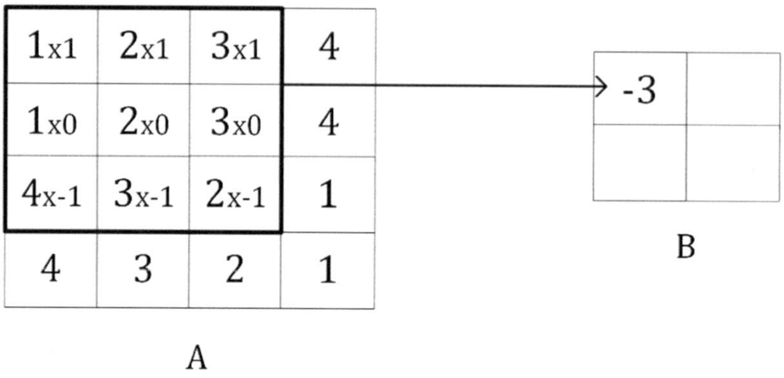

***Figure 8-2.** Visualization of convolution with the kernel $\Im_H$*

In Figure 8-3, you can see an illustrative example of convolution with stride $s = 2$.

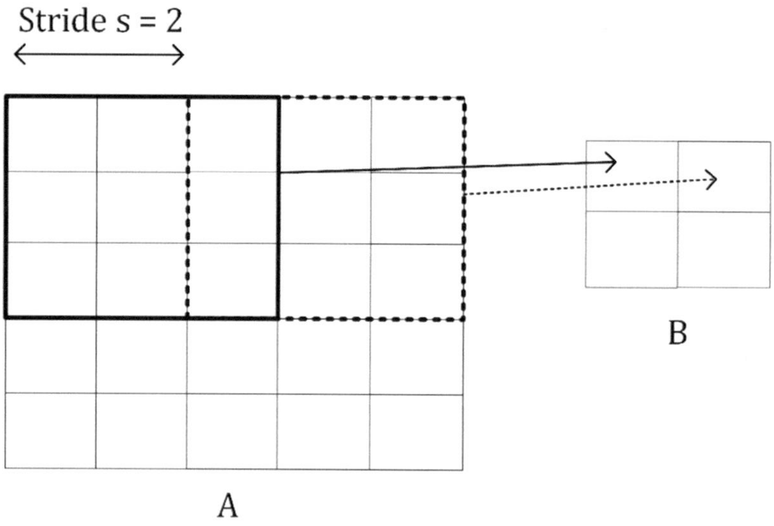

***Figure 8-3.** Visual explanation of convolution with stride $s = 2$*

The reason why the dimension of the output matrix takes only the floor (the integer part) of $\frac{n_A - n_K}{s} + 1$ can be seen intuitively in Figure 8-4. If $s > 1$, what can happen, depending on the dimensions of A, is that at a certain point, you cannot shift your window on matrix A (the black square in Figure 8-3, for example) anymore, and you cannot cover all of matrix A completely. In Figure 8-4, you can see how you would need an additional column on the right of matrix A (marked by many Xs), to be able to perform the convolution operation. In Figure 8-4, $s = 3$, and since we have $n_A = 5$ and $n_K = 3$, B will a scalar as a result.

$$n_B = \left\lfloor \frac{n_A - n_K}{s} + 1 \right\rfloor = \left\lfloor \frac{5-3}{3} + 1 \right\rfloor = \left\lfloor \frac{5}{3} \right\rfloor = 1$$

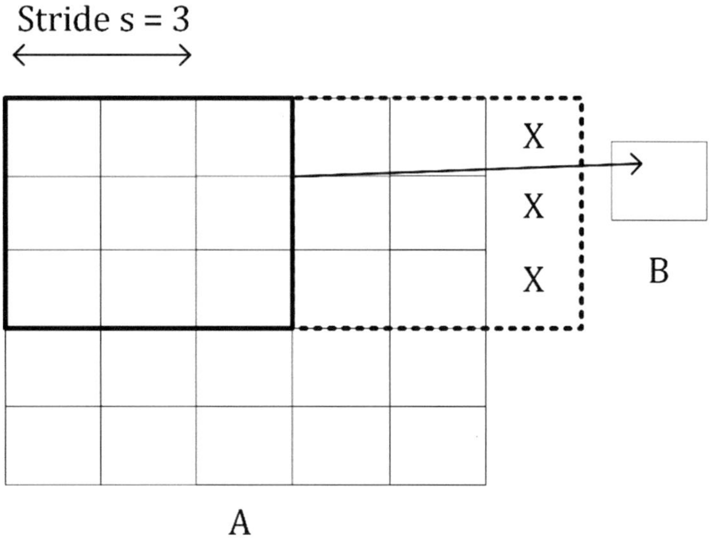

Figure 8-4. *Visual explanation of why the floor function is required when evaluating the resulting matrix B dimensions*

You can easily see from Figure 8-4 how with a 3 × 3 region you can only cover the top-left region of A, because with stride $s = 3$, you would end up outside A and, therefore, could consider only one region for the convolution operation, thereby ending up with a scalar for the resulting tensor B.

Let's now consider a few additional examples, to make this formula even clearer. Let's start with a small matrix 3 × 3.

$$A = \begin{pmatrix} 1 & 2 & 3 \\ 4 & 5 & 6 \\ 7 & 8 & 9 \end{pmatrix}$$

And let's consider the kernel

$$K = \begin{pmatrix} k_1 & k_2 & k_3 \\ k_4 & k_5 & k_6 \\ k_7 & k_8 & k_9 \end{pmatrix}$$

and the stride $s = 1$. The convolution will be given by

$$B = A * K = 1 \cdot k_1 + 2 \cdot k_2 + 3 \cdot k_3 + 4 \cdot k_4 + 5 \cdot k_5 + 6 \cdot k_6 + 7 \cdot k_7 + 8 \cdot k_8 + 9 \cdot k_9$$

and the result B will be a scalar, because $n_A = 3$, $n_K = 3$, therefore

$$n_B = \left\lfloor \frac{n_A - n_K}{s} + 1 \right\rfloor = \left\lfloor \frac{3-3}{1} + 1 \right\rfloor = 1$$

If you consider now a matrix A with dimensions 4 × 4, or $n_A = 4$, $n_K = 3$ and $s = 1$, you will get as output a matrix B with dimensions 2 × 2, because

$$n_B = \left\lfloor \frac{n_A - n_K}{s} + 1 \right\rfloor = \left\lfloor \frac{4-3}{1} + 1 \right\rfloor = 2$$

For example, you can verify that given

$$A = \begin{pmatrix} 1 & 2 & 3 & 4 \\ 5 & 6 & 7 & 8 \\ 9 & 10 & 11 & 12 \\ 13 & 14 & 15 & 16 \end{pmatrix}$$

and

$$K = \begin{pmatrix} 1 & 2 & 3 \\ 4 & 5 & 6 \\ 7 & 8 & 9 \end{pmatrix}$$

we have with stride $s = 1$

$$B = A * K = \begin{pmatrix} 348 & 393 \\ 528 & 573 \end{pmatrix}$$

Let's verify one of the elements, B_{11}, with the formula I gave you. We have

$$\begin{aligned} B_{11} &= \sum_{f=0}^{2} \sum_{h=0}^{2} A_{1+f,1+h} K_{1+f,1+h} = \sum_{f=0}^{2} \left(\mathrm{A}_{1+\mathrm{f},\,1} K_{1+f,1} + \mathrm{A}_{1+\mathrm{f},\,2} K_{1+f,2} + \mathrm{A}_{1+\mathrm{f},\,3} K_{1+f,3} \right) \\ &= \left(\mathrm{A}_{1,\,1} K_{1,1} + \mathrm{A}_{1,\,2} K_{1,2} + \mathrm{A}_{1,\,3} K_{1,3} \right) + \left(\mathrm{A}_{2,\,1} K_{2,1} + \mathrm{A}_{2,\,2} K_{2,2} + \mathrm{A}_{2,\,3} K_{2,3} \right) \\ &\quad + \left(\mathrm{A}_{3,\,1} K_{3,1} + \mathrm{A}_{3,\,2} K_{3,2} + \mathrm{A}_{3,\,3} K_{3,3} \right) = (1 \cdot 1 + 2 \cdot 2 + 3 \cdot 3) + (5 \cdot 4 + 6 \cdot 5 + 7 \cdot 6) \\ &\quad + (9 \cdot 7 + 10 \cdot 8 + 11 \cdot 9) = 14 + 92 + 242 = 348 \end{aligned}$$

Note that the formula I gave you for the convolution works only for stride $s = 1$ but can be easily generalized for other values of s.

This calculation is very easy to implement in Python. The following function can evaluate the convolution of two matrices easily enough for $s = 1$. (You can do it in Python with already existing functions, but I think it is instructive to see how to do it from scratch.)

```
import numpy as np
def conv_2d(A, kernel):
    output = np.zeros([A.shape[0]-(kernel.shape[0]-1), A.shape[1]-(kernel.
    shape[0]-1)])

    for row in range(1,A.shape[0]-1):
        for column in range(1, A.shape[1]-1):
            output[row-1, column-1] = np.tensordot(A[row-1:row+2,
            column-1:column+2], kernel)

    return output
```

Note that the input matrix A does not even need to be a square one, but it is assumed that the kernel is, and that its dimension n_K is odd. The previous example can be evaluated with the following code:

```
A = np.array([[1,2,3,4],[5,6,7,8],[9,10,11,12],[13,14,15,16]])
K = np.array([[1,2,3],[4,5,6],[7,8,9]])
print(conv_2d(A,K))
```

This gives the result

```
[[ 348. 393.]
[ 528. 573.]]
```

Examples of Convolution

Now let's try to apply the kernels we have defined at the beginning to a test image and see the results. As a test image, let's create a chessboard having the dimensions 160 × 160 pixels, with the code

```
chessboard = np.zeros([8*20, 8*20])
for row in range(0, 8):
    for column in range (0, 8):
        if ((column+8*row) % 2 == 1) and (row % 2 == 0):
            chessboard[row*20:row*20+20, column*20:column*20+20] = 1
        elif ((column+8*row) % 2 == 0) and (row % 2 == 1):
            chessboard[row*20:row*20+20, column*20:column*20+20] = 1
```

In Figure 8-5, you can see how the chessboard looks.

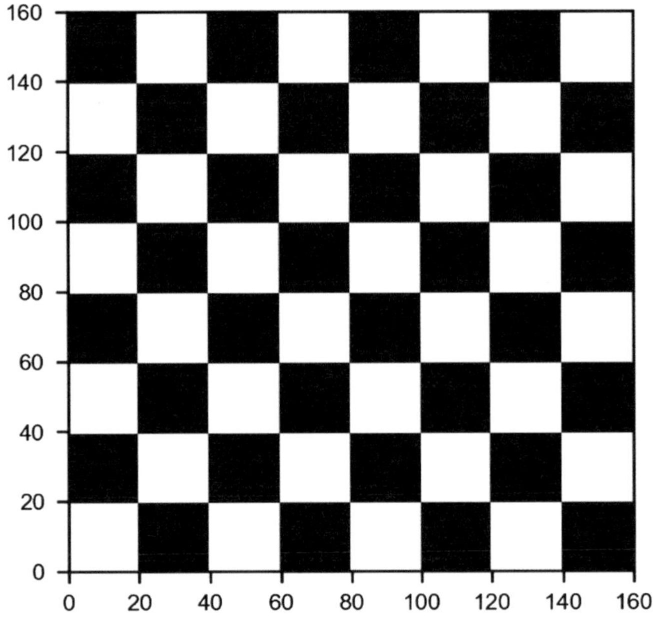

Figure 8-5. *Chessboard image generated with code*

Now let's try to apply convolution to this image with the different kernels with stride $s = 1$.

Using the kernel $\mathfrak{I}_H$ will detect the horizontal edges. This can be applied with the code

```
edgeh = np.matrix('1 1 1; 0 0 0; -1 -1 -1')
outputh = conv_2d (chessboard, edgeh)
```

In Figure 8-6, you can see what the output looks like.

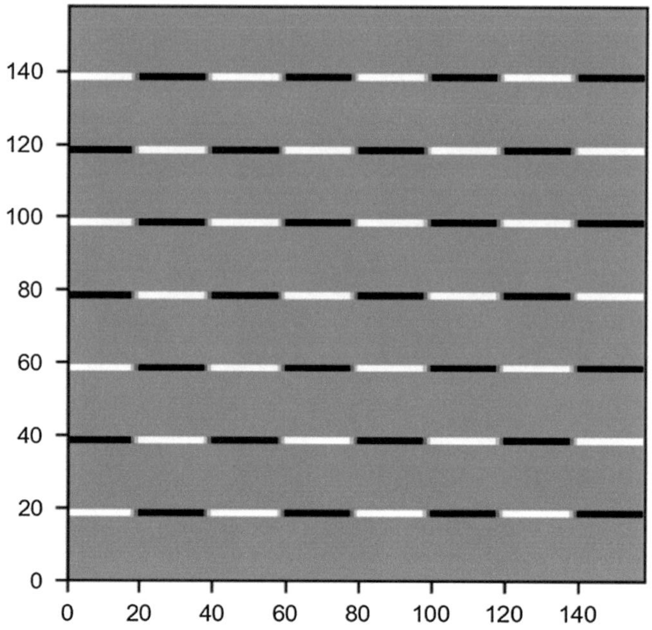

Figure 8-6. *Result of performing a convolution between the kernel $\mathfrak{I}_H$ and the chessboard image*

Now you can understand why I said that this kernel detects horizontal edges. Additionally, this kernel detects if you go from light to dark or vice versa. Note that this image is only 158 × 158 pixels, as expected, because

$$n_B = \left[\frac{n_A - n_K}{s} + 1\right] = \left[\frac{160-3}{1} + 1\right] = \left[\frac{157}{1} + 1\right] = [158] = 158$$

Now let's apply $\mathfrak{I}_V$ with the code

```
edgev = np.matrix('1 0 -1; 1 0 -1; 1 0 -1')
outputv = conv_2d (chessboard, edgev)
```

This gives the result shown in Figure 8-7.

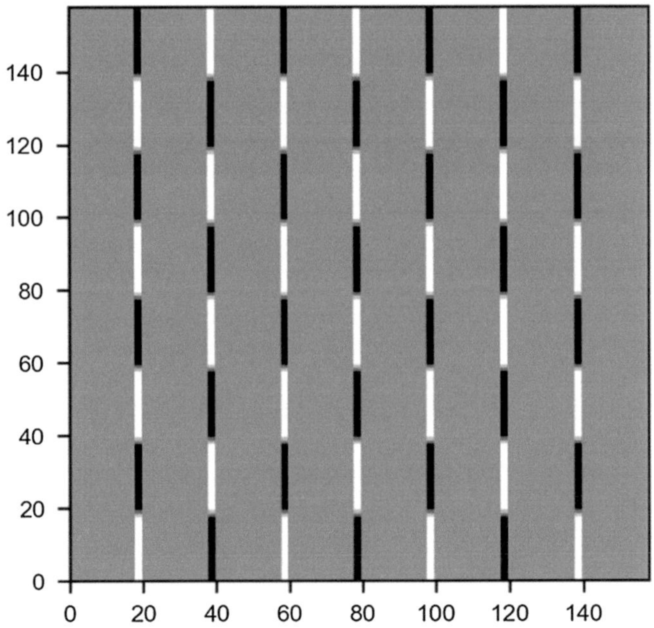

***Figure 8-7.** Result of performing a convolution between the kernel $\Im_V$ and the chessboard image*

Now we can use the kernel $\Im_L$

```
edgel = np.matrix ('-1 -1 -1; -1 8 -1; -1 -1 -1')
outputl = conv_2d (chessboard, edgel)
```

This gives the result shown in Figure 8-8.

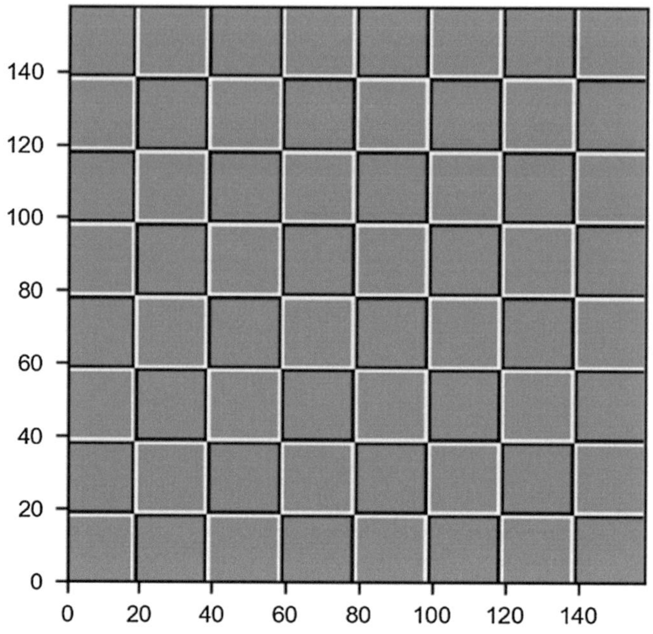

Figure 8-8. *Result of performing a convolution between the kernel $\mathfrak{I}_L$ and the chessboard image*

And, finally, we can apply the blurring kernel $\mathfrak{I}_B$.

```
edge_blur = -1.0/9.0*np.matrix('1 1 1; 1 1 1; 1 1 1')
output_blur = conv_2d (chessboard, edge_blur)
```

In Figure 8-9, you can see two plots: on the left, the blurred image, and on the right, the original one. The images show only a small region of the original chessboard, to make the blurring clearer.

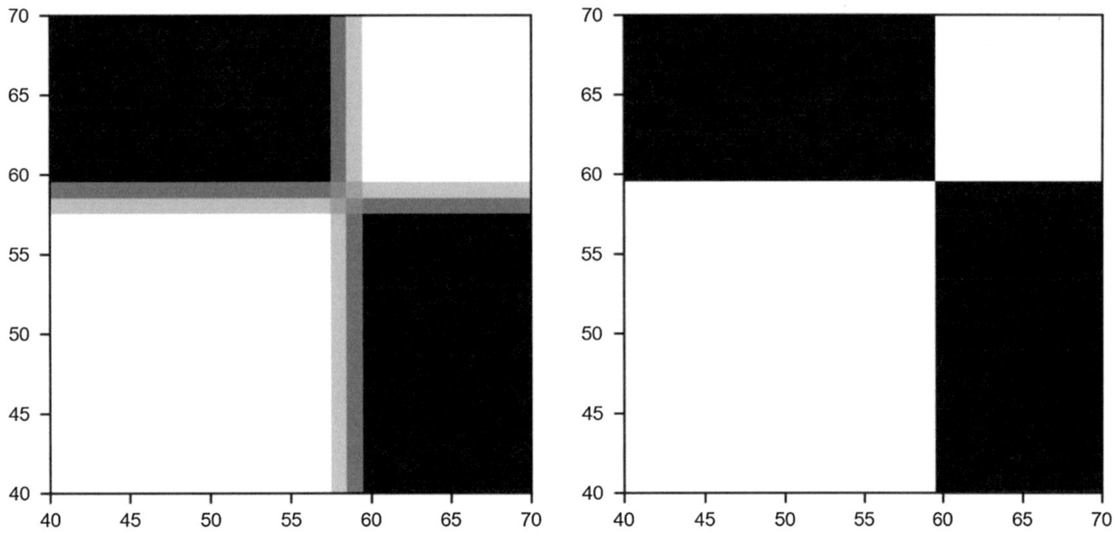

Figure 8-9. *Effect of the blurring kernel* $\mathfrak{I}_B$ *. On the left is the blurred image, and on the right, the original one.*

To finish this section let's try to understand better how the edges can be detected. Let's consider the following matrix with a sharp vertical transition, because the left part is full of tens and the right part full of zeros.

```
ex_mat = np.matrix('10 10 10 10 0 0 0 0; 10 10 10 10 0 0 0 0; 10 10 10 10 0 0 0 0; 10 10 10 10 0 0 0 0; 10 10 10 10 0 0 0 0; 10 10 10 10 0 0 0 0; 10 10 10 10 0 0 0 0; 10 10 10 10 0 0 0 0')
```

The result looks like this.

```
matrix([[10, 10, 10, 10, 0, 0, 0, 0],
        [10, 10, 10, 10, 0, 0, 0, 0],
        [10, 10, 10, 10, 0, 0, 0, 0],
        [10, 10, 10, 10, 0, 0, 0, 0],
        [10, 10, 10, 10, 0, 0, 0, 0],
        [10, 10, 10, 10, 0, 0, 0, 0],
        [10, 10, 10, 10, 0, 0, 0, 0],
        [10, 10, 10, 10, 0, 0, 0, 0]])
```

Now let's consider the kernel $\mathfrak{I}_V$. We can perform the convolution with the code

```
ex_out = conv_2d (ex_mat, edgev)
```

The result is

```
array([[ 0., 0., 30., 30., 0., 0.],
       [ 0., 0., 30., 30., 0., 0.],
       [ 0., 0., 30., 30., 0., 0.],
       [ 0., 0., 30., 30., 0., 0.],
       [ 0., 0., 30., 30., 0., 0.],
       [ 0., 0., 30., 30., 0., 0.]])
```

In Figure 8-10, you can see the original matrix (on the left) and the output of the convolution (on the right). The convolution with the kernel $\mathfrak{I}_V$ has clearly detected the sharp transition in the original matrix, marking with a vertical black line where the transition from black to white occurs. For example, consider $B_{11} = 0$.

$$B_{11} = \begin{pmatrix} 10 & 10 & 10 \\ 10 & 10 & 10 \\ 10 & 10 & 10 \end{pmatrix} * \mathfrak{I}_V = \begin{pmatrix} 10 & 10 & 10 \\ 10 & 10 & 10 \\ 10 & 10 & 10 \end{pmatrix} * \begin{pmatrix} 1 & 0 & -1 \\ 1 & 0 & -1 \\ 1 & 0 & -1 \end{pmatrix}$$
$$= 10\times1+10\times0+10\times-1+10\times1+10\times0+10\times-1+10\times1+10\times0+10\times-1=0$$

Note that in the input matrix

$$\begin{pmatrix} 10 & 10 & 10 \\ 10 & 10 & 10 \\ 10 & 10 & 10 \end{pmatrix}$$

there is no transition, as all the values are the same. On the contrary, if you consider B_{13}, you must consider this region of the input matrix

$$\begin{pmatrix} 10 & 10 & 0 \\ 10 & 10 & 0 \\ 10 & 10 & 0 \end{pmatrix}$$

where there is a clear transition, because the rightmost column is made up of zeros, and the rest of tens. You get now a different result.

$$B_{11} = \begin{pmatrix} 10 & 10 & 0 \\ 10 & 10 & 0 \\ 10 & 10 & 0 \end{pmatrix} * \Im_V = \begin{pmatrix} 10 & 10 & 0 \\ 10 & 10 & 0 \\ 10 & 10 & 0 \end{pmatrix} * \begin{pmatrix} 1 & 0 & -1 \\ 1 & 0 & -1 \\ 1 & 0 & -1 \end{pmatrix}$$
$$= 10\times1+10\times0+0\times-1+10\times1+10\times0+0\times-1+10\times1+10\times0+0\times-1=30$$

And this is exactly how, as soon as there is a big change in values along the horizontal direction, the convolution will return a high value, because the values multiplied by the column with 1 in the kernel will be bigger. When, conversely, there is a transition from small to high values along the horizontal axis, the elements multiplied by -1 will give a result that is bigger in absolute value, and, therefore, the final result will be negative and big in absolute value. This is the reason why this kernel can also detect if you pass from a light color to a darker color or vice versa. In fact, if you consider the opposite transition (from 0 to 10) in a hypothetical different matrix A, you would have

$$B_{11} = \begin{pmatrix} 0 & 10 & 10 \\ 0 & 10 & 10 \\ 0 & 10 & 10 \end{pmatrix} * \Im_V = \begin{pmatrix} 0 & 10 & 10 \\ 0 & 10 & 10 \\ 0 & 10 & 10 \end{pmatrix} * \begin{pmatrix} 1 & 0 & -1 \\ 1 & 0 & -1 \\ 1 & 0 & -1 \end{pmatrix}$$
$$= 0\times1+10\times0+10\times-1+0\times1+10\times0+10\times-1+0\times1+10\times0+10\times-1=-30$$

because, this time, we move from 0 to 10 along the horizontal direction.

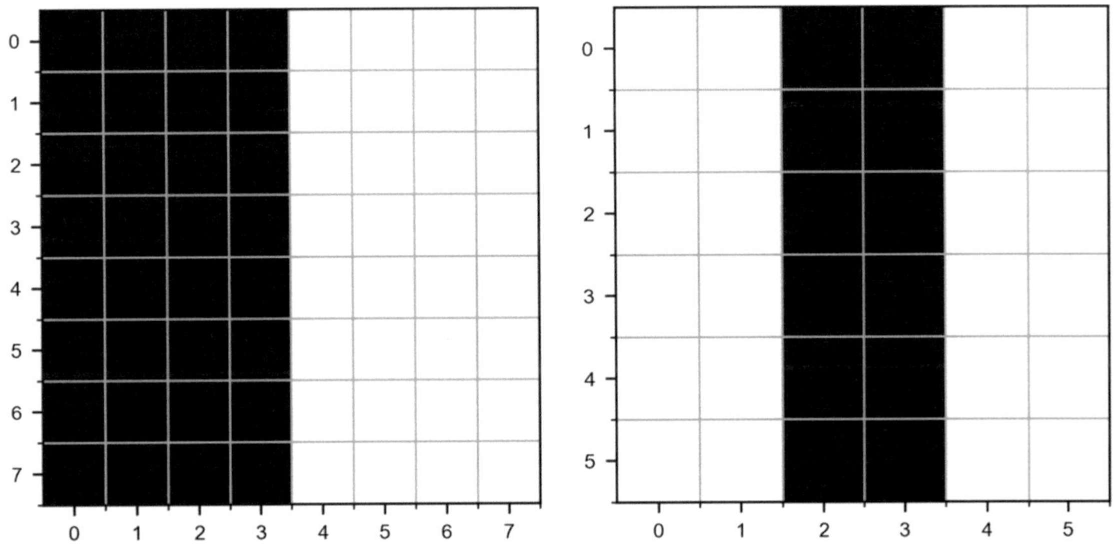

***Figure 8-10.** Result of the convolution of the matrix `ex_mat` with the kernel $\Im_V$, as described in the text*

Note how, as expected, the output matrix has dimensions 5 × 5, because the original matrix has dimensions 7 × 7, and the kernel is 3 × 3.

Pooling

Pooling is the second operation that is fundamental to CNNs. This operation is much easier to understand than convolution. To understand it, let's again consider a concrete example and what is called max pooling. Let's again use the 4 × 4 matrix from our discussion of convolution.

$$A = \begin{pmatrix} a_1 & a_2 & a_3 & a_4 \\ a_5 & a_6 & a_7 & a_8 \\ a_9 & a_{10} & a_{11} & a_{12} \\ a_{13} & a_{14} & a_{15} & a_{16} \end{pmatrix}$$

To perform max pooling, we must define a region of size $n_K \times n_K$, analogous to what we did for convolution. Let's consider $n_K = 2$. What we must do is start at the top-left corner of our matrix A and select a $n_K \times n_K$ region, in our case, 2 × 2, from A. Here, we select

$$\begin{pmatrix} a_1 & a_2 \\ a_5 & a_6 \end{pmatrix}$$

or the elements marked in boldface in matrix A, as follows:

$$A = \begin{pmatrix} \boldsymbol{a_1} & \boldsymbol{a_2} & a_3 & a_4 \\ \boldsymbol{a_5} & \boldsymbol{a_6} & a_7 & a_8 \\ a_9 & a_{10} & a_{11} & a_{12} \\ a_{13} & a_{14} & a_{15} & a_{16} \end{pmatrix}$$

From the elements selected, a_1, a_2, a_5, and a_6, the max pooling operation selects the maximum value, giving a result that we will indicate with B_1.

$$B_1 = \max_{i=1,2,5,6} a_i$$

Now we must shift our 2 × 2 window two columns, typically the same number of columns the selected region has, to the right and select the elements marked in boldface

$$A = \begin{pmatrix} a_1 & a_2 & \boldsymbol{a_3} & \boldsymbol{a_4} \\ a_5 & a_6 & \boldsymbol{a_7} & \boldsymbol{a_8} \\ a_9 & a_{10} & a_{11} & a_{12} \\ a_{13} & a_{14} & a_{15} & a_{16} \end{pmatrix}$$

or, in other words, the smaller matrix.

$$\begin{pmatrix} a_3 & a_4 \\ a_7 & a_8 \end{pmatrix}$$

The max-pooling algorithm will then select the maximum of the values, giving a result that we will indicate with B_2.

$$B_2 = \max_{i=3,4,7,8} a_i$$

At this point, we cannot shift the 2 × 2 region to the right anymore, so we shift it two rows down and start the process again, from the left side of A, selecting the elements marked in boldface and getting the maximum and calling it B_3, as follows:

$$A = \begin{pmatrix} a_1 & a_2 & a_3 & a_4 \\ a_5 & a_6 & a_7 & a_8 \\ \boldsymbol{a_9} & \boldsymbol{a_{10}} & a_{11} & a_{12} \\ \boldsymbol{a_{13}} & \boldsymbol{a_{14}} & a_{15} & a_{16} \end{pmatrix}$$

The stride s in this context has the same meaning already covered in the discussion on convolution. It is simply the number of rows or columns you move your region when selecting the elements. Finally, we select the last region, 2 × 2, in the bottom lower part of A, selecting the elements a_{11}, a_{12}, a_{15}, and a_{16}. We then get the maximum, and we then call it B_4. With the values we obtain in this process, in our example, the four values B_1, B_2, B_3 and B_4, we will build an output tensor.

$$B = \begin{pmatrix} B_1 & B_2 \\ B_3 & B_4 \end{pmatrix}$$

In the example, we have $s = 2$. Basically, this operation takes as input a matrix A, a stride s, and a kernel size n_K (the dimension of the region we selected in the previous example) and return a new matrix B, with dimensions given by the same formula we applied in the discussion of convolution.

$$n_B = \frac{n_A - n_K}{s} + 1$$

To reiterate, the idea is to start from the top left of your matrix A, take a region of dimensions $n_K \times n_K$, apply the max function to the selected elements, then shift the region of s elements toward the right, select a new region—again of dimensions $n_K \times n_K$—apply the function to its values, and so on. In Figure 8-11, you can see how you would select the elements from a matrix A with a stride $s = 2$

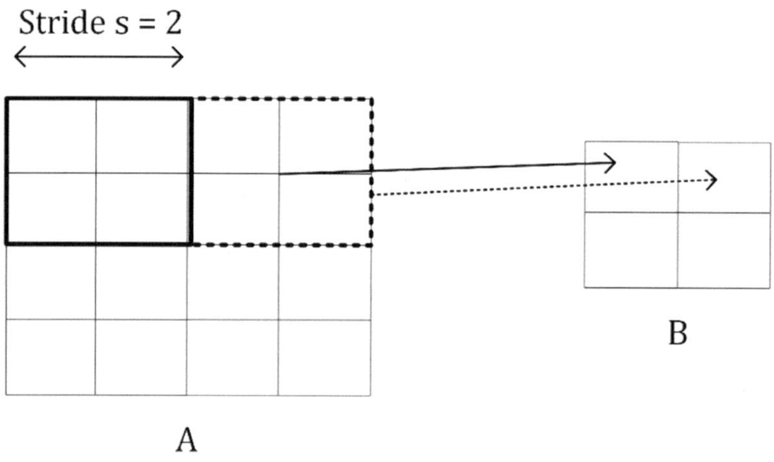

Figure 8-11. *Visualization of pooling with stride $s = 2$*

For example, applying max pooling to the input A

$$A = \begin{pmatrix} 1 & 3 & 5 & 7 \\ 4 & 5 & 11 & 3 \\ 4 & 1 & 21 & 6 \\ 13 & 15 & 1 & 2 \end{pmatrix}$$

will get you the result (it is very easy to verify)

$$B = \begin{pmatrix} 4 & 11 \\ 15 & 21 \end{pmatrix}$$

because 4 is the maximum of the values marked in boldface

$$A = \begin{pmatrix} \mathbf{1} & \mathbf{3} & 5 & 7 \\ \mathbf{4} & \mathbf{5} & 11 & 3 \\ 4 & 1 & 21 & 6 \\ 13 & 15 & 1 & 2 \end{pmatrix}$$

11 is the maximum of the values marked in boldface, as follows:

$$A = \begin{pmatrix} 1 & 3 & \mathbf{5} & \mathbf{7} \\ 4 & 5 & \mathbf{11} & \mathbf{3} \\ 4 & 1 & 21 & 6 \\ 13 & 15 & 1 & 2 \end{pmatrix}$$

and so on. It is worth mentioning another way of doing pooling, although not as widely used as max pooling: *average pooling*. Instead of returning the maximum of the selected values, it returns the average.

Note The most used pooling operation is *max pooling. Average pooling* is not as widely used but can be found in specific network architectures.

Padding

Worth mentioning is the concept of padding. Sometimes, when dealing with images, it is not optimal to get a result from a convolution operation that has dimensions that are different from those of the original image. So, sometimes, you do what is called *padding*. Basically, the idea is very simple: it consists of adding rows of pixels at the top, bottom, and columns of pixels on the right and on the left of the final images, filled with some values to make the resulting matrices the same size as the original one. Some strategies are to fill the added pixels with zeros, with the values of the closest pixels, and so on. In our example, our `ex_out` matrix with zero padding would look like this:

```
array([[ 0., 0., 0., 0., 0., 0., 0., 0.],
       [ 0., 0., 0., 30., 30., 0., 0., 0.],
       [ 0., 0., 0., 30., 30., 0., 0., 0.],
       [ 0., 0., 0., 30., 30., 0., 0., 0.],
       [ 0., 0., 0., 30., 30., 0., 0., 0.],
       [ 0., 0., 0., 30., 30., 0., 0., 0.],
       [ 0., 0., 0., 30., 30., 0., 0., 0.],
       [ 0., 0., 0., 0., 0., 0., 0., 0.]])
```

The use and reasons behind padding are beyond the scope of this book, but it is important to know that it exists. Only as a reference, in case you use padding p (the width of the rows and columns you use as padding), the final dimensions of the matrix B, in case of both convolution and pooling, is given by

$$n_B = \left\lfloor \frac{n_A + 2p - n_K}{s} + 1 \right\rfloor$$

Note When dealing with real images, you always code color images in three channels: RGB. This means that you must execute convolution and pooling in three dimensions: width, height, and color channel. This will add a layer of complexity to the algorithms.

Building Blocks of a CNN

Basically, convolutions and pooling operations are used to build the layers that are used in CNNs. Typically in CNNs, you can find the following layers:

- Convolutional layers
- Pooling layers
- Fully connected layers

Fully connected layers are exactly what you have seen in all previous chapters: a layer in which neurons are connected to all neurons of previous and subsequent layers. You already familiar with the layers listed, but the first two require some additional explanation.

Convolutional Layers

A convolutional layer takes as input a tensor (it can be three-dimensional, due to the three color channels), for example, an image of certain dimensions; applies a certain number of kernels, typically 10, 16, or even more; adds a bias; applies ReLU activation functions (for example), to introduce nonlinearity to the result of the convolution; and produces an output matrix B. If you remember the notation we used in the previous chapters, the result of the convolution will have the role of $W^{[l]}Z^{[l-1]}$ that was discussed in Chapter 3.

In the previous sections, I have shown you some examples of applying convolutions with just one kernel. How can you apply several kernels at the same time? Well, the answer is very simple. The final tensor (I now use the word *tensor*, because it will not be a simple matrix anymore) B will now have not 2 dimensions but 3. Let's indicate the number of kernels you want to apply with n_c (the c is used, because people sometimes refer to these as channels). You simply apply each filter to the input independently and stack the results. So, instead of a single matrix B with dimensions $n_B \times n_B$, you get a final tensor $\tilde{B}$ of dimensions $n_B \times n_B \times n_c$. That means that

$$\tilde{B}_{i,j,1} \quad \forall i,j \in [1,n_B]$$

will be the output of convolution of the input image with the first kernel,

$$\tilde{B}_{i,j,2} \quad \forall i,j \in [1,n_B]$$

will be the output of convolution with the second kernel, and so on. The convolution layer is nothing other than something that transforms the input into an output tensor. But what are the weights in this layer? The weights, or the parameter, that the network learns during the training phase, are the elements of the kernel themselves. We have discussed that we have n_c kernels, each of dimensions $n_K \times n_K$. That means that we have the $n_K^2 n_c$ parameter in a convolutional layer.

Note The number of parameters that you have in a convolutional layer, $n_K^2 n_c$, is independent of the input image size. This fact helps in reducing overfitting, especially when dealing with big size input images.

Sometimes, this layer is indicated with the word *POOL* and a number. In our case, we could indicate this layer with POOL1. In Figure 8-12, you can see a representation of a convolutional layer. The input image gets transformed by applying convolution with n_c kernels in a tensor of dimensions $n_A \times n_A \times n_c$.

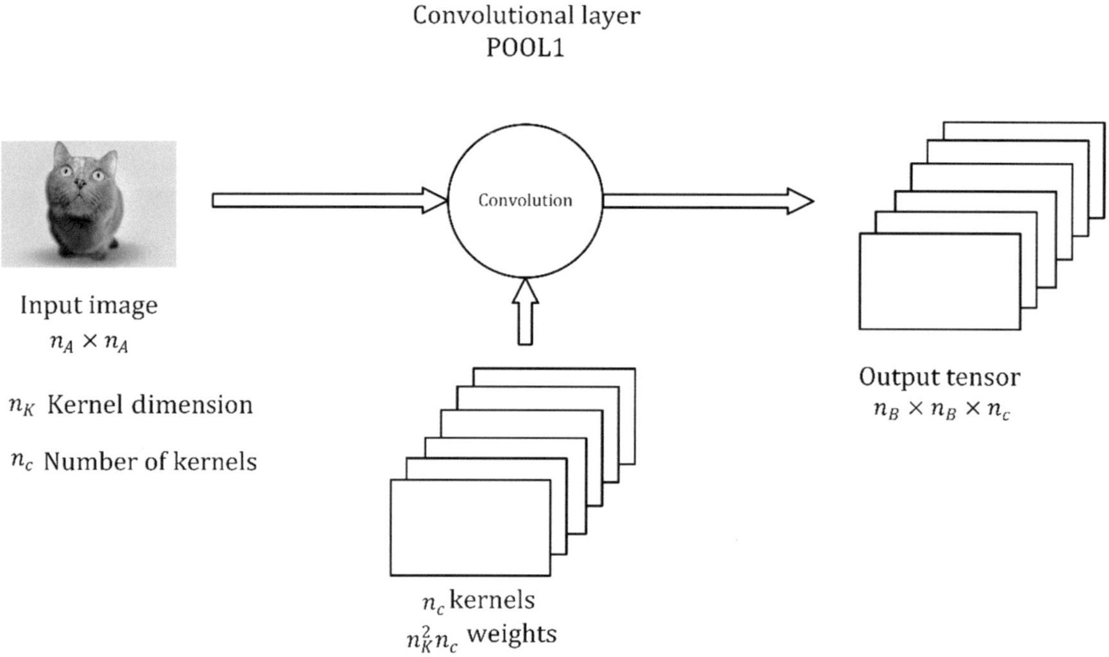

Figure 8-12. *Representation of a convolutional layer*[1]

A convolutional layer does not necessarily have to be placed immediately after the inputs. A convolutional layer may get as input the output of any other layer, of course. Keep in mind that usually your input image will have dimensions $n_A \times n_A \times 3$, because an image in color has three channels: RGB. A complete analysis of the tensors involved in a CNN when considering color images is beyond the scope of this book. Very often in diagrams, the layer is simply indicated as a cube or square.

[1]Cat image source: `www.shutterstock.com/`.

Pooling Layers

A pooling layer is usually indicated by *POOL* and a number: for example, POOL1. It takes as input a tensor and gives as output another tensor, after applying pooling to the input.

Note A pooling layer has no parameter to learn, but it introduces additional hyperparameters: n_K and stride s. Typically, in pooling layers, you don't use any padding, because one of the reasons to use pooling is often to reduce the dimensionality of the tensors.

Stacking Layers Together

In CNNs, you usually stack convolutional and pooling layers together, one after the other. In Figure 8-13, you can see a convolutional and a pooling layer stack. A convolutional layer is always followed by a pooling layer. Sometimes, the two together are called a layer. The reason is that a pooling layer has no learnable weights, and, therefore, it is seen as a simple operation that is associated with the convolutional layer. So, be aware when you read papers or blogs, and verify what they intend.

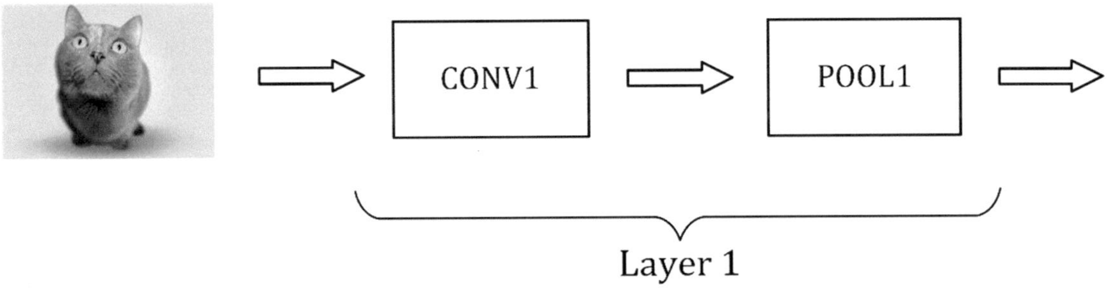

***Figure 8-13.** Representation of how to stack convolutional and pooling layers*

To conclude this discussion of CNNs, in Figure 8-14, you can see an example of a CNN. It is similar to the very famous LeNet-5 network, on which you can read more here: `https://goo.gl/hM1kAL`. You have the inputs, then two convolution-pooling layers twice, three fully connected layers, and an output layer, in which you may have your `softmax` function, in case, for example, you perform multiclass classification. I put some arbitrary numbers in the figure, to give you an idea of the size of the different layers.

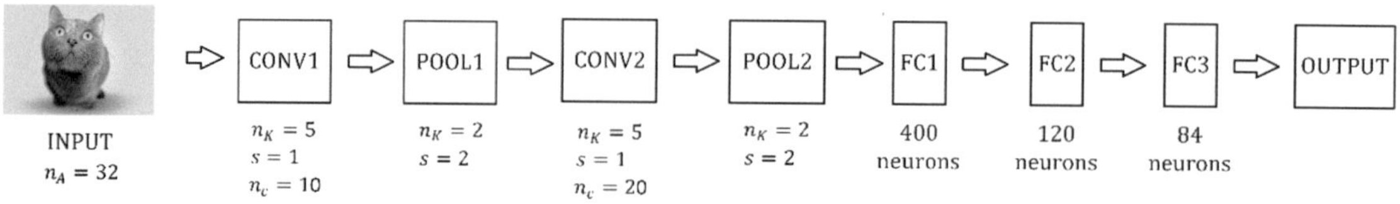

***Figure 8-14.** Representation of a CNN similar to the famous LeNet-5 network*

Example of a CNN

Let's try to build one such network, to give you a feel for how the process would work and what the code looks like. We will not do any hyperparameter tuning or optimization, to keep the section understandable. We will build the following architecture with the following layers, in this order:

- Convolution layer 1, with six filters 5 × 5, stride $s = 1$
- Max pooling layer 1, with a window 2 × 2, stride $s = 2$
- We then apply ReLU to the output of the previous layer.
- Convolution layer 2, with 16 filters 5 × 5, stride $s = 1$
- Max pooling layer 2, with a window 2 × 2, stride $s = 2$
- We then apply ReLU to the output of the previous layer.
- Fully connected layer, with 128 neurons and activation function ReLU
- Fully connected layer, with 10 neurons for classification of the Zalando dataset
- Softmax output neuron

We will import the Zalando dataset, as we did in Chapter 3, as follows:

```
data_train = pd.read_csv('fashion-mnist_train.csv', header = 0)
data_test = pd.read_csv('fashion-mnist_test.csv', header = 0)
```

See Chapter 3 for a detailed explanation of how to get the files. Next, let's prepare the data.

```
labels = data_train['label'].values.reshape(1, 60000)
labels_ = np.zeros((60000, 10))
labels_[np.arange(60000), labels] = 1
```

```
labels_ = labels_.transpose()
train = data_train.drop('label', axis=1)
```

and

```
labels_dev = data_test['label'].values.reshape(1, 10000)
labels_dev_ = np.zeros((10000, 10))
labels_dev_[np.arange(10000), labels_dev] = 1
test = data_dev.drop('label', axis=1)
```

Note that in this case, unlike in Chapter 3, we will use the transpose of all tensors, meaning that in each row, we will have an observation. In Chapter 3, each observation was in a column. If you check the dimensions with the code

```
print(labels_.shape)
print(labels_dev_.shape)
```

you will get the following results:

```
(60000, 10)
(10000, 10)
```

In Chapter 3, the dimensions were exchanged. The reason is that to develop the convolutional and pooling layers, we will use functions that are provided by TensorFlow, because developing them from scratch would require too much time. In addition, for some TensorFlow functions, it is easier if the tensors have different observations along the rows. As in Chapter 3, we must normalize the data.

```
train = np.array(train / 255.0)
dev = np.array(dev / 255.0)
labels_ = np.array(labels_)
labels_test_ = np.array(labels_test_)
```

We can now start to build our network.

```
x = tf.placeholder(tf.float32, shape=[None, 28*28])
x_image = tf.reshape(x, [-1, 28, 28, 1])
y_true = tf.placeholder(tf.float32, shape=[None, 10])
y_true_scalar = tf.argmax(y_true, axis=1)
```

The one line that requires an explanation is the second: `x_image = tf.reshape(x, [-1, 28, 28, 1])`. Remember that the convolutional layer will require the two-dimensional image and not a flattened list of gray values of the pixel, as was the case in Chapter 3, where our input was a vector with 784 (28 × 28) elements.

Note One of the biggest advantages of CNNs is that they use the two-dimensional information contained in the input image. This is why the input of convolutional layers are two-dimensional images and not a flattened vector.

When building CNNs, it is typical to define functions to build the different layers. In this way, hyperparameter tuning later will be easier, as we have seen previously. Another reason is that when we put all the pieces together with the functions, the code will be much more readable. The function names should be self-explanatory. Let's start with a function to build the convolutional layer. Note that TensorFlow documentation uses the term *filter*, so this is what we will use in the code.

```
def new_conv_layer(input, num_input_channels, filter_size, num_filters):
    shape = [filter_size, filter_size, num_input_channels, num_filters]
    weights = tf.Variable(tf.truncated_normal(shape, stddev=0.05))
    biases = tf.Variable(tf.constant(0.05, shape=[num_filters]))
    layer = tf.nn.conv2d(input=input, filter=weights, strides=[1, 1, 1, 1],
    padding='SAME')
    layer += biases
    return layer, weights
```

At this point, we will initialize the weights from a truncated normal distribution, the biases as a constant, and then we will use stride $s = 1$. The stride is a list, because it gives the stride in different dimensions. In our examples, we have gray images, but we could also have RGB, for example, thereby having more dimensions: the three color channels.

The pooling layer is easier, since it has no weights.

```
def new_pool_layer(input):
    layer = tf.nn.max_pool(value=input, ksize=[1, 2, 2, 1], strides=[1, 2,
    2, 1], padding='SAME')
    return layer
```

Now let's define a function that applies the activation function, in our case a ReLU, to the previous layer.

```
def new_relu_layer(input_layer):
    layer = tf.nn.relu(input_layer)
    return layer
```

Finally, we need a function to build the fully connected layer.

```
def new_fc_layer(input, num_inputs, num_outputs):
    weights = tf.Variable(tf.truncated_normal([num_inputs, num_outputs],
    stddev=0.05))
    biases = tf.Variable(tf.constant(0.05, shape=[num_outputs]))
    layer = tf.matmul(input, weights) + biases

    return layer
```

The new TensorFlow functions that we have used are `tf.nn.conv2d`, which builds a convolutional layer, and `tf.nn.max_pool`, which builds a pooling layer with max pooling, as you can imagine from the name. We don't have the space here to go into detail in what each function does, but you can find a lot of information in the official documentation. Now let's put everything together and actually build the network described at the beginning.

```
layer_conv1, weights_conv1 = new_conv_layer(input=x_image,
num_input_channels=1, filter_size=5, num_filters=6)
layer_pool1 = new_pool_layer(layer_conv1)
layer_relu1 = new_relu_layer(layer_pool1)
layer_conv2, weights_conv2 = new_conv_layer(input=layer_relu1,
num_input_channels=6, filter_size=5, num_filters=16)
layer_pool2 = new_pool_layer(layer_conv2)
layer_relu2 = new_relu_layer(layer_pool2)
```

We must create the fully connected layer, but to use `layer_relu2` as input, we first must flatten it, because it is still two-dimensional.

```
num_features = layer_relu2.get_shape()[1:4].num_elements()
layer_flat = tf.reshape(layer_relu2, [-1, num_features])
```

Then we can create the final layers.

```
layer_fc1 = new_fc_layer(layer_flat, num_inputs=num_features,
num_outputs=128)
layer_relu3 = new_relu_layer(layer_fc1)
layer_fc2 = new_fc_layer(input=layer_relu3, num_inputs=128, num_outputs=10)
```

Now let's evaluate the predictions, to be able to evaluate the accuracy later.

```
y_pred = tf.nn.softmax(layer_fc2)
y_pred_scalar = tf.argmax(y_pred, axis=1)
```

The array `y_pred_scalar` will contain the class number as a scalar. Now we need to define the cost function, and, again, we will use an existing TensorFlow function to make our life easier, and to keep the length of this chapter reasonable.

```
cost = tf.reduce_mean(tf.nn.softmax_cross_entropy_with_logits(logits=layer_
fc2, labels=y_true))
```

As usual, we need an optimizer.

```
optimizer = tf.train.AdamOptimizer(learning_rate=1e-4).minimize(cost)
```

Now we can finally define the operations to evaluate the accuracy.

```
correct_prediction = tf.equal(y_pred_scalar, y_true_scalar)
accuracy = tf.reduce_mean(tf.cast(correct_prediction, tf.float32))
```

It is time to train our network. We will use mini-batch gradient descent with a batch size of 100 and train our network for just ten epochs. We can define the variables as follows:

```
num_epochs = 10
batch_size = 100
```

The training can be achieved with

```
with tf.Session() as sess:
    sess.run(tf.global_variables_initializer())
    for epoch in range(num_epochs):
        train_accuracy = 0
```

```
for i in range(0, train.shape[0], batch_size):
    x_batch = train[i:i + batch_size,:]
    y_true_batch = labels_[i:i + batch_size,:]

    sess.run(optimizer, feed_dict={x: x_batch, y_true: y_true_batch})
    train_accuracy += sess.run(accuracy, feed_dict={x: x_batch,
    y_true: y_true_batch})

train_accuracy /= int(len(labels_)/batch_size)
dev_accuracy = sess.run(accuracy, feed_dict={x:dev,
y_true:labels_dev_})
```

If you run this code (it took roughly ten minutes on my laptop), it will start, after just one epoch, with a training accuracy of 63.7%, and after ten epochs, it will reach a training accuracy of 86% (also on the dev set). Remember that with the first dumb network we developed in Chapter 3 with five neurons in one layer, we reached 66% with mini-batch gradient descent. We have trained our network here only for ten epochs. You can get much higher accuracy if you train longer. Additionally, note that we have not done any hyperparameter tuning, so this would get you much better results, if you spent time tuning the parameters.

As you may have noticed, every time you introduce a convolutional layer, you will introduce new hyperparameters for each layer.

- Kernel size
- Stride
- Padding

These will have to be tuned, to get optimal results. Typically, researchers tend to use existing architectures for specific tasks that already have been optimized by other practitioners and are well documented in papers.

Introduction to RNNs

RNNs are very different from CNNs and, typically, are used when dealing with sequential information, in other words, for data for which the order matters. The typical example given is a series of words in a sentence. You can easily understand how the order of words in a sentence can make a big difference. For example, saying “the man ate the rabbit" has a different meaning than "the rabbit ate the man," the only difference being the order of the words, and who gets eaten by whom. You can use RNNs to predict, for example, the subsequent word in a sentence. Take, for example, the phrase "Paris is the capital of." It is easy to complete the sentence with "France," which means that there is information about the final word of the sentence encoded in the previous words, and that information is what RNNs exploit to predict the subsequent terms in a sequence. The name *recurrent* comes from how these networks work: they apply the same operation on each element of the sequence, accumulating information about the previous terms. To summarize

- RNNs make use of sequential data and use the information encoded in the order of the terms in the sequence.
- RNNs apply the same kind of operation to all terms in the sequence and build a memory of the previous terms in the sequence, to predict the next term.

Before trying to understand a bit better how RNNs work, let's consider a few important use cases in which they can be applied, to give you an idea of the potential range of applications.

- *Generating text*: Predicting probability of words, given a previous set of words. For example, you can easily generate text that looks like Shakespeare with RNNs, as A. Karpathy has done on his blog, available at `https://goo.gl/FodLp5`.
- *Translation*: Given a set of words in a language, you can get words in a different language.
- *Speech recognition*: Given a series of audio signals (words), we can predict the sequence of letters forming the words as spoken.
- *Generating image labels*: With CNNs, RNNs can be used to generate labels for images. Refer to A. Karpathy's paper on the subject: "Deep Visual-Semantic Alignments for Generating Image Descriptions," available at `https://goo.gl/8Ja3n2`. Be aware that this is a rather advanced paper that requires an extensive mathematical background.
- *Chatbots*: With a sequence of words given as input, RNNs try to generate answers to the input.

As you can imagine, to implement the preceding, you would require sophisticated architectures that are not easy to describe in a few sentences and call for a deeper (pun intended) understanding of how RNNs work, which is beyond the scope of this chapter and book.

Notation

Let's consider the sequence "Paris is the capital of France." This sentence will be fed to a RNN one word at a time: first "Paris," then "is", then "the," and so on. In our example,

- "Paris" will be the first word of the sequence: `w1 = 'Paris'`
- "is" will be the second word of the sequence: `w2 = 'is'`
- "the" will be the third word of the sequence: `w3 = 'the'`
- "capital" will be the fourth word of the sequence: `w4 = 'capital'`
- "of" will be the fifth word of the sequence: `w5 = 'of'`
- "France" will be the sixth word of the sequence: `w6 = 'France'`

The words will be fed into the RNN in the following order: `w1`, `w2`, `w3`, `w4`, `w5`, and `w6`. The different words will be processed by the network one after the other, or, as some like to say, at different time points. Usually, it is said that if word `w1` is processed at time t, then `w2` is processed at time $t+1$, `w3` at time $t+2$, and so on. The time t is not related to a real time but is meant to suggest the fact that each element in the sequence is processed sequentially and not in parallel. The time t is also not related to computing time or anything related to it. And the increment of 1 in $t+1$ does not have any meaning. It simply means that we are talking about the next element in our sequence. You may find the following notations when reading papers, blogs, or books:

- x_t: the input at time t. For example, `w1` could be the input at time 1 x_1, `w2` at time 2 x_2, and so on.
- s_t: This the notation with which the internal memory, that we have not defined yet, at time t is indicated. This quantity s_t contains the accumulated information on the previous terms in the sequence discussed previously. An intuitive understanding of it will have to suffice, because a more mathematical definition would require too detailed an explanation.

- o_t is the output of the network at time t or, in other words, after all the elements of the sequence until t, including the element x_t, have been fed to the network.

Basic Idea of RNNs

Typically, an RNN is indicated in the literature as the leftmost part of what is illustrated in Figure 8-15. The notation used is indicative—it simply indicates the different elements of the network: x refers to the inputs, s to the internal memory, W to one set of weights, and U to another set of weights. In reality, this schematic representation is simply a way of depicting the real structure of the network, which you can see at the right of Figure 8-15. Sometimes, this is called the unfolded version of the network.

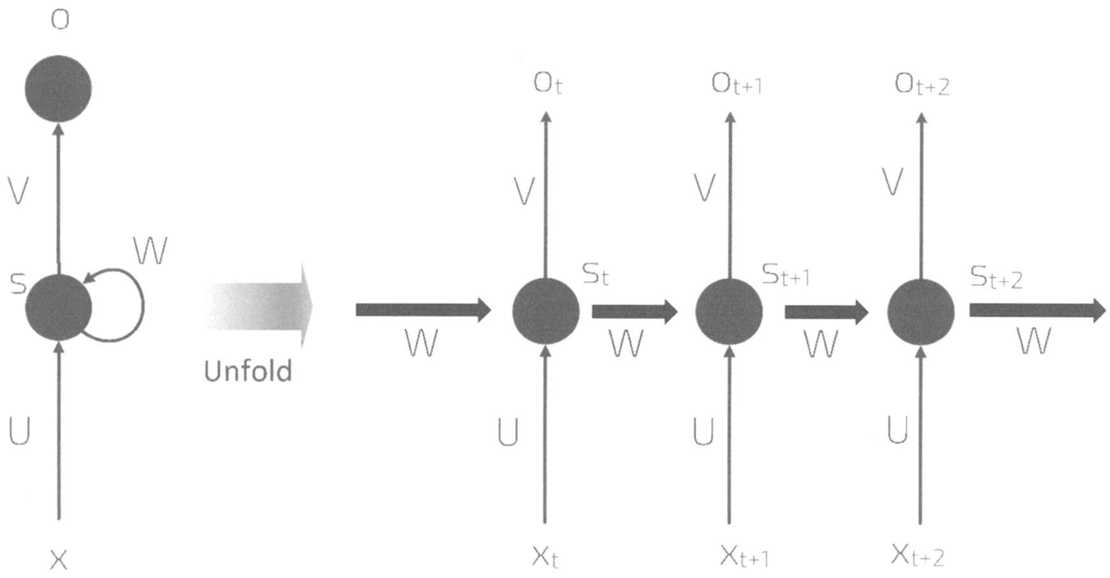

Figure 8-15. *Schematic representation of an RNN*

The right part of Figure 8-15 should be read left to right. The first neuron in the figure does its evaluation at an indicated time t, produces an output o_t, and creates an internal memory state s_t. The second neuron, which evaluates at a time $t + 1$, after the first neuron, gets as input both the next element in the sequence, x_{t+1}, and the previous memory state, s_t. The second neuron then generates an output, o_{t+1}, and a new internal memory state, s_{t+1}. The third neuron (the one at the extreme right of Figure 8-15) then gets as input the new element of the sequence x_{t+2} and the previous internal memory state s_{t+1}, and the process proceeds in this way for a finite number of neurons. You can see in Figure 8-15 that there are two sets of weights: *W* and *U*. One set (indicated by *W*) is used for the internal memory states, and one, *U*, for the sequence element. Typically, each neuron will generate the new internal memory state with a formula that will looks like this:

$$s_t = f\left(Ux_t + Ws_{t-1}\right)$$

where we have indicated with *f*() one of the activation functions, we have already seen as ReLU or tanh. Additionally, the previous formula will, of course, be multidimensional. s_t can be understood as the memory of the network at time *t*. The number of neurons (or time steps) that can be used is a new hyperparameter that must be tuned, depending on the problem. Research has shown that when this number is too big, the network has big problems during training.

Something very important to note is that at each time step, the weights do not change. The same operation is being performed at each step, simply changing the inputs every time an evaluation is performed. Additionally, in Figure 8-15, I have an output in the diagram (o_t, o_{t+1} and o_{t+2}) for every step, but, typically, this is not necessary. In our example, in which we want to predict the final word in a sentence, we may only require the final output.

Why the Name *Recurrent*?

I would like to discuss very briefly why the networks are called recurrent. I have said that the internal memory state at a time *t* is given by

$$s_t = f\left(Ux_t + Ws_{t-1}\right)$$

The internal memory state at time *t* is evaluated using the same memory state at time *t* – 1, the one at time *t* – 1 with the value at time *t* – 2, and so on. This is at the origin of the name *recurrent*.

Learning to Count

To give you an idea of their power, I would like to give you a very basic example of something RNNs are very good at and standard fully connected networks, such as the one you saw in the previous chapters, are really bad at. Let's try to teach a network to count. The problem we want to solve is the following: given a certain vector, which we will assume as being made of 15 elements and containing just 0 and 1, we want to build a neural network that is able to count the amount of 1s we have in the vector. This is a difficult problem for a standard network, but why? To understand intuitively why, let's consider the problem we have analyzed of distinguishing the one and two digits in the MNIST dataset.

If you remember that discussion of metric analysis, you will recall that the learning happens because the ones and the twos have black pixels in fundamentally different positions. A digit one will always differ (at least in the MNIST dataset) in the same way as the digit two, so the network identifies these differences, and as soon as they are detected, a clear identification can be made. In our case, this is no longer possible. Consider, for example, the simpler case of a vector with just five elements.

In this case, a one appears exactly one time. We have five possible cases: `[1,0,0,0,0]`, `[0,1,0,0,0]`, `[0,0,1,0,0]`, `[0,0,0,1,0]`, and `[0,0,0,0,1]`. There is no discernible pattern to be detected here. There is no easy weight configuration that could cover these cases at the same time. In the case of an image, this problem is similar to the problem of detecting the position of a black square in a white image. We can build a network in TensorFlow and check how good such networks are. Owing to the introductory nature of this chapter, however, I will not spend time on a discussion of hyperparameters, metric analysis, and so on. I will simply give you a basic network that can count.

Let's start by creating our vectors. We will create 10^5 vectors, which we will split into training and dev sets.

```
import numpy as np
import tensorflow as tf
from random import shuffle
```

Now let's create our list of vectors. The code is slightly more complicated, and we will look at it in a bit more detail.

```
nn = 15
ll = 2**15
train_input = ['{0:015b}'.format(i) for i in range(ll)]
shuffle(train_input)
train_input = [map(int,i) for i in train_input]
temp  = []
```

```
for i in train_input:
    temp_list = []
    for j in i:
            temp_list.append([j])
    temp.append(np.array(temp_list))
train_input = temp
```

We want to have all possible combinations of 1 and 0 in vectors of 15 elements. So, an easy way to do this is to take all numbers up to 2^{15} in a binary format. To understand why, let's suppose we want to do this with only four elements: we want all possible combinations of four 0 and 1. Consider all numbers up to 2^4 in binary that you can get with this code:

```
['{0:04b}'.format(i) for i in range(2**4)]
```

The code simply formats all the numbers that you get with the `range(2**4)` function, from `0` to `2**4`, in binary format, with `{0:04b}`, limiting the number of digits to 4. The result is the following:

```
['0000',
 '0001',
 '0010',
 '0011',
 '0100',
 '0101',
 '0110',
 '0111',
 '1000',
 '1001',
 '1010',
 '1011',
 '1100',
 '1101',
 '1110',
 '1111']
```

As you can easily verify, all possible combinations are listed. You have all possible combinations of the one appearing one time (`[0001]`, `[0010]`, `[0100]`, and `[1000]`), of the ones appearing two times, and so on. For our example, we will simply do this with 15 digits, which means that we will do it with numbers up to 2^{15}. The rest of the preceding code is there to simply transform a string such as `'0100'` in a list `[0,1,0,0]` and then concatenate all the lists with all the possible combinations. If you check the dimension of the output array, you will notice that you get (32768, 15, 1). Each observation is an array of dimensions (15, 1). Then we prepare the target variable, a one-hot encoded version of the counts. This means that if we have an input with four ones in the vector, our target vector will look like `[0,0,0,0,1,0,0,0,0,0,0,0,0,0,0,0]`. As expected, the `train_output` array will have the dimensions `(32768, 16)`. Now let's build our target variables.

```
train_output = []

for i in train_input:
    count = 0
    for j in i:
        if j[0] == 1:
            count+=1
    temp_list = ([0]*(nn+1))
    temp_list[count]=1
    train_output.append(temp_list)
```

Now let's split our set into a train and a dev set, as we have done now several times. We will do it here in a "dumb" way.

```
train_obs = ll-2000
dev_input = train_input[train_obs:]
dev_output = train_output[train_obs:]
train_input = train_input[:train_obs]
train_output = train_output[:train_obs]
```

Remember that this will work, because we have shuffled the vectors at the beginning, so we should have a random distribution of cases. We will use 2000 cases for the dev set and the rest (roughly 30,000) for the training. The `train_input` will have dimensions `(30768, 15, 1)`, and the `dev_input` will have dimensions `(2000, 15,1)`.

Now you can build a network with this code, and you should be able to understand almost all of it.

```
tf.reset_default_graph()

data = tf.placeholder(tf.float32, [None, nn,1])
target = tf.placeholder(tf.float32, [None, (nn+1)])

num_hidden_el = 24
RNN_cell = tf.nn.rnn_cell.LSTMCell(num_hidden_el, state_is_tuple=True)

val, state = tf.nn.dynamic_rnn(RNN_cell, data, dtype=tf.float32)
val = tf.transpose(val, [1, 0, 2])
last = tf.gather(val, int(val.get_shape()[0]) - 1)

W = tf.Variable(tf.truncated_normal([num_hidden, int(target.get_shape()
[1])]))
b = tf.Variable(tf.constant(0.1, shape=[target.get_shape()[1]]))

prediction = tf.nn.softmax(tf.matmul(last, W) + b)
cross_entropy = -tf.reduce_sum(target * tf.log(tf.clip_by_
value(prediction,1e-10,1.0)))
optimizer = tf.train.AdamOptimizer()
minimize = optimizer.minimize(cross_entropy)
errors = tf.not_equal(tf.argmax(target, 1), tf.argmax(prediction, 1))
error = tf.reduce_mean(tf.cast(errors, tf.float32))
```

Then let's train the network.

```
init_op = tf.global_variables_initializer()
sess = tf.Session()
sess.run(init_op)
mb_size = 1000
no_of_batches = int(len(train_input)/mb_size)
epoch = 50
for i in range(epoch):
    ptr = 0
```

```
    for j in range(no_of_batches):
        train, output = train_input[ptr:ptr+mb_size], train_
        output[ptr:ptr+mb_size]
        ptr+=mb_size
        sess.run(minimize,{data: train, target: output})
incorrect = sess.run(error,{data: test_input, target: test_output})
print('Epoch {:2d} error {:3.1f}%'.format(i + 1, 100 * incorrect))
```

The new part that you probably will not recognize is the following piece of code:

```
num_hidden_el = 24
RNN_cell = tf.nn.rnn_cell.LSTMCell(num_hidden_el,state_is_tuple=True)

val, state = tf.nn.dynamic_rnn(RNN_cell, data, dtype=tf.float32)
val = tf.transpose(val, [1, 0, 2])
last = tf.gather(val, int(val.get_shape()[0]) - 1)
```

For performance reasons, and to let you realize how efficient RNNs are, I am using here a long short-term memory (LSTM) kind of neuron. This has a special way of calculating the internal state. A discussion of LSTMs is well beyond the scope of this book. For the moment, you should focus on the results and not on the code. If you let the code run, you will get the following result:

```
Epoch 0 error 80.1%
Epoch 10 error 27.5%
Epoch 20 error 8.2%
Epoch 30 error 3.8%
Epoch 40 error 3.1%
Epoch 50 error 2.0%
```

After just 50 epochs, the network is right in 98% of the cases. Just let it run for more epochs, and you can reach incredible precision. After 100 epochs, you can achieve an error of 0.5%. An instructive exercise is to attempt to train a fully connected network (as the ones we have discussed so far) to count. You will see how this is not possible.

You should now have a basic understanding of how CNNs and RNNs work, and on what principles they operate. The research on those networks is immense, since they are really flexible, but the discussion in the previous sections should have given you enough information to understand how these architectures work.

CHAPTER 9

A Research Project

Typically, when talking about deep learning, people think about image recognition, speech recognition, image detection, and so on. These are the most well-known applications, but the possibilities of deep neural networks are endless. In this chapter, I will show you how deep neural networks can be successfully applied to a less conventional problem: the extraction of a parameter in sensing applications. For this specific problem, we will develop the algorithms for a sensor, which I will describe later, to determine the oxygen concentration in a medium, for example, a gas.

The chapter is organized as follows: first, I will discuss the research problem to be solved, then I will explain some introductory material required to solve it, and, finally, I will show you the first results of this ongoing research project.

The Problem Description

The functioning principle of many sensor devices is based on the measurement of a physical quantity, such as voltage, volume, or light intensity, that is typically easy to measure. This quantity must be strongly correlated with another physical quantity, which is the one to be determined and, typically, difficult to measure directly, such as temperature or, in this example, gas concentration. If we know how the two quantities are correlated (typically, via a mathematical model), from the first quantity, we can derive the second, the one we are really interested in. So, in a simplified way, we can imagine a sensor as a black box, which, when given an input (temperature, gas concentration, and so on), produces an output (voltage, volume, or light intensity). The dependence of the output from the input is characteristic of the type of sensing and may be extremely complex. This makes the implementation of the necessary algorithms in real hardware very difficult, or even impossible. Here, we will use the approach to determine the output from the input, using neural networks instead of a set of formulas.

U. Michelucci, *Applied Deep Learning*, https://doi.org/10.1007/978-1-4842-3790-8_9

This research project deals with the measurement of oxygen concentration, using the principle of "luminescence quenching": a sensitive element, a dye substance, is in contact with a gas, of which we want to measure the oxygen content. The dye is illuminated with a so-called excitation light (typically, in the blue part of the light spectrum) and, after absorbing a part of it, it reemits light in a different part of the spectrum (typically, in the red part). The intensity and duration of the emitted light is strongly dependent on the oxygen concentration in the gas in contact with the dye. If the gas has some oxygen in it, part of the emitted light from the dye is suppressed, or "quenched" (from here, the name of the measurement principle), this effect being strongest the higher the amount of oxygen in the gas. The goal of the project is to develop new algorithms to determine the oxygen concentration (input) from a measured signal, the so-called phase shift (output) between the exciting and emitted light. If you don't understand what this means, don't worry. it is not required in order for you to understand the content of this chapter. It is enough to intuitively understand that this phase shift measures the change between the light exciting the dye and the one emitted after the "quenching" effect and that this "change" is strongly affected by the oxygen contained in the gas.

The difficulty in the sensor realization is that the response of the system depends (nonlinearly) on several parameters. This dependency is, for most dye molecules, so complex that it is almost impossible to write down equations for the oxygen concentration as a function of all these influencing parameters. The typical approach is, therefore, to develop a very sophisticated empirical model, with many parameters manually tuned.

The typical setup for luminescence measurements is shown schematically in Figure 9-1. This setup was used to get the data for the validation dataset. A sample containing the luminescent dye substance is illuminated by an excitation light (the blue light in the figure), emitted by a light-emitting diode, or laser, focused with a lens. The emitted luminescence (the red light at the right of the figure) is collected by a detector with the help of another lens. The sample holder contains the dye and the gas, indicated with the sample in the figure, for which we want to measure the oxygen concentration.

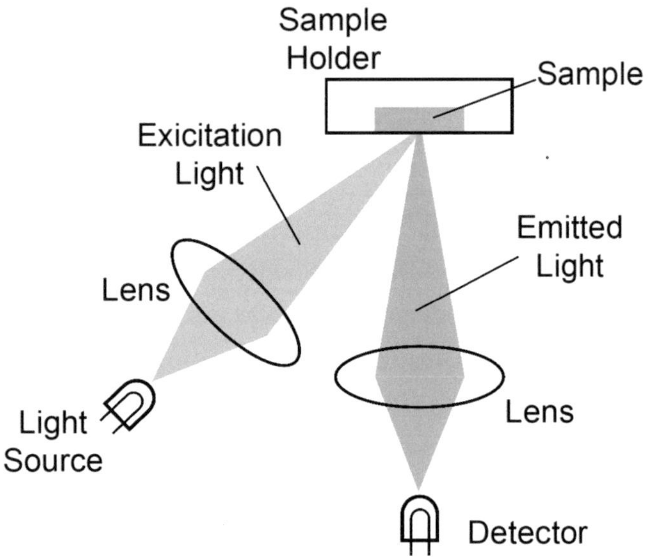

Figure 9-1. *Schematic setup of a luminescence measurement system*

The luminescence intensity collected by the detector is not constant in time but, rather, decreases. How fast it decreases depends on the amount of oxygen present, typically quantified by a decay time, indicated with τ. The simplest description of this decay is by a single exponential decay function, $e^{-t/\tau}$, characterized by a decay time, τ. A common technique used in practice to determine such a decay time is to modulate the intensity of the excitation light, or, in other words, to vary the intensity in a periodic way, with a frequency $f = 2\pi\omega$, where ω is the so-called angular frequency. The reemitted luminescence light has an intensity that is also modulated, or, in other words, it varies periodically but is characterized by a phase shift θ. This phase shift is related to the decay time τ as $\tan\theta = \omega\tau$. To give you an intuitive understanding of what this phase shift is, consider the light to be represented (if you are a physicist reading this, forgive me), in its simplest form, as a wave with an amplitude varying as a trigonometric function.

$$\sin(\omega t + \theta)$$

The quantity θ is called the phase constant of the wave. Now what happens is that the light that excites the dye has a phase constant θ_{exc}, and the light emitted has a different phase constant, $\theta_{emitted}$. The measurement principle measures exactly this phase change, $\theta \equiv \theta_{exc} - \theta_{emitted}$, because this change is strongly influenced by the oxygen content in the gas. Please keep in mind that this explanation is highly intuitive and, from a physics point of view, not completely correct, but it should give you an approximate understanding of what we are measuring.

To summarize, the measured signal is this phase shift θ, simply called phase in the following text, while the searched quantity (the one we want to predict) is the oxygen concentration in the gas in contact with the dye.

In real life, the situation is, unfortunately, even more complicated. The light phase shift not only depends on the modulation frequency ω and the oxygen concentration $O2$ in the gas but also nonlinearly on the temperature and chemical composition of the surrounding of the dye molecule. Additionally, only rarely can the decay of the light intensity be described by only one decay time. Most frequently, at least two decay times are needed, further increasing the number of the parameters required to describe the system. Given a laser modulation frequency ω, a temperature T in degrees Celsius, and an oxygen concentration $O2$ (expressed in % of oxygen contained in air), the system returns the phase θ. In Figure 9-2, you can see a plot of a typical measured $\tan\theta$ for $T = 45^\circ C$ and $O2 = 4\%$.

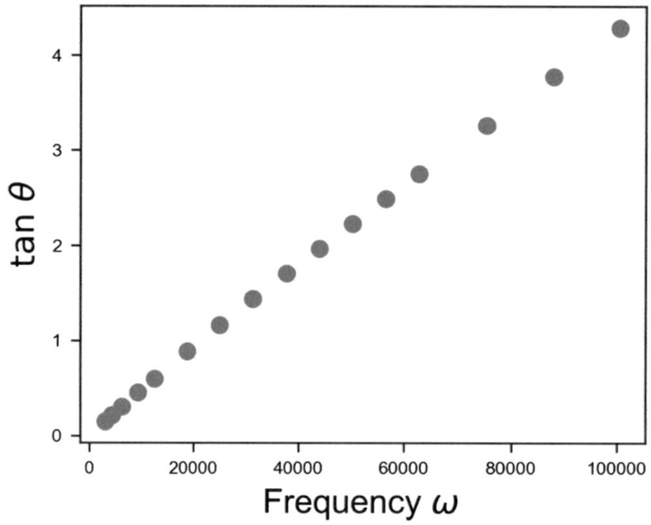

Figure 9-2. *Plot of the measured* $\tan\theta$ *for* $T = 45^\circ C$ *and* $O2 = 4\%$

The idea of this research project is to be able to get the oxygen concentration from data without the need of developing any theoretical model for the behavior of the sensor. To do this, we will try to use deep neural networks and let them learn from artificially created data what the oxygen concentration in the gas is for any given phase, and then we will apply our model to real experimental data.

The Mathematical Model

Let's look at one of the mathematical models that can be used to determine the oxygen concentration. For one thing, it gives an idea of how complicated it is, and for another, it will be used in this chapter to generate the training data set. Without going into the physics involved in the measurement technique, which is beyond the scope of this book, a simple model describing how the phase θ is linked to the oxygen concentration $O2$ can be described by the following formula:

$$\frac{\tan\theta(\omega,T,O2)}{\tan\theta(\omega,T,O2=0)} = \frac{f(\omega,T)}{1+KSV_1(\omega,T)\cdot O2} + \frac{1-f(\omega,T)}{1+KSV_2(\omega,T)\cdot O2}$$

The quantities $f(\omega, T)$, $KSV_1(\omega, T)$, and $KSV_2(\omega, T)$ are parameters whose analytical form is unknown and that are specific to the dye molecule used, how old it is, how the sensor is built, and other factors. Our goal is to train a neural network in the laboratory and later deploy it on a sensor that can be used in the field. The main problem here is to determine the frequency- and temperature-dependent function form of f, KSV_1, and KSV_2. For this reason, commercial sensors usually rely on polynomial or exponential approximations, with enough parameters and on fitting procedures to determine a good enough approximation of the quantities.

In this chapter, we will create the training dataset with the mathematical model just described, then we will apply it to experimental data, to see how well we can predict the oxygen concentration. The goal is a feasibility study to check how well such a method works.

Preparing the training dataset in this case is a bit tricky and convoluted, so before starting, let's look at a similar but much easier problem, so that you get an understanding of what we want to do in the more complicated case.

Regression Problem

Let's consider first the following problem. Given a function $L(x)$ with a parameter A, we want to train a neural network to extract the parameter value A from a set of values of the function. In other words, given a set of values of the input variable x_i for $i = 1, \ldots, N$, we will calculate an array of N values $L_i = L(x_i)$ for $i = 1, \ldots, N$ and use them as input for a neural network. We will train the network to give us as output A. As a concrete example, let's consider the following function:

$$L(x) = \frac{A^2}{A^2 + x^2}$$

This is the so called Lorentzian function, with a maximum in $x = 0$ and with $L(0) = 1$. The problem we want to solve here is to determine A, given a certain number of data points of this function. In this case, this is rather simple, because we can do it, for example, with a classical nonlinear fit, or even by solving a simple quadratic equation, but suppose we want to teach a neural network to do that. We want a neural network to learn how to perform a nonlinear fit for this function. With all you learned in this book, this will not prove to be too difficult. Let's start by creating a training dataset. First, let's define a function for $L(x)$

```
def L(x,A):
    y = A**2/(A**2+x**2)
    return y
```

Let's now consider 100 points and generate an array of all the x points we want to use.

```
number_of_x_points = 100
min_x = 0.0
max_x = 5.0
x = np.arange(min_x, max_x, (max_x-min_x)/number_of_x_points )
```

Finally, let's generate 1000 observations, which we will use as input for our network.

```
number_of_samples = 1000
np.random.seed(20)
A_v = np.random.normal(1.0, 0.4, number_of_samples)

for i in range(len(A_v)):
    if A_v[i] <= 0:
        A_v[i] = np.random.random_sample([1])
data = np.zeros((number_of_samples, number_of_x_points))
targets = np.reshape(A_v, [1000,1])
```

```
for i in range(number_of_samples):
    data[i,:] = L(x, A_v[i])
```

The array data will now contain all observations, each one on a row. Note that to avoid having negative values for *A*, we have built a check into the code.

```
if A_v[i] <= 0:
        A_v[i] = np.random.random_sample([1])
```

In this way, if the random value chosen for *A* is negative, a new random value is assigned instead. You may have noticed that in the equation for $L(x)$, the quantity *A* always appears squared, so on first sight, a negative value would not be a problem. But remember that this negative value will be the target variable we want to predict. When first developing this model, I had a few negative values for *A*. The network was not able to distinguish between positive and negative values, thus getting wrong results.

If you check the shape of the array A_v, you get

```
(1000, 100)
```

This translates as 1000 observations, each having 100 values that are the different value of *L*, are calculated at the values of *x* that we have generated. We also need a dev dataset, of course.

```
number_of_dev_samples = 1000

np.random.seed(42)
A_v_dev = np.random.normal(1.0, 0.4, number_of_samples)

for i in range(len(A_v_dev)):
    if A_v_dev[i] <= 0:
        A_v_dev[i] = np.random.random_sample([1])

data_dev = np.zeros((number_of_samples, number_of_x_points))
targets_dev = np.reshape(A_v_dev, [1000,1])

for i in range(number_of_samples):
    data_dev[i,:] = L(x, A_v_dev[i])
```

In Figure 9-3, you can see four random examples of the functions we will use as input.

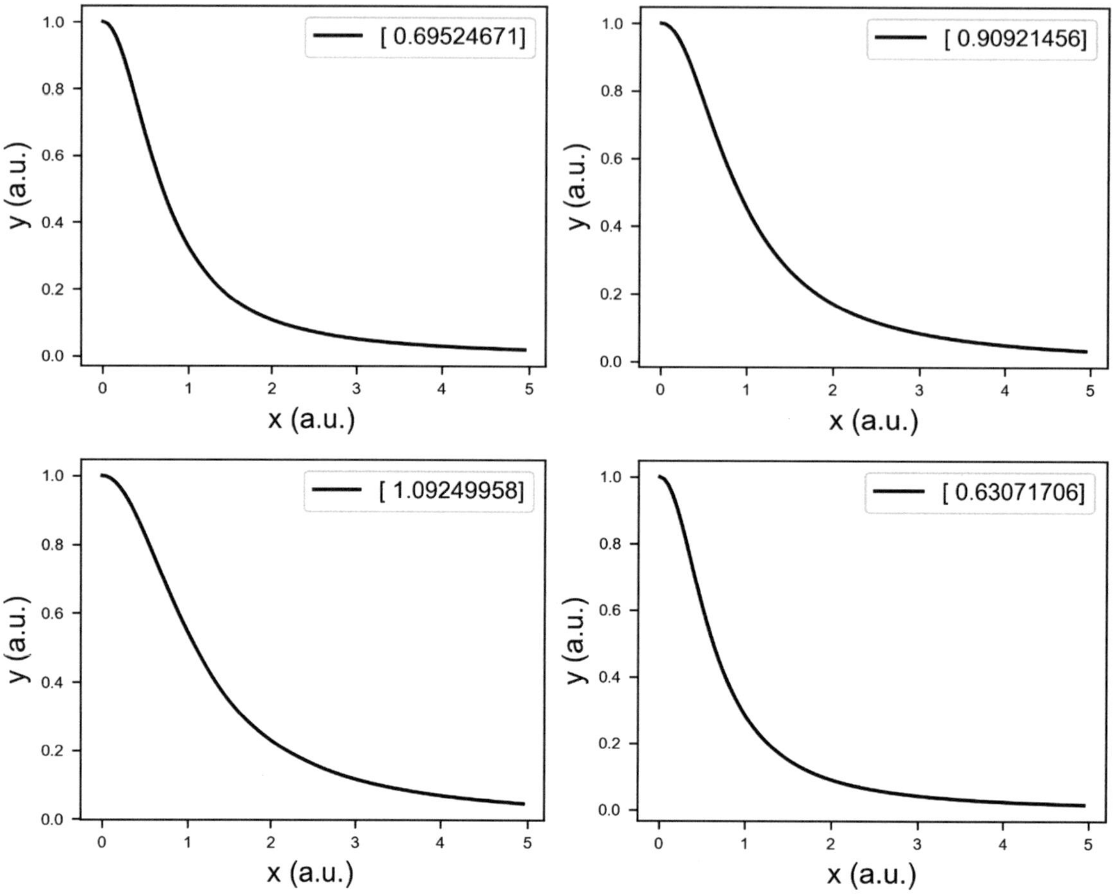

Figure 9-3. *Four random examples of the function L(x). In the legend, you see the values used for A for the plot.*

Now let's build a simple network with one layer and ten neurons, to try to extract this value.

```
tf.reset_default_graph()

n1 = 10
nx = number_of_x_points
n2 = 1

W1 = tf.Variable(tf.random_normal([n1,nx]))/500.0
b1 = tf.Variable(tf.ones((n1,1)))/500.0
W2 = tf.Variable(tf.random_normal([n2,n1]))/500.0
b2 = tf.Variable(tf.ones((n2,1)))/500.0
```

```
X = tf.placeholder(tf.float32, [nx, None]) # Inputs
Y = tf.placeholder(tf.float32, [1, None]) # Labels

Z1 = tf.matmul(W1,X)+b1
A1 = tf.nn.sigmoid(Z1)
Z2 = tf.matmul(W2,A1)+b2
y_ = Z2
cost = tf.reduce_mean(tf.square(y_-Y))
learning_rate = 0.1
training_step = tf.train.AdamOptimizer(learning_rate).minimize(cost)

init = tf.global_variables_initializer()
```

Note that we have initialized the weights randomly, and we will not use mini-batch gradient descent. Let's train the network for 20,000 epochs.

```
sess = tf.Session()
sess.run(init)

training_epochs = 20000
cost_history = np.empty(shape=[1], dtype = float)

train_x = np.transpose(data)
train_y = np.transpose(targets)

cost_history = []
for epoch in range(training_epochs+1):
    sess.run(training_step, feed_dict = {X: train_x, Y: train_y})
    cost_ = sess.run(cost, feed_dict={ X:train_x, Y: train_y})
    cost_history = np.append(cost_history, cost_)

    if (epoch % 1000 == 0):
        print("Reached epoch",epoch,"cost J =", cost_)
```

The model converges very fast. The MSE (the cost function) goes from 1.1 at the beginning to ca. $2.5 \cdot 10^{-4}$ after 10,000 epochs. After 20,000 epochs, the MSE reaches 10^{-6}. We can plot the predicted vs. the real values, to get a visual check on how the system is doing. In Figure 9-4, you can see how well the system is working.

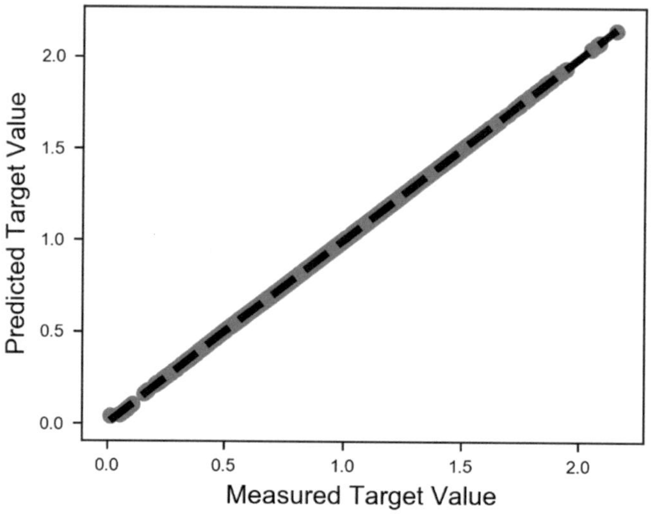

***Figure 9-4.** Predicted vs. real values of A*

By the way, the MSE on the dev set is $3 \cdot 10^{-5}$, so we are probably slightly overfitting the training dataset. One of the reasons is that we are considering a relatively narrow x range: only from 0 to 5. Therefore, when you are dealing with very big values of A (of the order of 2.5, for example), the system tends not to do so well. If you check the same plot as in Figure 9-4 but for the dev dataset (Figure 9-5), you can see how the model has problems with big values of A.

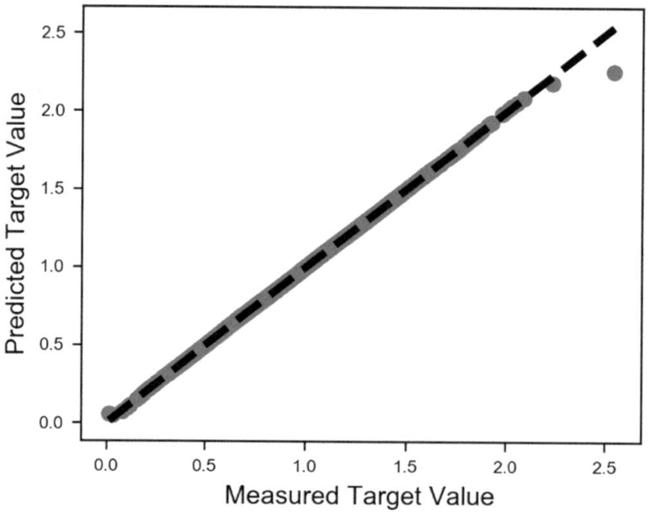

***Figure 9-5.** Predicted vs. real values of A for the dev dataset*

There is another reason for these bad predictions at higher values of A. When we generated the training data, we used the following line of code for the values of A:

```
A_v = np.random.normal(1.0, 0.4, number_of_samples)
```

This means that the chosen values for A are distributed according to a normal distribution, with an average of 1.0 and a standard deviation of 0.4. There will be very few observations with A bigger than 2.0. You can redo the entire exercise we have done, but this time, choose the values of A from a uniform distribution with the code

```
A_v = np.random.random_sample([number_of_dev_samples])*3.0
```

This line of code will give you random numbers between 0 and 3.0. After 20,000 epochs, now we will get $MSE_{train} = 3.8 \cdot 10^{-6}$ and $MSE_{dev} = 1.7 \cdot 10^{-6}$. This time, our predictions on the dev dataset are much better, and there appears to be no overfitting.

Note When you are generating training data artificially, you should always check it for extreme values. Your training data should cover all possible cases that you expect to see in real life; otherwise, your predictions will fail.

Dataset Preparation

Now let's start to generate the dataset we will need for the project. This is going to be slightly more difficult, and, as you will see, we will have to spend more time doing this than developing and tuning our network. The goal of this chapter is to show you how you can use neural networks for research projects that are outside the "classical" use-case basis, such as for image recognition. The experimental data consists of 50 measurements of θ; 5 temperatures: 5°C, 15°C, 25°C, 35°C, and 45°C; and 10 different oxygen concentration values: 0%, 4%, 8%, 15%, 20%, 30%, 40%, 60%, 80 % , and 100%. Each measurement is composed of 22 frequency measurements for the following values of ω:

```
0 62.831853
1 282.743339
2 628.318531
3 1256.637061
4 3141.592654
```

```
5 4398.229715
6 6283.185307
7 9424.777961
8 12566.370614
9 18849.555922
10 25132.741229
11 31415.926536
12 37699.111843
13 43982.297150
14 50265.482457
15 56548.667765
16 62831.853072
17 75398.223686
18 87964.594301
19 100530.964915
20 113097.335529
21 125663.706144
```

For the training dataset, we will use only frequencies between 3000 *Hz* and 100,000 *Hz*. Owing to the limitations of the experimental setup, artifacts and errors begin to appear below 3000 *Hz* and above 10,000 *Hz*. Trying to use all the data made the network perform much worse. That will not be a limitation.

Even if you don't have the data files, I will explain how I prepared them, so that you can reuse the code for your case. First, the files were saved in one folder called `data`. I created a list with the names of all the files we wanted to load:

```
files = os.listdir('./data')
```

Such information as the temperature and oxygen concentration are encoded in the file name, so we must extract them from it. The file's name looks like this: `20180515_PST3-1_45C_Mix8_00.txt`. The `45C` is the temperature, and `8_00` is the oxygen concentration. To extract the information, I wrote one function.

```
def get_T_O2(filename):
    T_ = float(filename[17:19])
    O2_ = float(filename[24:-4].replace('_','.'))
    return T_, O2_
```

This will return two values, one containing the temperature value (T_), and one containing the value of oxygen concentration (O2_). Then I convert the content of the file in a panda data frame, to be able to work with it.

```
def get_df(filename):
    frame = pd.read_csv('./data/'+filename, header = 10, sep = '\t')
    frame = frame.drop(frame.columns[6], axis=1)

    frame.columns=['f', 'ref_r', 'ref_phi', 'raw_r', 'raw_phi', 'sample_phi']

    return frame
```

This function was written this way, according to how the files were structured, of course. This is how the first rows of a file look:

```
StereO2

Probe: PST3-1
Medium: N2+Mix, Mix 0 %
Temperatur: 5 °C
Detektionsfilter: LP594 + SP682
HW Config Ref:
D:\Projekt\20180515_Quarzglas_Reference_00.ini
HW Config Sample: D:\Projekt\20180515_PST3_Sample_00.ini
Date, Time: 15.05.2018, 10:37
Filename: D:\Projekt\20180515_ PST3-1_05C_Mix0_00.txt
$Data$
Frequency (Hz)  Reference R (V)  Reference Phi (deg)  Sample Raw R (V)
Sample Raw Phi (deg)  Sample Phi (deg)
10.00E+0        247.3E-3         18.00E-3             371.0E-3
258.0E-3              240.0E-3
45.00E+0        247.4E-3         72.00E-3             371.0E-3
1.164E+0              1.092E+0
100.0E+0        248.4E-3         108.0E-3             370.9E-3
2.592E+0              2.484E+0
200.0E+0        247.5E-3         396.0E-3             369.8E-3
5.232E+0              4.836E+0
```

If you want to do something similar, naturally you may have to modify the functions. Now let's loop over all the files and create lists with the values of *T*, *O*2, and the data frames. In the folder `data` there are 50 files.

```
frame = pd.DataFrame()
df_list = []
T_list = []
O2_list = []

for file_ in files:
    df = get_df(file_)
    T_, O2_ = get_T_O2(file_)

    df_list.append(df)
    T_list.append(T_)
    O2_list.append(O2_)
```

We can check the content of one of the files. Let's type, for example,

```
get_df(files[2]).head()
```

You can see in Figure 9-6 the first five records of the file with index 2.

	f	ref_r	ref_phi	raw_r	raw_phi	sample_phi
0	10.0	0.2473	0.018	0.2501	0.192	0.174
1	45.0	0.2474	0.072	0.2502	0.846	0.774
2	100.0	0.2484	0.108	0.2501	1.902	1.794
3	200.0	0.2475	0.396	0.2498	3.798	3.402
4	500.0	0.2474	1.008	0.2471	9.456	8.448

Figure 9-6. *First five records of the file with index 2*

The file contains more information than we require.

We have the frequency f, which we must convert to the angular frequency ω (there is a factor 2π between the two), and we must calculate the tangent of θ. We do this with the following code:

```
for df_ in df_list:
    df_['w'] = df_['f']*2*np.pi
    df_['tantheta'] = np.tan(df_['sample_phi']*np.pi/180.0)
```

adding, in this way, two new columns to each data frame. At this point, we must find a good approximation for f, KSV_1, and KSV_2, to be able to create our dataset. To give you an example and to make this chapter more concise, let's consider only one temperature: $T = 45°C$. Let's filter from all our data only that which were measured at this temperature. To do this, we can use the following code:

```
T = 45

Tdf = pd.DataFrame(T_list, columns = ['T'])
Odf = pd.DataFrame(O2_list, columns = ['O2'])
filesdf = pd.DataFrame(files, columns = ['filename'])

files45 = filesdf[Tdf['T'] == T]
filesref = filesdf[(Tdf['T']==T) & (Odf['O2']==0)]
fileref_idx = filesref.index[0]
O5 = Odf[Tdf['T'] == T]
dfref = df_list[fileref_idx]
```

First, we convert the lists `T_list` and `O2_list` to pandas data frames, because, in this format, it is easier to select the right data. Then you may notice that we select all files with $T = 45°C$ in a data frame `files45`. Additionally, we select the data frame for $T = 45°C$ and $O2 = 0\%$, and we call it `dfref`. The reason is that at the beginning, I gave you a formula for θ that involved $\tan\theta\,(\omega, T, O2 = 0)$. `dfref` will contain exactly the measured data for $\tan\theta\,(\omega, T, O2 = 0)$. Remember that we must model the quantity

$$\frac{\tan\theta\left(\omega, T = 45^\circ C\right)}{\tan\theta\left(\omega, T = 45^\circ C, O2 = 0\right)}$$

I know this is getting complicated, but hold on, we are almost done. Selecting the right data frame from the list of data frames is slightly more complicated but can be done in this way:

```
from itertools import compress
A = Tdf['T'] == T
data = list(compress(df_list, A))

B = (Tdf['T']==T) & (Odf['O2']==0)
dataref_ = list(compress(df_list, B))
```

`compress` is easy to understand. You can find more information on the official documentation page, available at `https://goo.gl/xNZEHH`. Basically, the idea is that given two lists, `d` and `s`, the output of `compress(d,s)` is given by a new list equal to `[(d[0] if s[0]), (d[1] if s[1]), ...]`. In our case, `A` and `B` are lists made up of Boolean values, so the code returns only the values of `df_list` for the position in the list `A` that have `True`.

Using nonlinear fitting, we will find the values for f, KSV_1, and KSV_2 for each value of ω we have at our disposal. We must loop over all the values of ω, fit the function

$$\frac{\tan\theta\left(\omega,T=45^\circ C,O2\right)}{\tan\theta\left(\omega,T=45^\circ C,O2=0\right)}$$

with respect to $O2$, using the function

```
def fitfunc(x,  f, KSV, KSV2):
    return (f/(1.0+KSV*x)+ (1.0-f)/(1+KSV2*x))
```

to extract f, KSV_1, and KSV_2 for each $O2$ value. I did it with this code:

```
f = []
KSV = []
KSV2 = []

for w_ in wred:

    # Let's prepare the file

    O2x = []
    tantheta = []
```

```
    #tantheta0 = float(dfref[dfref['w']==w_]['tantheta'])
    tantheta0 = float(dataref_[0][dataref_[0]['w']==w_]['tantheta'])

    # Loop over the files
    for idx, df_ in enumerate(data_train):
        O2xvalue = float(Odf.loc[idx])
        O2x.append(O2xvalue)

        tanthetavalue = float(df_[df_['w'] == w_]['tantheta'])
        tantheta.append(tanthetavalue)

    popt, pcov = curve_fit(fitfunc_2, O2x, np.array(tantheta)/tantheta0,
    p0 = [0.4,0.06, 0.003])

    f.append(popt[0])
    KSV.append(popt[1])
    KSV2.append(popt[2])
```

Take some time to study the code. The code is so convoluted because each file contains data at a fixed *O*2 value. We want to build, for each frequency value, an array containing the values we want to fit as a function of *O*2. That is why we must do some data wrangling. In the lists f, KSV, and KSV2, we now have the values we found with respect to the frequency. Let's first select only the values for angular frequencies between 3000 and 100,000.

```
w_  = w[4:20]
f_  = f[4:20]
KSV_  = KSV[4:20]
```

In Figure 9-7, you can see how *f*, KSV_1, and KSV_2 depend on the angular frequency.

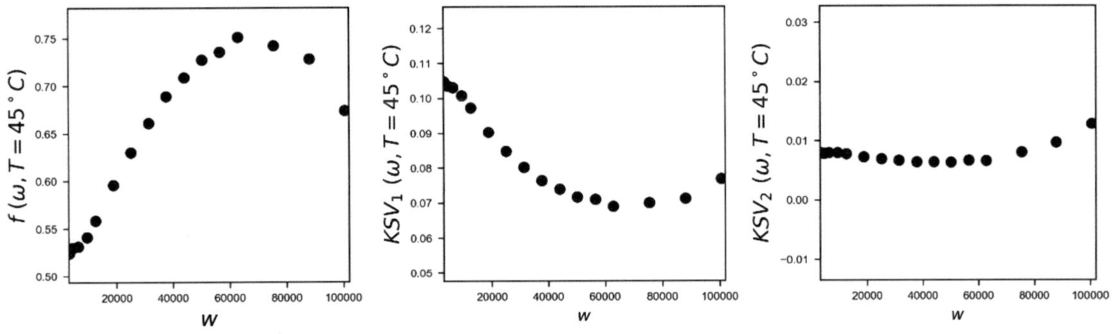

***Figure 9-7.** Dependency of f, KSV_1, and KSV_2 on the angular frequency*

There is another small problem we must overcome. We must be able to calculate *f*, *KSV*, and KSV_2 for any value of ω, not only for the ones we have obtained. To do this, we must use interpolation. To save some time, we will not develop the interpolation functions from scratch. Instead, we will use the `interp1d` function from the SciPy package.

```
from scipy.interpolate import interp1d
```

We will do it in this way:

```
finter = interp1d(wred, f, kind='cubic')
KSVinter = interp1d(wred, KSV, kind = 'cubic')
KSV2inter = interp1d(wred, KSV2, kind = 'cubic')
```

Note that `finter`, `KSVinter`, and `KSV2inter` are functions that accept as input a value for ω, as a NumPy array and return the value of *f*, KSV_1, and KSV_2, respectively. The continuous line in Figure 9-8 shows the interpolated functions obtained by the points in Figure 9-7.

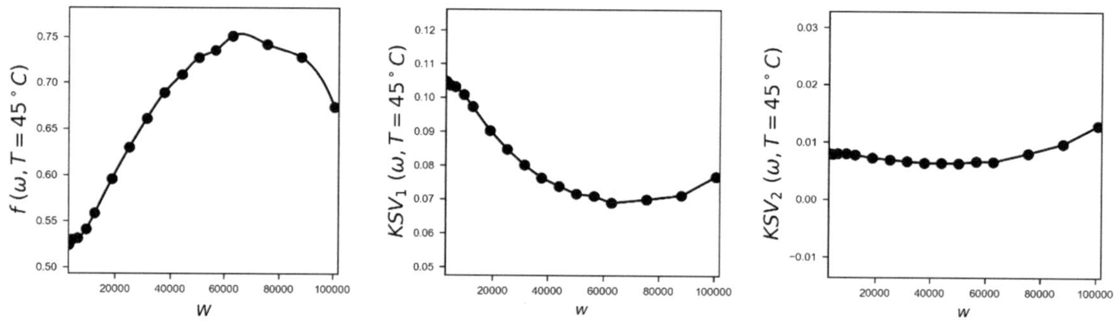

***Figure 9-8.** Dependency of f, KSV_1, and KSV_2 on the angular frequency. The continous line is the interpolated function.*

At this point, we have all the ingredients we need. We can finally create our training dataset with the formula

$$\frac{\tan\theta(\omega,T,O2)}{\tan\theta(\omega,T,O2=0)} = \frac{f(\omega,T)}{1+KSV_1(\omega,T)\cdot O2} + \frac{1-f(\omega,T)}{1+KSV_2(\omega,T)\cdot O2}$$

Let's now create 5000 observations for random values of $O2$.

```
number_of_samples = 5000
number_of_x_points = len(w_)
np.random.seed(20)
O2_v = np.random.random_sample([number_of_samples])*100.0
```

We need the preceding mathematical function

```
def fitfunc2(x, O2, ffunc, KSVfunc, KSV2func):
    output = []
    for x_ in x:
        KSV_ = KSVfunc(x_)
        KSV2_ = KSV2func(x_)
        f_ = ffunc(x_)
        output_ = f_/(1.0+KSV_*O2)+(1.0-f_)/(1.0+KSV2_*O2)
        output.append(output_)
    return output
```

to calculate

$$\frac{\tan\theta(\omega,T,O2)}{\tan\theta(\omega,T,O2=0)}$$

for a value of the angular frequency and of $O2$. The data can be generated with the code

```
data = np.zeros((number_of_samples, number_of_x_points))
targets = np.reshape(O2_v, [number_of_samples,1])

for i in range(number_of_samples):
    data[i,:] = fitfunc2(w_, float(targets[i]), finter, KSVinter,
KSV2inter)
```

In Figure 9-9, you can see a few random examples of the data we generated.

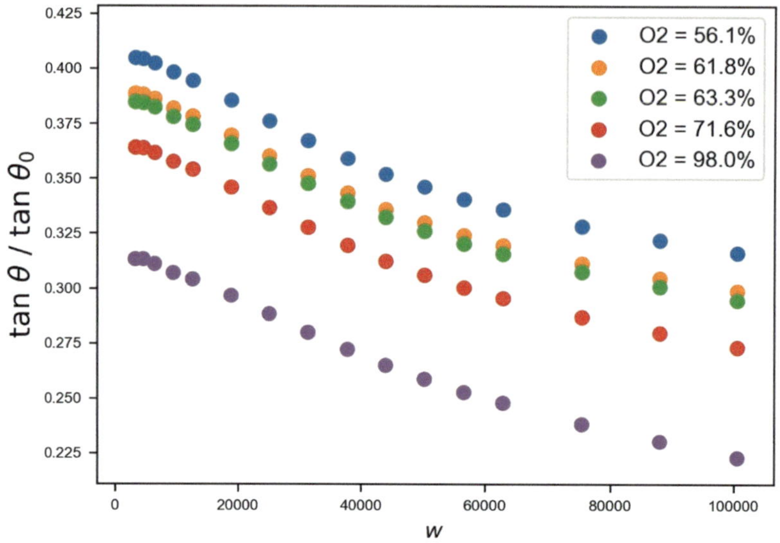

Figure 9-9. *Random examples of the data we generated*

Model Training

Let's start to build the network. We will limit ourselves here, for space reasons, to a simple three-layer network with five neurons in each layer.

```
tf.reset_default_graph()

n1 = 5 # Number of neurons in layer 1
n2 = 5 # Number of neurons in layer 2
n3 = 5 # Number of neurons in layer 3
nx = number_of_x_points
n_dim = nx
n4 = 1

stddev_f = 2.0

tf.set_random_seed(5)

X = tf.placeholder(tf.float32, [n_dim, None])
Y = tf.placeholder(tf.float32, [10, None])
W1 = tf.Variable(tf.random_normal([n1, n_dim], stddev=stddev_f))
b1 = tf.Variable(tf.constant(0.0, shape = [n1,1]) )
W2 = tf.Variable(tf.random_normal([n2, n1], stddev=stddev_f))
```

```
b2 = tf.Variable(tf.constant(0.0, shape = [n2,1]))
W3 = tf.Variable(tf.random_normal([n3,n2], stddev = stddev_f))
b3 = tf.Variable(tf.constant(0.0, shape = [n3,1]))
W4 = tf.Variable(tf.random_normal([n4,n3], stddev = stddev_f))
b4 = tf.Variable(tf.constant(0.0, shape = [n4,1]))

X = tf.placeholder(tf.float32, [nx, None]) # Inputs
Y = tf.placeholder(tf.float32, [1, None]) # Labels

# Let's build our network

Z1 = tf.nn.sigmoid(tf.matmul(W1, X) + b1) # n1 x n_dim * n_dim x n_obs = n1
x n_obs
Z2 = tf.nn.sigmoid(tf.matmul(W2, Z1) + b2) # n2 x n1 * n1 * n_obs = n2 x
n_obs
Z3 = tf.nn.sigmoid(tf.matmul(W3, Z2) + b3)
Z4 = tf.matmul(W4, Z3) + b4
y_ = Z2
```

This, at least, is how I began. I chose as output of the network a neuron with an identity activation function y_= Z2. Unfortunately, the training was not working and very unstable. Because I had to predict a percentage, I needed an output between 0 and 100. So, I decided to try a sigmoid activation function multiplied by 100.

```
y_ = tf.sigmoid(Z2)*100.0
```

Suddenly, the training worked beautifully. I used the Adam optimizer.

```
cost = tf.reduce_mean(tf.square(y_-Y))
learning_rate = 1e-3
training_step = tf.train.AdamOptimizer(learning_rate).minimize(cost)
init = tf.global_variables_initializer()
```

This time, I used mini-batches of size 100.

```
batch_size = 100
sess = tf.Session()
sess.run(init)
training_epochs = 25000
cost_history = np.empty(shape=[1], dtype = float)
```

```
train_x = np.transpose(data)
train_y = np.transpose(targets)
cost_history = []
for epoch in range(training_epochs+1):

    for i in range(0, train_x.shape[0], batch_size):
        x_batch = train_x[i:i + batch_size,:]
        y_batch = train_y[i:i + batch_size,:]

        sess.run(training_step, feed_dict = {X: x_batch, Y: y_batch})

    cost_ = sess.run(cost, feed_dict={ X:train_x, Y: train_y})
    cost_history = np.append(cost_history, cost_)

    if (epoch % 1000 == 0):
        print("Reached epoch",epoch,"cost J =", cost_)
```

You should understand this code now without too many explanations. It is basically what we have used several times previously. You may have noticed that I have initialized the weights randomly. I tried several strategies, but this seemed to be the one that worked best. It is very instructive to check how the training is going. In Figure 9-10, you can see the cost function evaluated on the training dataset and on the experimental dev dataset. You can see how it oscillates. There are mainly two reasons for this.

- The first is that we are using mini-batches, and, therefore, the cost function oscillates
- The second reason is that the experimental data is noisy, because the measuring apparatus is not perfect. The gas mixer, for example, has an absolute error of roughly 1–2%, which means that if we have an experimental observation for $O2 = 60\%$, it could be as low as 58% or 59% and as high as 61% or 62%.

Given this error, one should expect to have, on average, an absolute error of ca. 1% in our prediction.

Note Roughly speaking, the output of a well-trained network will never be able to exceed the accuracy of the target variables used. Remember to always check the errors you may have on your target variables, to estimate how accurate they are. In the preceding example, because our target values for *O2* have a maximum absolute error of ±1% (that is, the experimental error), the expected error for the results of the network will be of this order of magnitude.

Caution The network will learn the function that produces a certain output, given a specific input. If the output is wrong, the learned function will also be wrong.

Finally, let's check how the network performs.

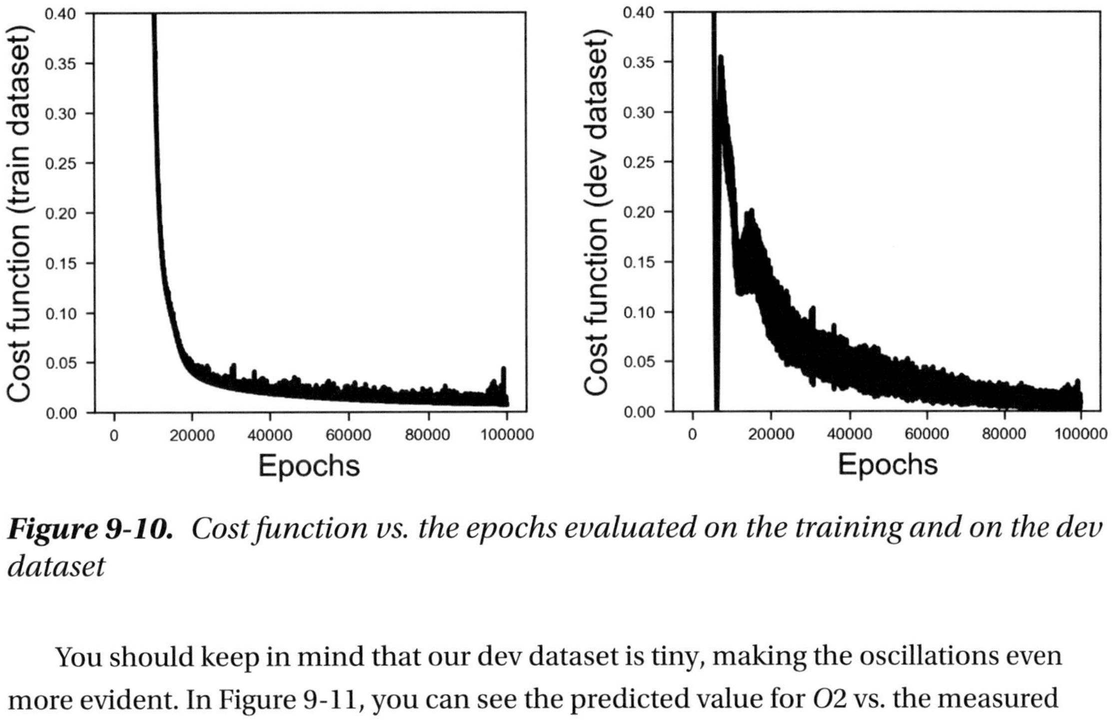

***Figure 9-10.** Cost function vs. the epochs evaluated on the training and on the dev dataset*

You should keep in mind that our dev dataset is tiny, making the oscillations even more evident. In Figure 9-11, you can see the predicted value for *O2* vs. the measured value. As you can see, they lie beautifully on the diagonal.

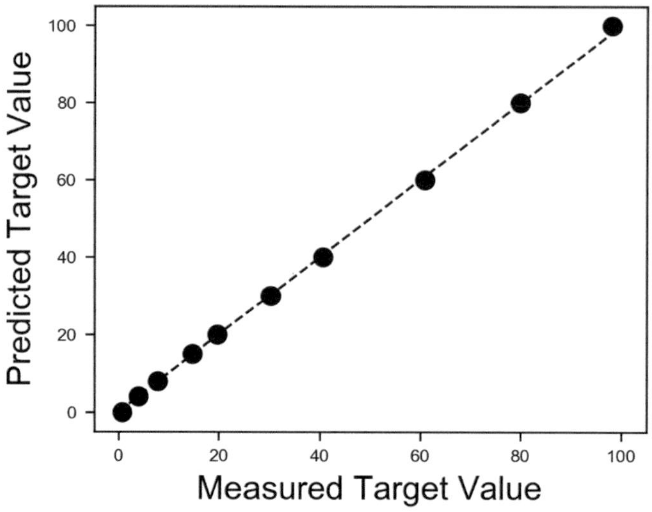

***Figure 9-11.** Predicted value for O2 vs. the measured value*

In Figure 9-12, you can see the absolute error calculated on the dev dataset for $O2 \in [0,100]$.

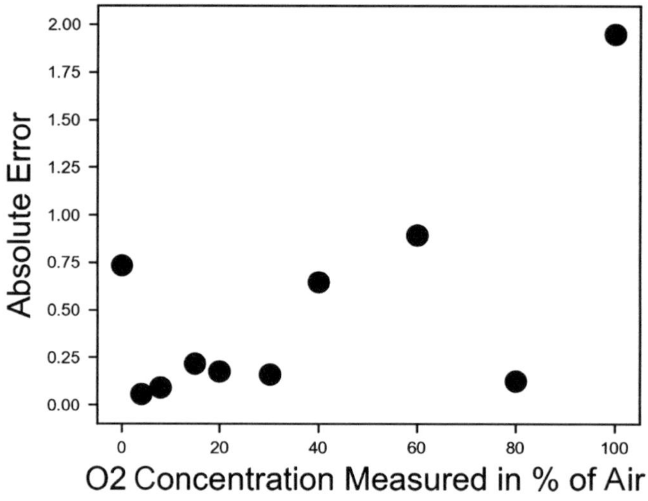

***Figure 9-12.** Absolute error calculated on the dev dataset for $O2 \in [0,100]$*

The results are stunningly good. For all values of *O2*, except for 100%, the error lies below 1%. Remember that our network learned from an artificially created dataset. This network could now be used in this type of sensor without the need of implementing complicated mathematical equations for the estimation of *O2*. The next phase of this project will be to get automatically ca. 10,000 measurements at various values of the temperature *T* and the oxygen concentration *O2* and use those measurements as a training set to predict both *T* and *O2* at the same time.

CHAPTER 10

Logistic Regression from Scratch

In Chapter 2, we developed a logistic regression model for binary classification with one neuron and applied it to two digits of the MNIST dataset. The actual Python code for the computational graph construction was just ten lines of code (excluding the part that performs the training of the model; review Chapter 2, if you don't remember what we did there).

```
tf.reset_default_graph()

X = tf.placeholder(tf.float32, [n_dim, None])
Y = tf.placeholder(tf.float32, [1, None])
learning_rate = tf.placeholder(tf.float32, shape=())

W = tf.Variable(tf.zeros([1, n_dim]))
b = tf.Variable(tf.zeros(1))

init = tf.global_variables_initializer()
y_ = tf.matmul(tf.transpose(W),X)+b
cost = tf.reduce_mean(tf.square(y_-Y))
training_step = tf.train.GradientDescentOptimizer(learning_rate).
minimize(cost)
```

This code is very compact and very quick to write. There is really a lot going on behind the scenes that you don't see with this Python code. TensorFlow does a lot of things in the background that you may not be aware of. It will be very instructive to try to develop this exact model completely from scratch, mathematically and in Python, without using TensorFlow, to observe what is really going on. The next sections lay out the entire mathematical formulation required, and its implementation in Python (with just `numpy`). The goal is to build a model that we can train for binary classification.

U. Michelucci, *Applied Deep Learning*, https://doi.org/10.1007/978-1-4842-3790-8_10

I will not spend too much time on the notation or the ideas behind the mathematics, because you have seen these several times in previous chapters. The discussion of dataset preparation will also be very brief, as it has already been described in Chapter 2.

I will not go through all the Python code line by line, because, if you read the previous chapters, you should have quite a good grasp of the practices and ideas used here. There are no real new concepts; you have already seen almost everything. Consider this chapter as a reference, to learn how to implement a logistic model completely from scratch. I strongly suggest that you try to understand all the mathematics and implement it in Python once. It is very instructive and will teach you a lot about debugging, about how important it is to write good code, and how comfortable libraries such as TensorFlow are.

Mathematics Behind Logistic Regression

Let's start with some notation and a reminder of what we are going to do. Our prediction will be a variable $\hat{y}$ that can only be 0 or 1. (We will indicate with 0 and 1 the two classes we are trying to predict.)

$$Prediction \rightarrow \hat{y} \in \{0,1\}$$

What our method will give as output, or as a prediction, will be the probability of $\hat{y}$ being 1, given the input case *x*. Or, in a more mathematical form,

$$\hat{y} = P(y=1|x)$$

We will then define an input observation to be of class 1, if $\hat{y} \geq 0.5$, and of class 0, if $\hat{y} < 0.5$. As we have in Chapter 2 (see Figure 2-2), we will consider n_x inputs and one neuron with the sigmoid (indicated with σ) activation function. Our neuron output $\hat{y}$ can be easily written for observation *i* as

$$\hat{y}^{[i]} = \sigma\left(z^{[i]}\right) = \sigma\left(\boldsymbol{w}^T \boldsymbol{x}^{[i]} + b\right) = \sigma\left(w_1 x_1^{[i]} + w_2 x_2^{[i]} + \ldots + w_{n_x} x_{n_x}^{[i]} + b\right)$$

To find the best weights and bias, we will minimize the cost function that is written here for one observation

$$\mathcal{L}\left(\hat{y}^{[i]}, y^{[i]}\right) = -\left(y^{[i]} \log \hat{y}^{[i]} + \left(1 - y^{[i]}\right) \log\left(1 - \hat{y}^{[i]}\right)\right)$$

where, with y, we have indicated our labels. We will use the gradient descent algorithm, as described in Chapter 2, so we will need the partial derivatives of our cost function with respect to the weights and the bias. You will remember that at iteration $n+1$ (we will indicate here the iteration with an index in square brackets as subscript), we will update our weights from iteration n with the equations

$$w_{j,[n+1]} = w_{j,[n]} - \gamma \frac{\partial \mathcal{L}\left(\hat{y}^{[i]}, y^{[i]}\right)}{\partial w_j}$$

and, for the bias,

$$b_{[n+1]} = b_{j,[n]} - \gamma \frac{\partial \mathcal{L}\left(\hat{y}^{[i]}, y^{[i]}\right)}{\partial b}$$

where γ is the learning rate. The derivatives are not so complicated and can be calculated easily with the chain rule

$$\frac{\partial \mathcal{L}\left(\hat{y}^{[i]}, y^{[i]}\right)}{\partial w_j} = \frac{\partial \mathcal{L}\left(\hat{y}^{[i]}, y^{[i]}\right)}{\partial \hat{y}^{[i]}} \frac{d\hat{y}^{[i]}}{dz^{[i]}} \frac{\partial z^{[i]}}{\partial w_j}$$

as can b

$$\frac{\partial \mathcal{L}\left(\hat{y}^{[i]}, y^{[i]}\right)}{\partial b} = \frac{\partial \mathcal{L}\left(\hat{y}^{[i]}, y^{[i]}\right)}{\partial \hat{y}^{[i]}} \frac{d\hat{y}^{[i]}}{dz^{[i]}} \frac{\partial z^{[i]}}{\partial b}$$

Now, calculating the derivatives, you can verify that

$$\frac{\partial \mathcal{L}\left(\hat{y}^{[i]}, y^{[i]}\right)}{\partial \hat{y}^{[i]}} = -\frac{y^{[i]}}{\hat{y}^{[i]}} + \frac{1-y^{[i]}}{1-\hat{y}^{[i]}}$$

$$\frac{d\hat{y}^{[i]}}{dz^{[i]}} = \hat{y}^{[i]}\left(1-\hat{y}^{[i]}\right)$$

$$\frac{\partial z^{[i]}}{\partial w_j} = x_j^{[i]}$$

$$\frac{\partial z^{[i]}}{\partial b} = 1$$

When we put all this together, we get

$$w_{j,[n+1]} = w_{j,[n]} - \gamma \frac{\partial \mathcal{L}\left(\hat{y}^{[i]}, y^{[i]}\right)}{\partial w_j} = w_{j,[n]} - \gamma\left(1-\hat{y}^{[i]}\right)x_j^{[i]}$$

$$b_{[n+1]} = b_{[n]} - \gamma \frac{\partial \mathcal{L}\left(\hat{y}^{[i]}, y^{[i]}\right)}{\partial b} = b_{j,[n]} - \gamma\left(1 - \hat{y}^{[i]}\right)$$

These equations are valid only for one training case; therefore, as we have already done, let's generalize them to many training cases, remembering that we define our cost function J for many observations as

$$J(\boldsymbol{w}, b) = \frac{1}{m}\sum_{i=1}^{m} \mathcal{L}\left(\hat{y}^{[i]}, y^{[i]}\right)$$

where, as usual, we have indicated the number of observations with m. The bold $\boldsymbol{w}$ is simply a vector of all the weights $\boldsymbol{w} = \left(w_1, w_2, \ldots, w_{n_x}\right)$. We will also need our beloved matrix formalism here (which you have seen several times in previous chapters)

$$Z = W^T X + B$$

where we have indicated with B a matrix of dimensions $(1, n_x)$ (to make it consistent with the notation we are using now here) and with all elements equal to b (in Python, we will not have to define it, because broadcasting will take care of it for us). X will contain our observations and features and have dimensions (n_x, m) (observations on columns, features on rows), and W^T will be the transpose of the matrix containing all the weights, which, in our cases, has the dimensions $(1, n_x)$, because it is transposed. Our neuron output in matrix form will be

$$\hat{Y} = \sigma(Z)$$

where the sigmoid function acts element by element. The equations for the partial derivatives now become

$$\frac{\partial J(\boldsymbol{w}, b)}{\partial w_j} = \frac{1}{m}\sum_{i=1}^{m} \frac{\partial \mathcal{L}\left(\hat{y}^{[i]}, y^{[i]}\right)}{\partial w_j} = \frac{1}{m}\sum_{i=1}^{m} \frac{\partial \mathcal{L}\left(\hat{y}^{[i]}, y^{[i]}\right)}{\partial \hat{y}^{[i]}} \frac{d\hat{y}^{[i]}}{dz^{[i]}} \frac{\partial z^{[i]}}{\partial w_j} = \frac{1}{m}\sum_{i=1}^{m}\left(1 - \hat{y}^{[i]}\right) x_j^{[i]}$$

and for b

$$\frac{\partial J(\boldsymbol{w}, b)}{\partial b} = \frac{1}{m}\sum_{i=1}^{m} \frac{\partial \mathcal{L}\left(\hat{y}^{[i]}, y^{[i]}\right)}{\partial b} = \frac{1}{m}\sum_{i=1}^{m} \frac{\partial \mathcal{L}\left(\hat{y}^{[i]}, y^{[i]}\right)}{\partial \hat{y}^{[i]}} \frac{d\hat{y}^{[i]}}{dz^{[i]}} \frac{\partial z^{[i]}}{\partial b} = \frac{1}{m}\sum_{i=1}^{m}\left(1 - \hat{y}^{[i]}\right)$$

These equations can be written in matrix form (where ∇_w indicates the gradient with respect to $\boldsymbol{w}$) as

$$\nabla_w J(\boldsymbol{w}, b) = \frac{1}{m} X\left(\hat{Y} - Y\right)^T$$

and for *b*,

$$\frac{\partial J(\boldsymbol{w}, b)}{\partial b} = \frac{1}{m}\sum_{i=1}^{m}\left(\hat{Y}_i - Y_i\right)$$

Finally, the equation we need to implement for the gradient descent algorithm is

$$\boldsymbol{w}_{[n+1]} = \boldsymbol{w}_{[n]} - \gamma \frac{1}{m} X\left(\hat{Y} - Y\right)^T$$

and for *b*,

$$b_{[n+1]} = b_{[n]} - \gamma \frac{1}{m}\sum_{i=1}^{m}\left(\hat{Y}_i - Y_i\right)$$

At this point, you should already have gained a completely new appreciation of TensorFlow. The library does all this for you in the background, and, more important, all automatically. Remember: We are dealing here with just one neuron. You can easily see how complicated it can get when you want to calculate the same equations for networks with many layers and neurons, or for something as a convolutional or recurrent neural network.

We now have all the mathematics we need to implement logistic regression completely from scratch. Let's move on to some Python.

Python Implementation

Let's start importing the necessary libraries.

```
import numpy as np
%matplotlib inline
import matplotlib.pyplot as plt
```

Note that we don't import TensorFlow. We will not need it here. Let's write a function for the sigmoid activation function `sigmoid(z)`.

```
def sigmoid(z):
    s = 1.0 / (1.0 + np.exp(-z))
    return s
```

We will also require a function to initialize the weights. In this basic case, we can simply initialize everything with zeros. Logistic regression will work anyway.

```
def initialize(dim):
    w = np.zeros((dim,1))
    b = 0
    return w,b
```

Then we must implement the following equations, which we have calculated in the previous section:

$$\nabla_w J(\boldsymbol{w}, b) = \frac{1}{m} X\left(\hat{Y} - Y\right)^T$$

and

$$\frac{\partial J(\boldsymbol{w}, b)}{\partial b} = \frac{1}{m} \sum_{i=1}^{m} \left(\hat{Y}_i - Y_i\right)$$

```
def derivatives_calculation(w, b, X, Y):
    m = X.shape[1]
    z = np.dot(w.T,X)+b
    y_ = sigmoid(z)

    cost = -1.0/m*np.sum(Y*np.log(y_)+(1.0-Y)*np.log(1.0-y_))

    dw = 1.0/m*np.dot(X, (y_-Y).T)
    db = 1.0/m*np.sum(y_-Y)

    derivatives = {"dw": dw, "db":db}
    return derivatives, cost
```

Now we need the function that will update the weights.

```
def optimize(w, b, X, Y, num_iterations, learning_rate, print_cost = False):

    costs = [] for i in range(num_iterations):
        derivatives, cost = derivatives_calculation(w, b, X, Y)
```

```
        dw = derivatives ["dw"]
        db = derivatives ["db"]

        w = w - learning_rate*dw
        b = b - learning_rate*db

        if i % 100 == 0:
            costs.append(cost)

        if print_cost and i % 100 == 0:
            print ("Cost (iteration %i) = %f" %(i, cost))

    derivatives = {"dw": dw, "db": db}
    params = {"w": w, "b": b}

    return params, derivatives, costs
```

The next function, predict(), creates a matrix of dimensions $(1, m)$ that contains the predictions of the model given the inputs $\boldsymbol{w}$ and b.

```
def predict (w, b, X):
    m = X.shape[1]

    Y_prediction = np.zeros((1,m))
    w = w.reshape(X.shape[0],1)
    A = sigmoid (np.dot(w.T, X)+b)

    for i in range(A.shape[1]):

        if (A[:,i] > 0.5):
            Y_prediction[:, i] = 1
        elif (A[:,i] <= 0.5):
            Y_prediction[:, i] = 0
    return Y_prediction
```

Finally, let's put everything together in the model() function.

```
def model (X_train, Y_train, X_test, Y_test, num_iterations = 1000,
learning_rate = 0.5, print_cost = False):

    w, b = initialize(X_train.shape[0])
    parameters, derivatives, costs = optimize(w, b, X_train, Y_train,
    num_iterations, learning_rate, print_cost)
```

```
    w = parameters["w"]
    b = parameters["b"]

    Y_prediction_test = predict (w, b, X_test)
    Y_prediction_train = predict (w, b, X_train)

    train_accuracy = 100.0 - np.mean(np.abs(Y_prediction_train-Y_train)*100.0)
    test_accuracy = 100.0 - np.mean(np.abs(Y_prediction_test-Y_test)*100.0)

    d = {"costs": costs, "Y_prediction_test": Y_prediction_test, "Y_
    prediction_train": Y_prediction_train, "w": w, "b": b, "learning_rate":
    learning_rate, "num_iterations": num_iterations}

    print ("Accuracy Test: ", test_accuracy)
    print ("Accuracy Train: ", train_accuracy)

    return d
```

Test of the Model

After building the model, we must see what results it can achieve with some data. In the next section, I will first prepare the dataset we have already used in Chapter 2, the two digits one and two from the MNIST dataset, and then train our neuron on the dataset and check what results we get.

Dataset Preparation

As an optimizing metric, we chose accuracy, so let's see what value we can reach with our model. We will use the same dataset as in Chapter 2: a subset of the MNIST dataset consisting of the digits one and two. Here, you can find the code to get the data without explanation, because we have already dissected it extensively in Chapter 2.

The code we require is the following:

```
from sklearn.datasets import fetch_mldata
mnist = fetch_mldata('MNIST original')
X,y = mnist["data"], mnist["target"]
```

```
X_12 = X[np.any([y == 1,y == 2], axis = 0)]
y_12 = y[np.any([y == 1,y == 2], axis = 0)]
```

Because we loaded all images in one block, we must create a dev and a train dataset (the split being 80% train and 20% dev), as follows:

```
shuffle_index = np.random.permutation(X_12.shape[0])
X_12_shuffled, y_12_shuffled = X_12[shuffle_index], y_12[shuffle_index]

train_proportion = 0.8
train_dev_cut = int(len(X_12)*train_proportion)
X_train, X_dev, y_train, y_dev = \
    X_12_shuffled[:train_dev_cut], \
    X_12_shuffled[train_dev_cut:], \
    y_12_shuffled[:train_dev_cut], \
    y_12_shuffled[train_dev_cut:]
```

As usual, we normalize the inputs,

```
X_train_normalised = X_train/255.0
X_dev_normalised = X_test/255.0
```

bring the matrices in the right format,

```
X_train_tr = X_train_normalised.transpose()
y_train_tr = y_train.reshape(1,y_train.shape[0])
X_dev_tr = X_dev_normalised.transpose()
y_dev_tr = y_dev.reshape(1,y_dev.shape[0])
```

and define some constants.

```
dim_train = X_train_tr.shape[1]
dim_dev = X_dev_tr.shape[1]
```

Now let's shift our labels (remember this from Chapter 2?). We have here 1 and 2, and we need 0 and 1.

```
y_train_shifted = y_train_tr - 1
y_test_shifted = y_test_tr - 1
```

Running the Test

Finally, we can test the model with the call

```
d = model (Xtrain, ytrain, Xtest, ytest, num_iterations = 4000, learning_
rate = 0.05, print_cost = True)
```

Although your numbers may vary, you should get an output similar to the following, in which I have omitted a few iterations for space reasons:

```
Cost (iteration 0) = 0.693147
Cost (iteration 100) = 0.109078
Cost (iteration 200) = 0.079466
Cost (iteration 300) = 0.067267
Cost (iteration 400) = 0.060286

.........

Cost (iteration 3600) = 0.031350
Cost (iteration 3700) = 0.031148
Cost (iteration 3800) = 0.030955
Cost (iteration 3900) = 0.030769
Accuracy Test: 99.092131809
Accuracy Train: 99.1003111074
```

Not so bad for a result.[1]

[1]In case you are wondering why we get a different result that we had in Chapter 2, remember that we are using a slightly different training set for learning, giving rise to this difference.

Conclusion

You should really try to understand all the steps I have outlined in this chapter, to understand how much is done for you by a library. Remember: We have here an incredibly simple model with just one neuron. Theoretically, you could write all the equations for more complex network architectures, but this would be very difficult and extremely error-prone. TensorFlow calculates all the derivatives for you, regardless of the complexity of the network. In case you are interested in learning what TensorFlow can do, I suggest you read the official documentation, available at `https://goo.gl/E5DpHK`.

Note You should now appreciate a library such as TensorFlow and realize how much is going on in the background when you use it. You should also be aware of the complexity of the calculations and the importance of understanding the details of the algorithm and how these are implemented, to optimize and debug your models.

Index

U. Michelucci, *Applied Deep Learning*, https://doi.org/10.1007/978-1-4842-3790-8

I

J

K

L

M

S

T

U, V, W, X, Y

Z

Made in the USA
Las Vegas, NV
03 November 2026

57423825R00259